Alive
The Final Evolution

1

Story by Tadashi Kawashima
Art by Adachitoka

Translated and adapted by
Anastasia Moreno

Lettered by
North Market Street Graphics

Ballantine Books • New York

Alive volume 1 is a work of fiction. Names, characters, places, and incidents are the products of the author's imagination or are used fictitiously. Any resemblance to actual events, locales, or persons, living or dead, is entirely coincidental.

A Del Rey Trade Paperback Original

Published in the United States by Del Rey Books, an imprint of The Random House Publishing Group, a division of Random House, Inc., New York.

Publication rights arranged through Kodansha Ltd.

First published in Japan in 2005 by Kodansha Ltd., Tokyo

ISBN 978-0-345-49746-8

Printed in the United States of America

www.delreymanga.com

9 8 7 6 5 4 3 2 1

Translator/Adapter—Anastasia Moreno
Lettering—North Market Street Graphics

741.5952
ALI
v.1

Contents

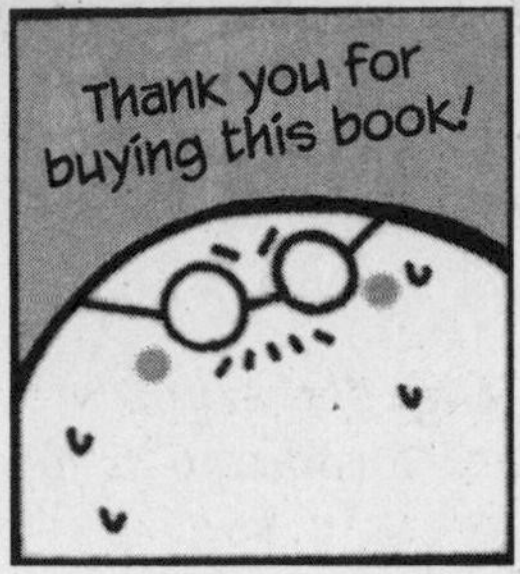
Thank you for buying this book!

Tadashi Kawashima

Oh, don't worry about me. Please buy the book to help out Adachitoka-kun, please ♡

Just kidding [LAUGH]

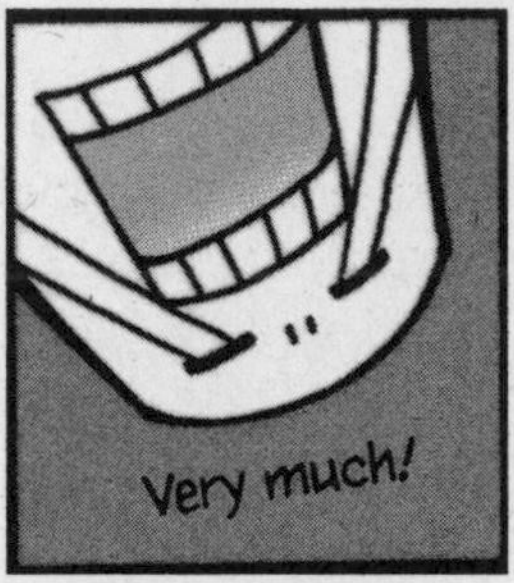
Very much!

Adachitoka

It began.
Alive volume 1.
Please enjoy this series, including the manga shorts at the end.

Honorifics Explained

Throughout the Del Rey Manga books, you will find Japanese honorifics left intact in the translations. For those not familiar with how the Japanese use honorifics and, more important, how they differ from American honorifics, we present this brief overview.

Politeness has always been a critical facet of Japanese culture. Ever since the feudal era, when Japan was a highly stratified society, use of honorifics—which can be defined as polite speech that indicates relationship or status—has played an essential role in the Japanese language. When addressing someone in Japanese, an honorific usually takes the form of a suffix attached to one's name (example: "Asuna-san"), is used as a title at the end of one's name, or appears in place of the name itself (example: "Negi-sensei," or simply "Sensei!").

Honorifics can be expressions of respect or endearment. In the context of manga and anime, honorifics give insight into the nature of the relationship between characters. Many English translations leave out these important honorifics and therefore distort the feel of the original Japanese. Because Japanese honorifics contain nuances that English honorifics lack, it is our policy at Del Rey not to translate them. Here, instead, is a guide to some of the honorifics you may encounter in Del Rey Manga.

-san: This is the most common honorific and is equivalent to Mr., Miss, Ms., or Mrs. It is the all-purpose honorific and can be used in any situation where politeness is required.

-sama: This is one level higher than "-san" and is used to confer great respect.

-dono: This comes from the word "tono," which means "lord." It is an even higher level than "-sama" and confers utmost respect.

-kun: This suffix is used at the end of boys' names to express familiarity or endearment. It is also sometimes used by men among friends, or when addressing someone younger or of a lower station.

-chan: This is used to express endearment, mostly toward girls. It is also used for little boys, pets, and even among lovers. It gives a sense of childish cuteness.

Bozu: This is an informal way to refer to a boy, similar to the English terms "kid" and "squirt."

Sempai/
Senpai: This title suggests that the addressee is one's senior in a group or organization. It is most often used in a school setting, where underclassmen refer to their upperclassmen as "sempai." It can also be used in the workplace, such as when a newer employee addresses an employee who has seniority in the company.

Kohai: This is the opposite of "sempai" and is used toward underclassmen in school or newcomers in the workplace. It connotes that the addressee is of a lower station.

Sensei: Literally meaning "one who has come before," this title is used for teachers, doctors, or masters of any profession or art.

-[blank]: This is usually forgotten in these lists, but it is perhaps the most significant difference between Japanese and English. The lack of honorific means that the speaker has permission to address the person in a very intimate way. Usually, only family, spouses, or very close friends have this kind of permission. Known as *yobisute,* it can be gratifying when someone who has earned the intimacy starts to call one by one's name without an honorific. But when that intimacy hasn't been earned, it can be very insulting.

Alive

1

Writer/ Tadashi Kawashima
Artist/ Adachitoka

contents

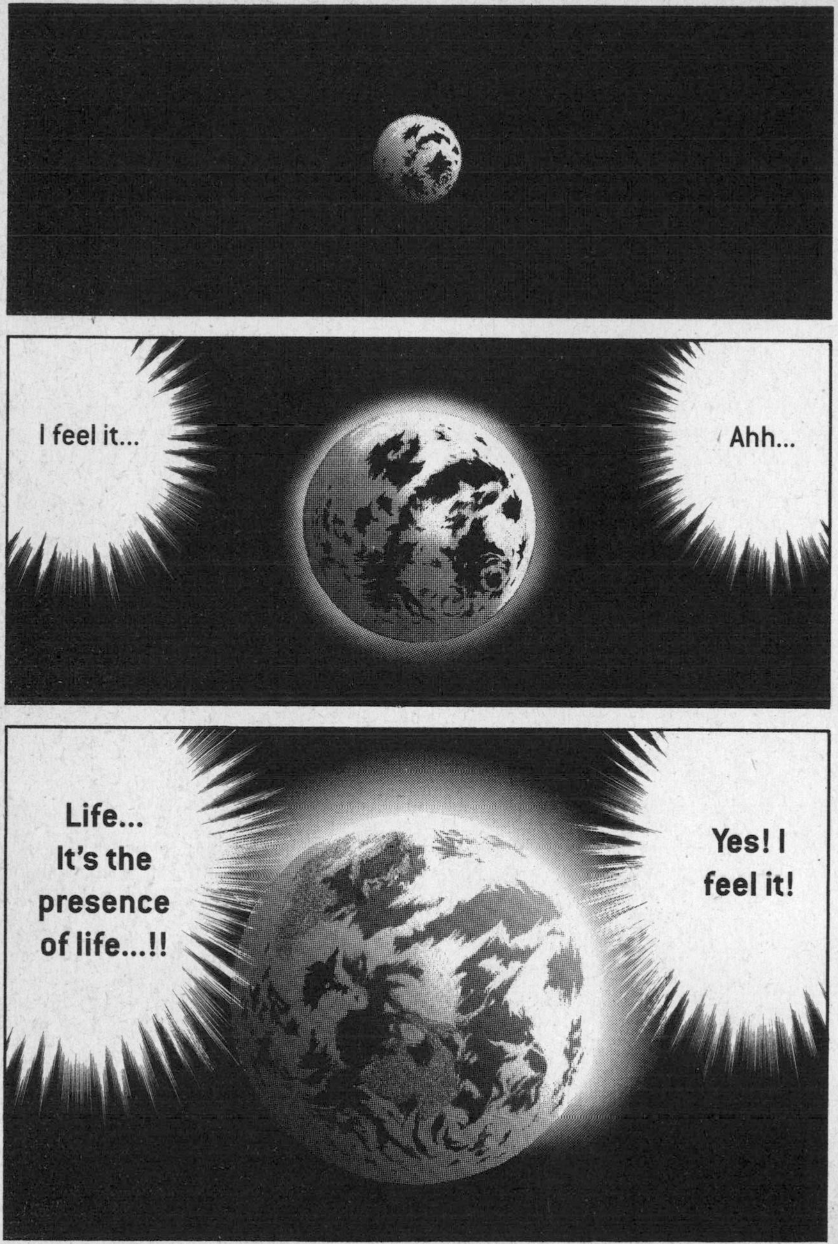
Ahh...
I feel it...
Yes! I feel it!
Life... It's the presence of life...!!

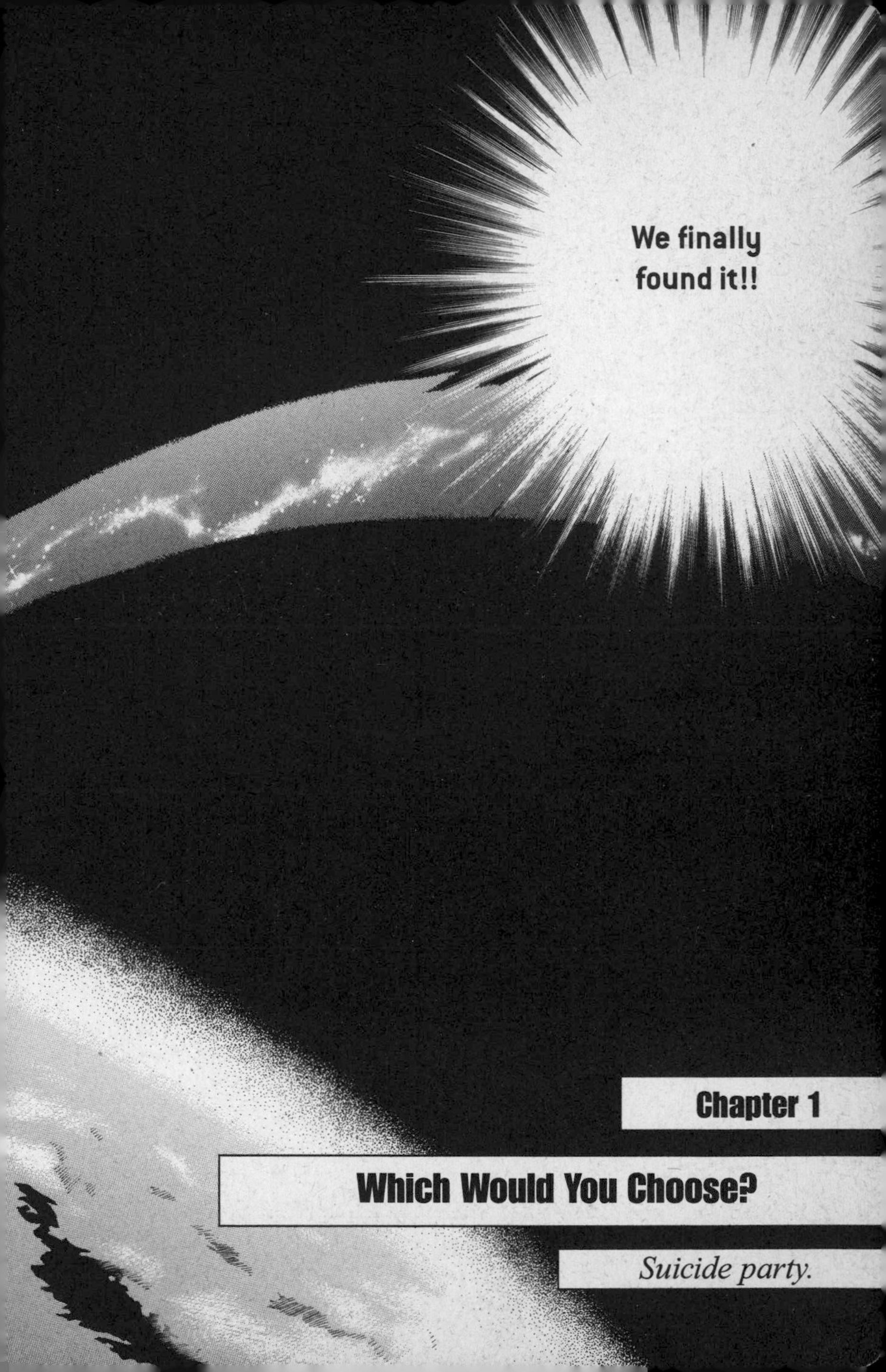
We finally found it!!
Chapter 1
Which Would You Choose?
Suicide party.

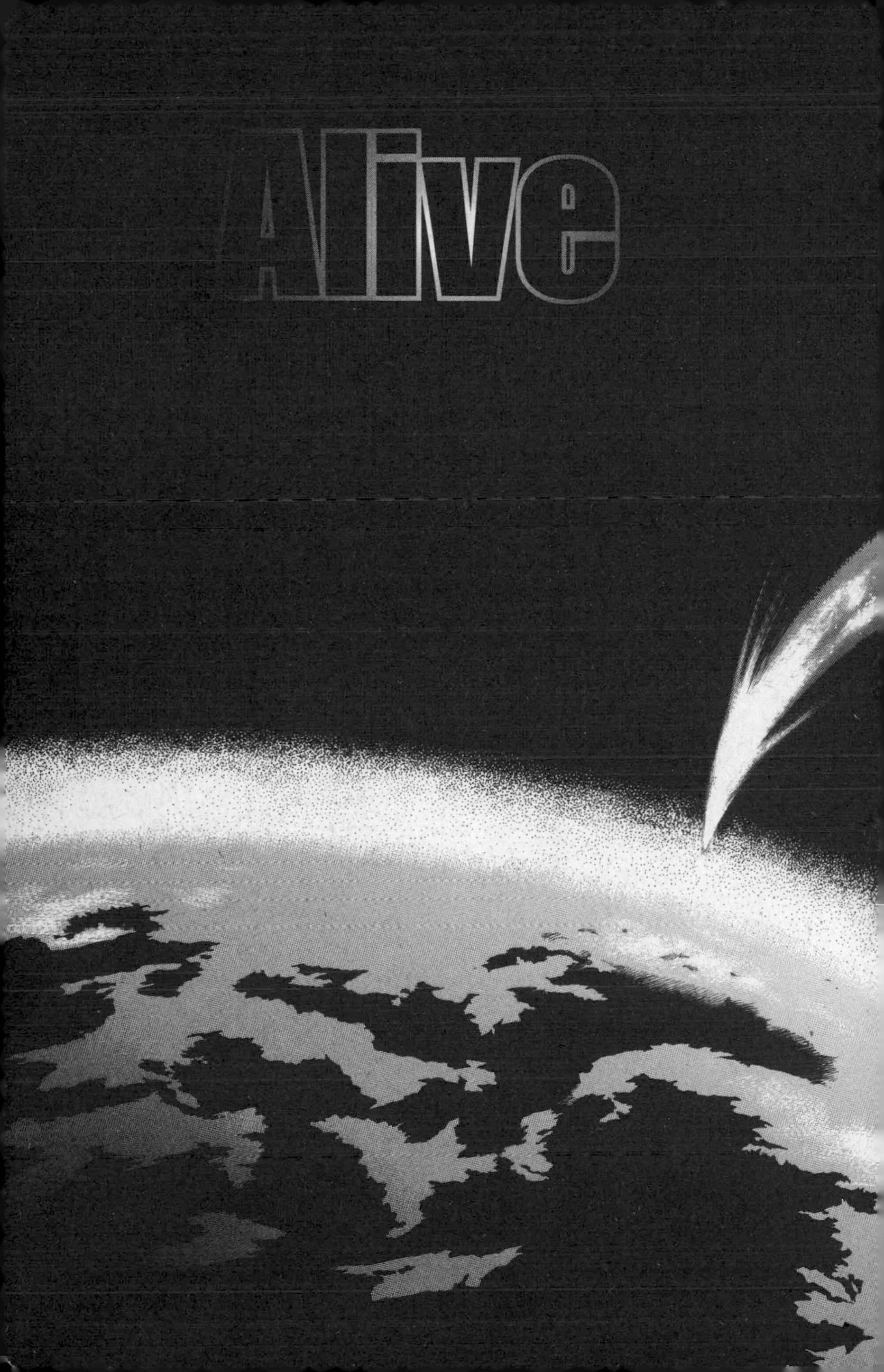
Alive

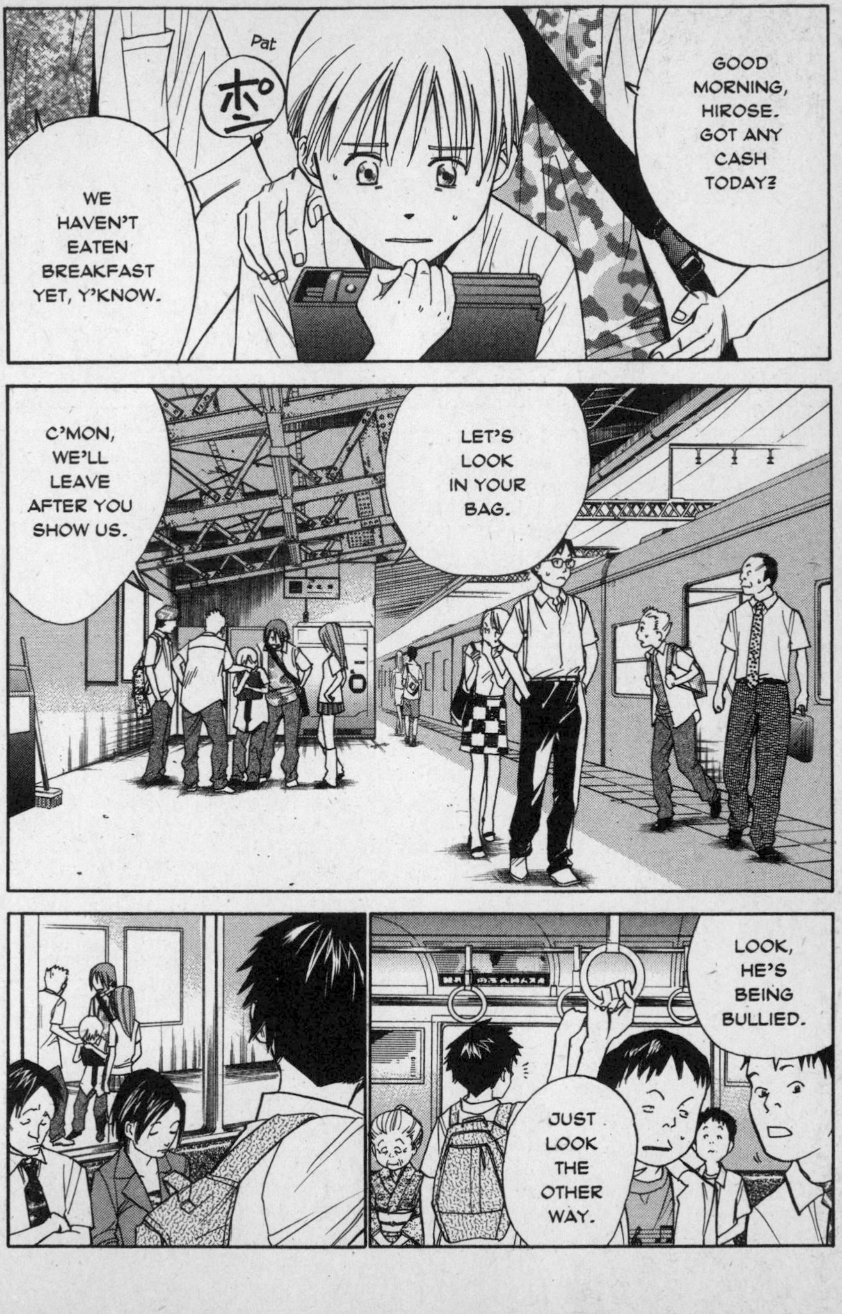
GOOD MORNING, HIROSE. GOT ANY CASH TODAY?
Pat
WE HAVEN'T EATEN BREAKFAST YET, Y'KNOW.
LET'S LOOK IN YOUR BAG.
C'MON, WE'LL LEAVE AFTER YOU SHOW US.
LOOK, HE'S BEING BULLIED.
JUST LOOK THE OTHER WAY.

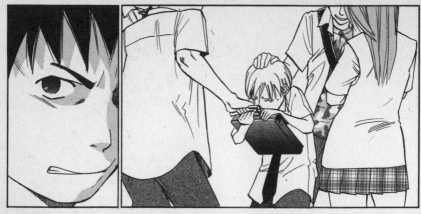

HIRO...

SLAM!

KSSSHH

KA....
KANŌ-
KUN?

VWEEM

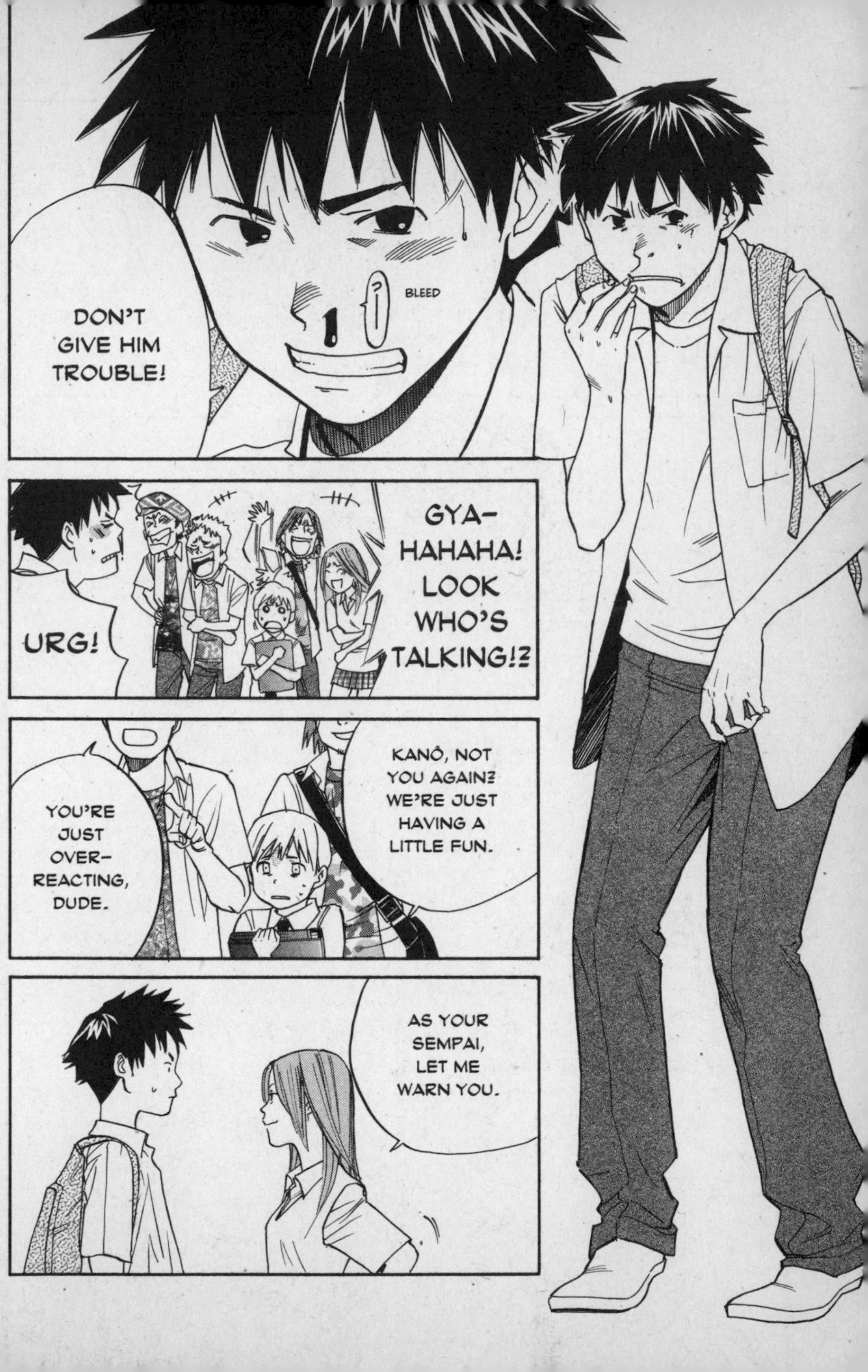
BLEED
DON'T GIVE HIM TROUBLE!
GYA-HAHAHA! LOOK WHO'S TALKING!?
URG!
KANÔ, NOT YOU AGAIN? WE'RE JUST HAVING A LITTLE FUN.
YOU'RE JUST OVER-REACTING, DUDE.
AS YOUR SEMPAI, LET ME WARN YOU.

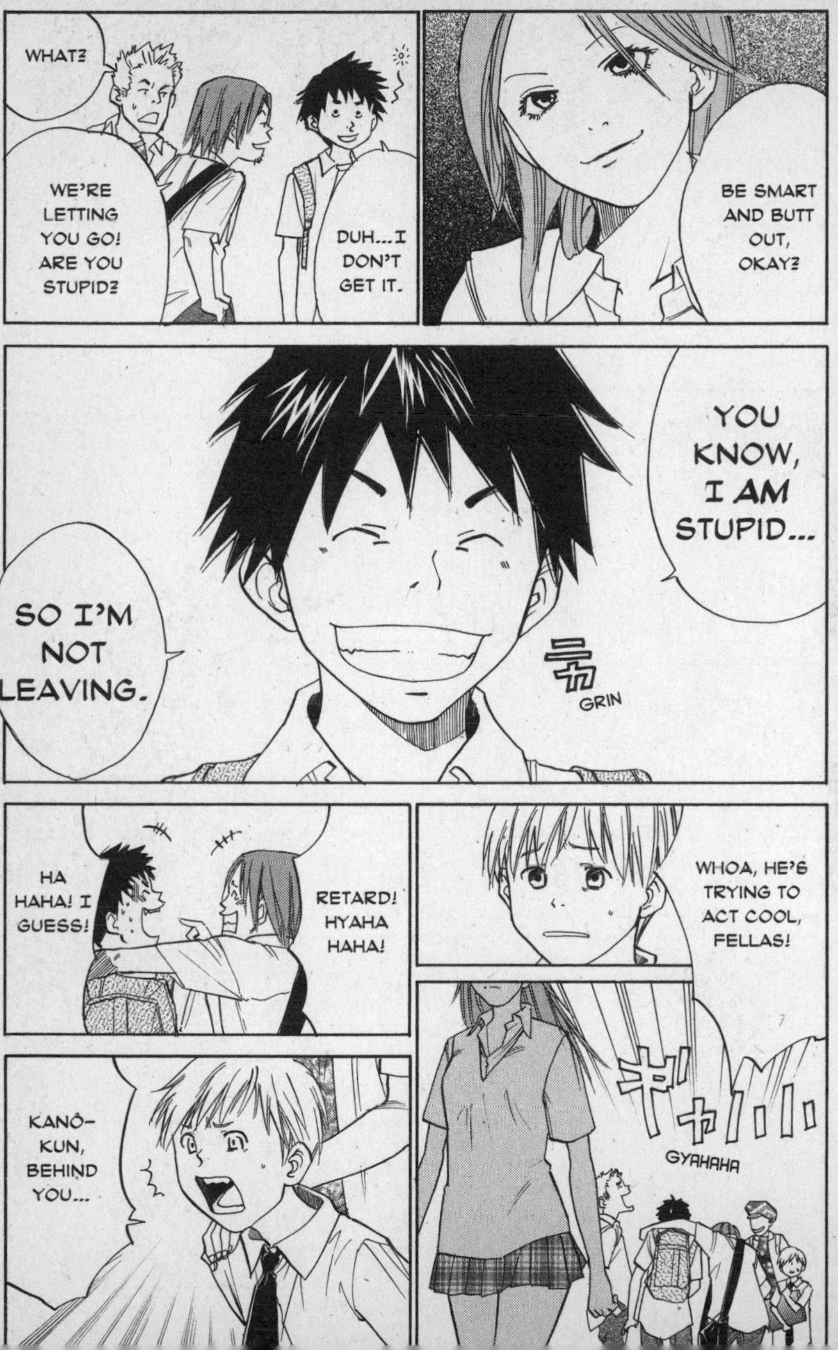
BE SMART AND BUTT OUT, OKAY?
DUH...I DON'T GET IT.
WHAT?
WE'RE LETTING YOU GO! ARE YOU STUPID?
YOU KNOW, I AM STUPID...
SO I'M NOT LEAVING.
GRIN
WHOA, HE'S TRYING TO ACT COOL, FELLAS!
RETARD! HYAHA HAHA!
HA HAHA! I GUESS!
GYAHAHA
KANÔ-KUN, BEHIND YOU...

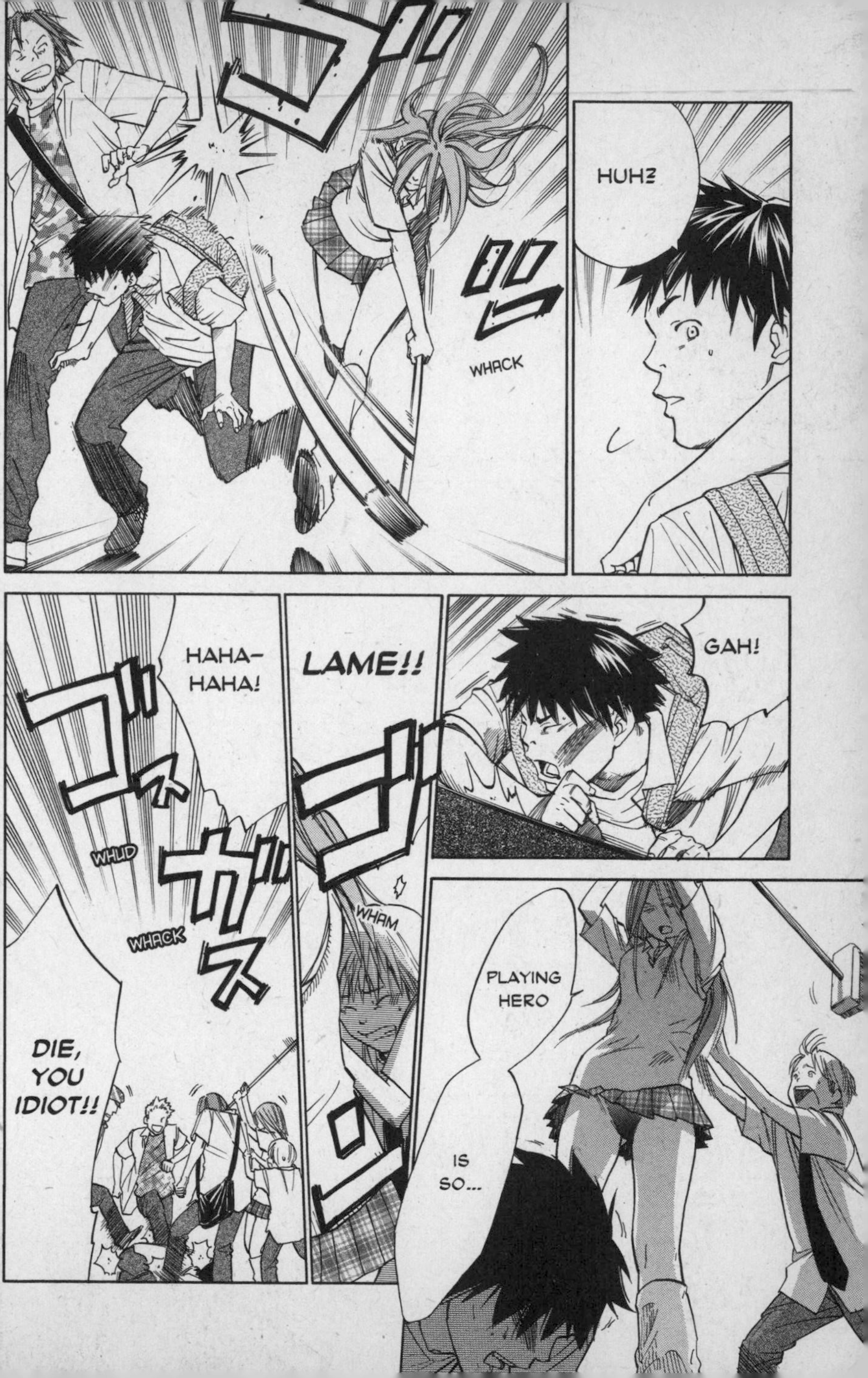
HUH?
WHACK
GAH!
PLAYING HERO
IS SO...
LAME!!
WHAM
HAHA-HAHA!
WHUD
WHACK
DIE, YOU IDIOT!!

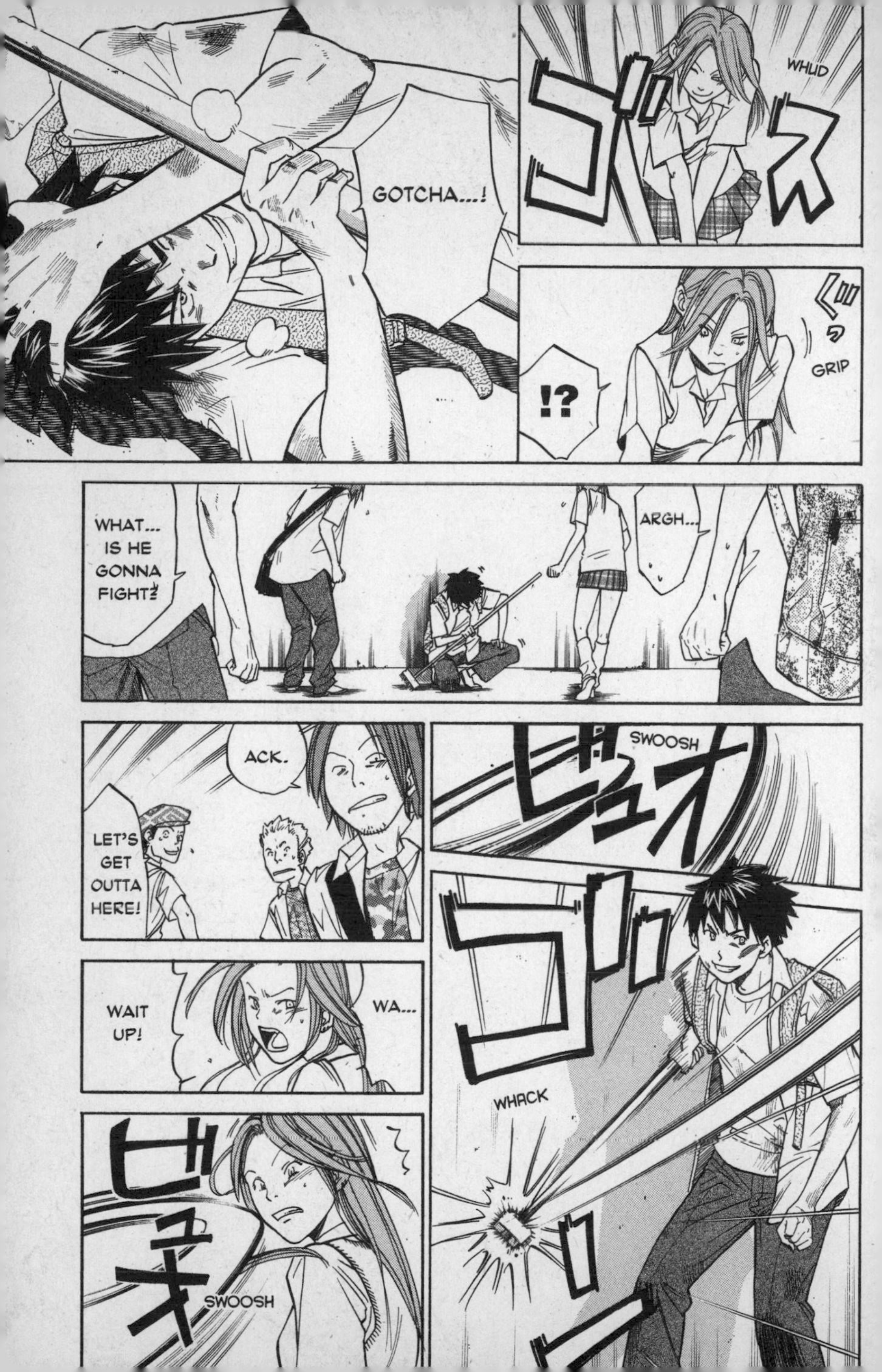
WHUD
GRIP
!?
GOTCHA...!
...
ARGH...
WHAT... IS HE GONNA FIGHT?!
SWOOSH
WHACK
ACK.
LET'S GET OUTTA HERE!
WA...
WAIT UP!
SWOOSH

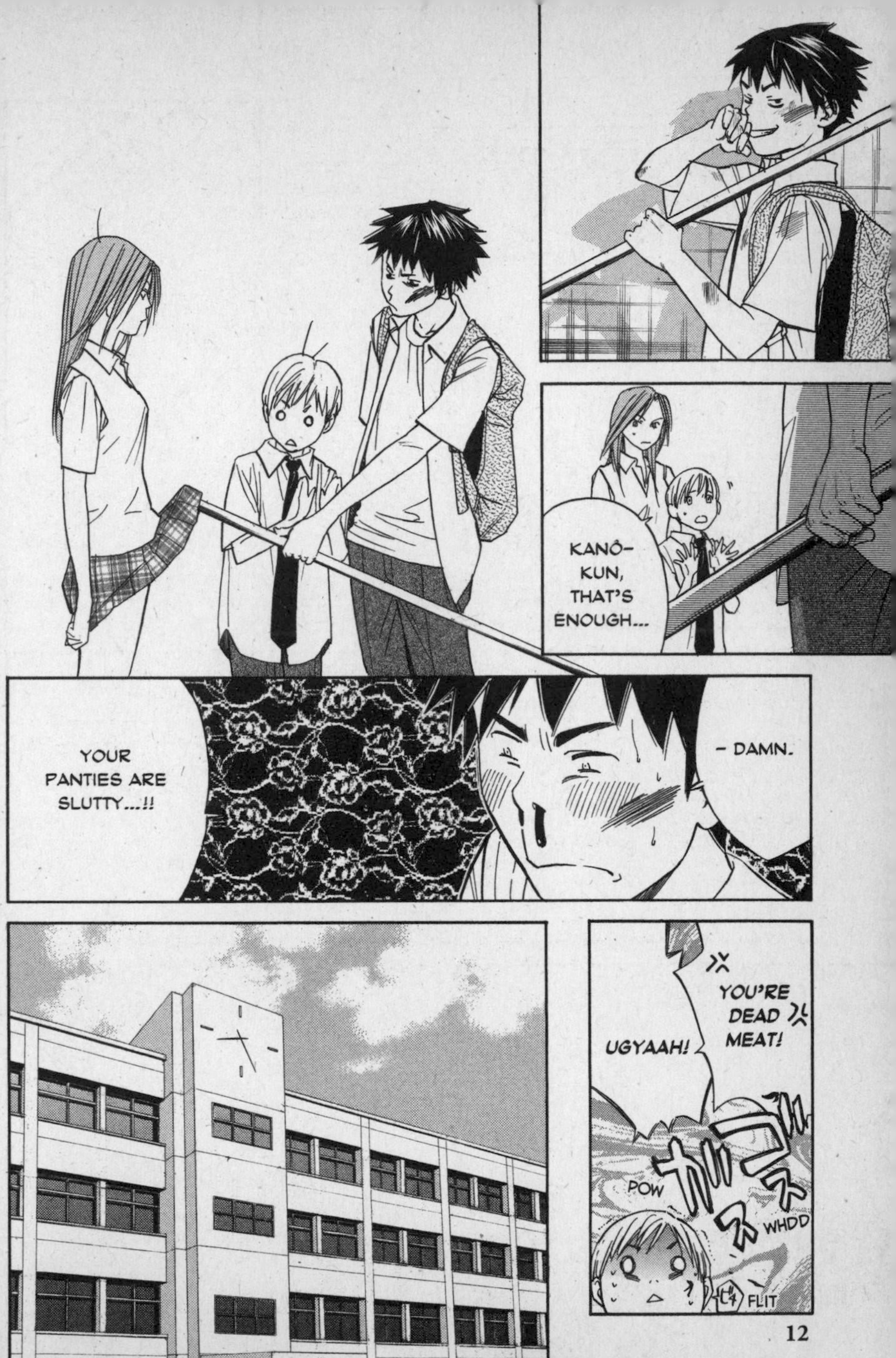
KANÔ-KUN, THAT'S ENOUGH...
- DAMN.
YOUR PANTIES ARE SLUTTY...!!
YOU'RE DEAD MEAT!
UGYAAH!
POW
WHDD
FLIT

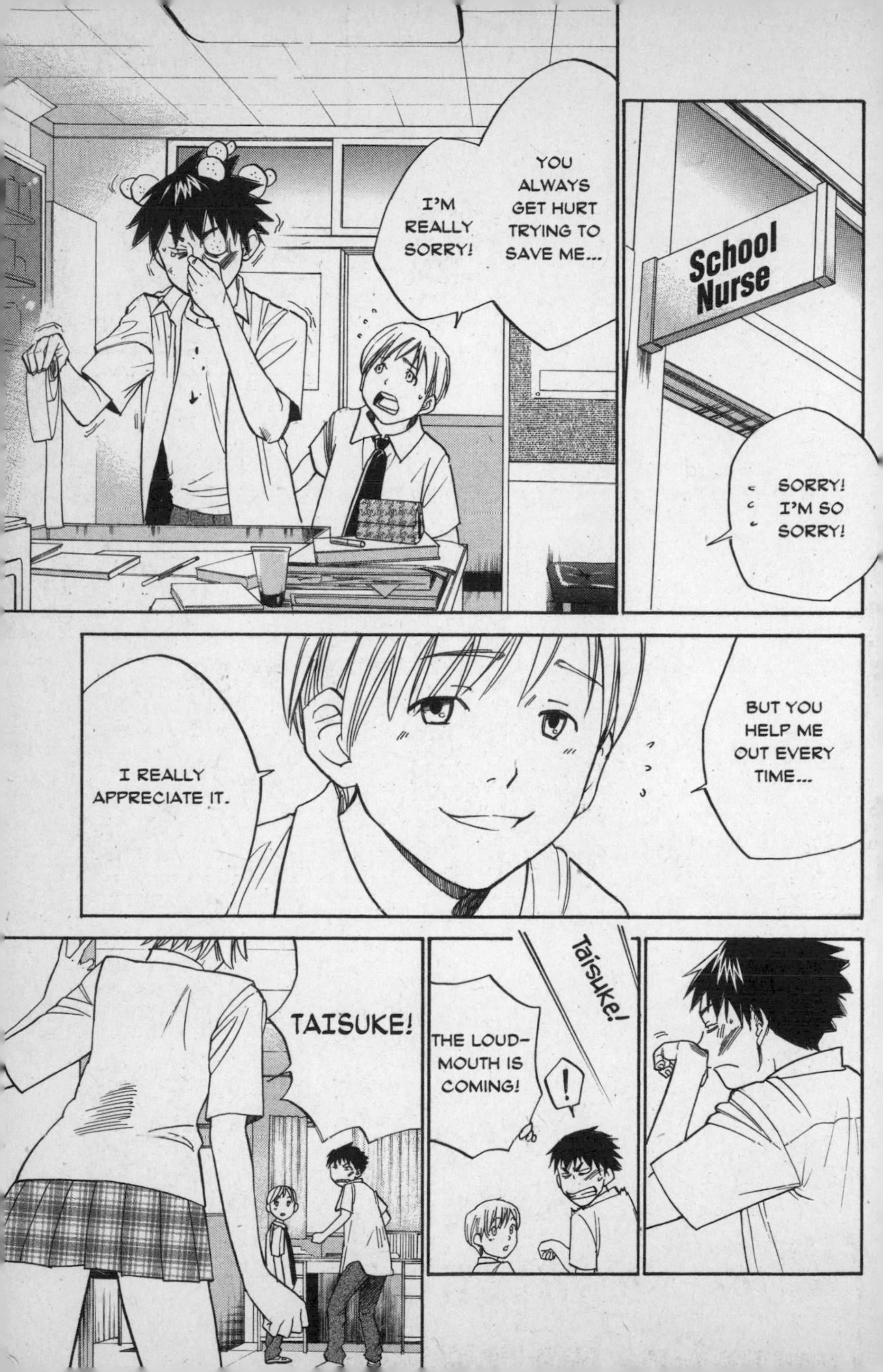
School Nurse
SORRY! I'M SO SORRY!
YOU ALWAYS GET HURT TRYING TO SAVE ME...
I'M REALLY SORRY!
BUT YOU HELP ME OUT EVERY TIME...
I REALLY APPRECIATE IT.
Taisuke!
THE LOUD-MOUTH IS COMING!
!
TAISUKE!

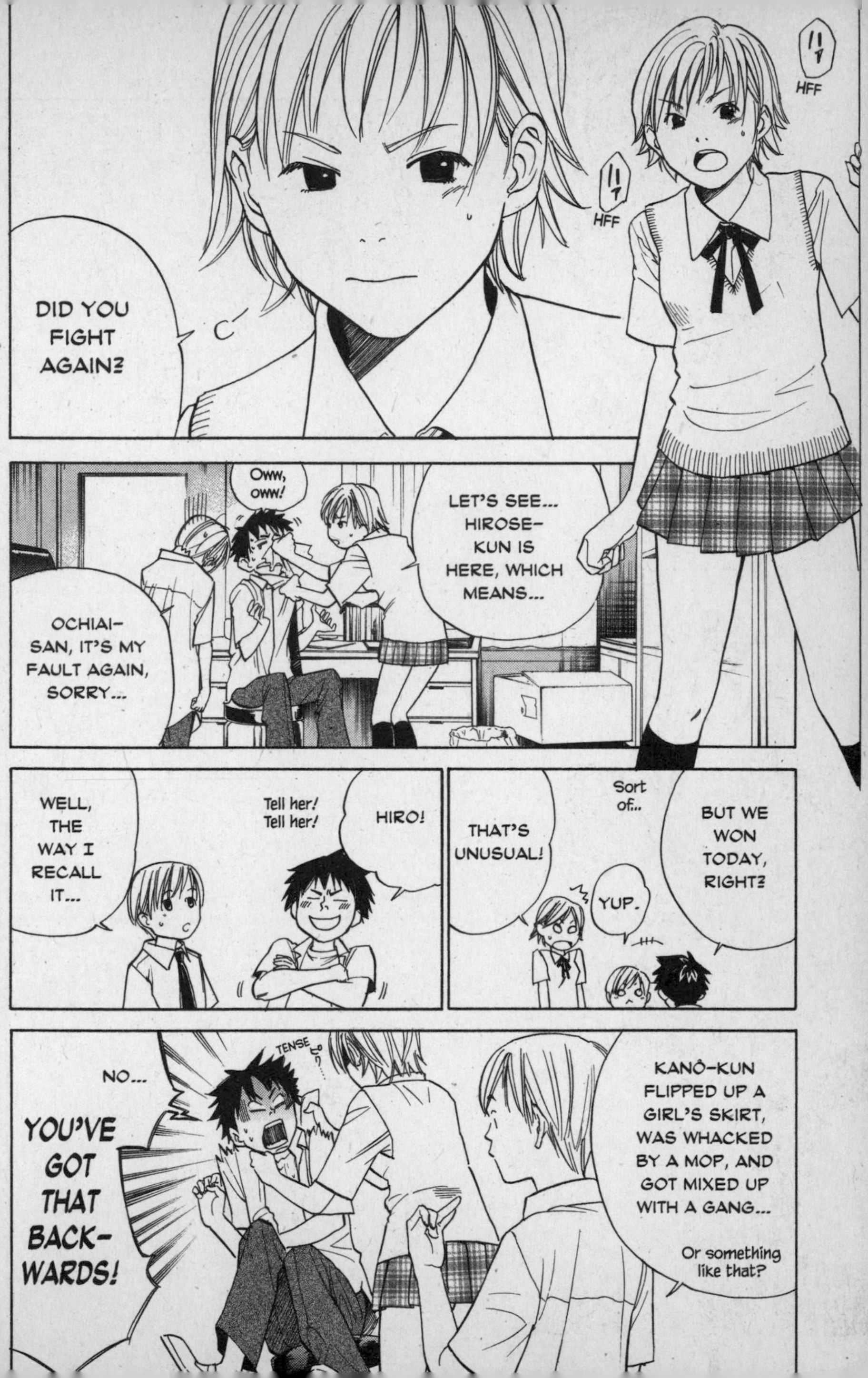
ハァ
HFF
ハァ
HFF
DID YOU FIGHT AGAIN?
LET'S SEE... HIROSE-KUN IS HERE, WHICH MEANS...
Oww, oww!
OCHIAI-SAN, IT'S MY FAULT AGAIN, SORRY...
BUT WE WON TODAY, RIGHT?
Sort of...
THAT'S UNUSUAL!
YUP.
HIRO!
Tell her! Tell her!
WELL, THE WAY I RECALL IT...
KANÔ-KUN FLIPPED UP A GIRL'S SKIRT, WAS WHACKED BY A MOP, AND GOT MIXED UP WITH A GANG...
Or something like that?
TENSE
NO...
YOU'VE GOT THAT BACK-WARDS!

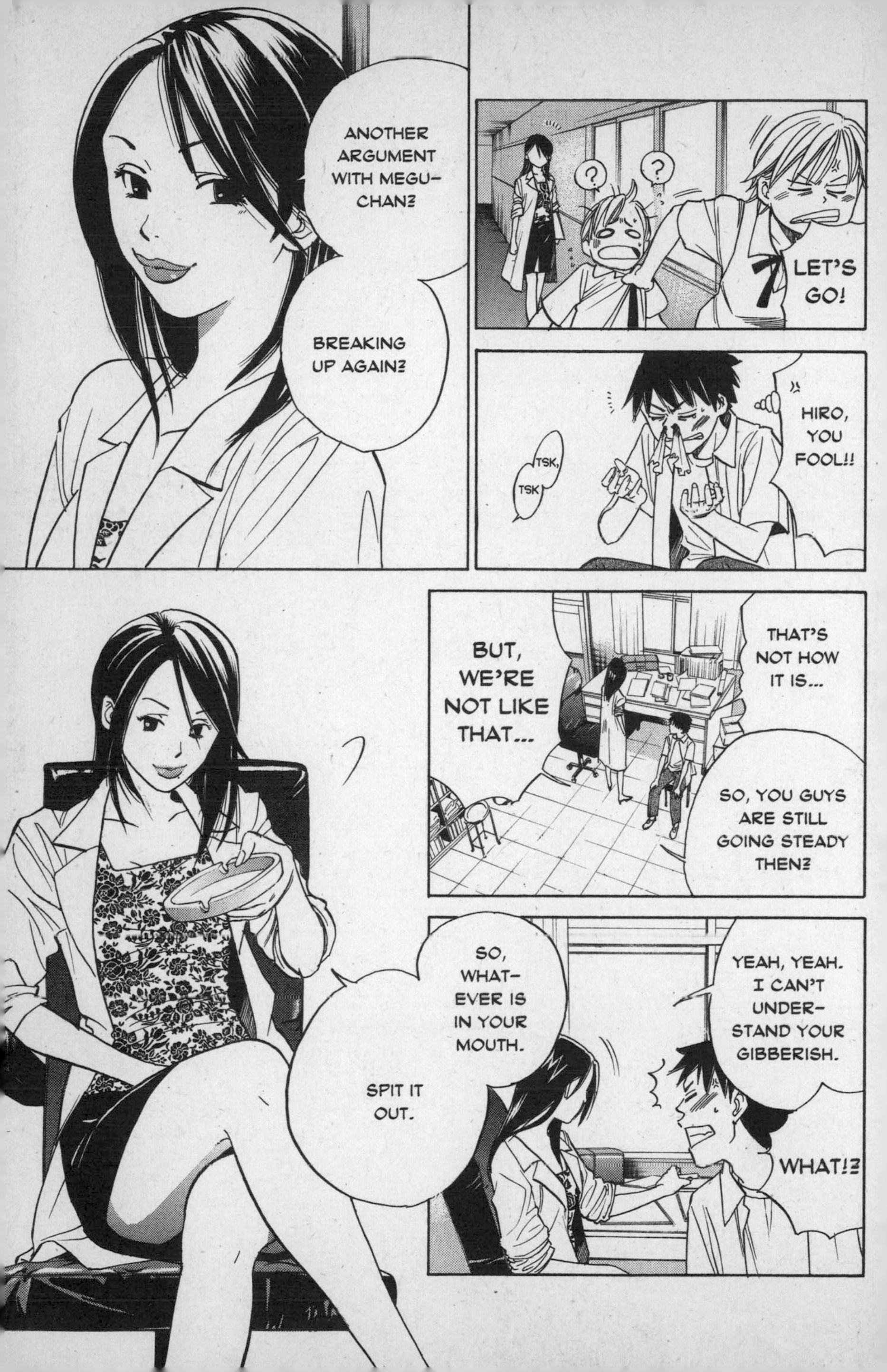
LET'S GO!
HIRO, YOU FOOL!!
TSK, TSK
ANOTHER ARGUMENT WITH MEGU-CHAN?
BREAKING UP AGAIN?
THAT'S NOT HOW IT IS...
SO, YOU GUYS ARE STILL GOING STEADY THEN?
BUT, WE'RE NOT LIKE THAT...
YEAH, YEAH. I CAN'T UNDER-STAND YOUR GIBBERISH.
WHAT!?
SO, WHAT-EVER IS IN YOUR MOUTH.
SPIT IT OUT.

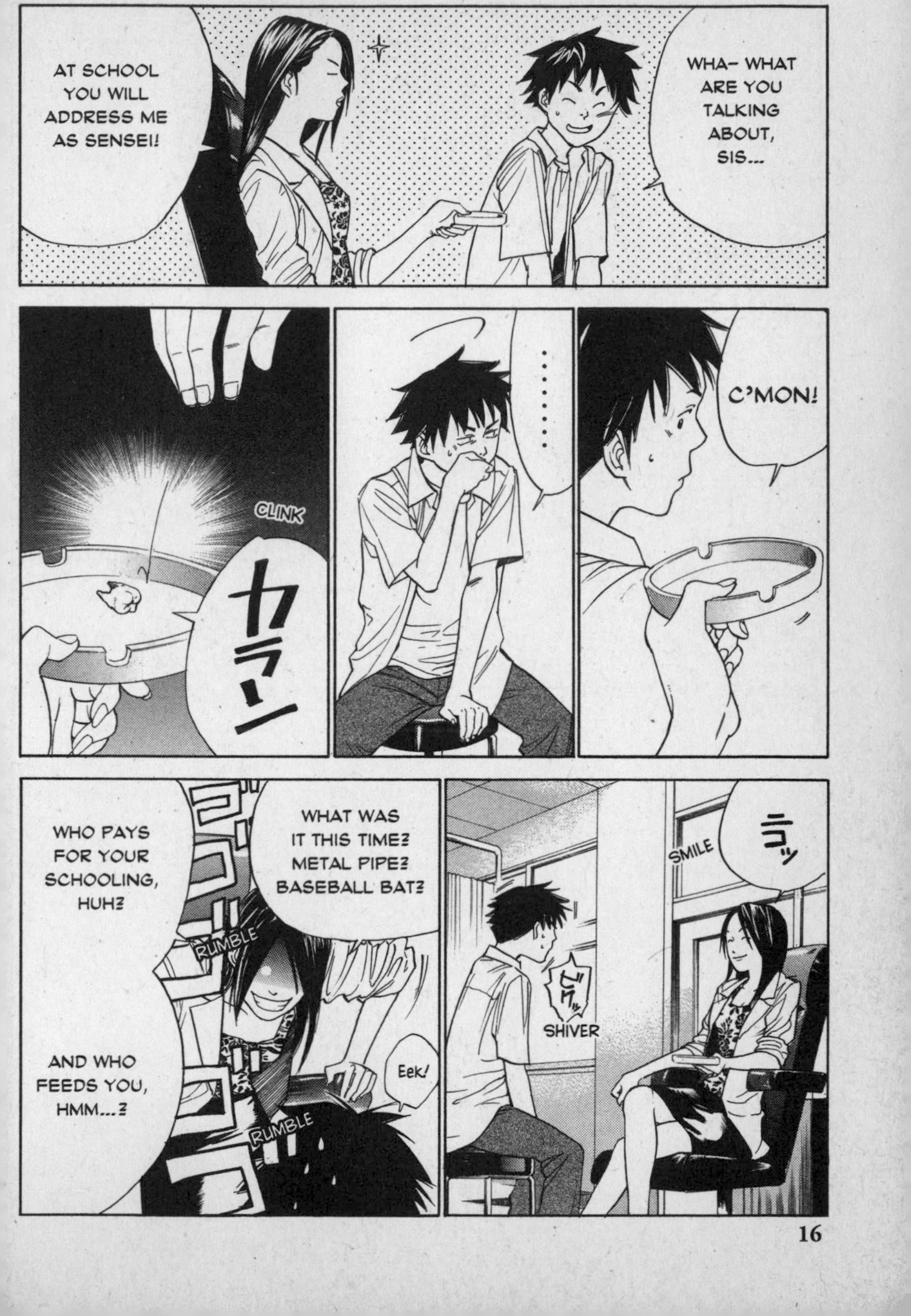
WHA- WHAT ARE YOU TALKING ABOUT, SIS...
AT SCHOOL YOU WILL ADDRESS ME AS SENSEI!
C'MON!
......
CLINK
カラーン
SMILE
ニコッ
ビクッ
SHIVER
WHAT WAS IT THIS TIME? METAL PIPE? BASEBALL BAT?
WHO PAYS FOR YOUR SCHOOLING, HUH?
RUMBLE
Eek!
AND WHO FEEDS YOU, HMM...?
RUMBLE

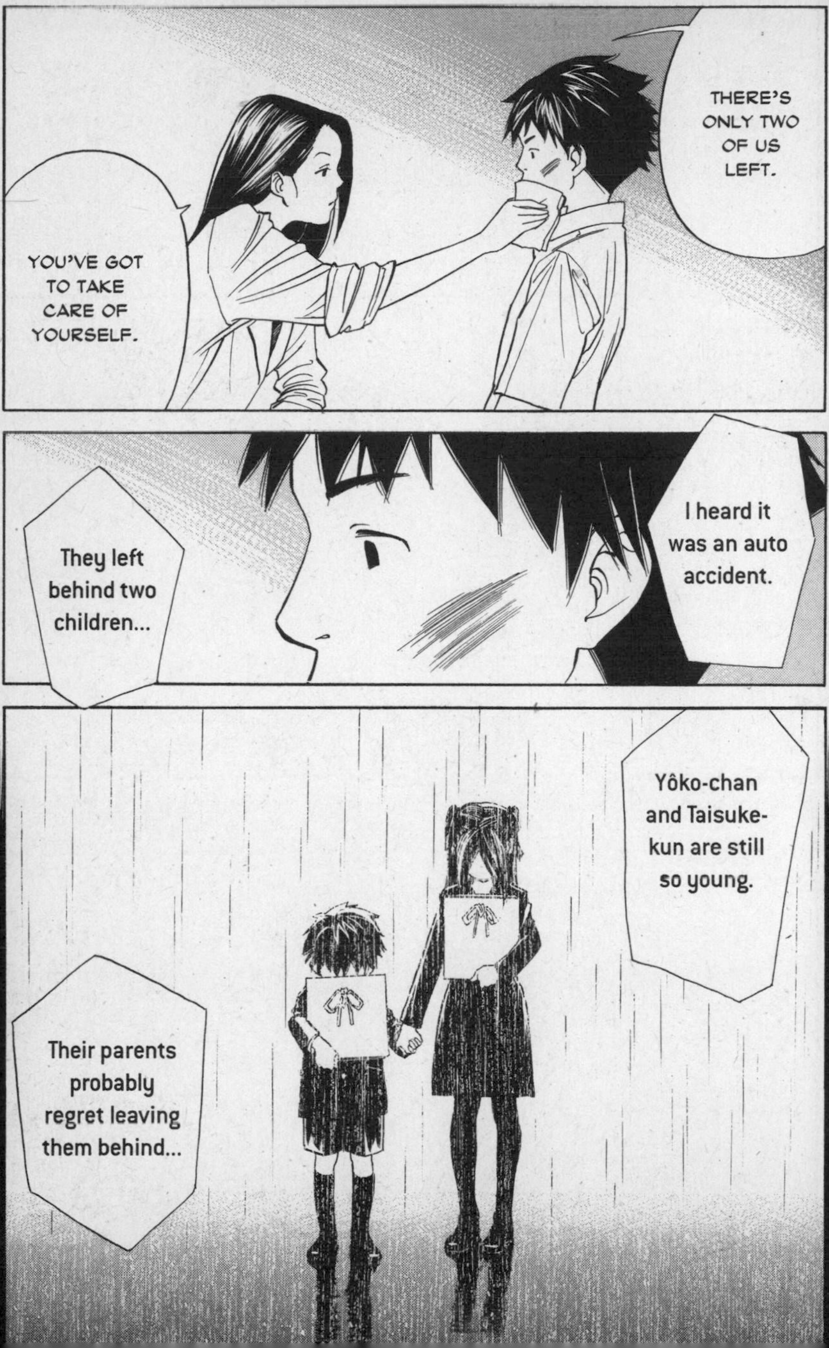
THERE'S ONLY TWO OF US LEFT.
YOU'VE GOT TO TAKE CARE OF YOURSELF.
I heard it was an auto accident.
They left behind two children...
Yôko-chan and Taisuke-kun are still so young.
Their parents probably regret leaving them behind...

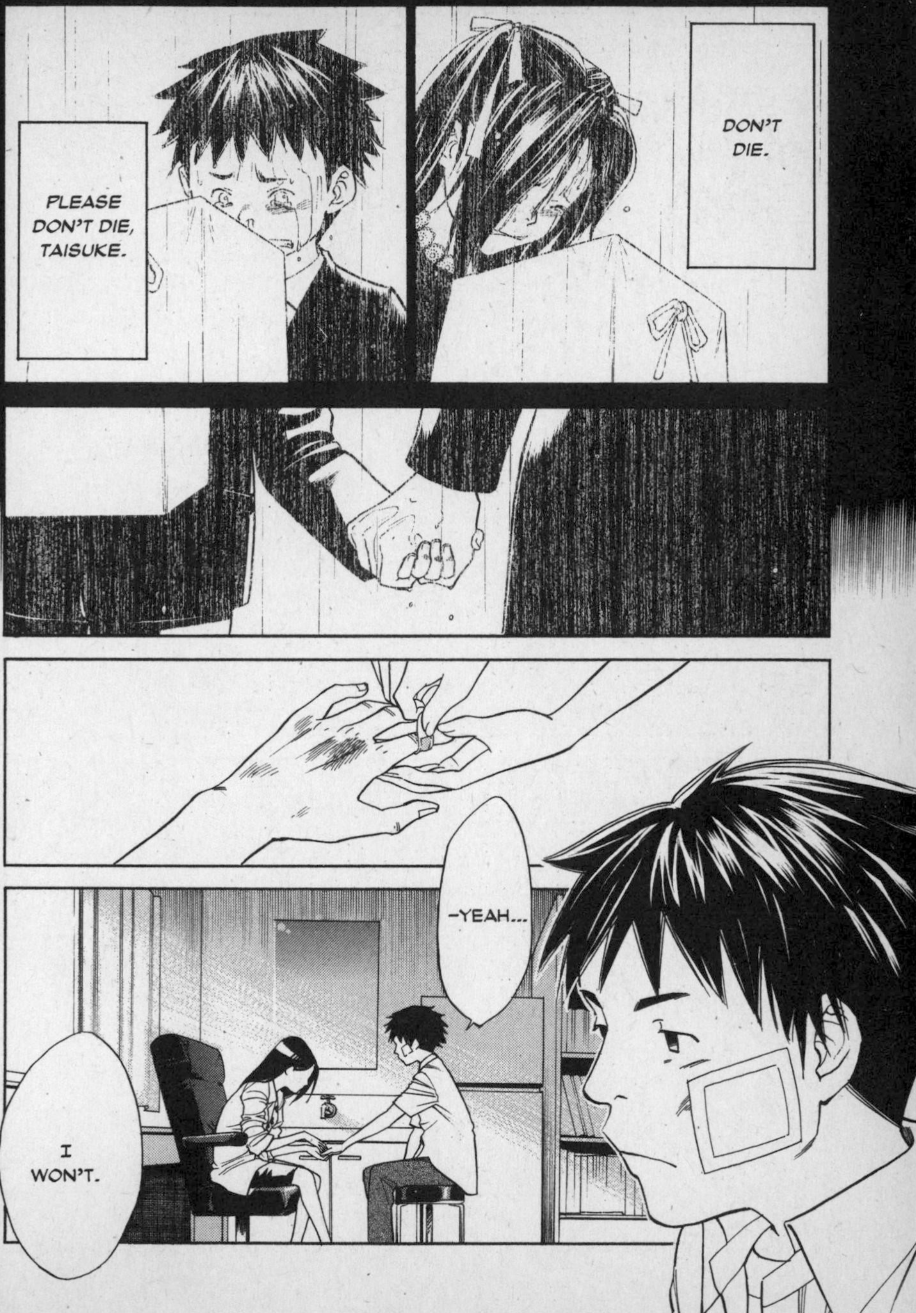
DON'T DIE.
PLEASE DON'T DIE, TAISUKE.
-YEAH...
I WON'T.

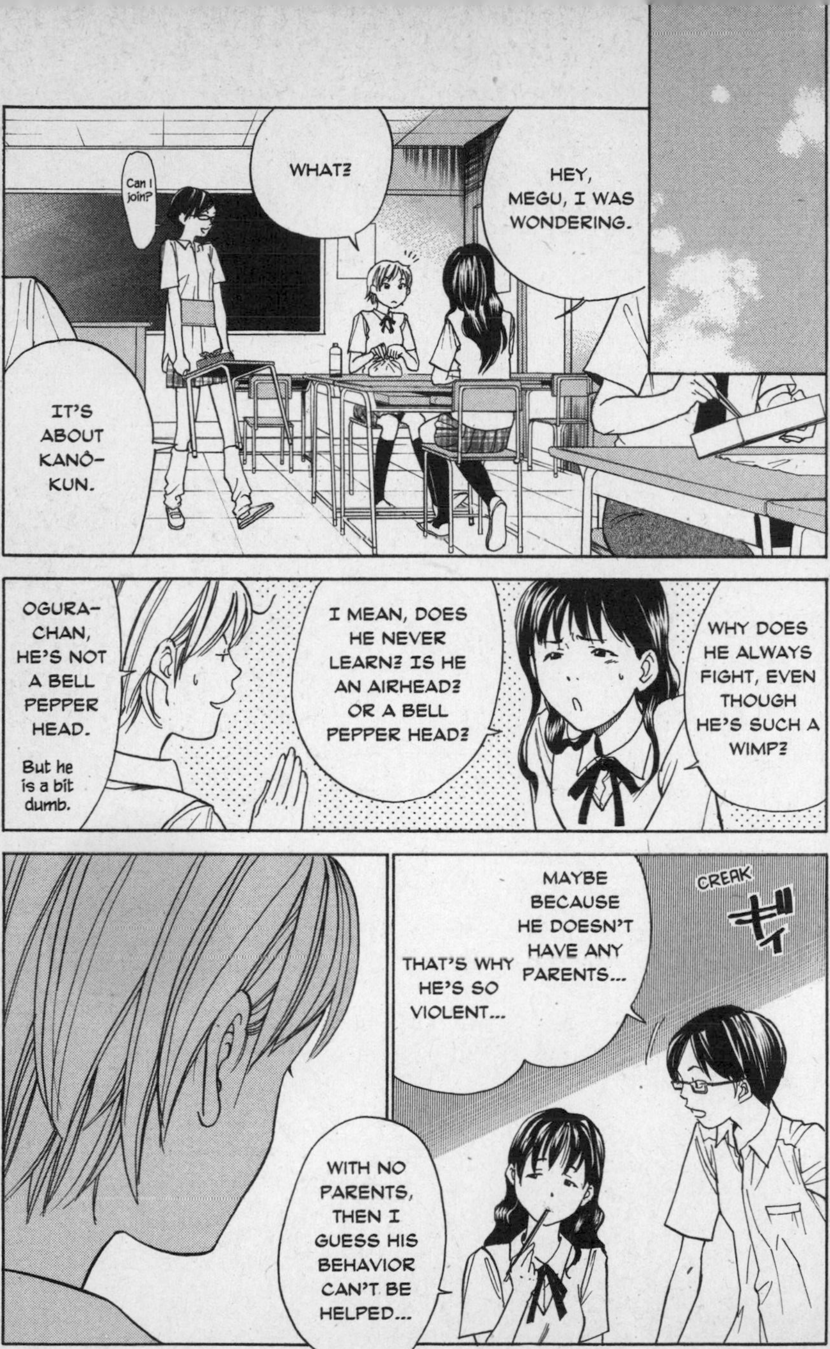
HEY, MEGU, I WAS WONDERING.
WHAT?
Can I join?
IT'S ABOUT KANÔ-KUN.
WHY DOES HE ALWAYS FIGHT, EVEN THOUGH HE'S SUCH A WIMP?
I MEAN, DOES HE NEVER LEARN? IS HE AN AIRHEAD? OR A BELL PEPPER HEAD?
OGURA-CHAN, HE'S NOT A BELL PEPPER HEAD.
But he is a bit dumb.
CREAK
ギィ
MAYBE BECAUSE HE DOESN'T HAVE ANY PARENTS...
THAT'S WHY HE'S SO VIOLENT...
WITH NO PARENTS, THEN I GUESS HIS BEHAVIOR CAN'T BE HELPED...

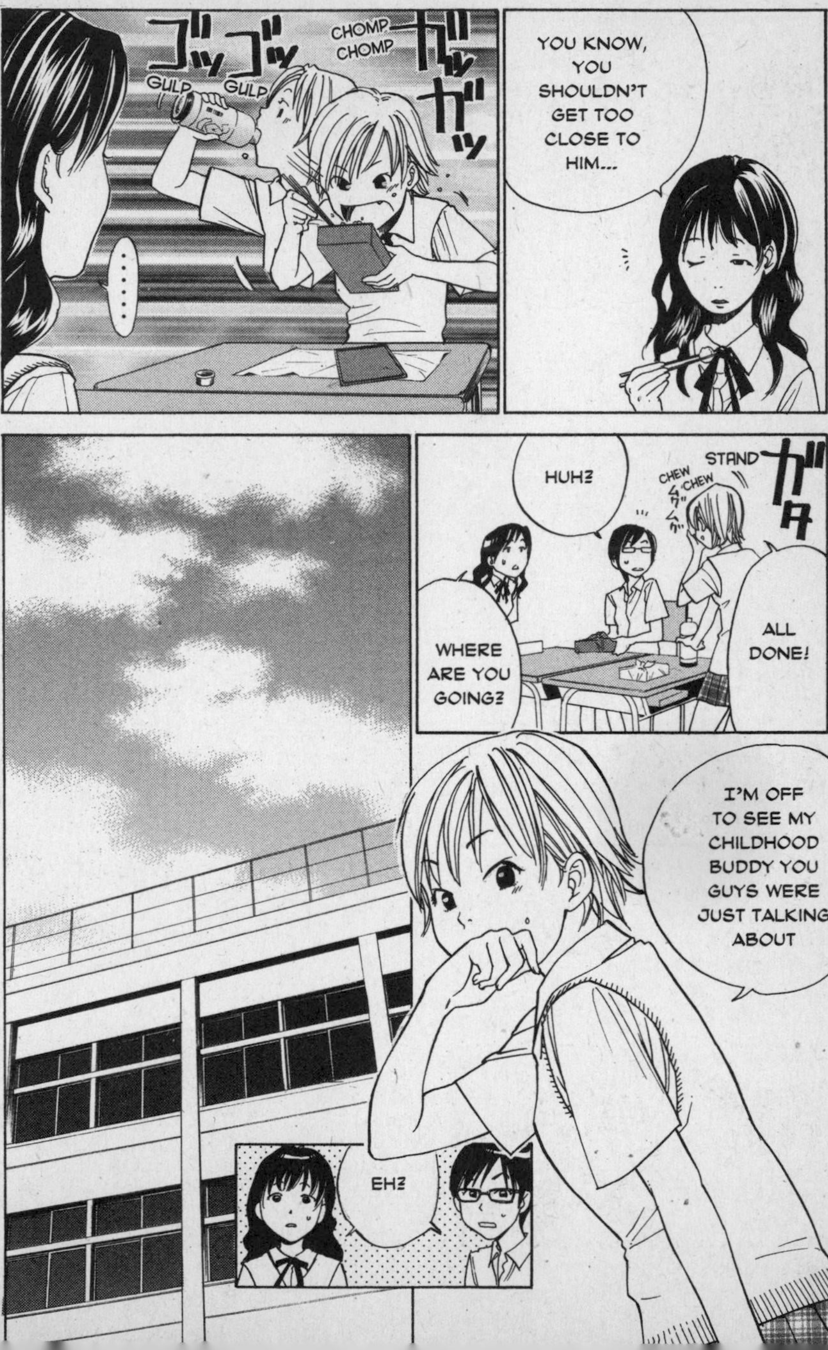
YOU KNOW, YOU SHOULDN'T GET TOO CLOSE TO HIM...
ガッ ガッ
CHOMP CHOMP
ゴッ ゴッ
GULP GULP
......
STAND
ガタ
CHEW CHEW
HUH?
ALL DONE!
WHERE ARE YOU GOING?
I'M OFF TO SEE MY CHILDHOOD BUDDY YOU GUYS WERE JUST TALKING ABOUT
EH?

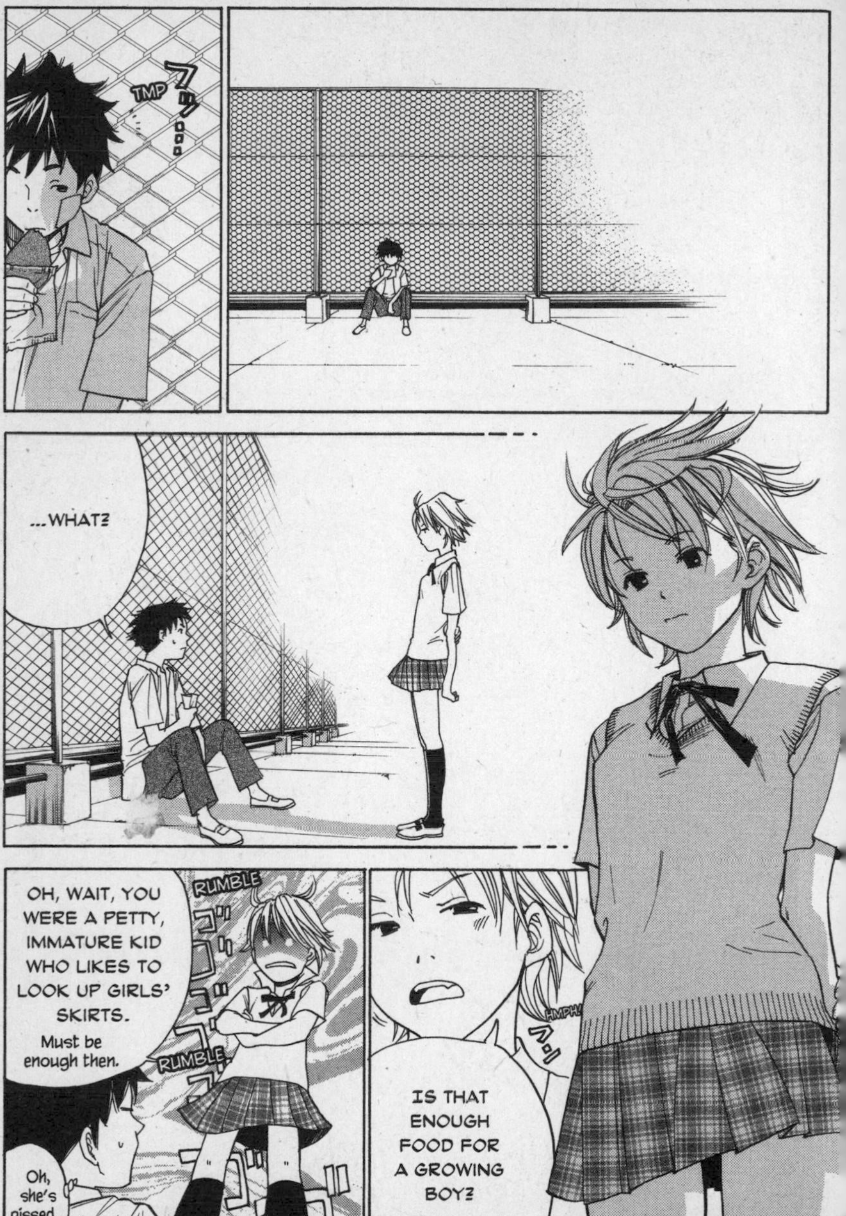
TMP
...WHAT?
IS THAT ENOUGH FOOD FOR A GROWING BOY?
HMPH!
OH, WAIT, YOU WERE A PETTY, IMMATURE KID WHO LIKES TO LOOK UP GIRLS' SKIRTS.
RUMBLE
RUMBLE
Must be enough then.
Oh, she's pissed...

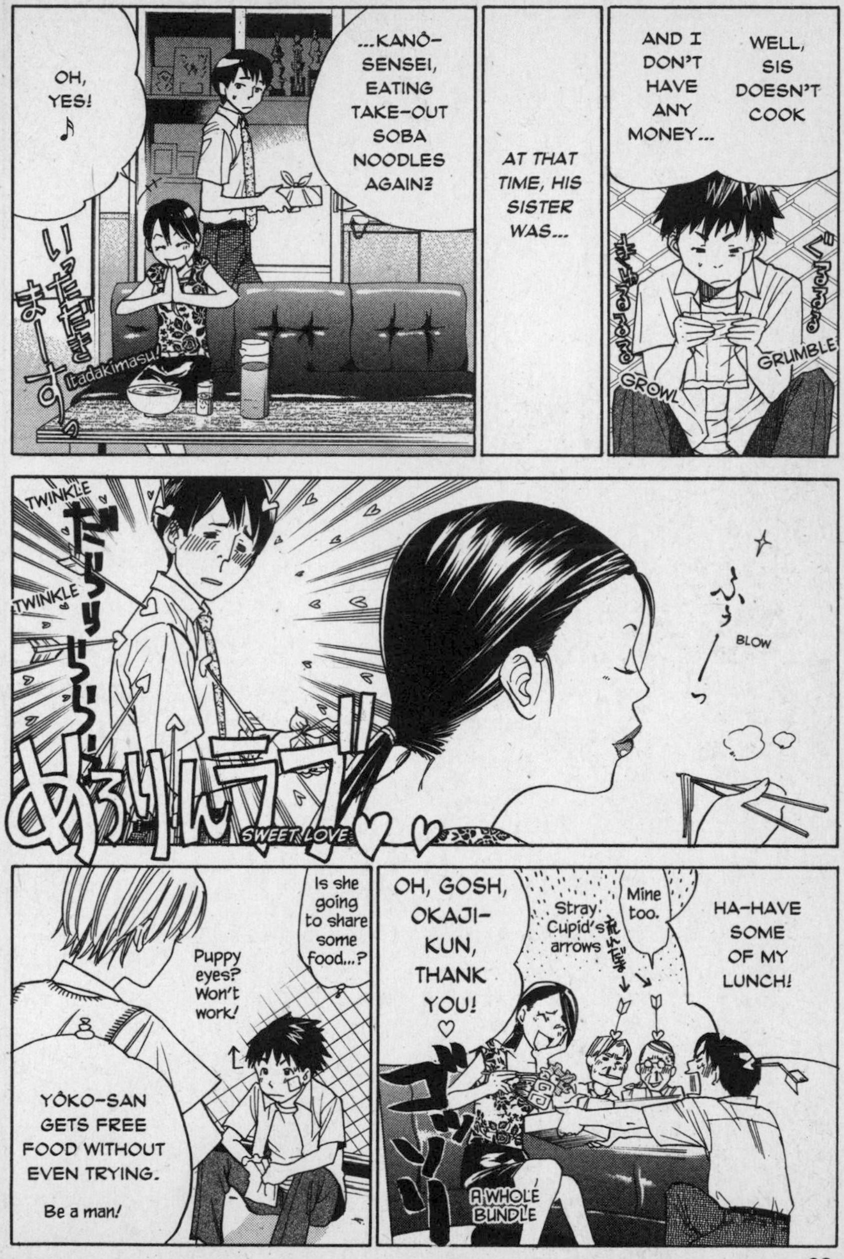
WELL, SIS DOESN'T COOK
AND I DON'T HAVE ANY MONEY...
GRUMBLE
GROWL
AT THAT TIME, HIS SISTER WAS...
...KANÔ-SENSEI, EATING TAKE-OUT SOBA NOODLES AGAIN?
OH, YES! ♪
いただきまーす
Itadakimasu!
BLOW
TWINKLE
TWINKLE
めろりんラブ
SWEET LOVE
HA-HAVE SOME OF MY LUNCH!
Mine too.
Stray Cupid's arrows
OH, GOSH, OKAJI-KUN, THANK YOU! ♡
A WHOLE BUNDLE
Is she going to share some food...?
Puppy eyes? Won't work!
YÔKO-SAN GETS FREE FOOD WITHOUT EVEN TRYING.
Be a man!

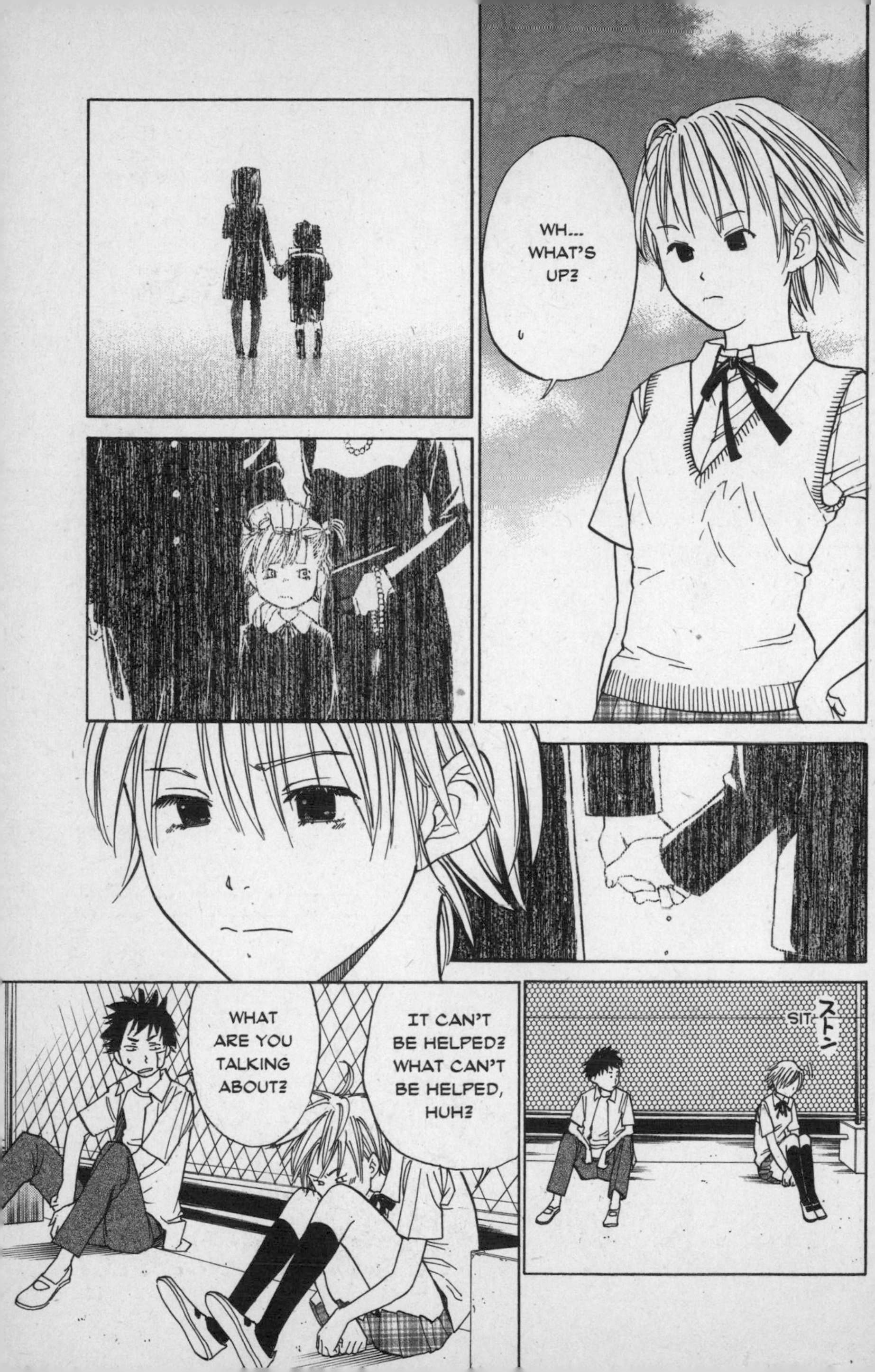
WH... WHAT'S UP?
SIT ストン
IT CAN'T BE HELPED? WHAT CAN'T BE HELPED, HUH?
WHAT ARE YOU TALKING ABOUT?

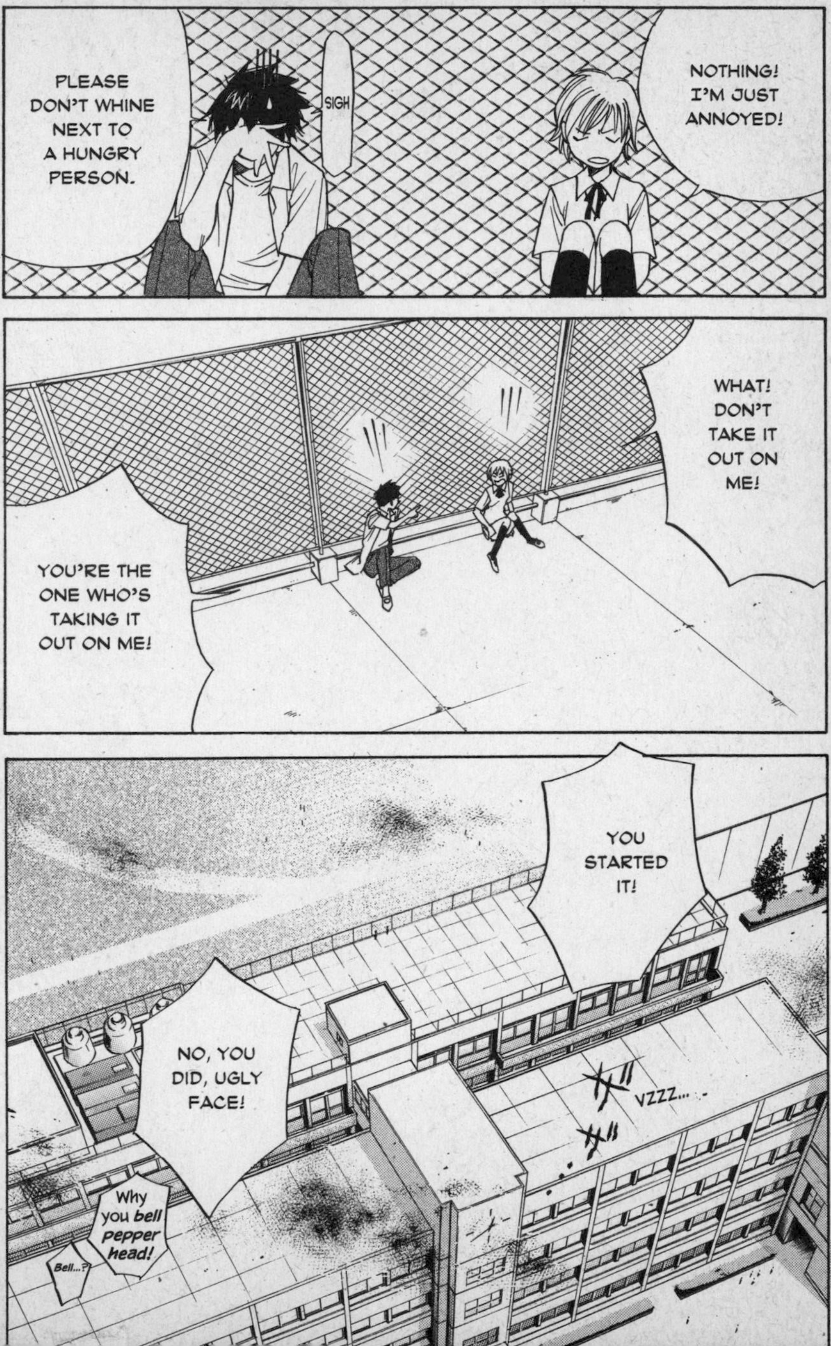
NOTHING! I'M JUST ANNOYED!
SIGH
PLEASE DON'T WHINE NEXT TO A HUNGRY PERSON.
WHAT! DON'T TAKE IT OUT ON ME!
YOU'RE THE ONE WHO'S TAKING IT OUT ON ME!
YOU STARTED IT!
VZZZ...
NO, YOU DID, UGLY FACE!
Why you *bell pepper head!*
Bell...?

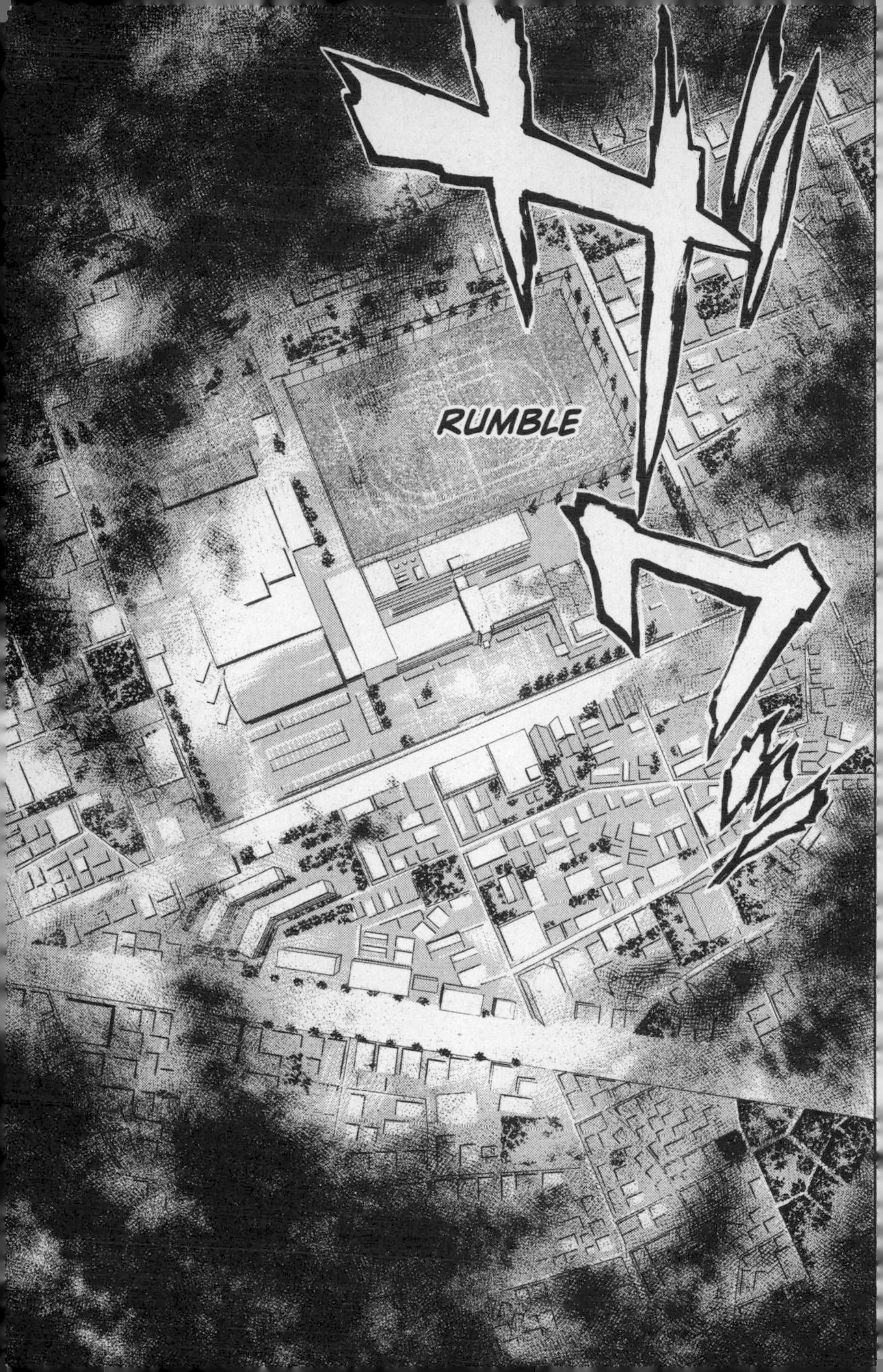
RUMBLE

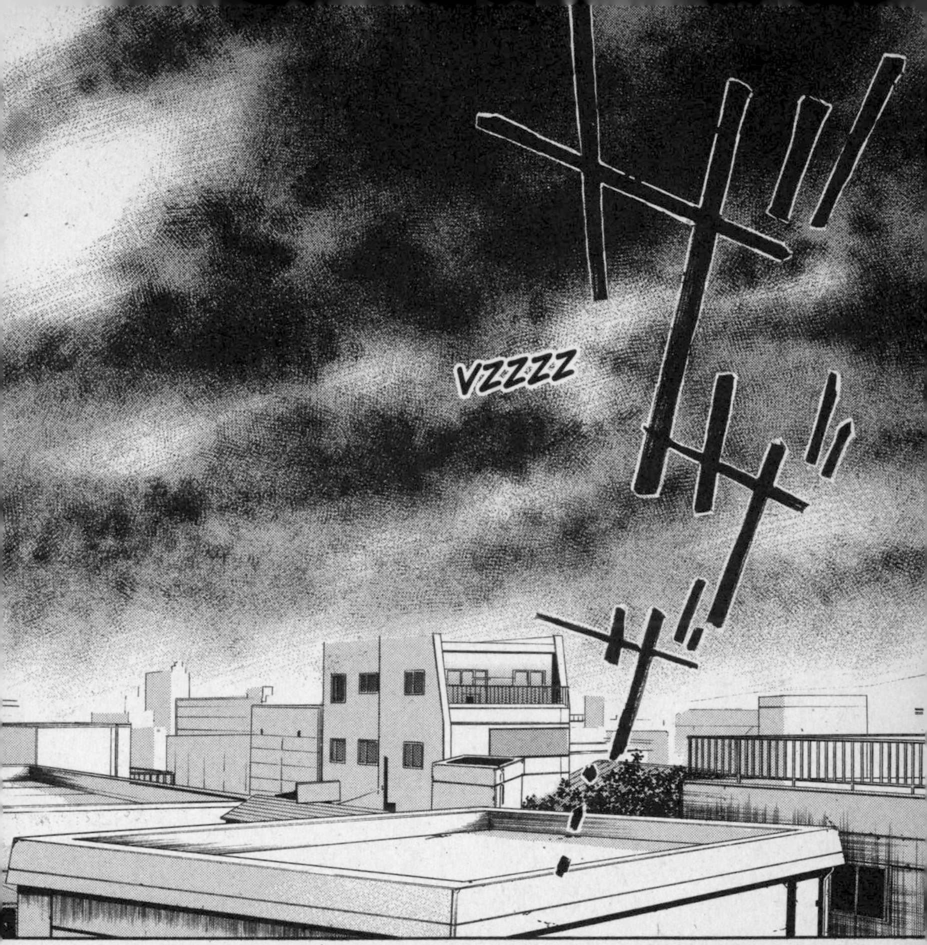
VZZZZ
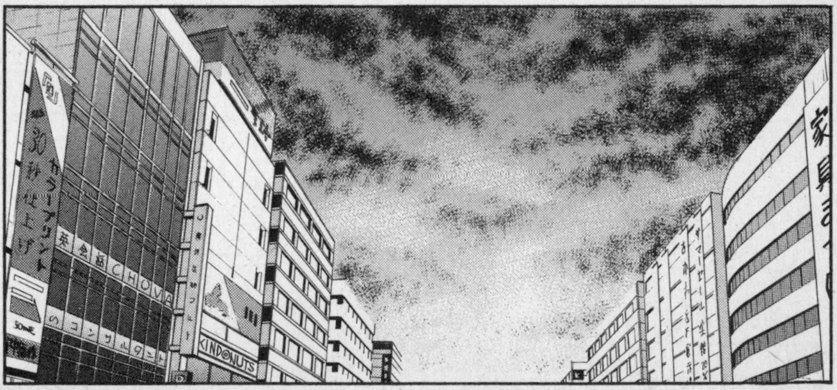

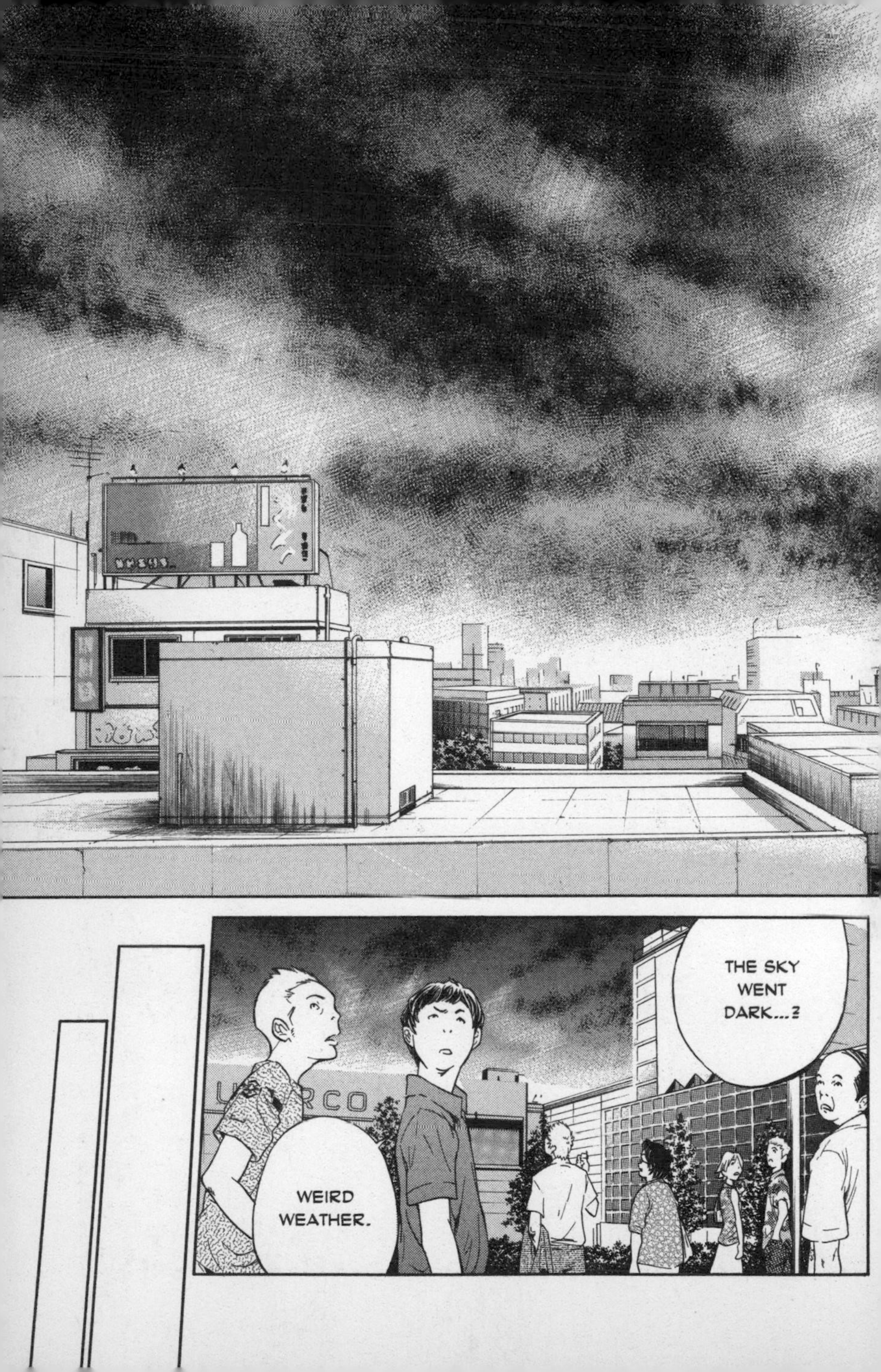
THE SKY WENT DARK...?
WEIRD WEATHER.

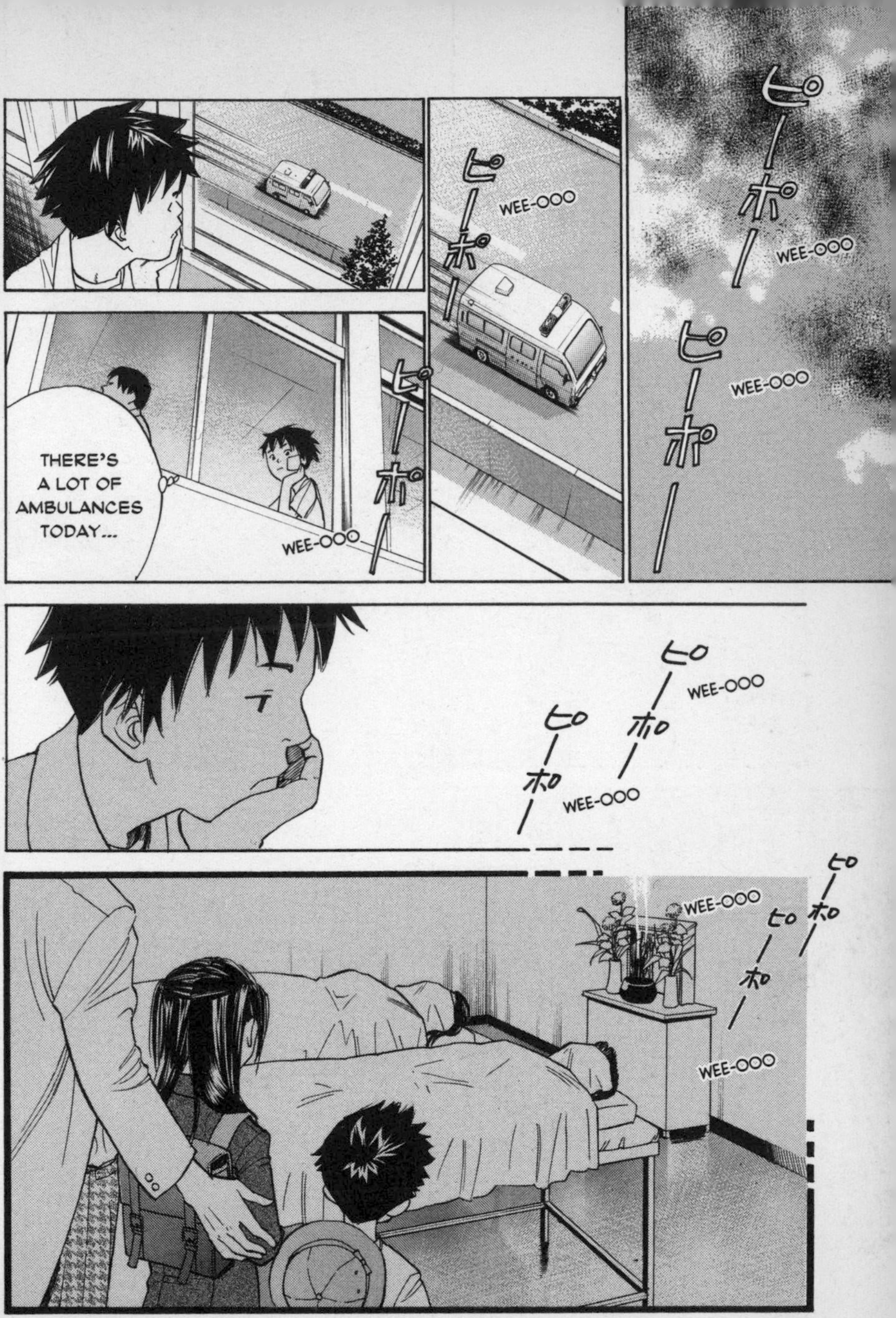
ピーポー
WEE-OOO
ピーポー
WEE-OOO
ピーポー
WEE-OOO
ピーポー
WEE-OOO
THERE'S A LOT OF AMBULANCES TODAY...
ピーポー
WEE-OOO
ピーポー
WEE-OOO
ピーポー
WEE-OOO
ピーポー
WEE-OOO

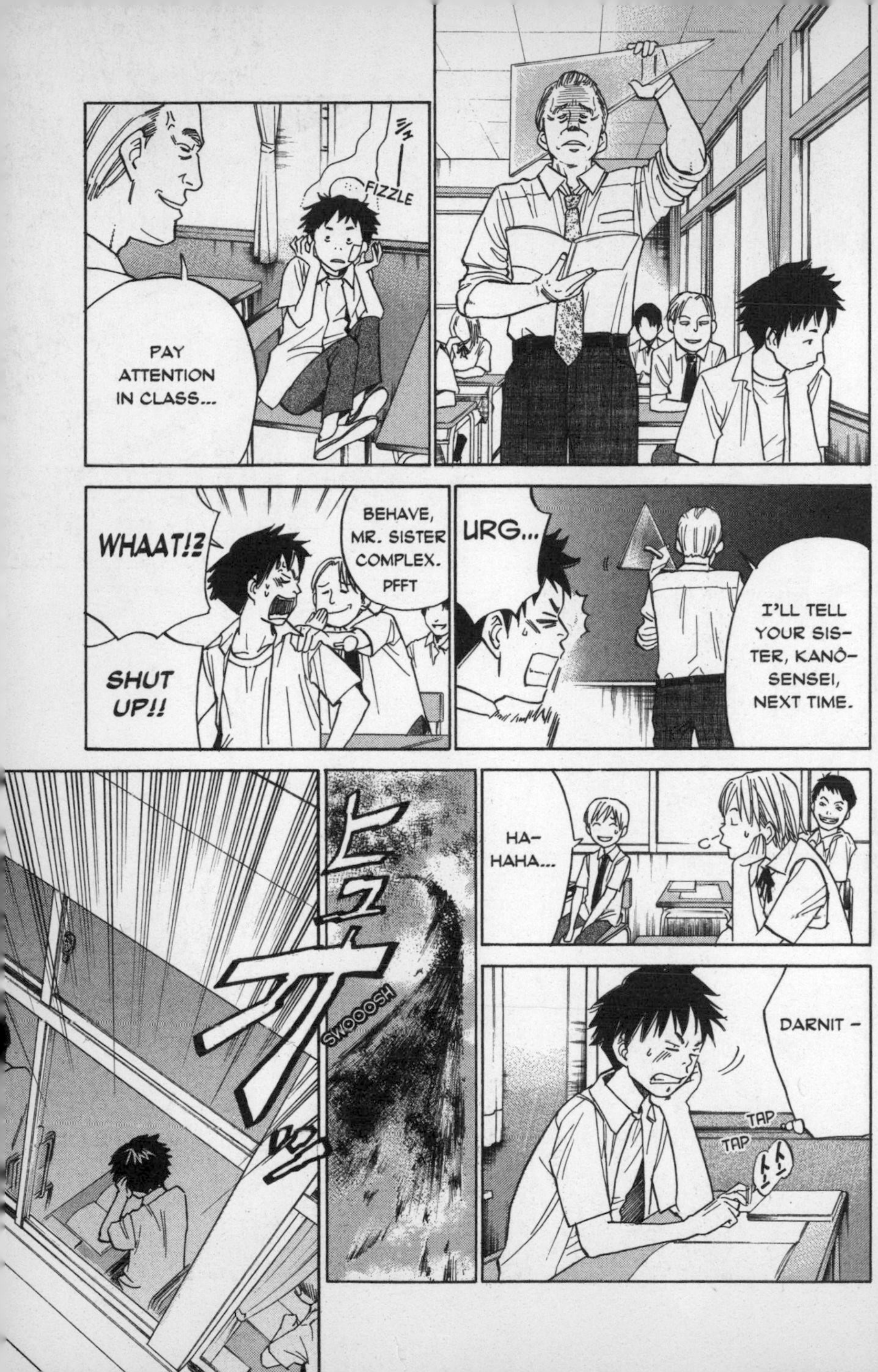
FIZZLE
PAY ATTENTION IN CLASS...
I'LL TELL YOUR SISTER, KANÔ-SENSEI, NEXT TIME.
URG...
BEHAVE, MR. SISTER COMPLEX. PFFT
WHAAT!?
SHUT UP!!
HA-HAHA...
DARNIT –
TAP
TAP
SWOOOSH

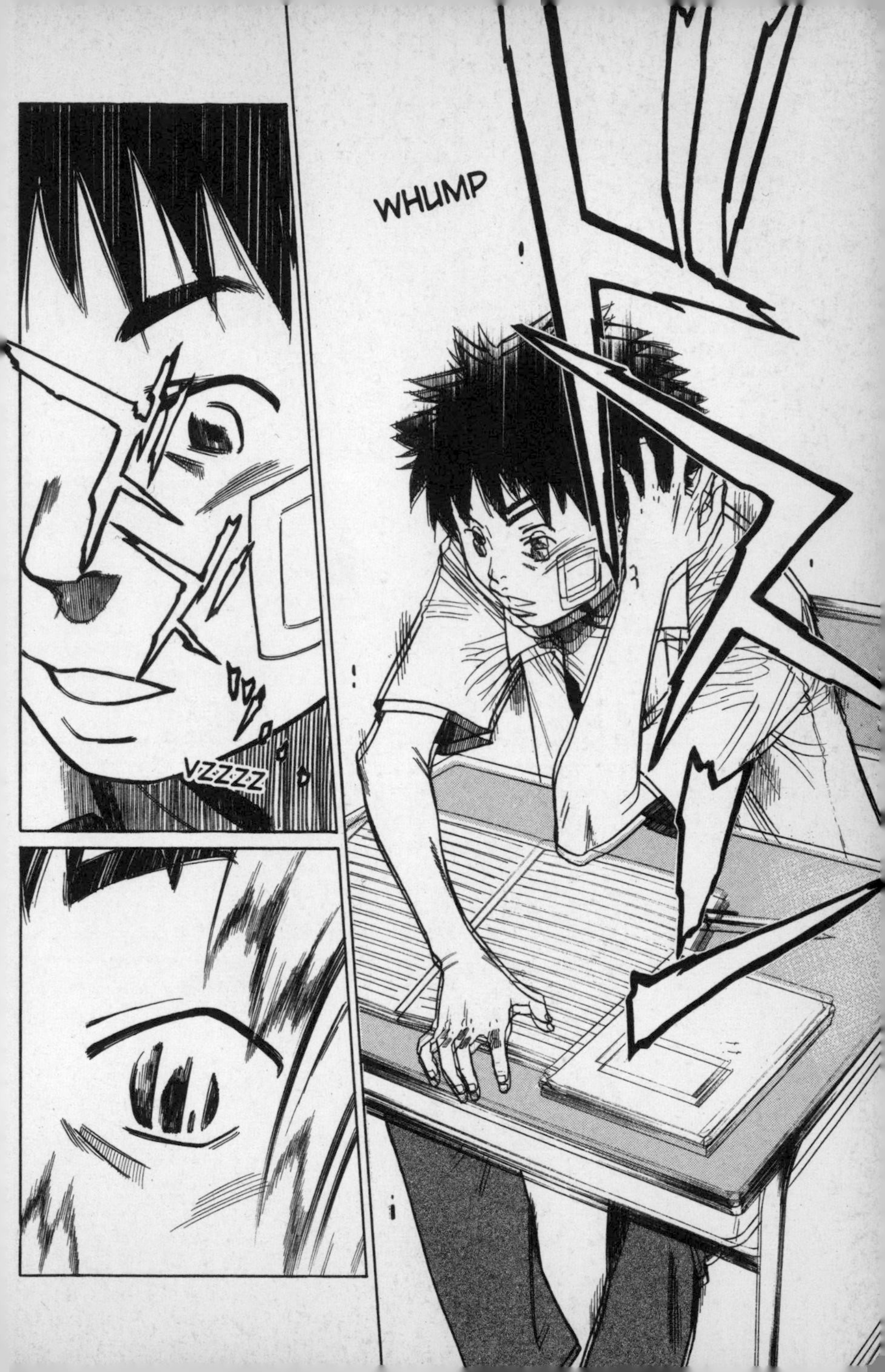
WHUMP
VZZZZ

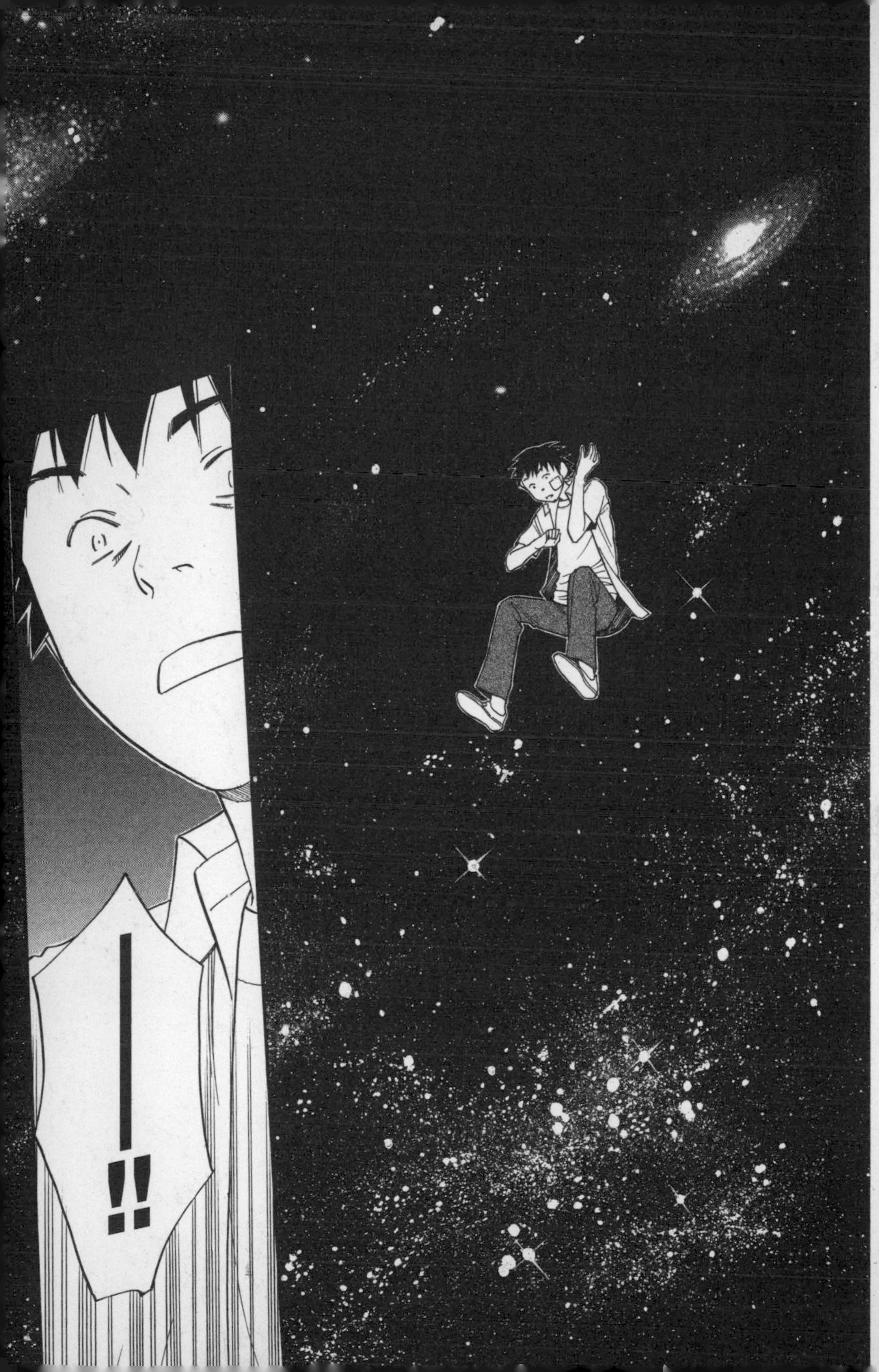
—!!

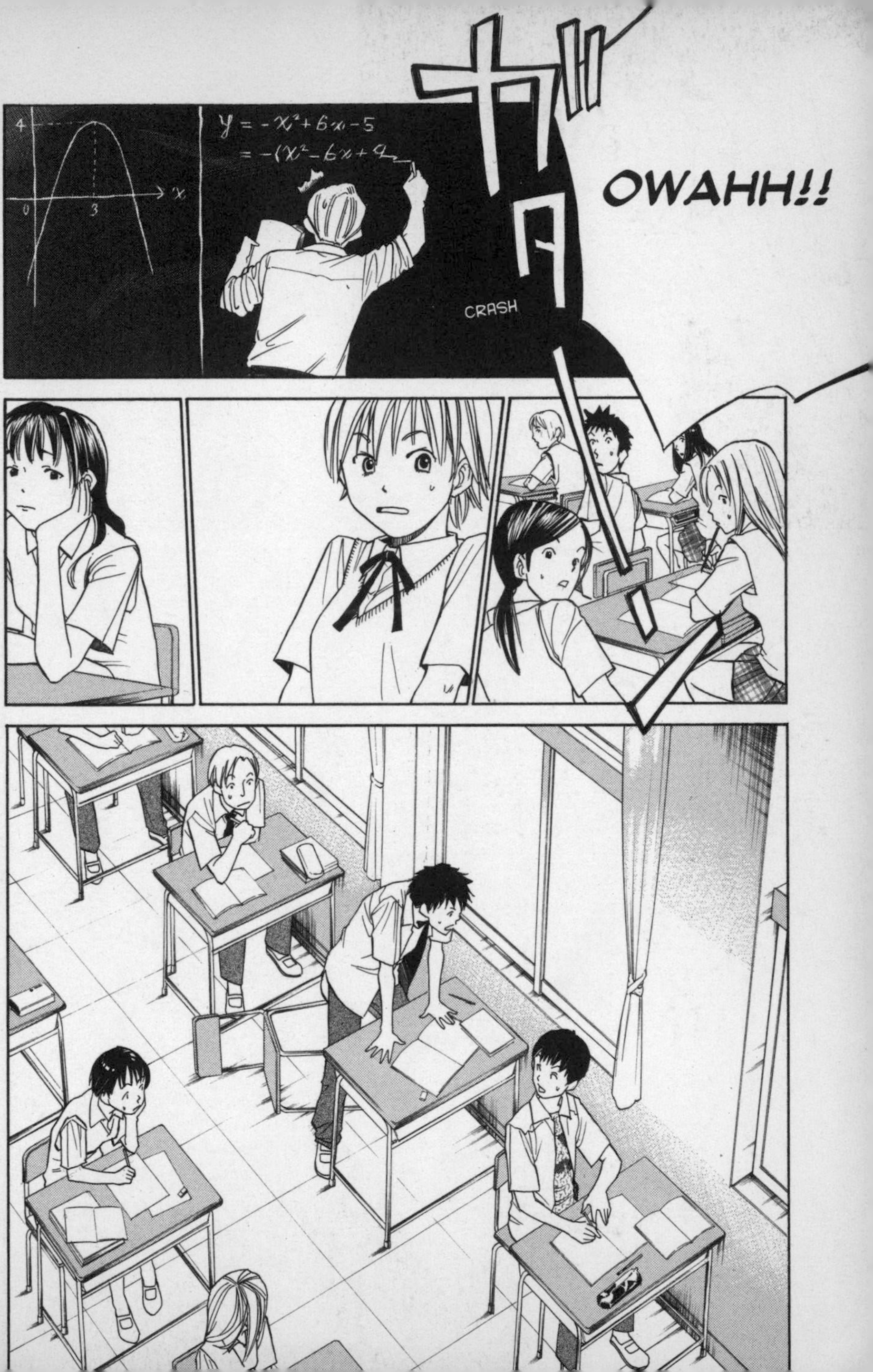
$y = -x^2 + 6x - 5$
OWAHH!!
CRASH

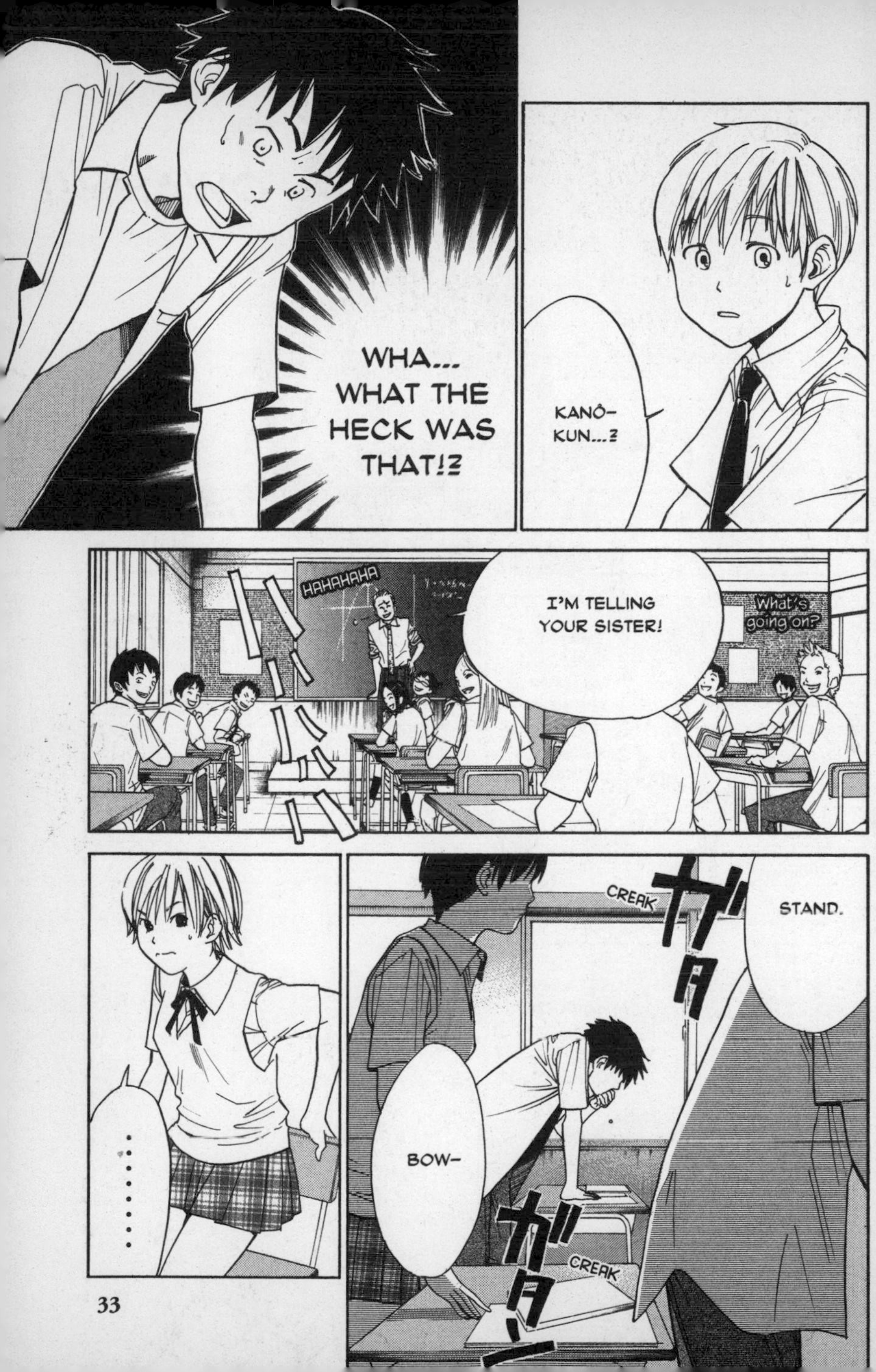
KANÔ-KUN...!?
WHA... WHAT THE HECK WAS THAT!?
What's going on?
I'M TELLING YOUR SISTER!
HAHAHAHA
STAND.
CREAK
BOW-
CREAK
....

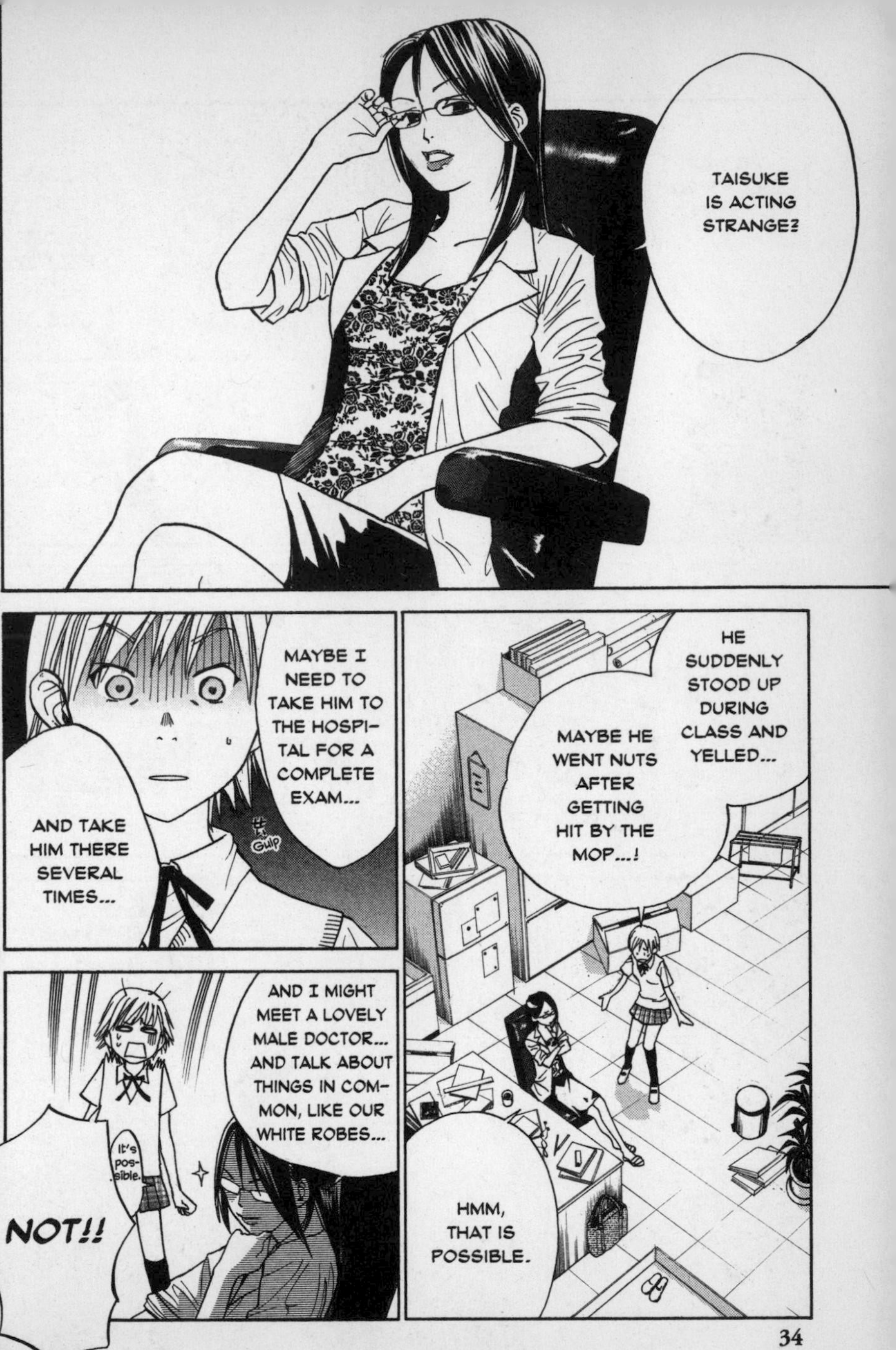
TAISUKE IS ACTING STRANGE?
HE SUDDENLY STOOD UP DURING CLASS AND YELLED...
MAYBE HE WENT NUTS AFTER GETTING HIT BY THE MOP...!
HMM, THAT IS POSSIBLE.
MAYBE I NEED TO TAKE HIM TO THE HOSPITAL FOR A COMPLETE EXAM...
AND TAKE HIM THERE SEVERAL TIMES...
Gulp
AND I MIGHT MEET A LOVELY MALE DOCTOR... AND TALK ABOUT THINGS IN COMMON, LIKE OUR WHITE ROBES...
It's possible.
NOT!!

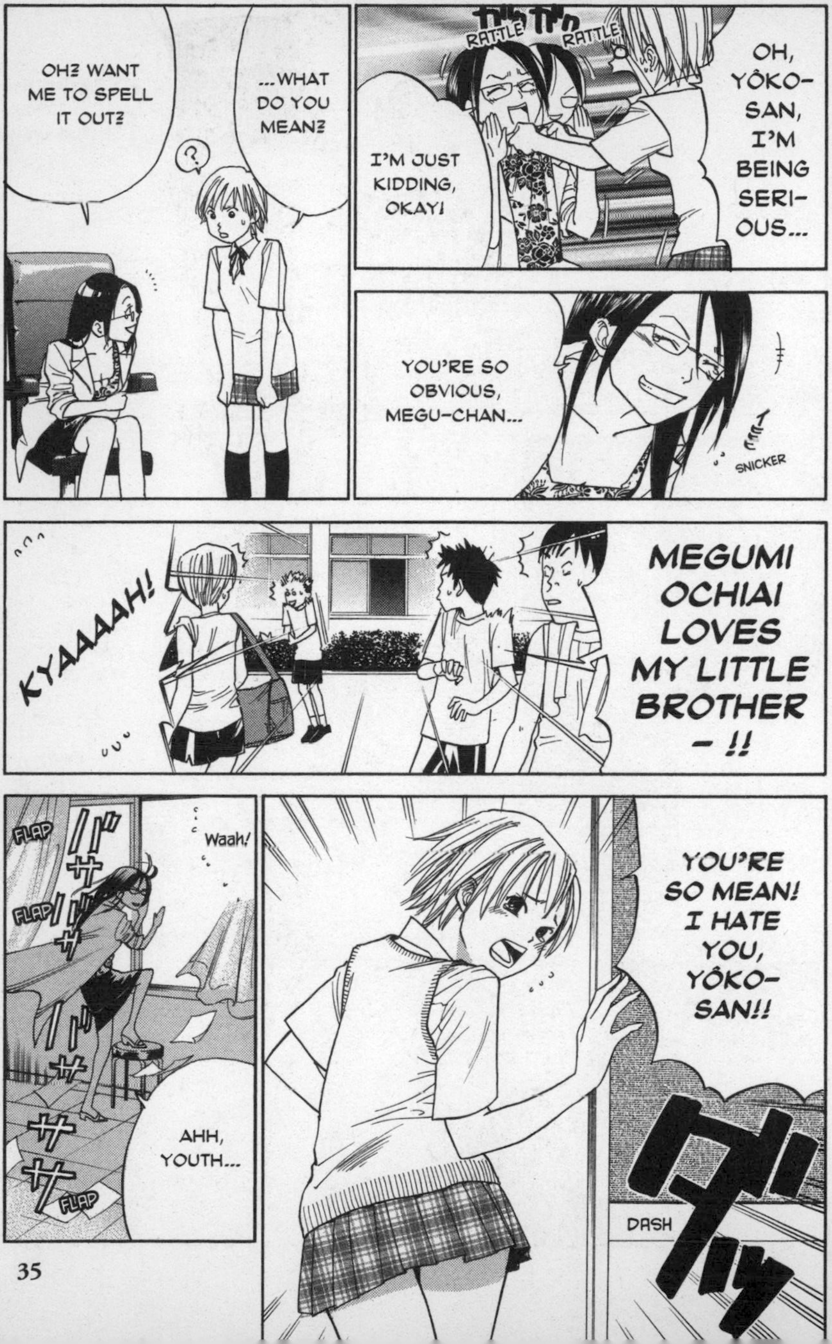
RATTLE RATTLE
OH, YÔKO-SAN, I'M BEING SERIOUS...
I'M JUST KIDDING, OKAY!
YOU'RE SO OBVIOUS, MEGU-CHAN...
SNICKER
...WHAT DO YOU MEAN?
OH? WANT ME TO SPELL IT OUT?
MEGUMI OCHIAI LOVES MY LITTLE BROTHER – !!
KYAAAAH!
YOU'RE SO MEAN! I HATE YOU, YÔKO-SAN!!
DASH
Waah!
FLAP
FLAP
AHH, YOUTH...
FLAP

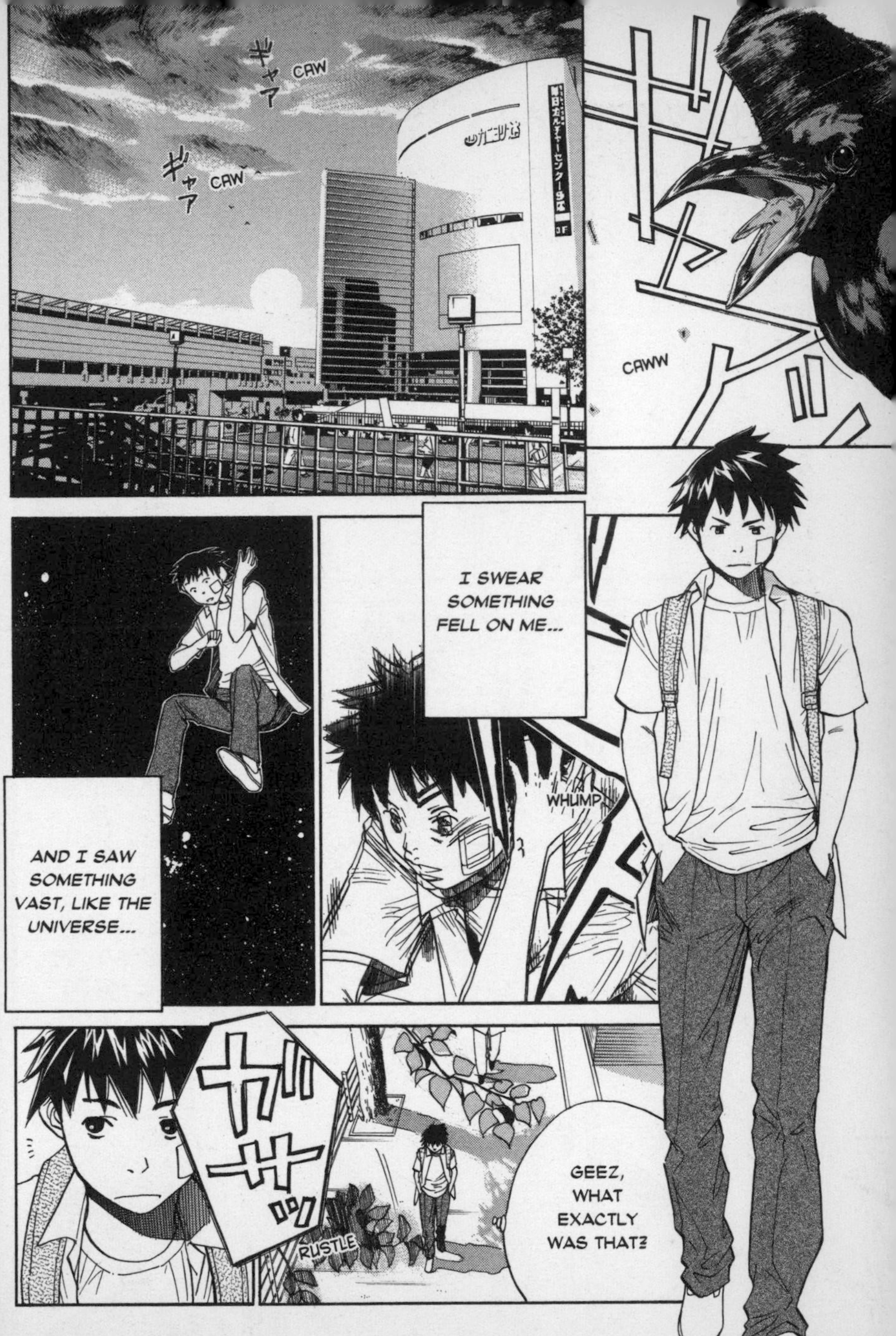
CAWW
ギャア
CAW
ギャア
CAW
I SWEAR SOMETHING FELL ON ME...
WHUMP
AND I SAW SOMETHING VAST, LIKE THE UNIVERSE...
GEEZ, WHAT EXACTLY WAS THAT?
RUSTLE

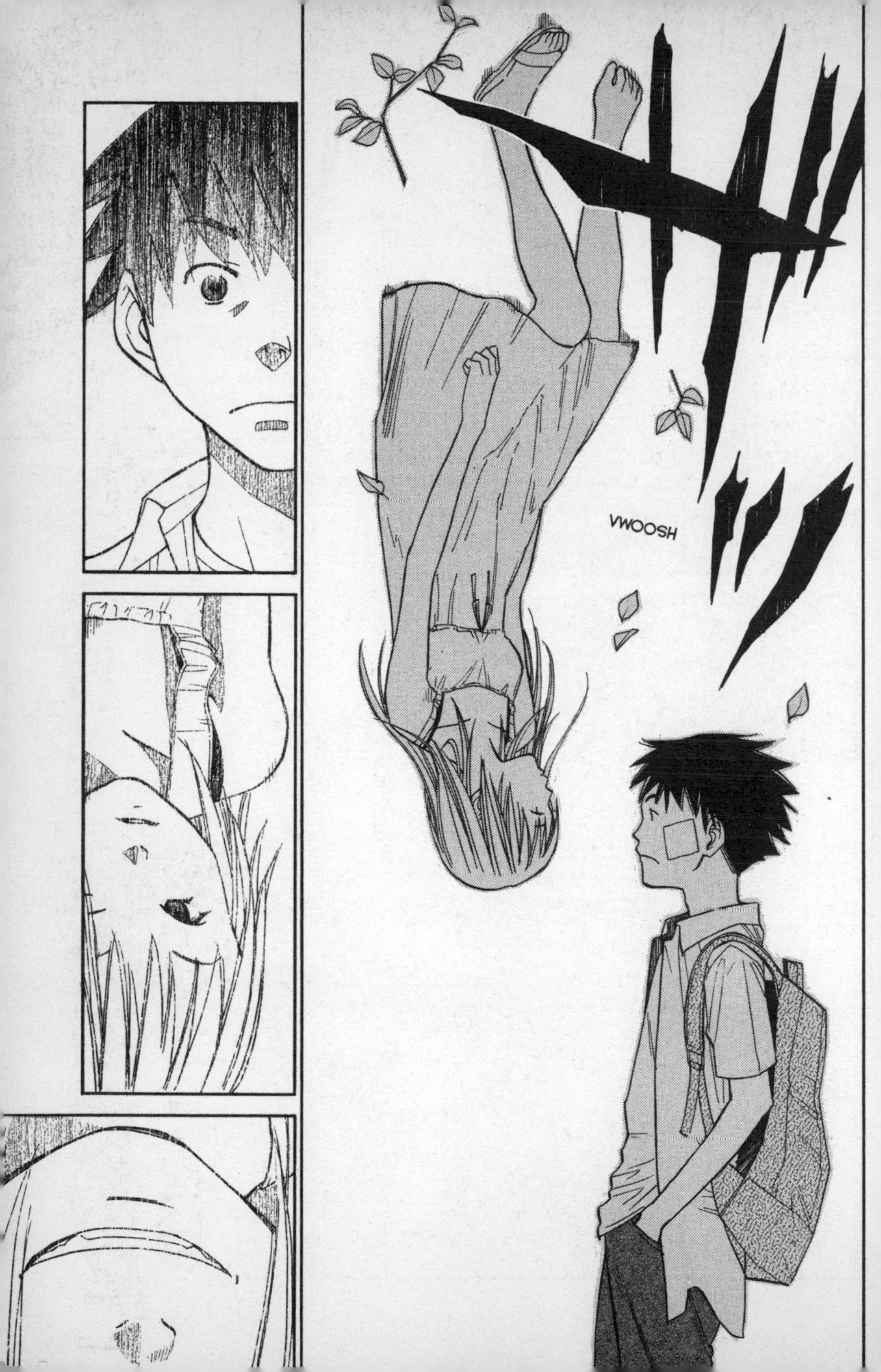
VWOOSH

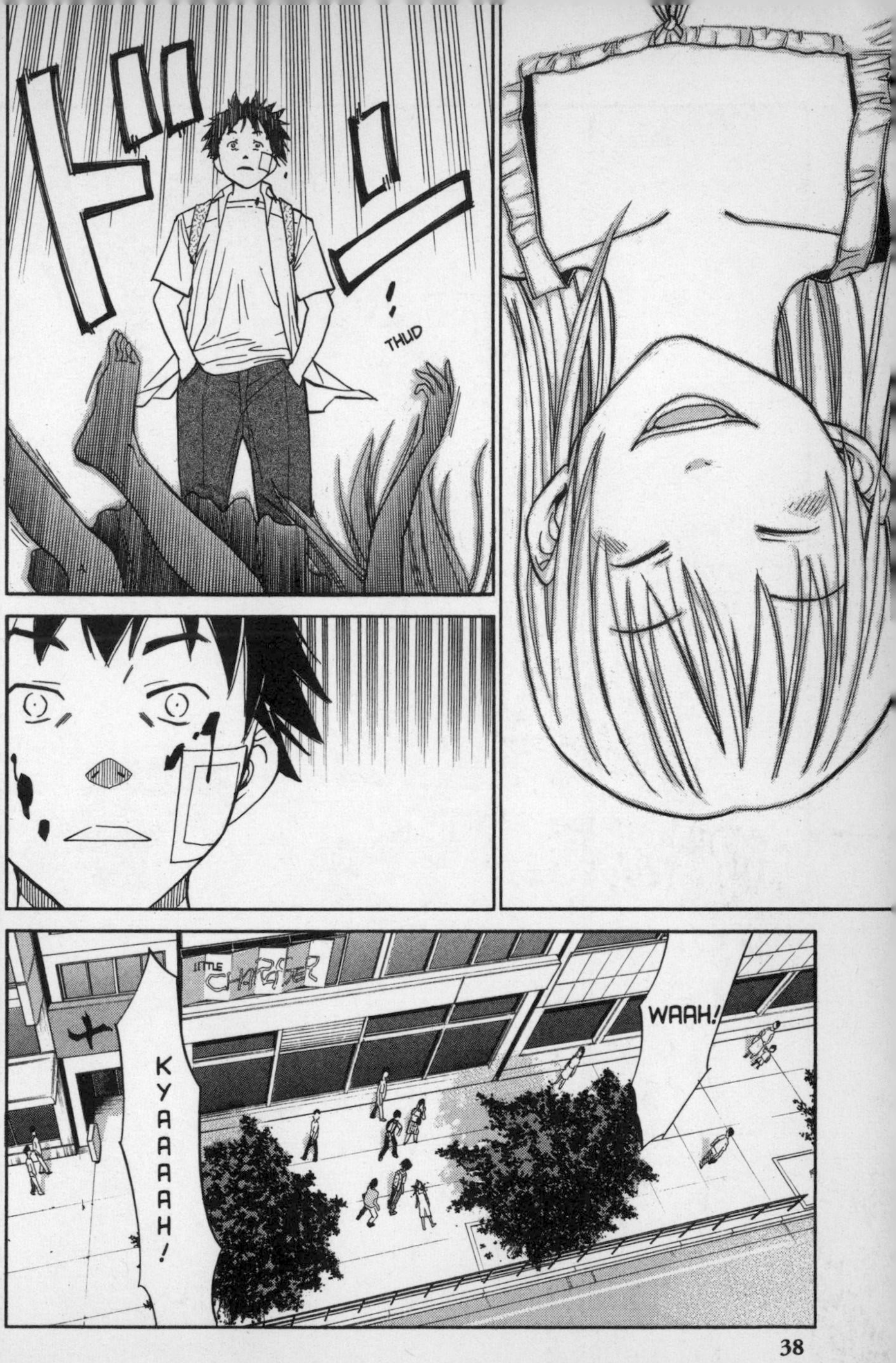
THUD
WAAH!
KYAAAAAH!

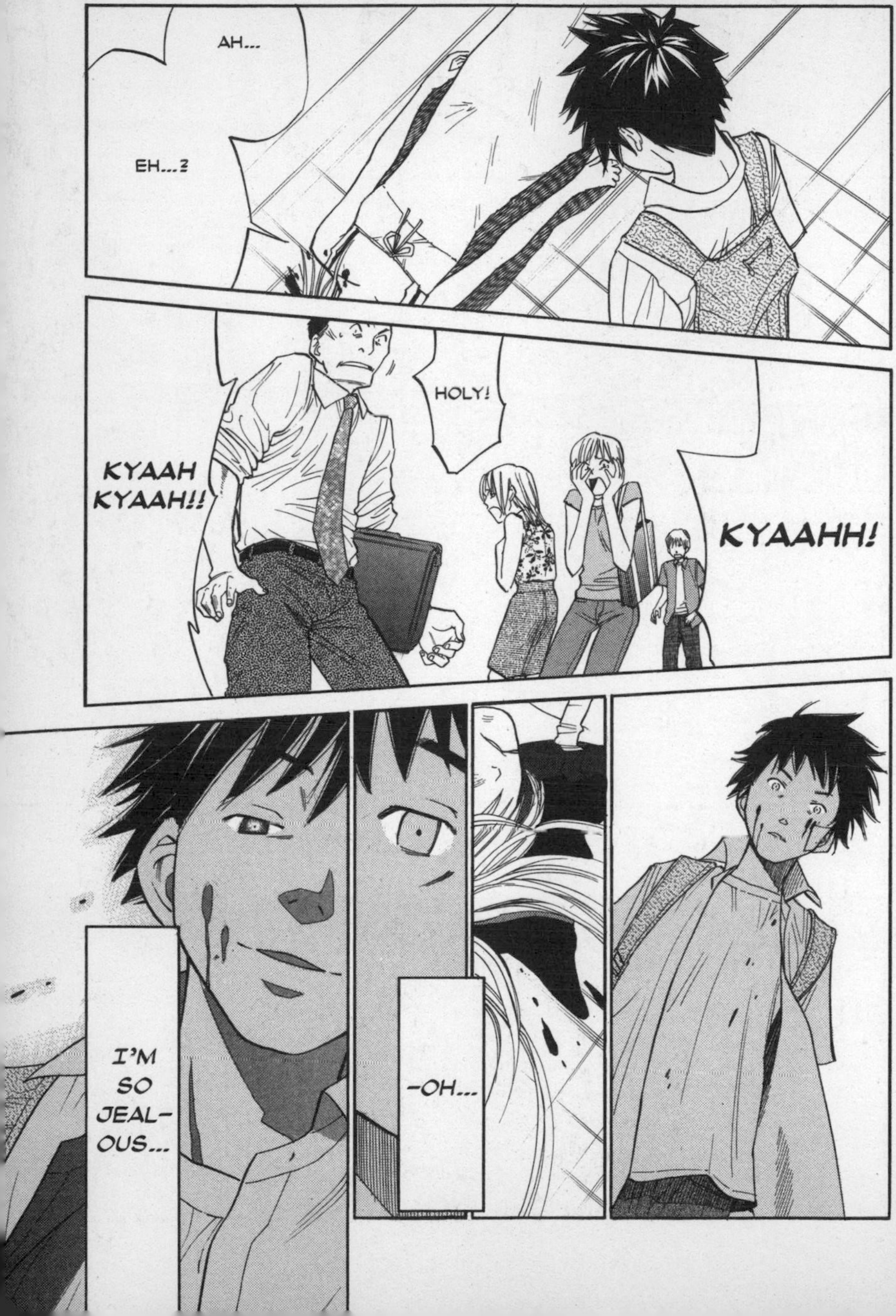
AH...
EH...?
HOLY!
KYAAHH!
KYAAH KYAAH!!
-OH...
I'M SO JEAL-OUS...

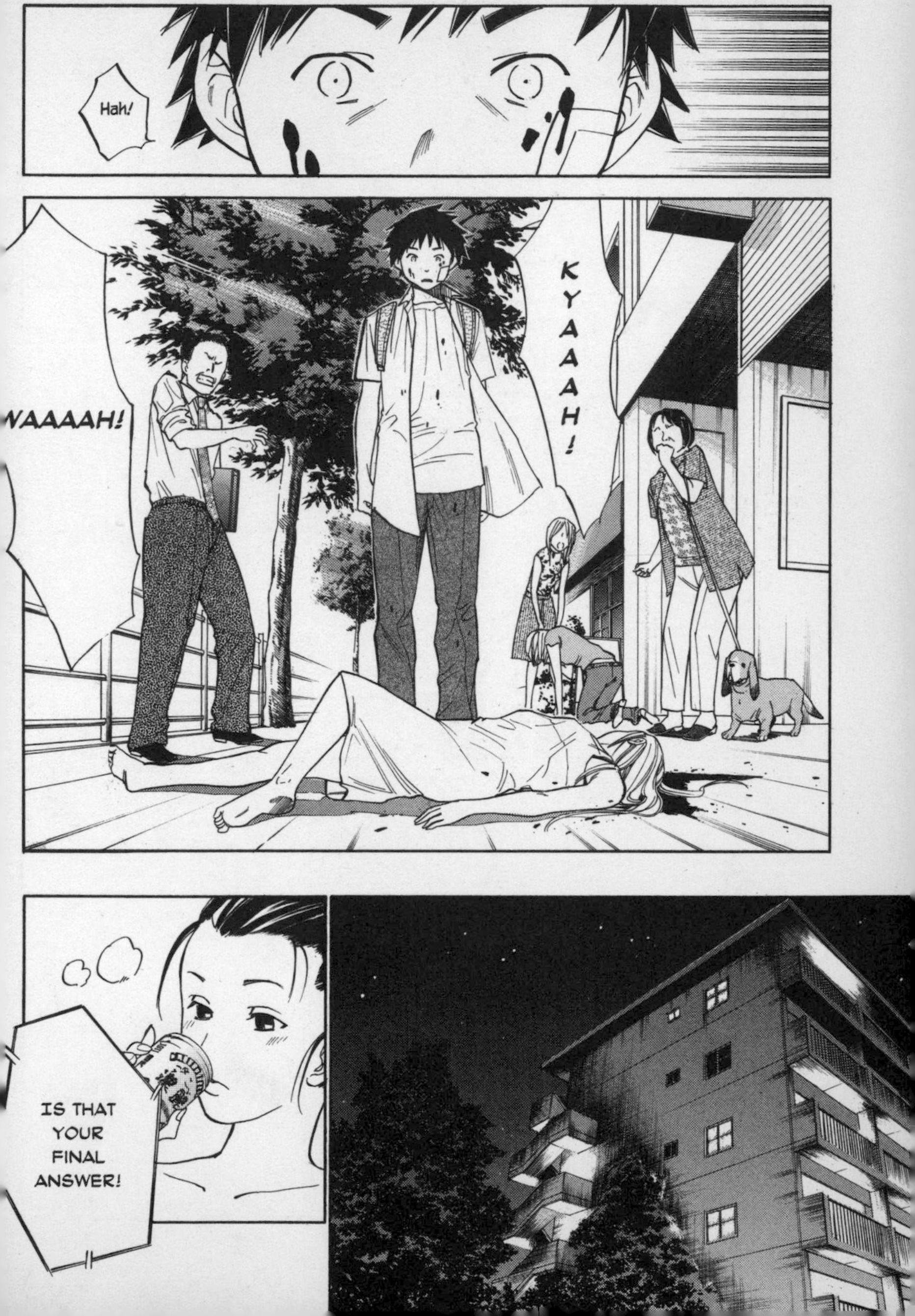
Hah!
KYAAAAH!
WAAAAH!
IS THAT YOUR FINAL ANSWER!

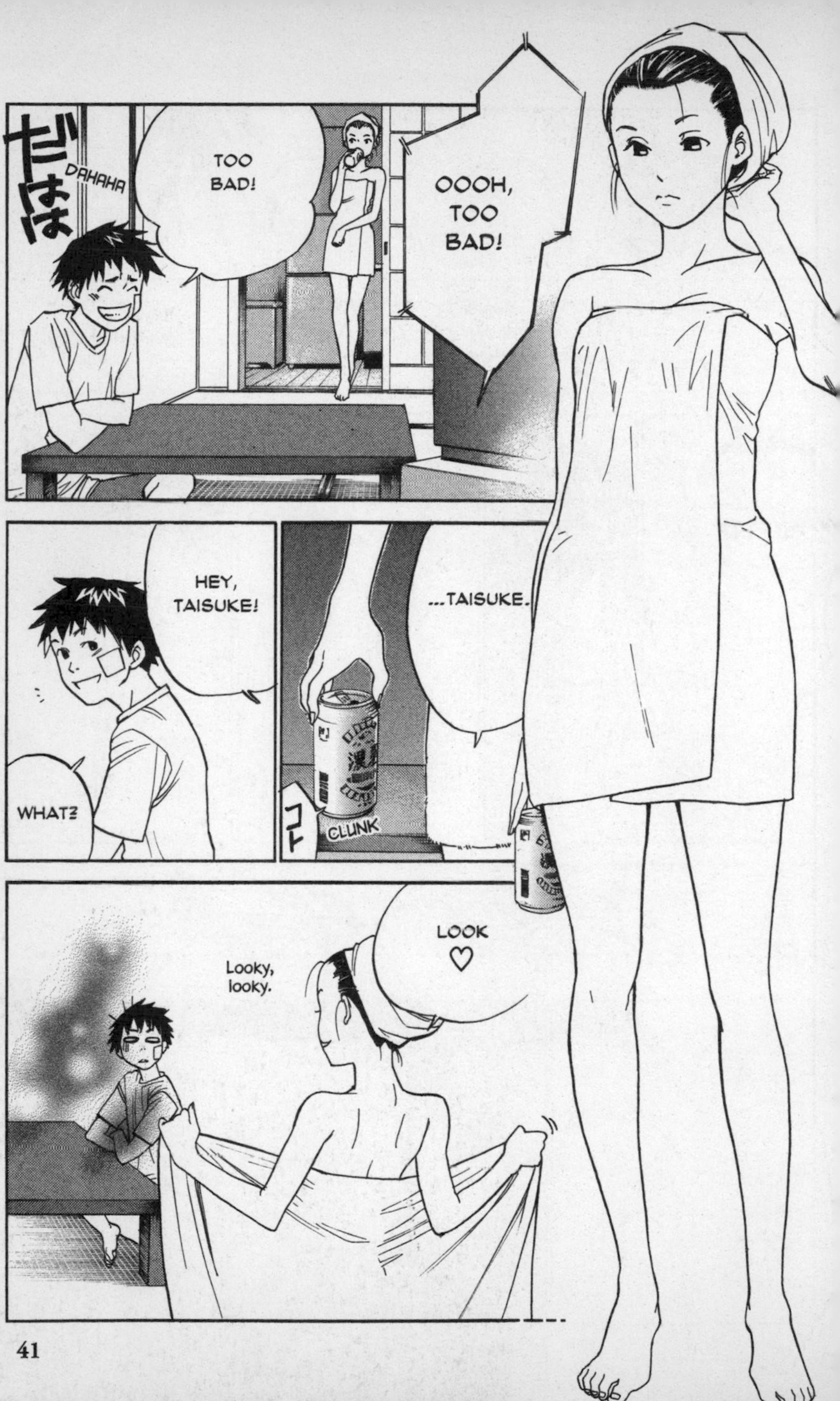
OOOH, TOO BAD!
だはは
DAHAHA
TOO BAD!
...TAISUKE.
コト
CLUNK
HEY, TAISUKE!
WHAT?
LOOK ♡
Looky, looky.

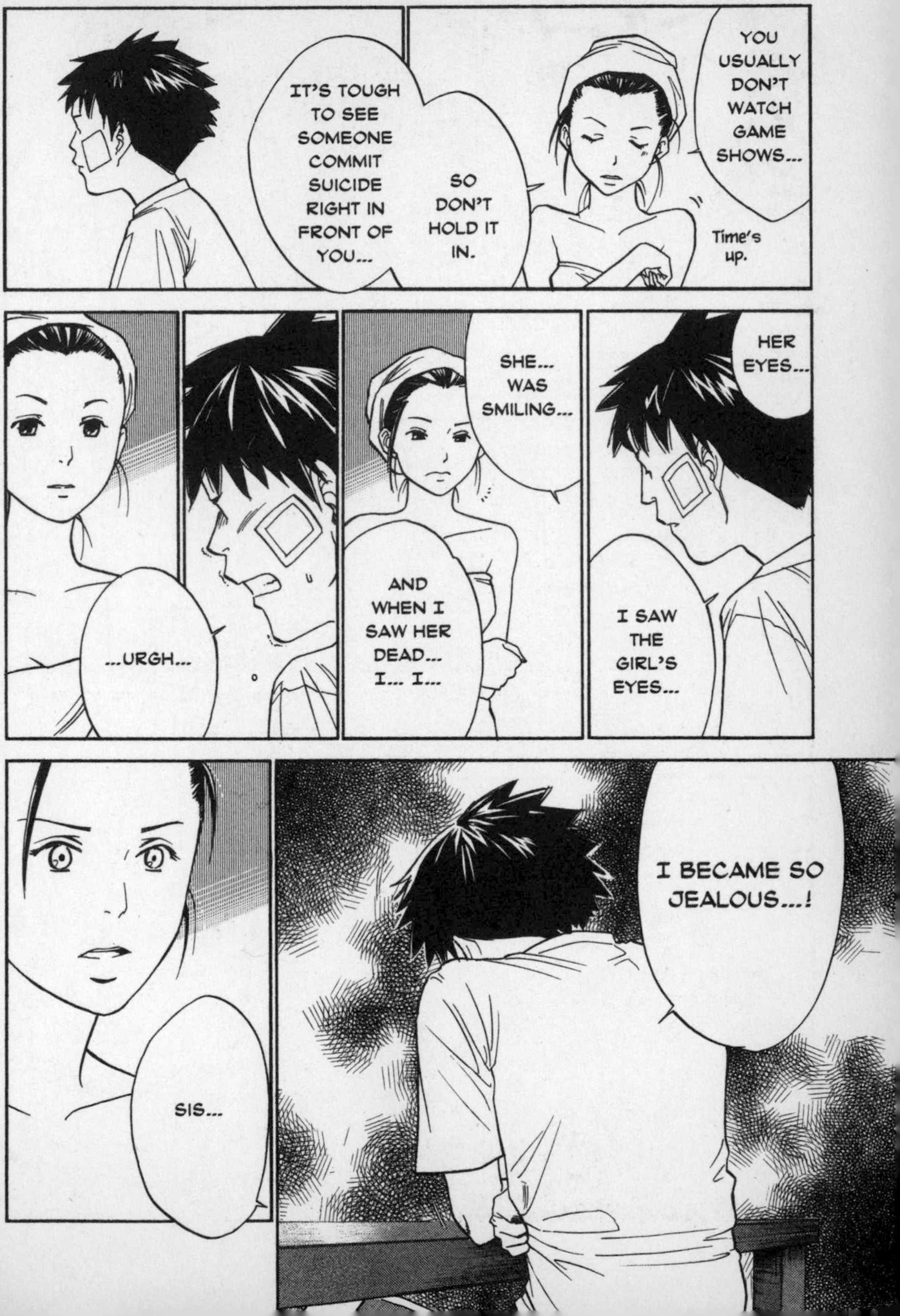
YOU USUALLY DON'T WATCH GAME SHOWS...
Time's up.
IT'S TOUGH TO SEE SOMEONE COMMIT SUICIDE RIGHT IN FRONT OF YOU...
SO DON'T HOLD IT IN.
HER EYES...
I SAW THE GIRL'S EYES...
SHE... WAS SMILING...
AND WHEN I SAW HER DEAD... I... I...
...URGH...
I BECAME SO JEALOUS...!
SIS...

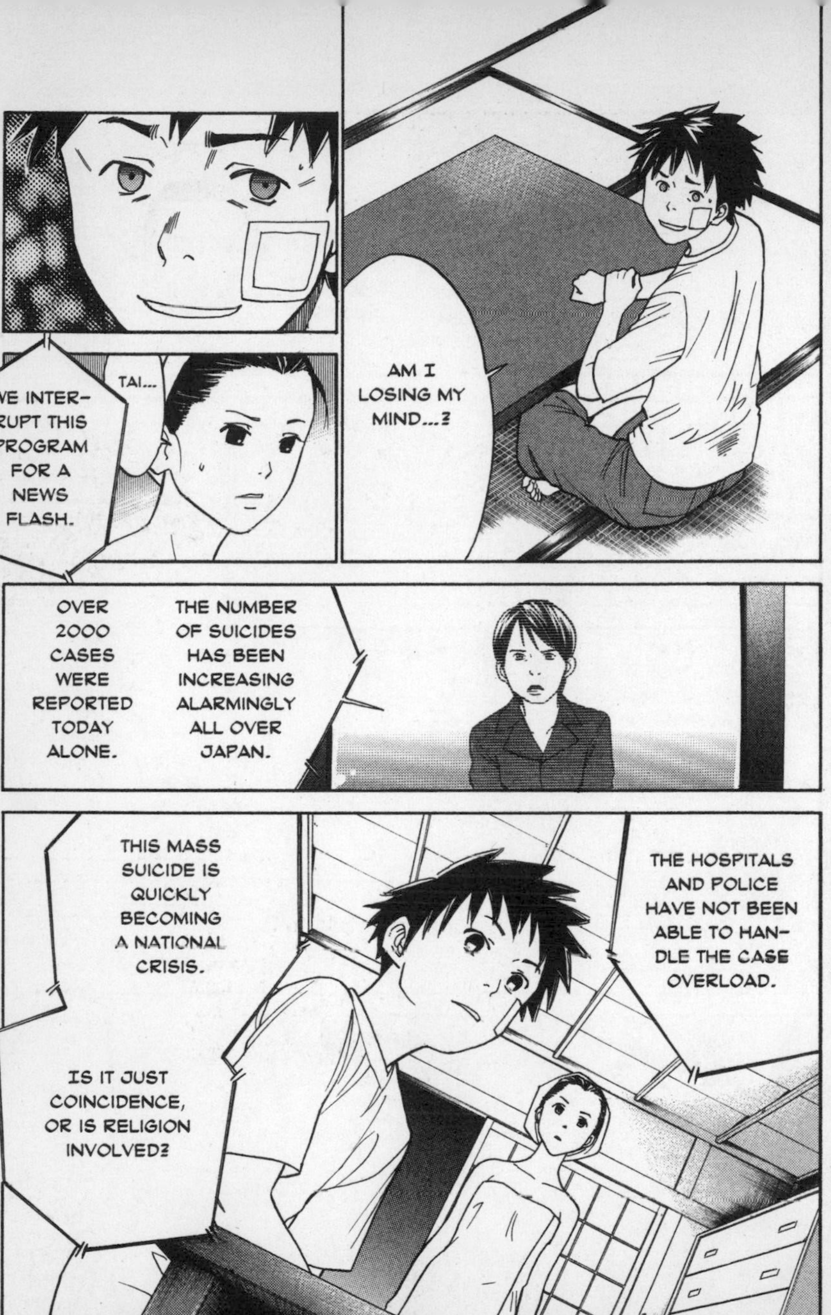
AM I LOSING MY MIND...?
TAI...
WE INTER-RUPT THIS PROGRAM FOR A NEWS FLASH.
THE NUMBER OF SUICIDES HAS BEEN INCREASING ALARMINGLY ALL OVER JAPAN.
OVER 2000 CASES WERE REPORTED TODAY ALONE.
THE HOSPITALS AND POLICE HAVE NOT BEEN ABLE TO HAN-DLE THE CASE OVERLOAD.
THIS MASS SUICIDE IS QUICKLY BECOMING A NATIONAL CRISIS.
IS IT JUST COINCIDENCE, OR IS RELIGION INVOLVED?

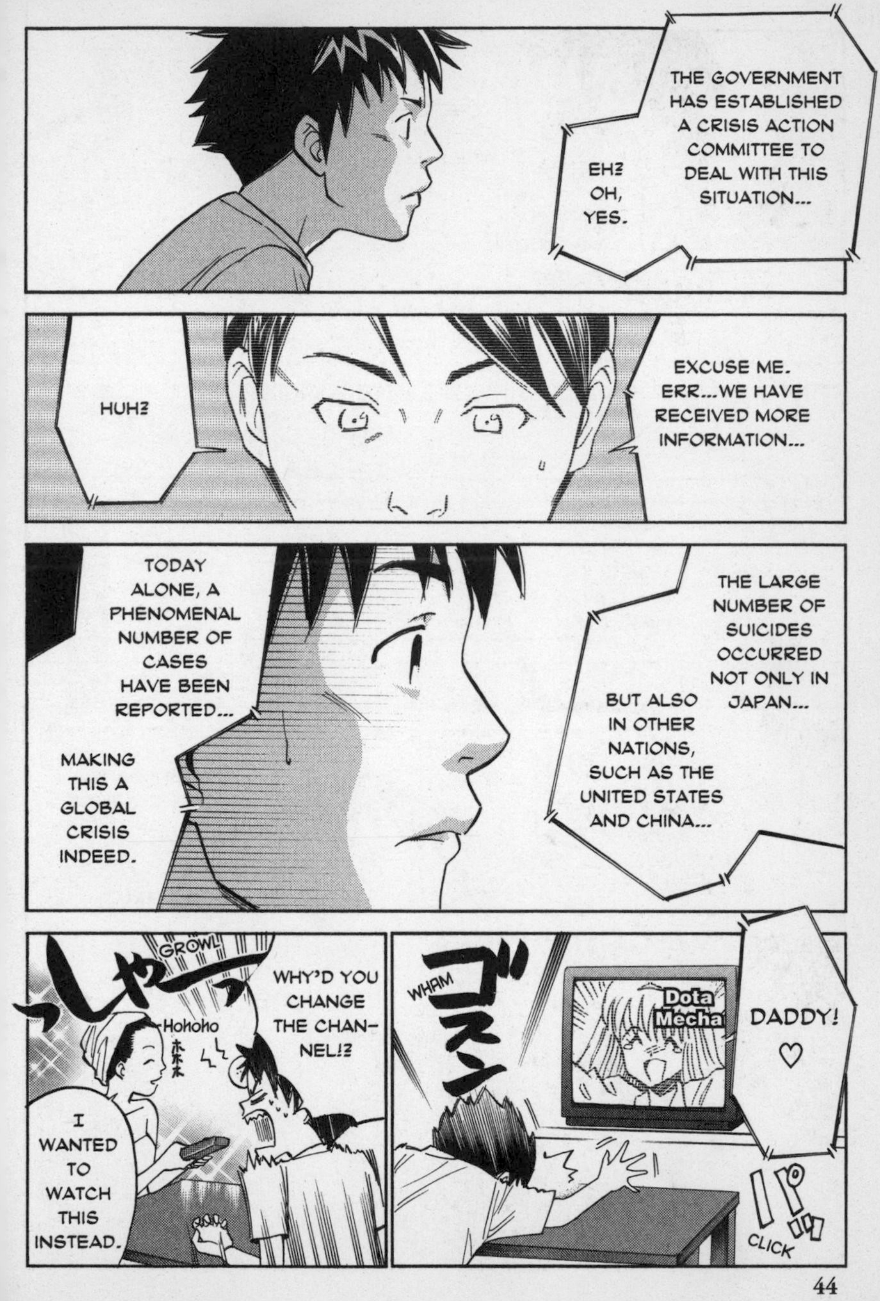
THE GOVERNMENT HAS ESTABLISHED A CRISIS ACTION COMMITTEE TO DEAL WITH THIS SITUATION...
EH? OH, YES.
EXCUSE ME. ERR...WE HAVE RECEIVED MORE INFORMATION...
HUH?
THE LARGE NUMBER OF SUICIDES OCCURRED NOT ONLY IN JAPAN...
BUT ALSO IN OTHER NATIONS, SUCH AS THE UNITED STATES AND CHINA...
TODAY ALONE, A PHENOMENAL NUMBER OF CASES HAVE BEEN REPORTED...
MAKING THIS A GLOBAL CRISIS INDEED.
DADDY! ♡
Dota Mecha
ゴスッ
WHAM
パッ
CLICK
WHY'D YOU CHANGE THE CHAN-NEL!?
GROWL
Hohoho
I WANTED TO WATCH THIS INSTEAD.

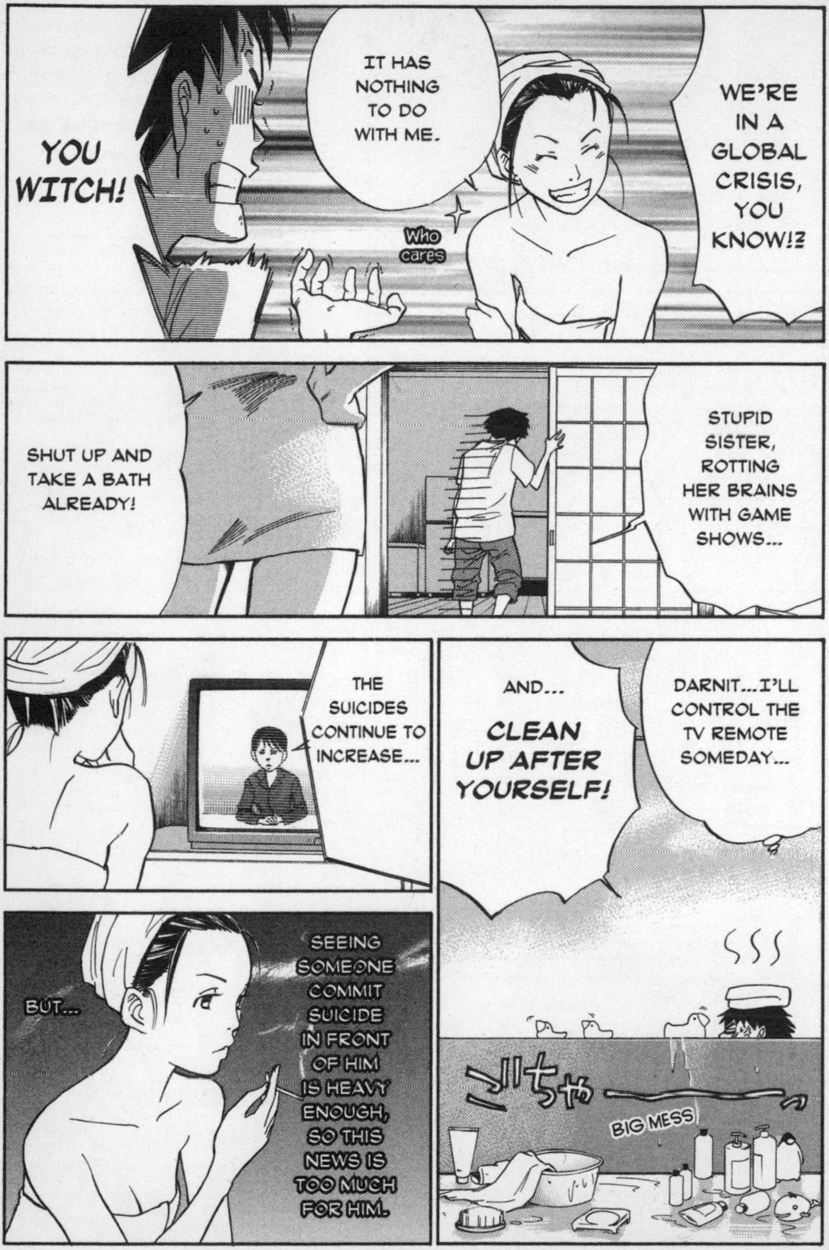
WE'RE IN A GLOBAL CRISIS, YOU KNOW!?
IT HAS NOTHING TO DO WITH ME.
Who cares
YOU WITCH!
STUPID SISTER, ROTTING HER BRAINS WITH GAME SHOWS...
SHUT UP AND TAKE A BATH ALREADY!
DARNIT...I'LL CONTROL THE TV REMOTE SOMEDAY...
AND... CLEAN UP AFTER YOURSELF!
BIG MESS
THE SUICIDES CONTINUE TO INCREASE...
SEEING SOMEONE COMMIT SUICIDE IN FRONT OF HIM IS HEAVY ENOUGH, SO THIS NEWS IS TOO MUCH FOR HIM.
BUT...

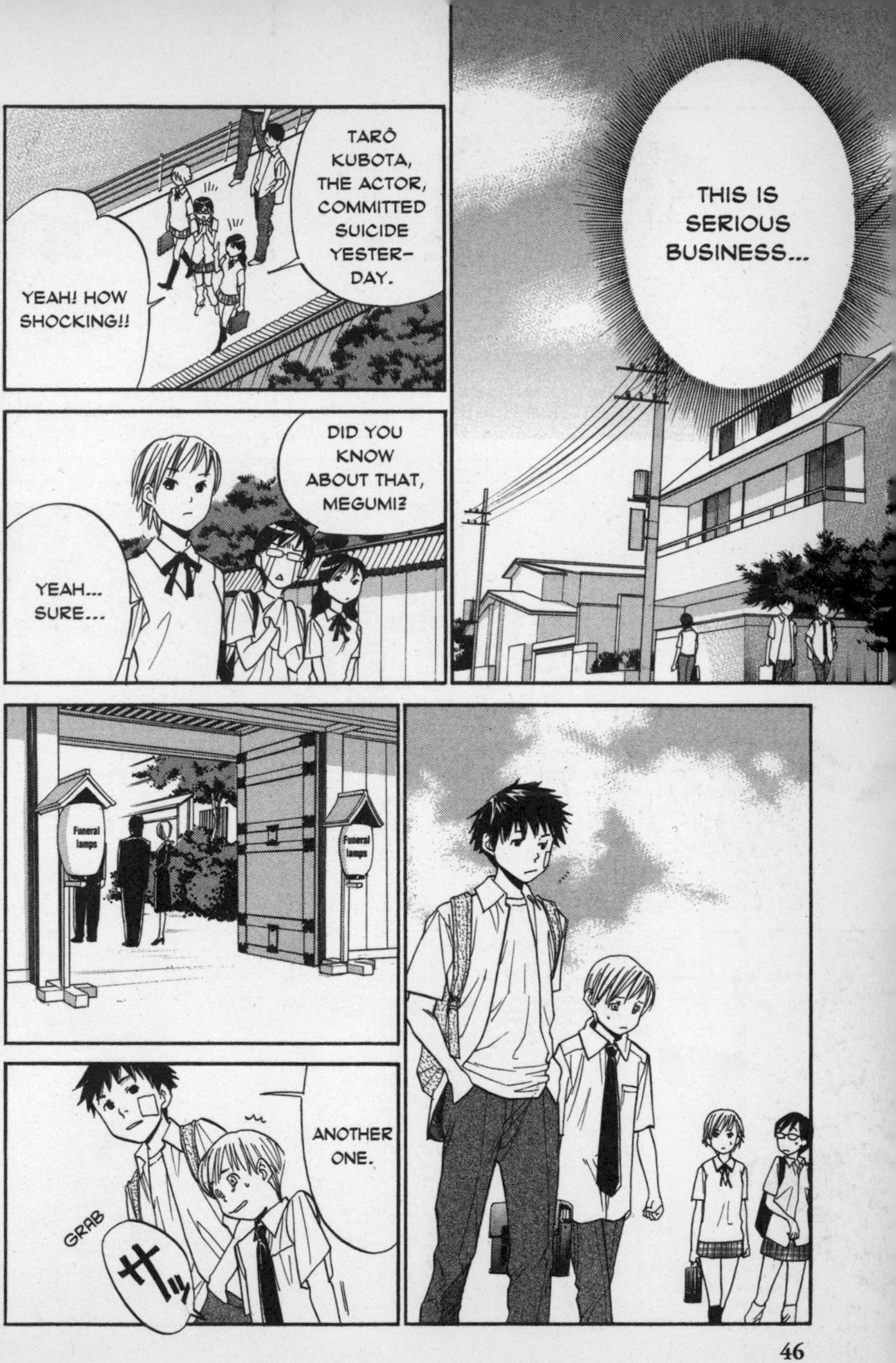
THIS IS SERIOUS BUSINESS...
TARÔ KUBOTA, THE ACTOR, COMMITTED SUICIDE YESTER-DAY.
YEAH! HOW SHOCKING!!
DID YOU KNOW ABOUT THAT, MEGUMI?
YEAH... SURE...
Funeral lamps
Funeral lamps
ANOTHER ONE.
GRAB
サッ

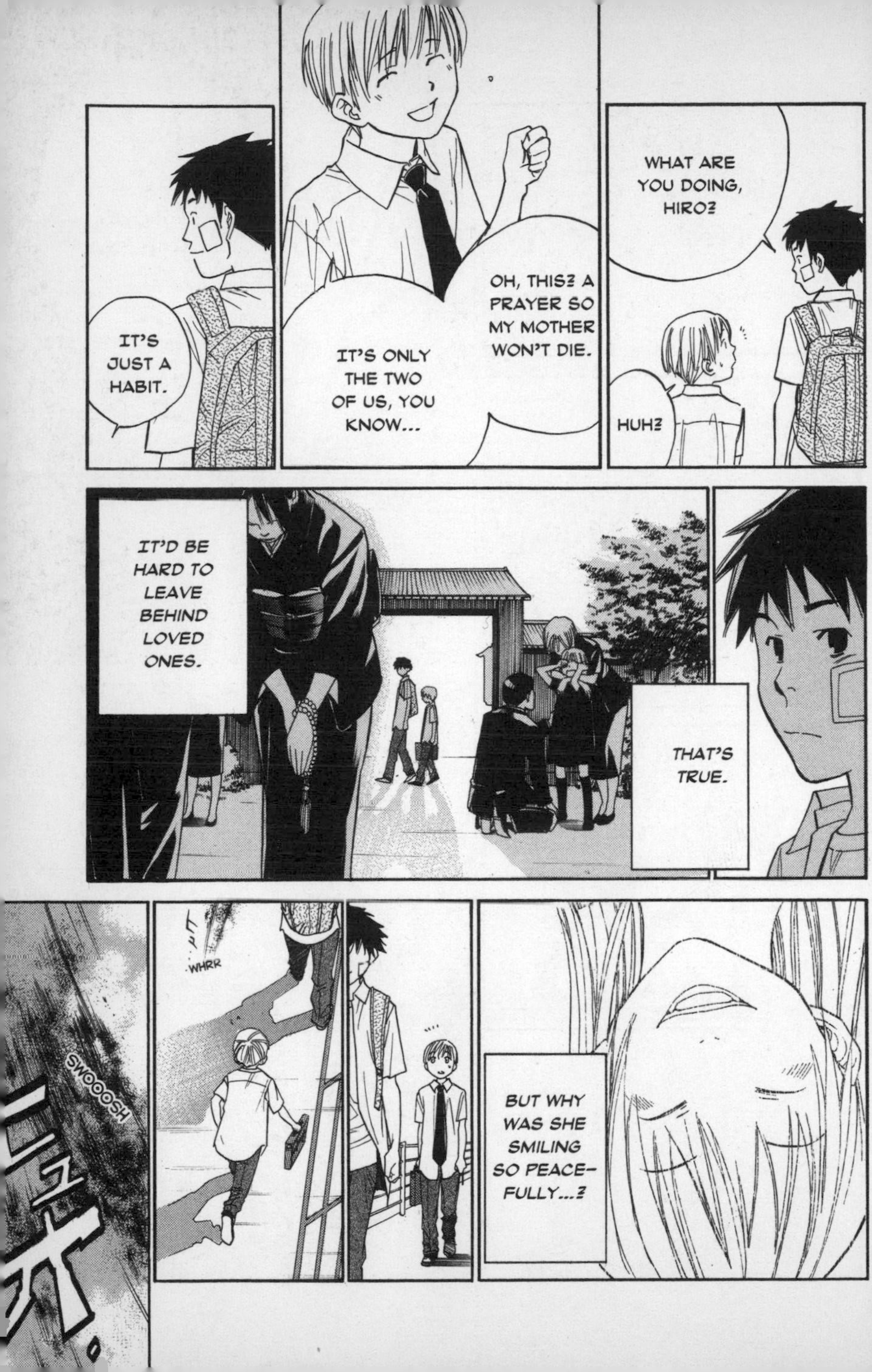
WHAT ARE YOU DOING, HIRO?
HUH?
OH, THIS? A PRAYER SO MY MOTHER WON'T DIE.
IT'S ONLY THE TWO OF US, YOU KNOW...
IT'S JUST A HABIT.
THAT'S TRUE.
IT'D BE HARD TO LEAVE BEHIND LOVED ONES.
BUT WHY WAS SHE SMILING SO PEACE-FULLY...?
WHRR
SWOOOSH

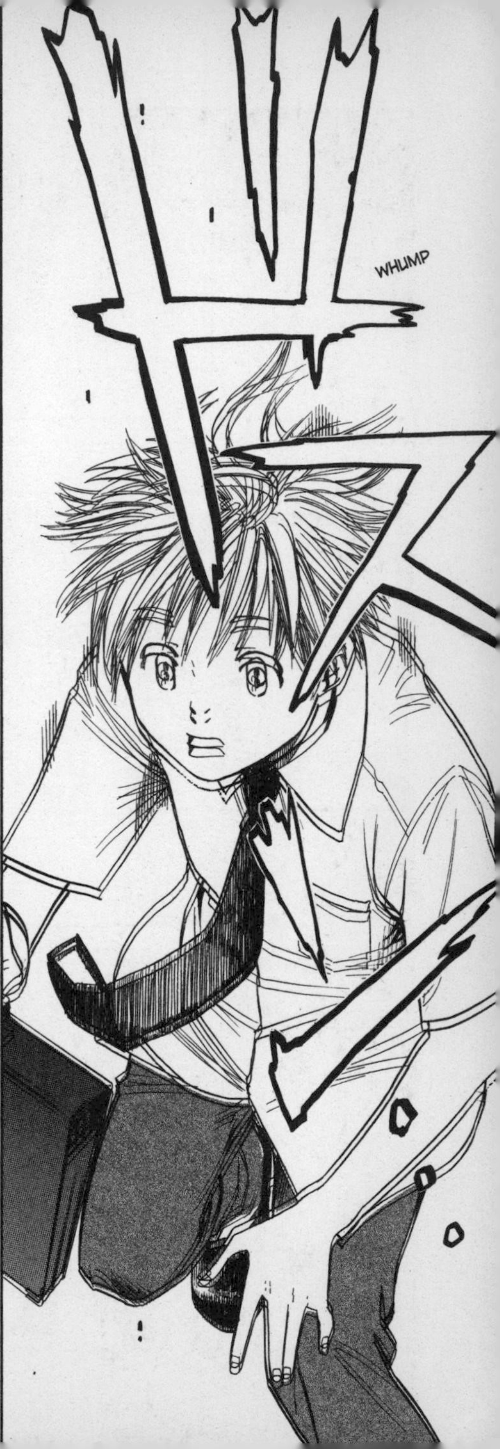
WHUMP

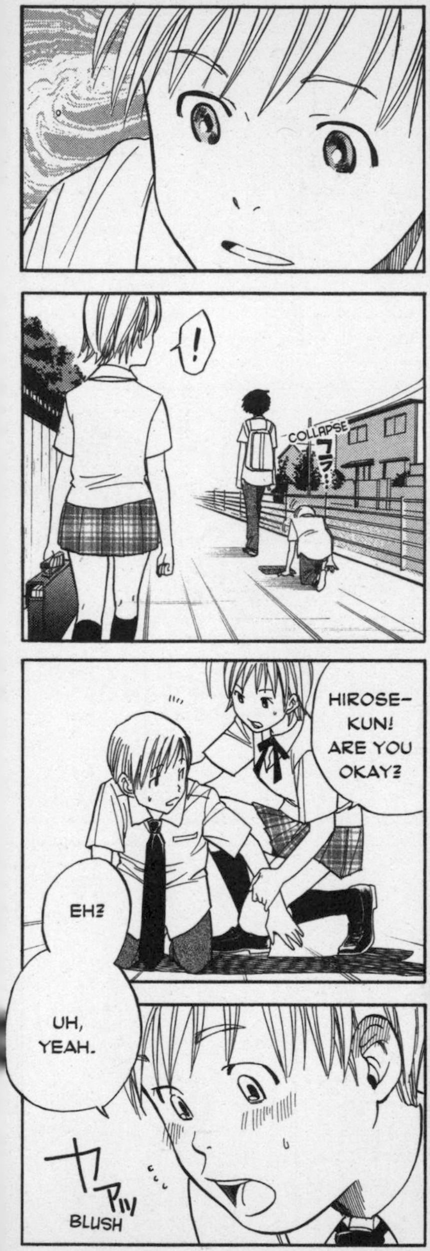
!
COLLAPSE
HIROSE-KUN! ARE YOU OKAY?
EH?
UH, YEAH.
BLUSH

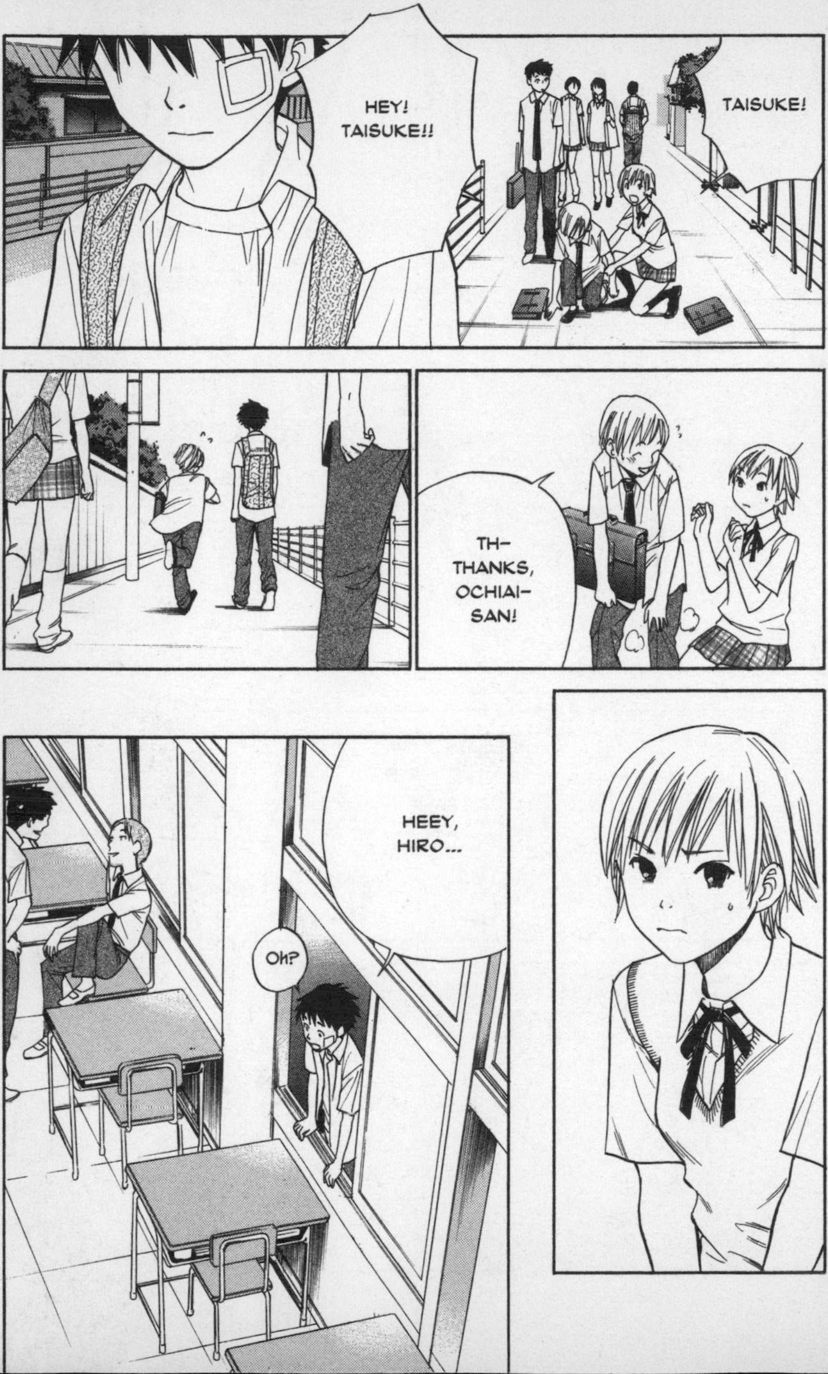
TAISUKE!
HEY! TAISUKE!!
TH-THANKS, OCHIAI-SAN!
HEEY, HIRO...
Oh?

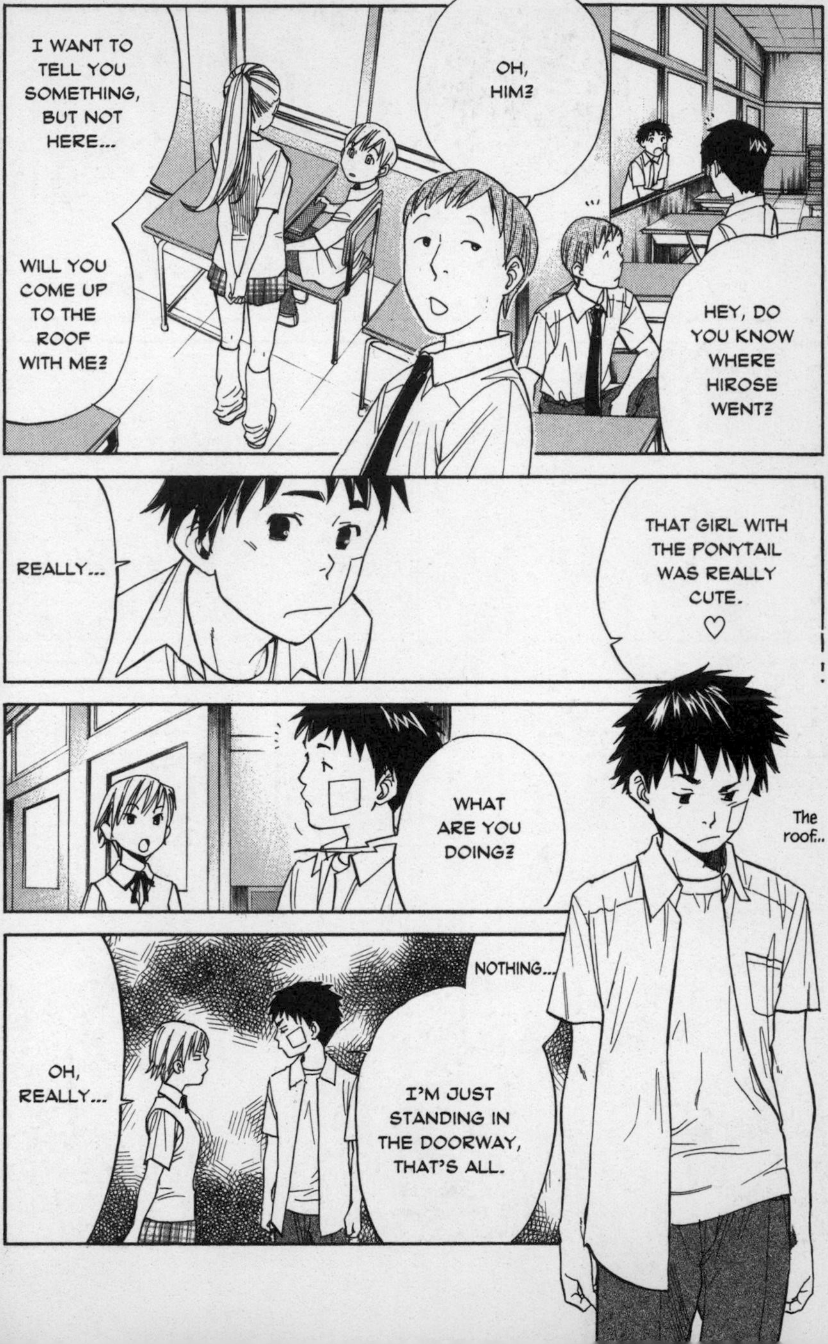
HEY, DO YOU KNOW WHERE HIROSE WENT?
OH, HIM?
I WANT TO TELL YOU SOMETHING, BUT NOT HERE...
WILL YOU COME UP TO THE ROOF WITH ME?
THAT GIRL WITH THE PONYTAIL WAS REALLY CUTE. ♡
REALLY...
The roof...
WHAT ARE YOU DOING?
NOTHING...
I'M JUST STANDING IN THE DOORWAY, THAT'S ALL.
OH, REALLY...

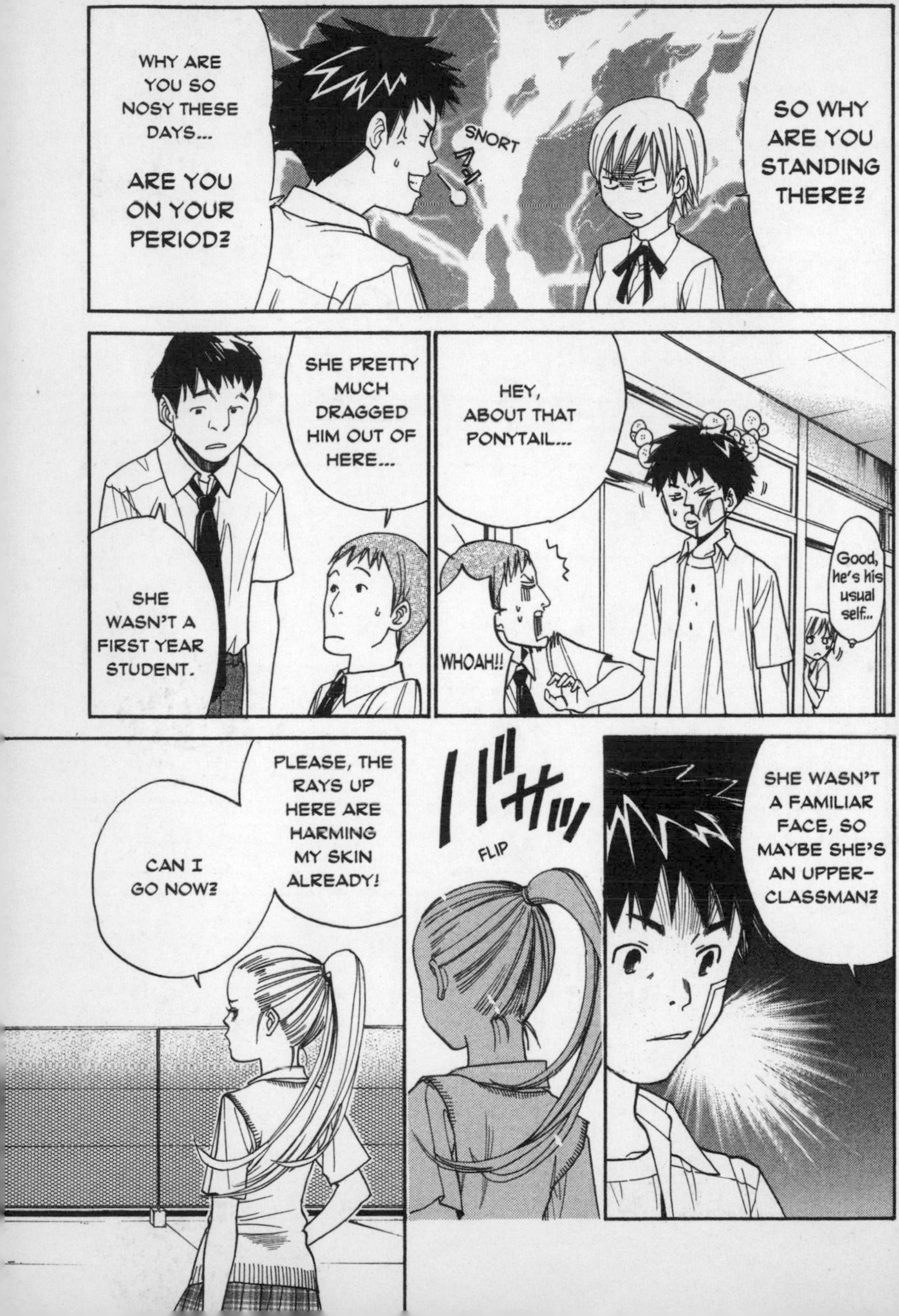
SO WHY ARE YOU STANDING THERE?
SNORT
WHY ARE YOU SO NOSY THESE DAYS...
ARE YOU ON YOUR PERIOD?
HEY, ABOUT THAT PONYTAIL...
Good, he's his usual self...
WHOAH!!
SHE PRETTY MUCH DRAGGED HIM OUT OF HERE...
SHE WASN'T A FIRST YEAR STUDENT.
SHE WASN'T A FAMILIAR FACE, SO MAYBE SHE'S AN UPPER-CLASSMAN?
FLIP
PLEASE, THE RAYS UP HERE ARE HARMING MY SKIN ALREADY!
CAN I GO NOW?

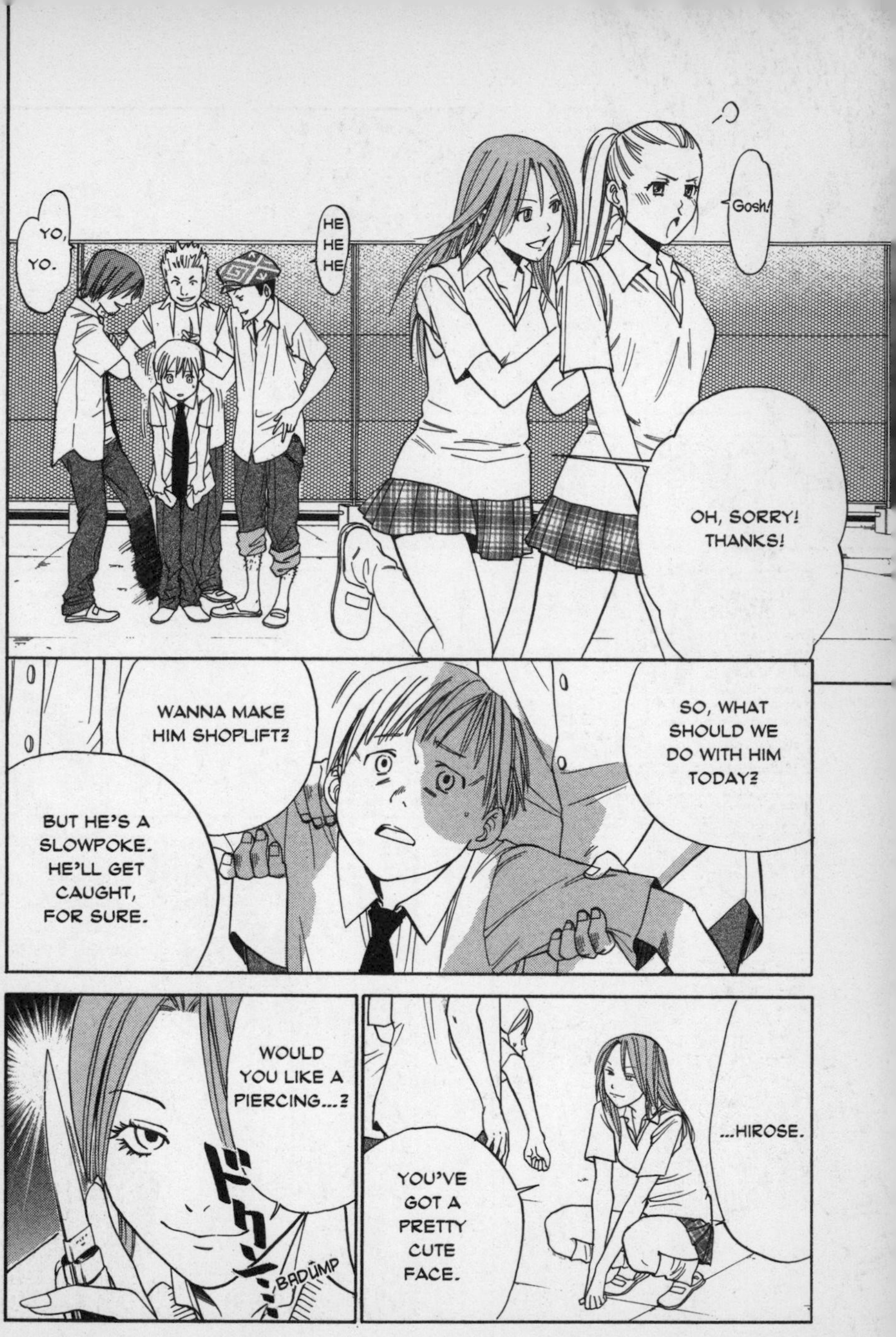
Gosh!
HE HE HE
YO, YO.
OH, SORRY! THANKS!
SO, WHAT SHOULD WE DO WITH HIM TODAY?
WANNA MAKE HIM SHOPLIFT?
BUT HE'S A SLOWPOKE. HE'LL GET CAUGHT, FOR SURE.
...HIROSE.
YOU'VE GOT A PRETTY CUTE FACE.
WOULD YOU LIKE A PIERCING...?
ドクン…
BADUMP

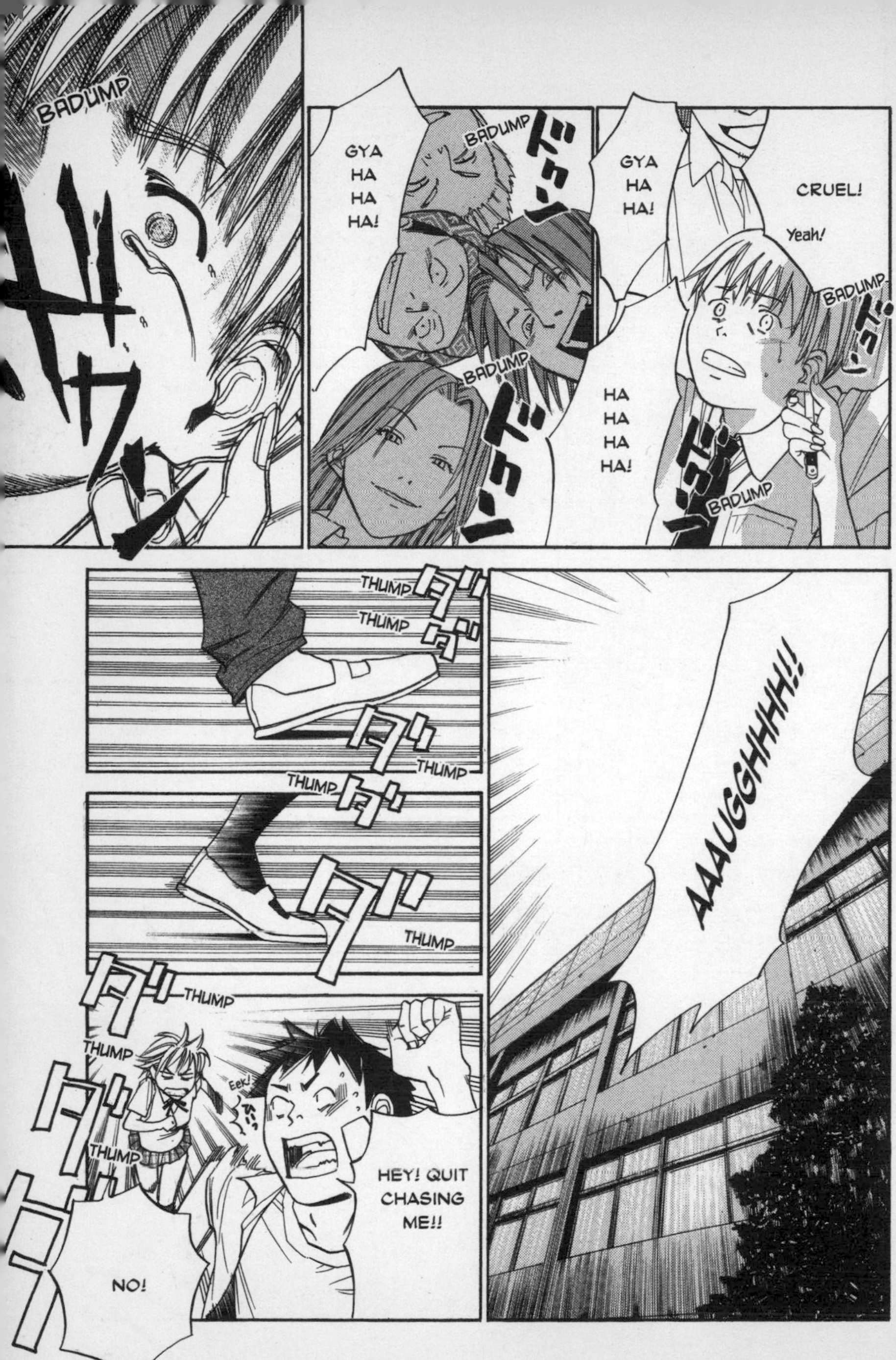
GYA HA HA!
CRUEL!
Yeah!
BADUMP
HA HA HA HA!
BADUMP
GYA HA HA HA!
BADUMP
BADUMP
BADUMP
AAAUGHHH!!
THUMP
THUMP
THUMP
THUMP
THUMP
THUMP
THUMP
THUMP
Eek!
HEY! QUIT CHASING ME!!
NO!

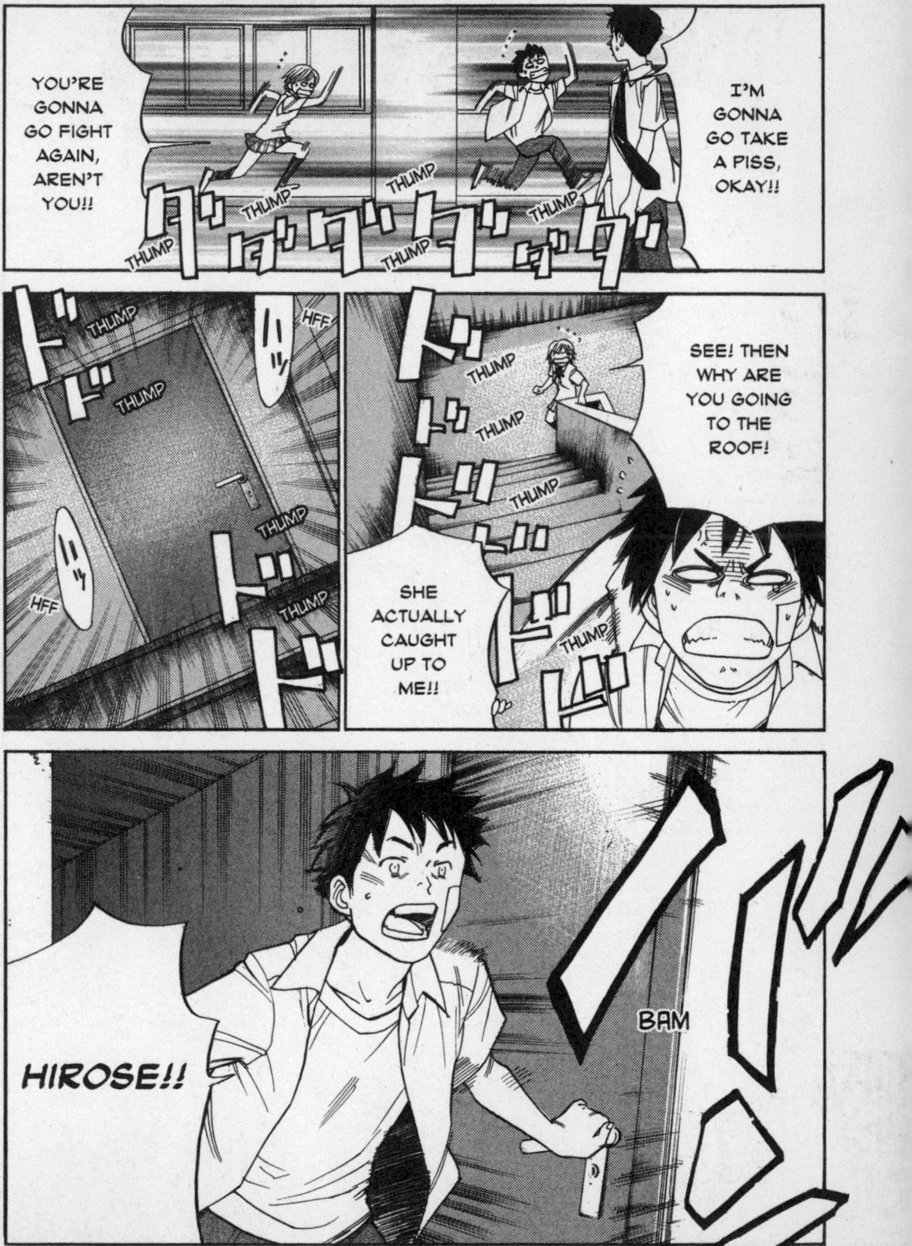
I'M GONNA GO TAKE A PISS, OKAY!!
THUMP
THUMP
THUMP
THUMP
THUMP
YOU'RE GONNA GO FIGHT AGAIN, AREN'T YOU!!
SEE! THEN WHY ARE YOU GOING TO THE ROOF!
THUMP
THUMP
THUMP
THUMP
SHE ACTUALLY CAUGHT UP TO ME!!
HFF
THUMP
THUMP
THUMP
THUMP
HFF
BAM
HIROSE!!

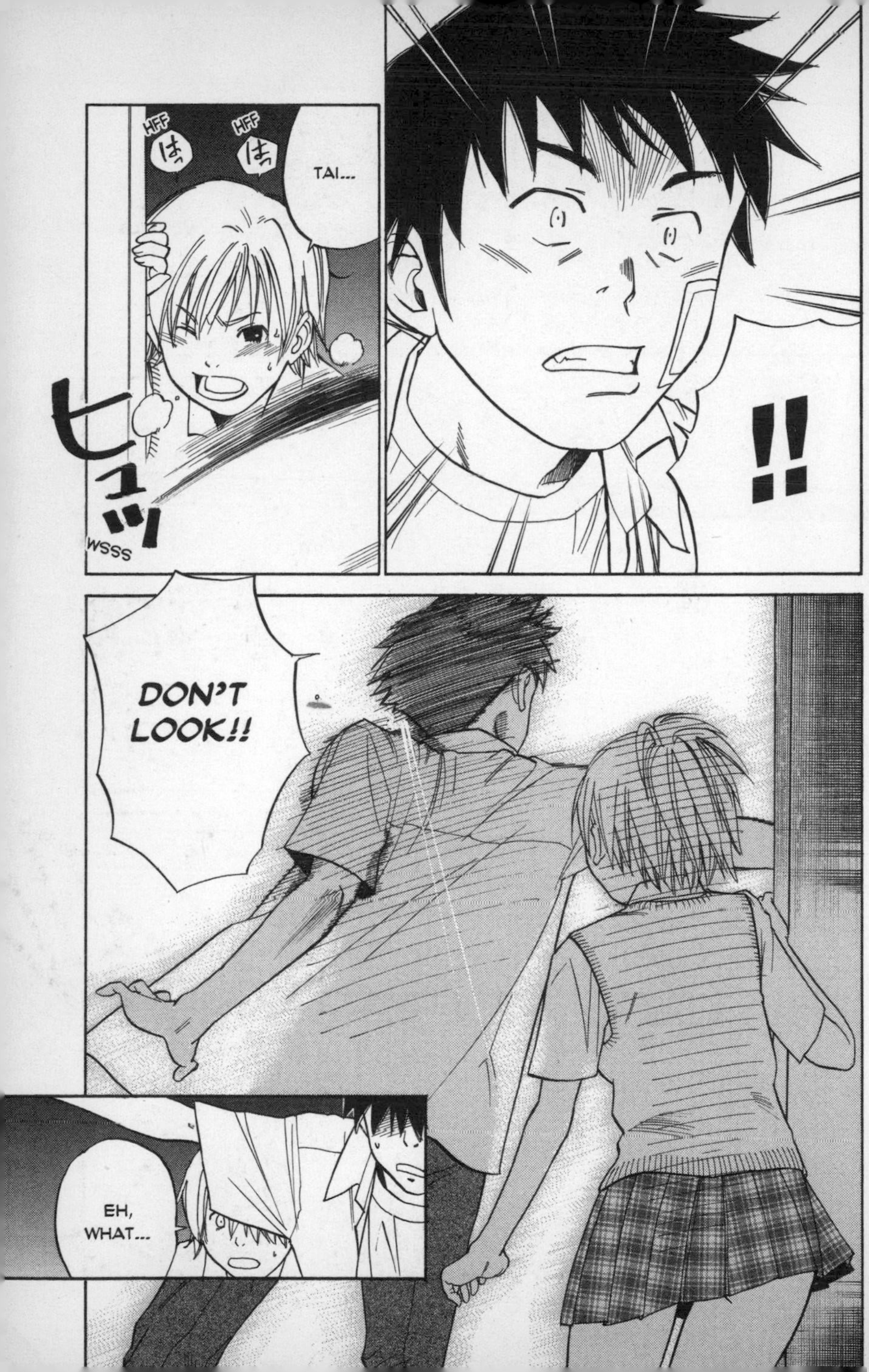
!!
TAI...
HFF
はっ
HFF
はっ
ヒュッ
WSSS
DON'T LOOK!!
EH, WHAT...

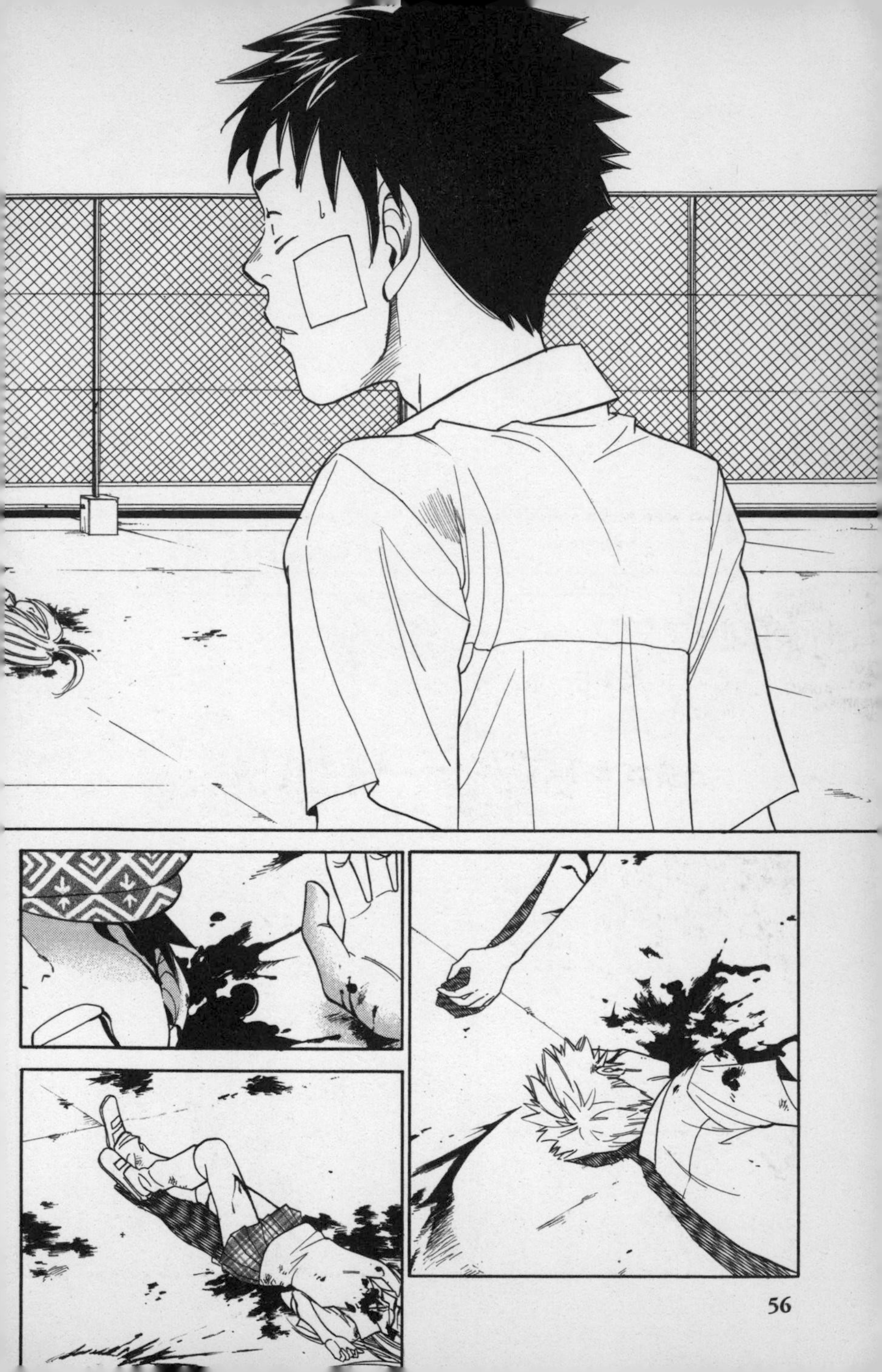

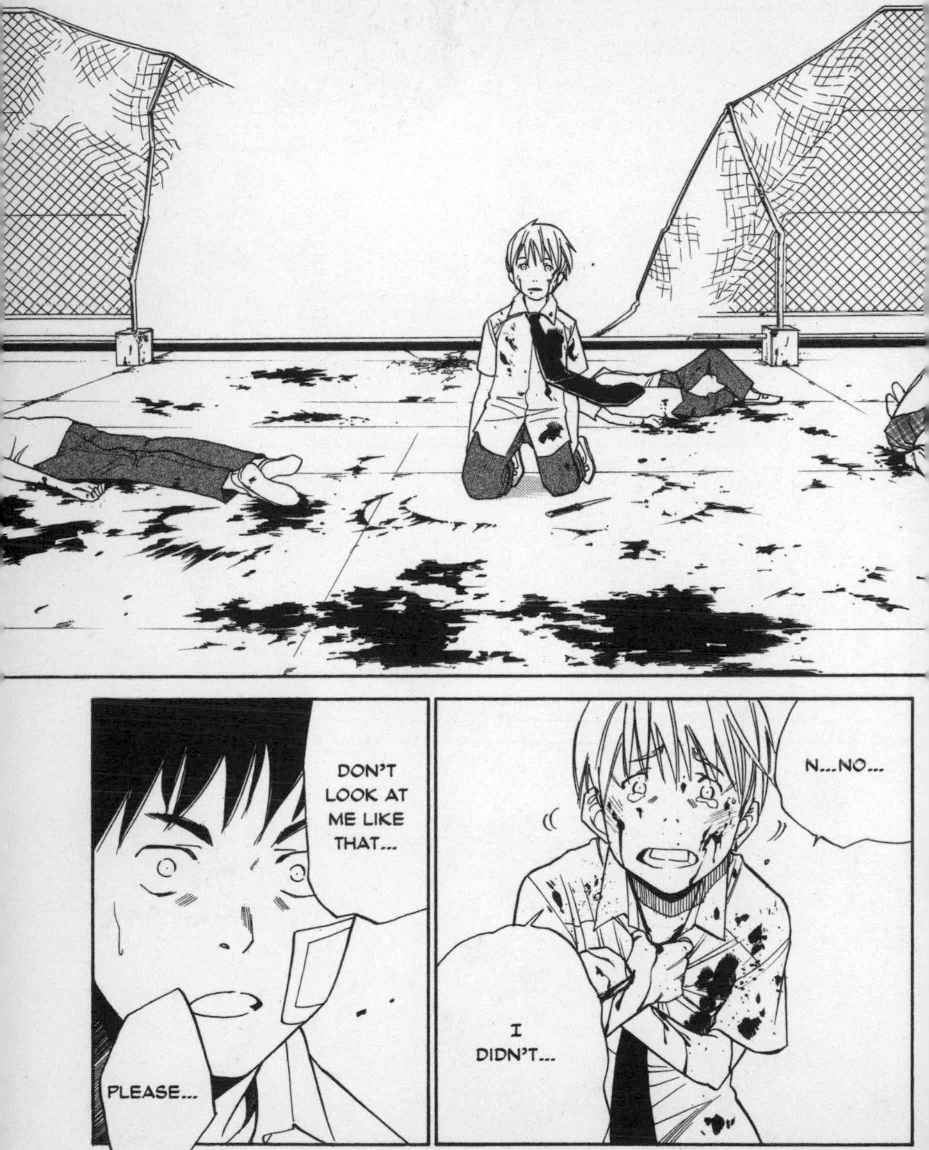
N...NO...
I DIDN'T...
DON'T LOOK AT ME LIKE THAT...
PLEASE...

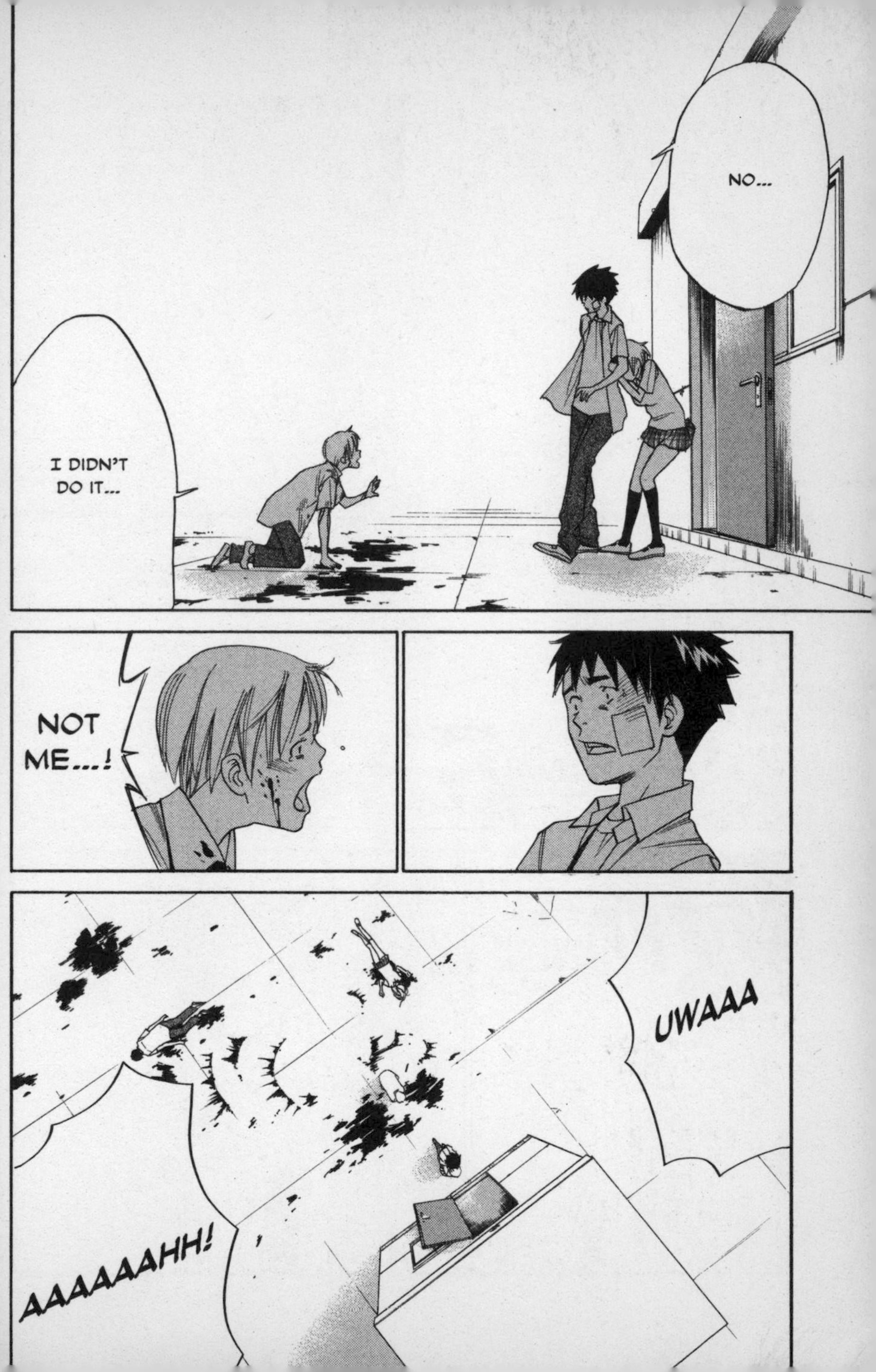
NO...
I DIDN'T DO IT...
NOT ME...!
UWAAA
AAAAAAHH!

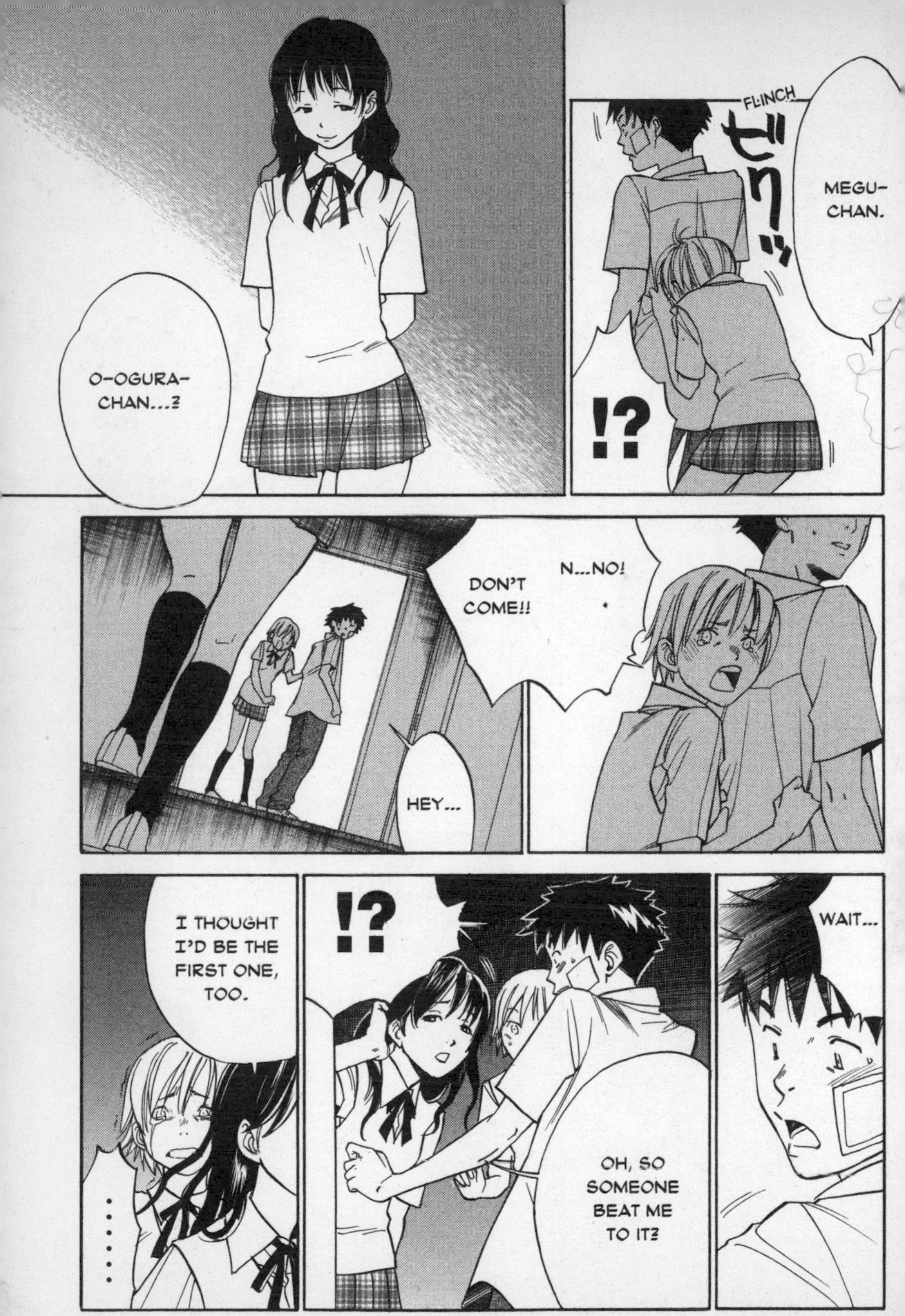
FLINCH
MEGU-CHAN.
!?
O-OGURA-CHAN...?
N...NO!
DON'T COME!!
HEY...
WAIT...
!?
OH, SO SOMEONE BEAT ME TO IT?
I THOUGHT I'D BE THE FIRST ONE, TOO.
......

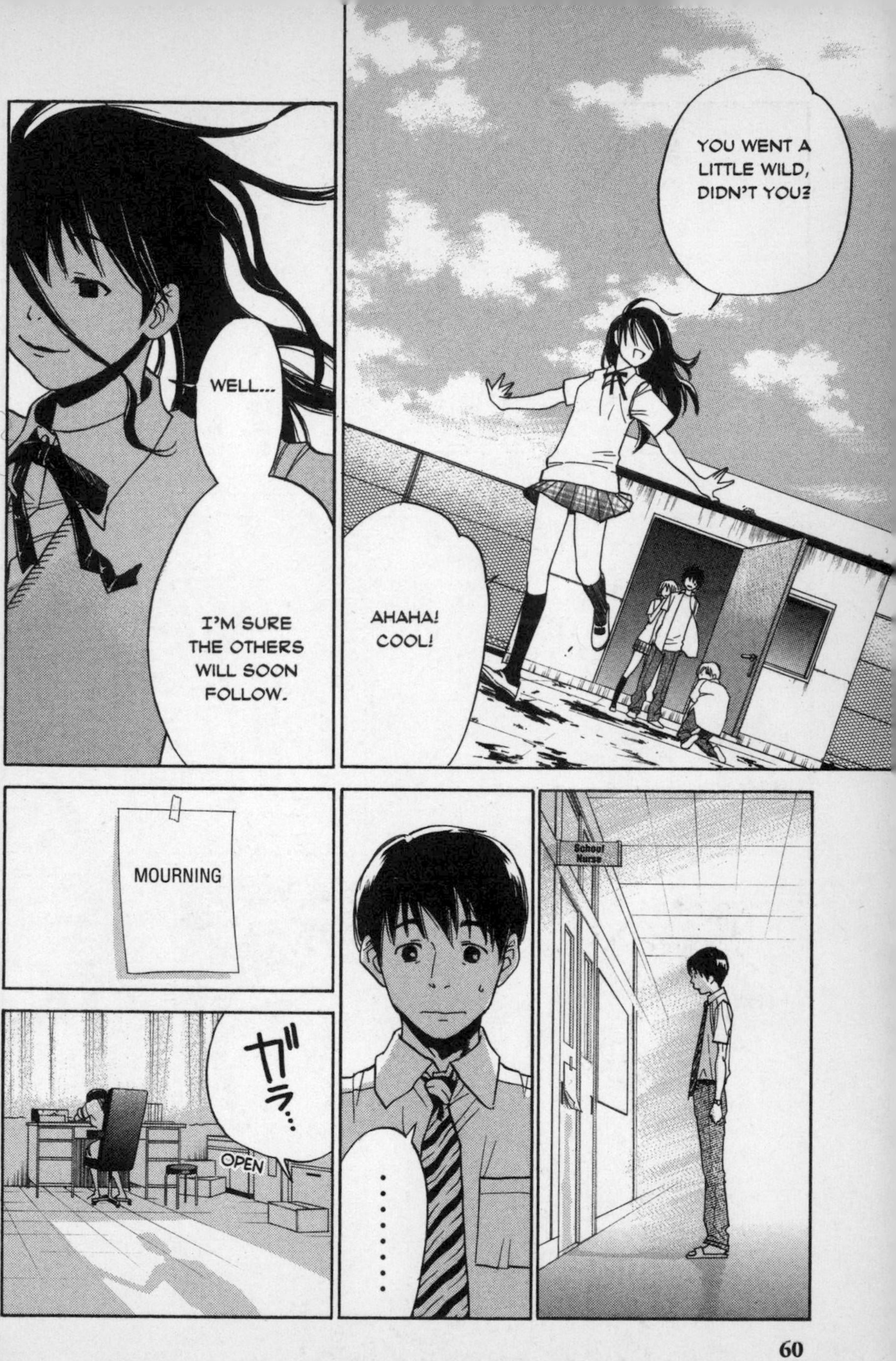
YOU WENT A LITTLE WILD, DIDN'T YOU?
AHAHA! COOL!
WELL...
I'M SURE THE OTHERS WILL SOON FOLLOW.
School Nurse
......
MOURNING
ガラ...
OPEN

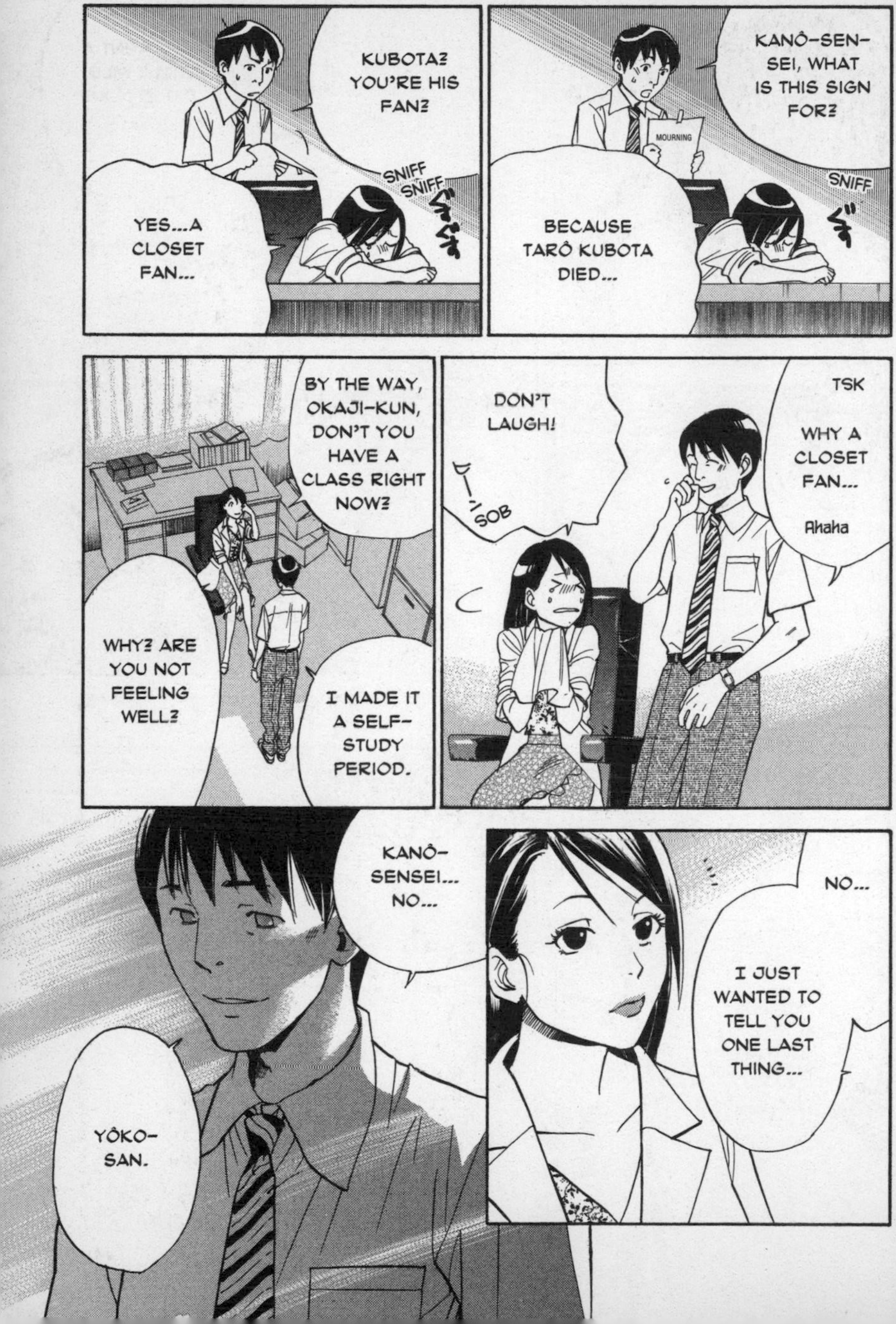
KANÔ-SENSEI, WHAT IS THIS SIGN FOR?
MOURNING
SNIFF
BECAUSE TARÔ KUBOTA DIED...
KUBOTA? YOU'RE HIS FAN?
SNIFF SNIFF
YES...A CLOSET FAN...
TSK
WHY A CLOSET FAN...
Ahaha
DON'T LAUGH!
SOB
BY THE WAY, OKAJI-KUN, DON'T YOU HAVE A CLASS RIGHT NOW?
WHY? ARE YOU NOT FEELING WELL?
I MADE IT A SELF-STUDY PERIOD.
NO...
I JUST WANTED TO TELL YOU ONE LAST THING...
KANÔ-SENSEI... NO...
YÔKO-SAN.

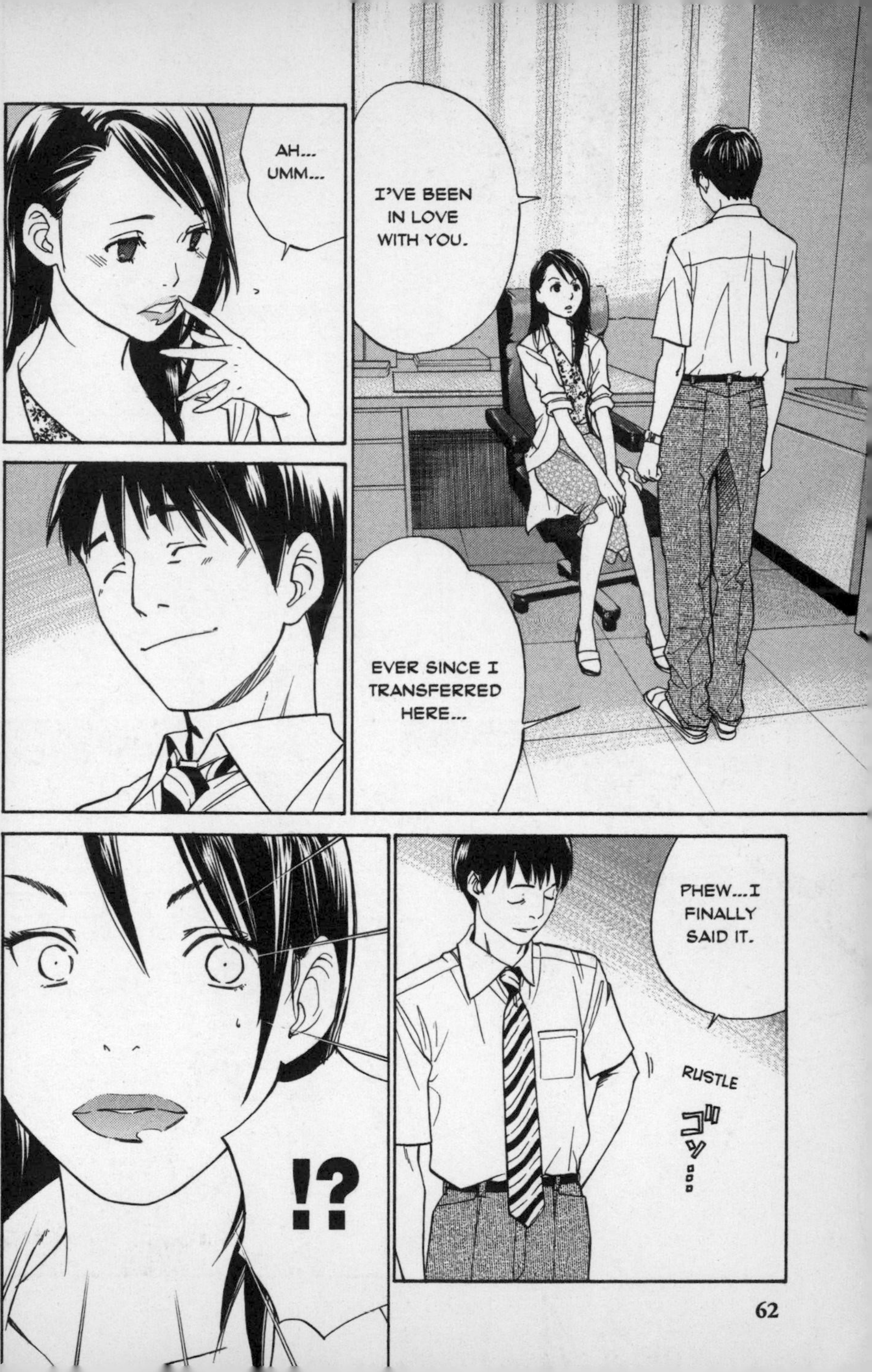
I'VE BEEN IN LOVE WITH YOU.
EVER SINCE I TRANSFERRED HERE...
AH... UMM...
PHEW...I FINALLY SAID IT.
RUSTLE
ゴッ...
!?

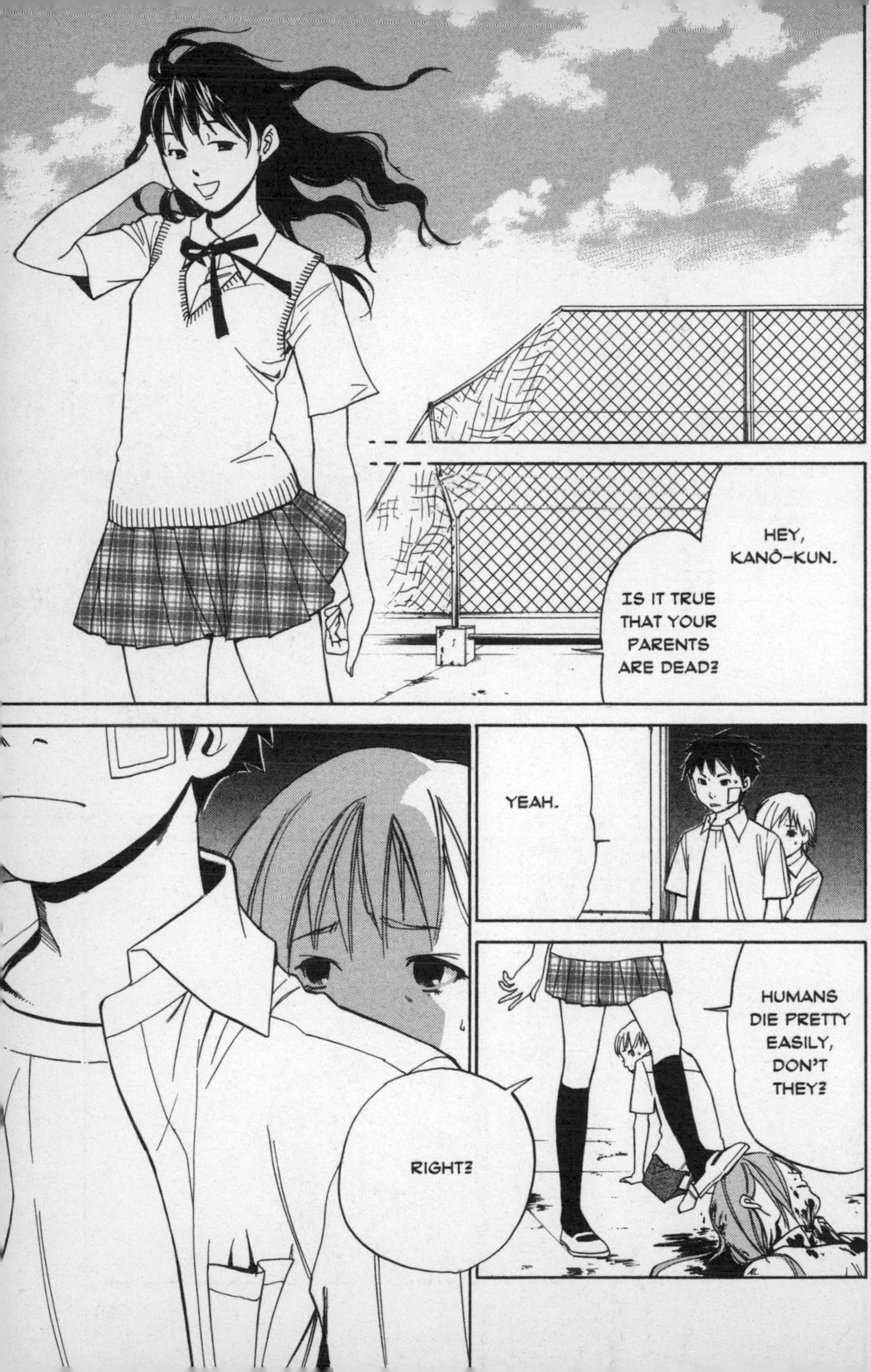
HEY, KANÔ-KUN.
IS IT TRUE THAT YOUR PARENTS ARE DEAD?
YEAH.
HUMANS DIE PRETTY EASILY, DON'T THEY?
RIGHT?

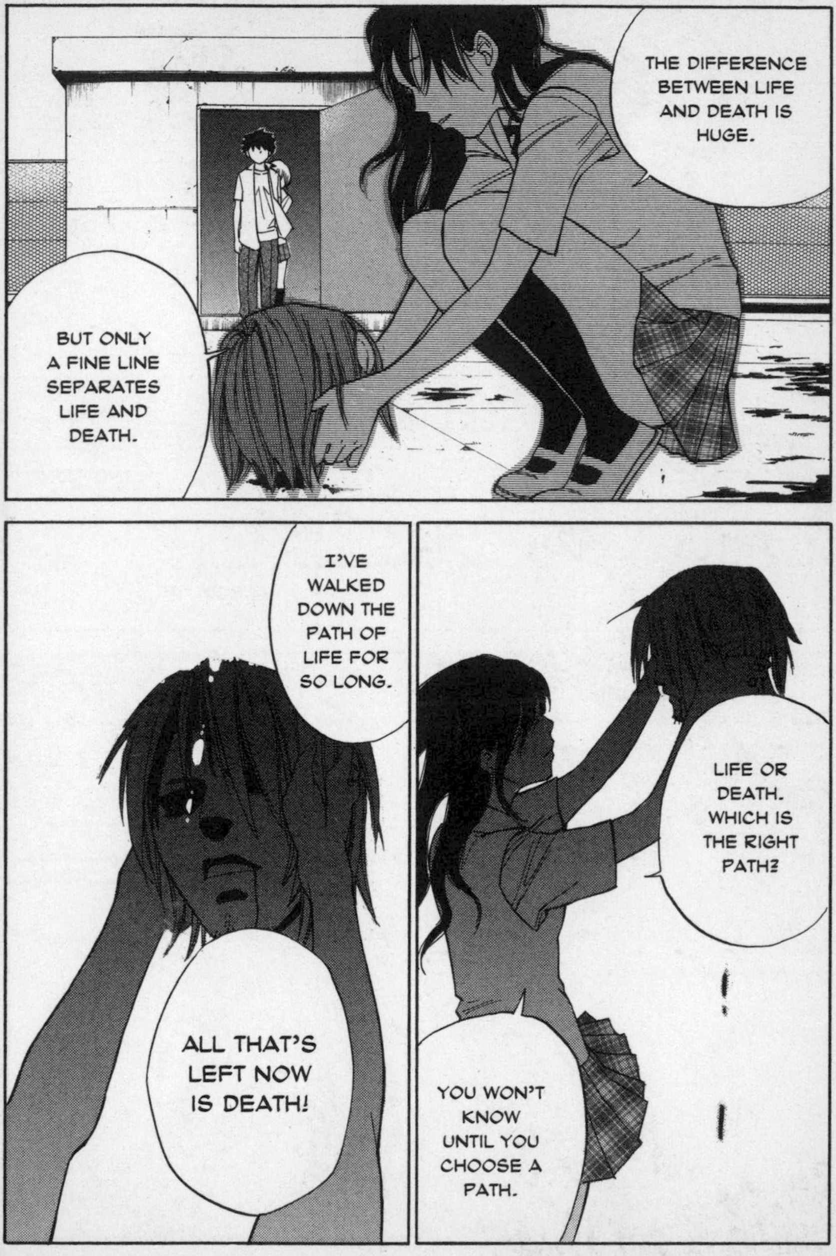
THE DIFFERENCE BETWEEN LIFE AND DEATH IS HUGE.
BUT ONLY A FINE LINE SEPARATES LIFE AND DEATH.
LIFE OR DEATH. WHICH IS THE RIGHT PATH?
YOU WON'T KNOW UNTIL YOU CHOOSE A PATH.
I'VE WALKED DOWN THE PATH OF LIFE FOR SO LONG.
ALL THAT'S LEFT NOW IS DEATH!

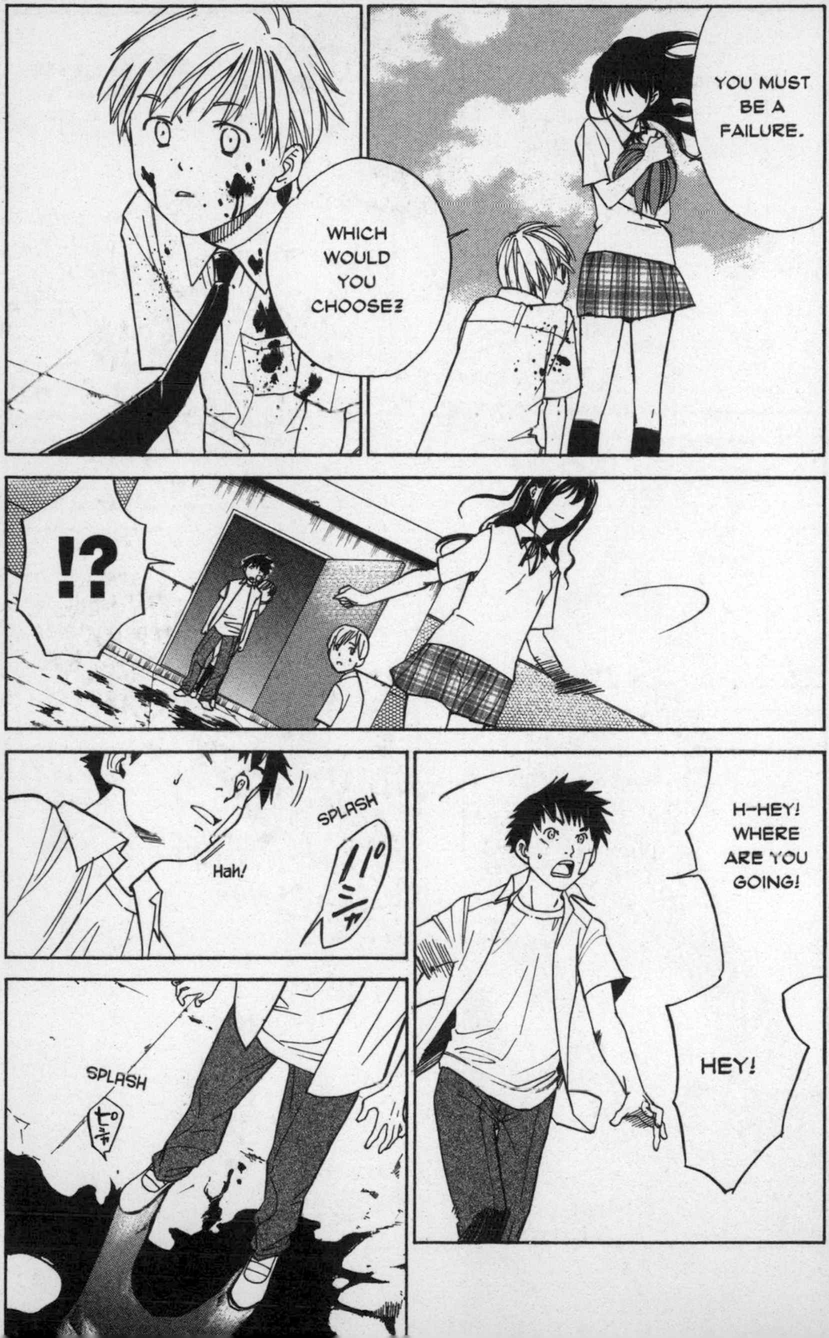
YOU MUST BE A FAILURE.
WHICH WOULD YOU CHOOSE?
!?
H-HEY! WHERE ARE YOU GOING!
HEY!
SPLASH
パシャ
Hah!
SPLASH

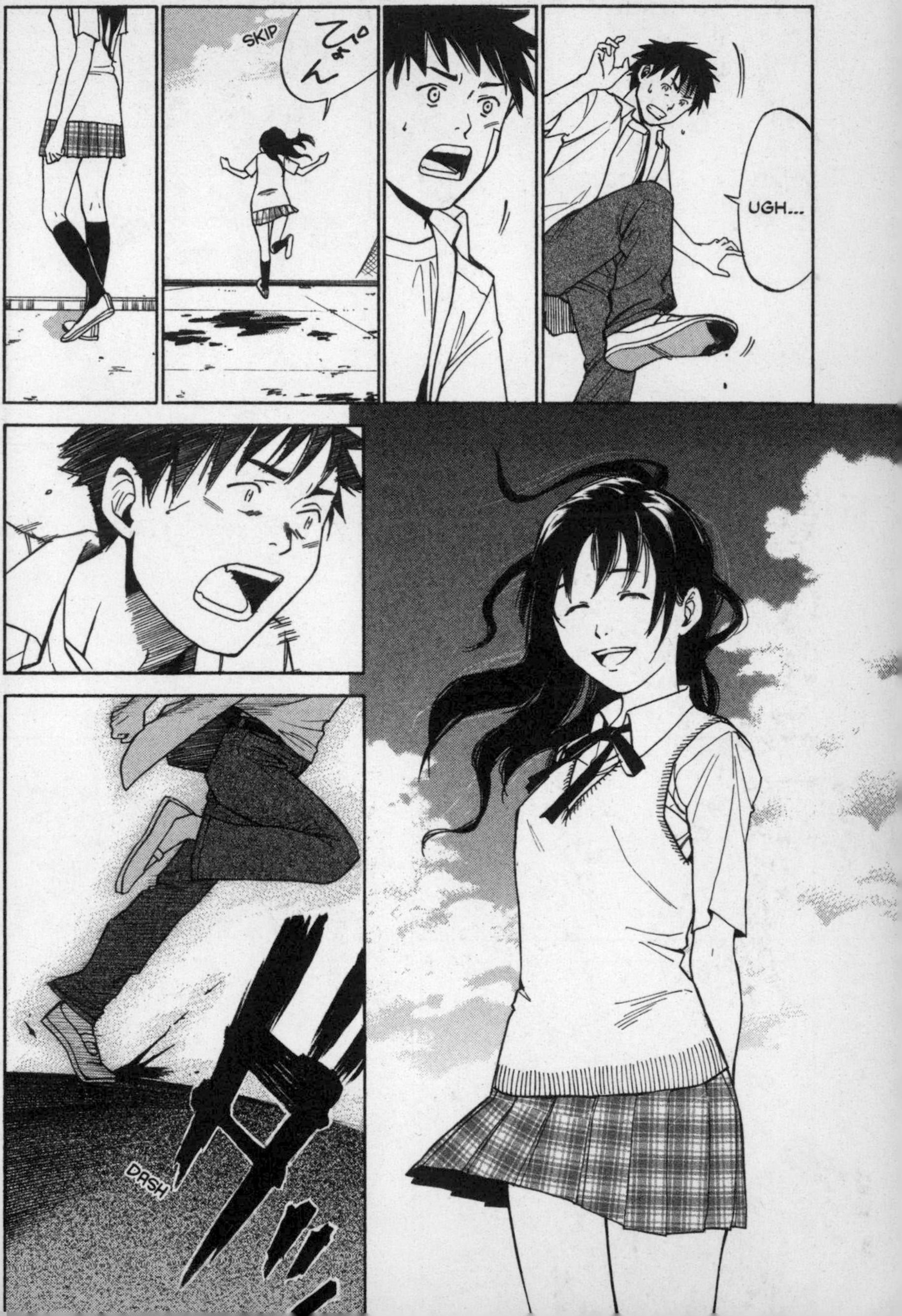
UGH...
ぴょん
SKIP
DASH

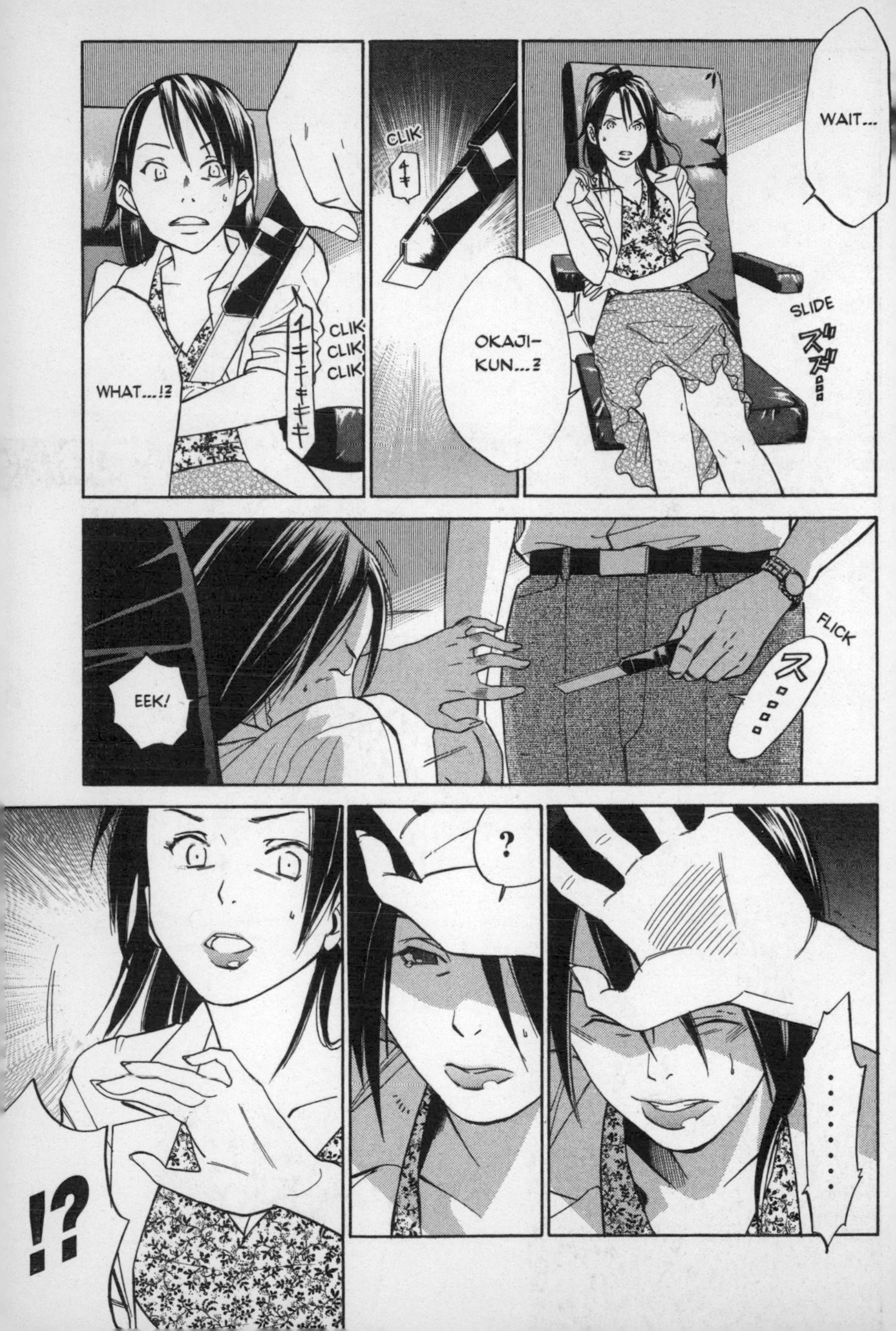

WAIT...
SLIDE
OKAJI-KUN...?
CLIK
CLIK
CLIK
CLIK
WHAT...!?
FLICK
ス....
EEK!
....
?
!?

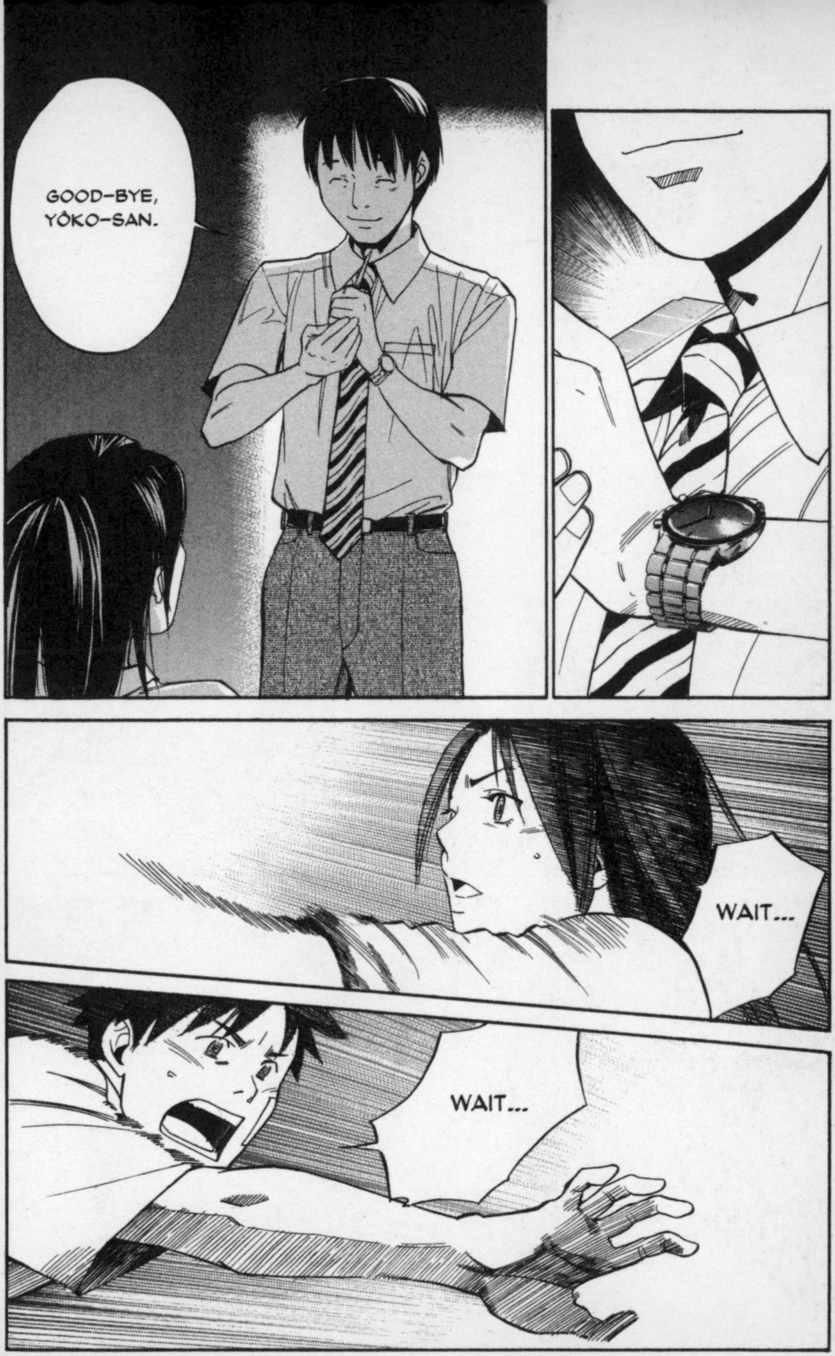
GOOD-BYE, YÔKO-SAN.
WAIT...
WAIT...

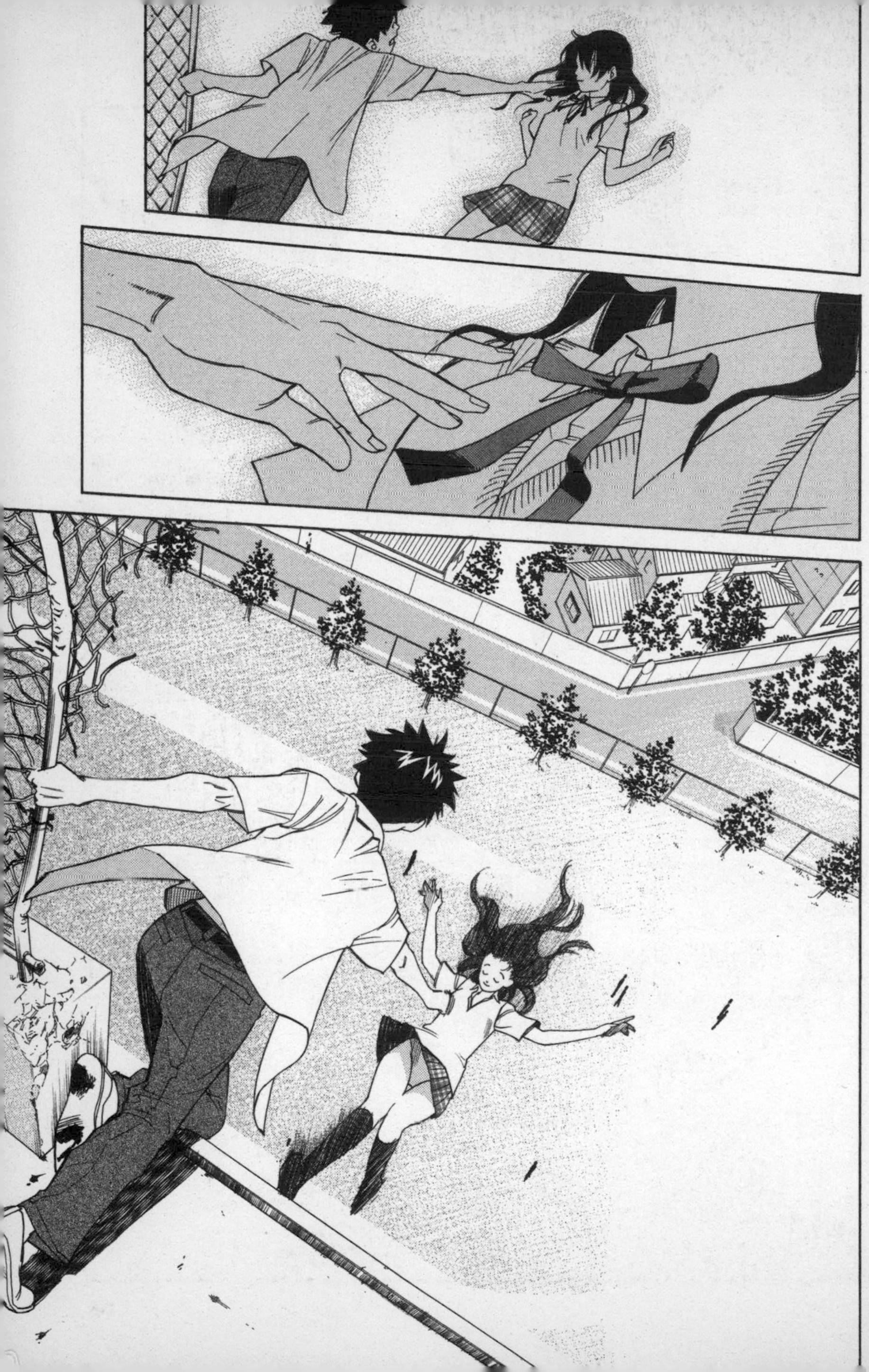

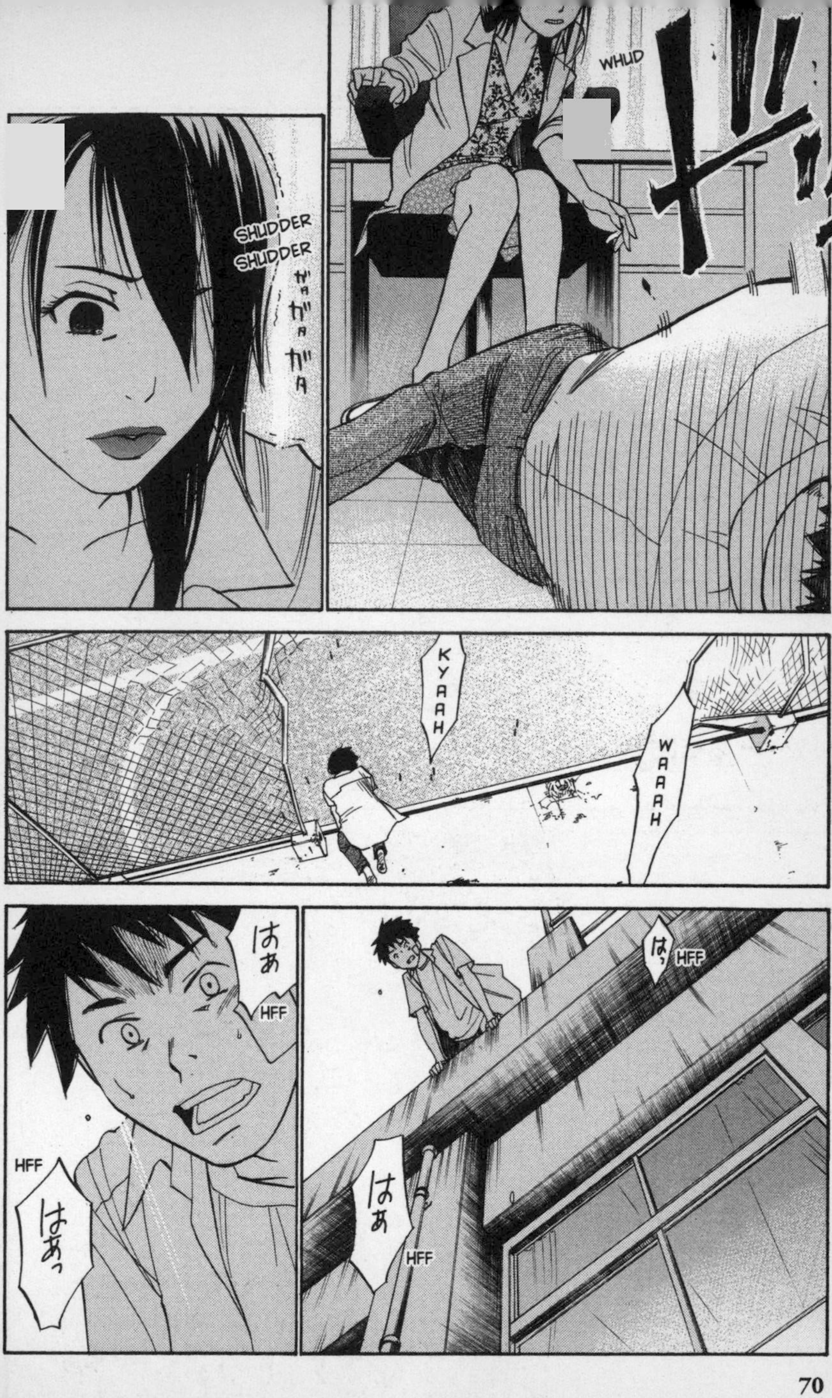
WHUD
SHUDDER
SHUDDER
ガタガタガタ
WAAAAH
KYAAAH
は、
HFF
はあ
HFF
はあ
HFF
HFF
はあっ

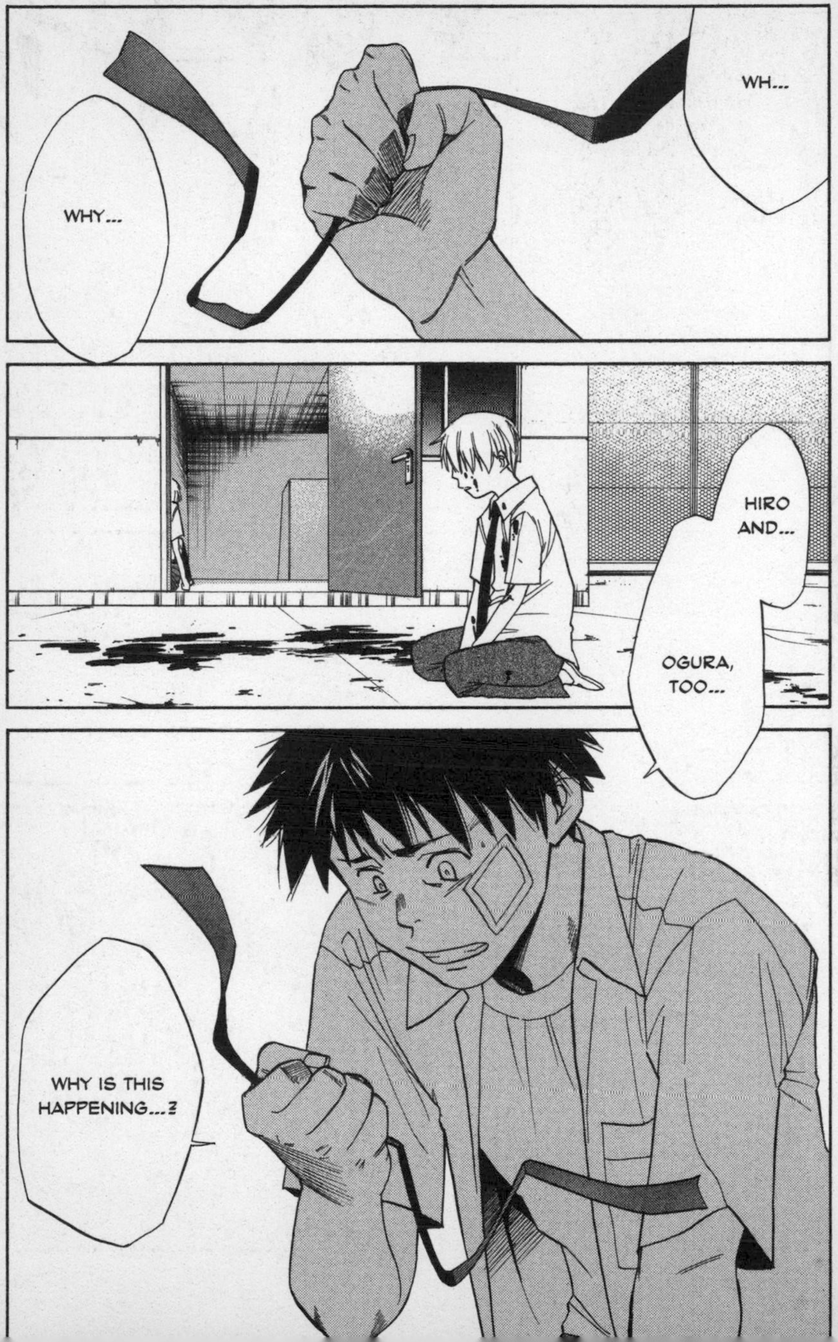
WH...
WHY...
HIRO AND...
OGURA, TOO...
WHY IS THIS HAPPENING...?

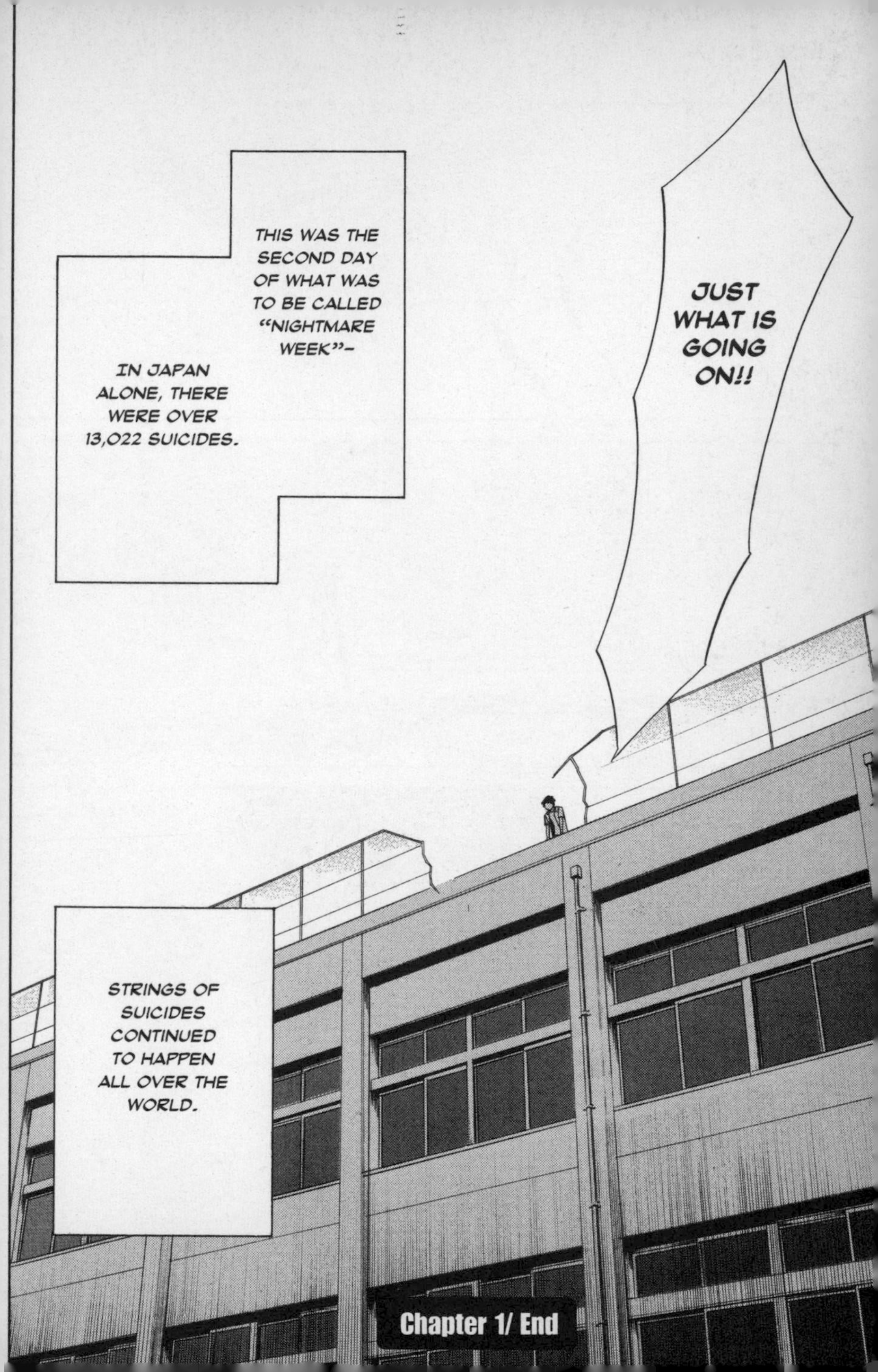
JUST WHAT IS GOING ON!!
THIS WAS THE SECOND DAY OF WHAT WAS TO BE CALLED "NIGHTMARE WEEK"–
IN JAPAN ALONE, THERE WERE OVER 13,022 SUICIDES.
STRINGS OF SUICIDES CONTINUED TO HAPPEN ALL OVER THE WORLD.
Chapter 1/ End

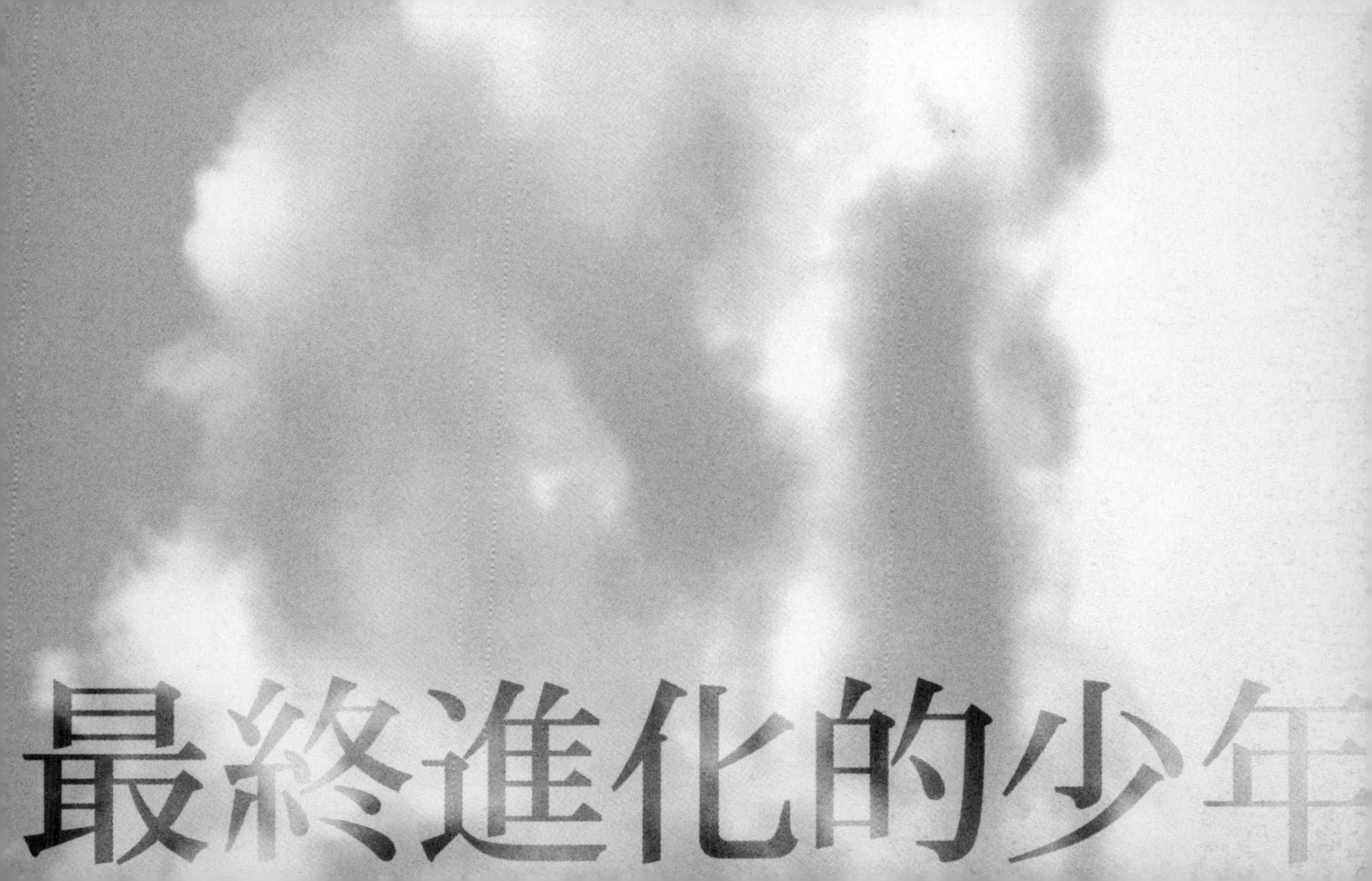
最終進化的少年

Alive

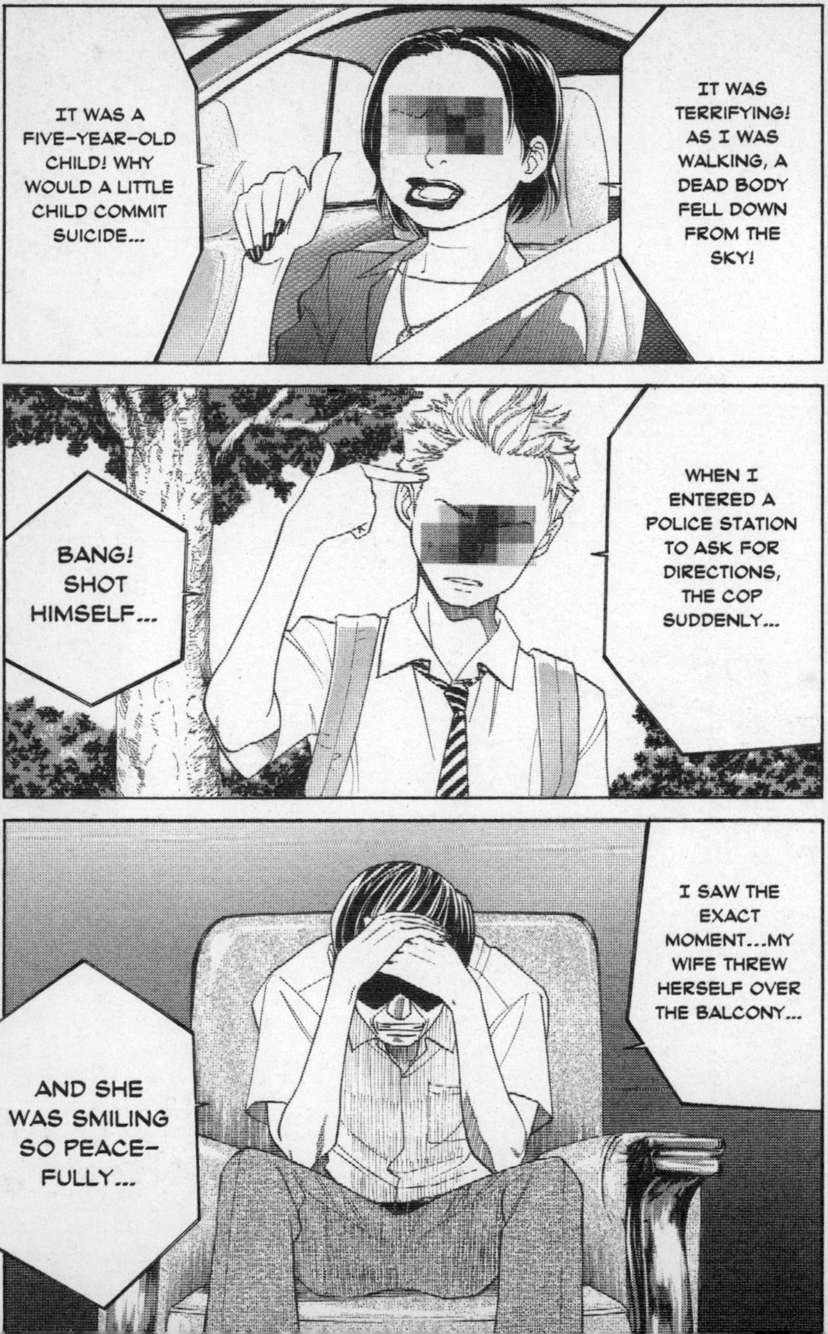
IT WAS TERRIFYING! AS I WAS WALKING, A DEAD BODY FELL DOWN FROM THE SKY!
IT WAS A FIVE-YEAR-OLD CHILD! WHY WOULD A LITTLE CHILD COMMIT SUICIDE...
WHEN I ENTERED A POLICE STATION TO ASK FOR DIRECTIONS, THE COP SUDDENLY...
BANG! SHOT HIMSELF...
I SAW THE EXACT MOMENT...MY WIFE THREW HERSELF OVER THE BALCONY...
AND SHE WAS SMILING SO PEACE-FULLY...

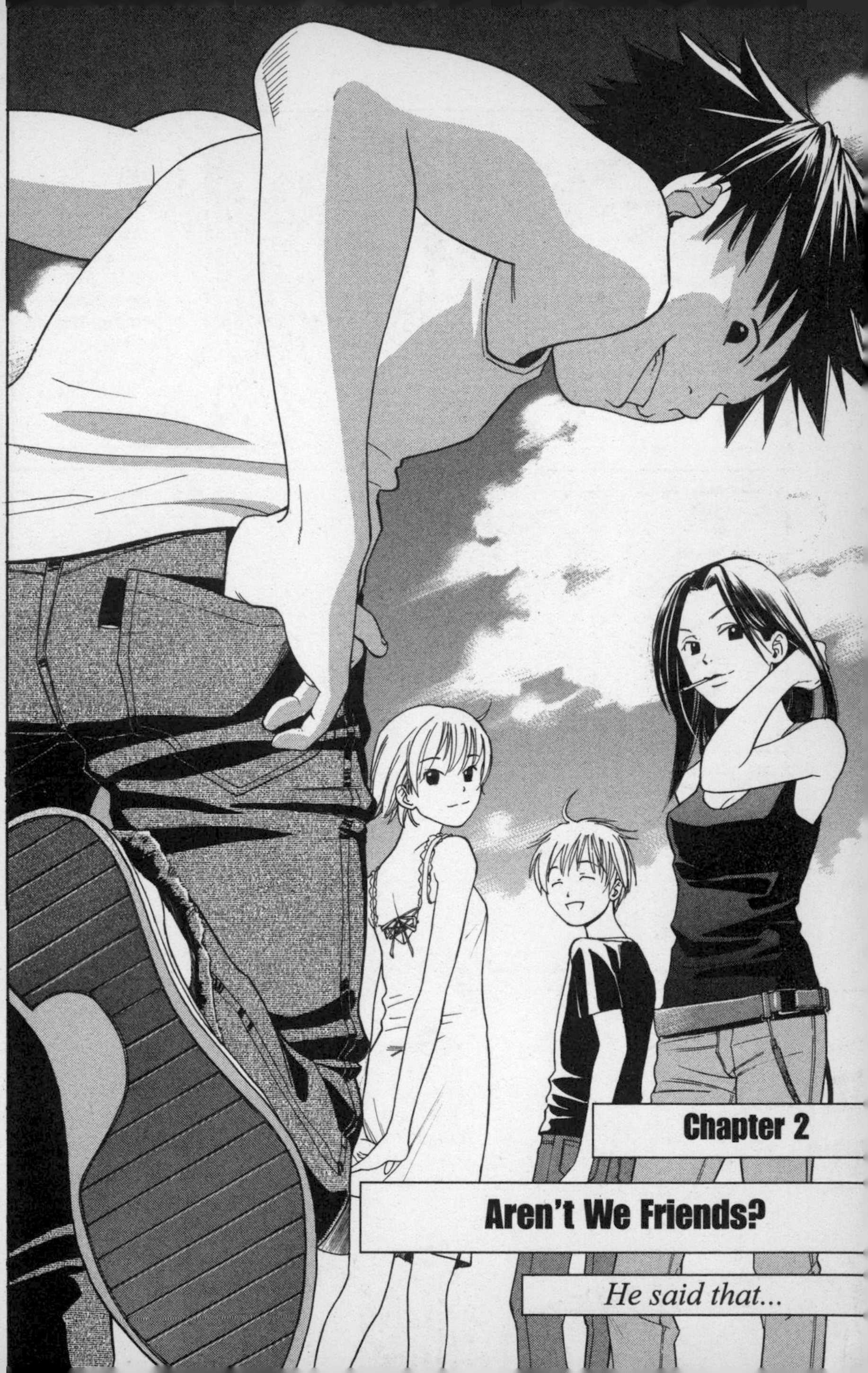
Chapter 2
Aren't We Friends?
He said that...

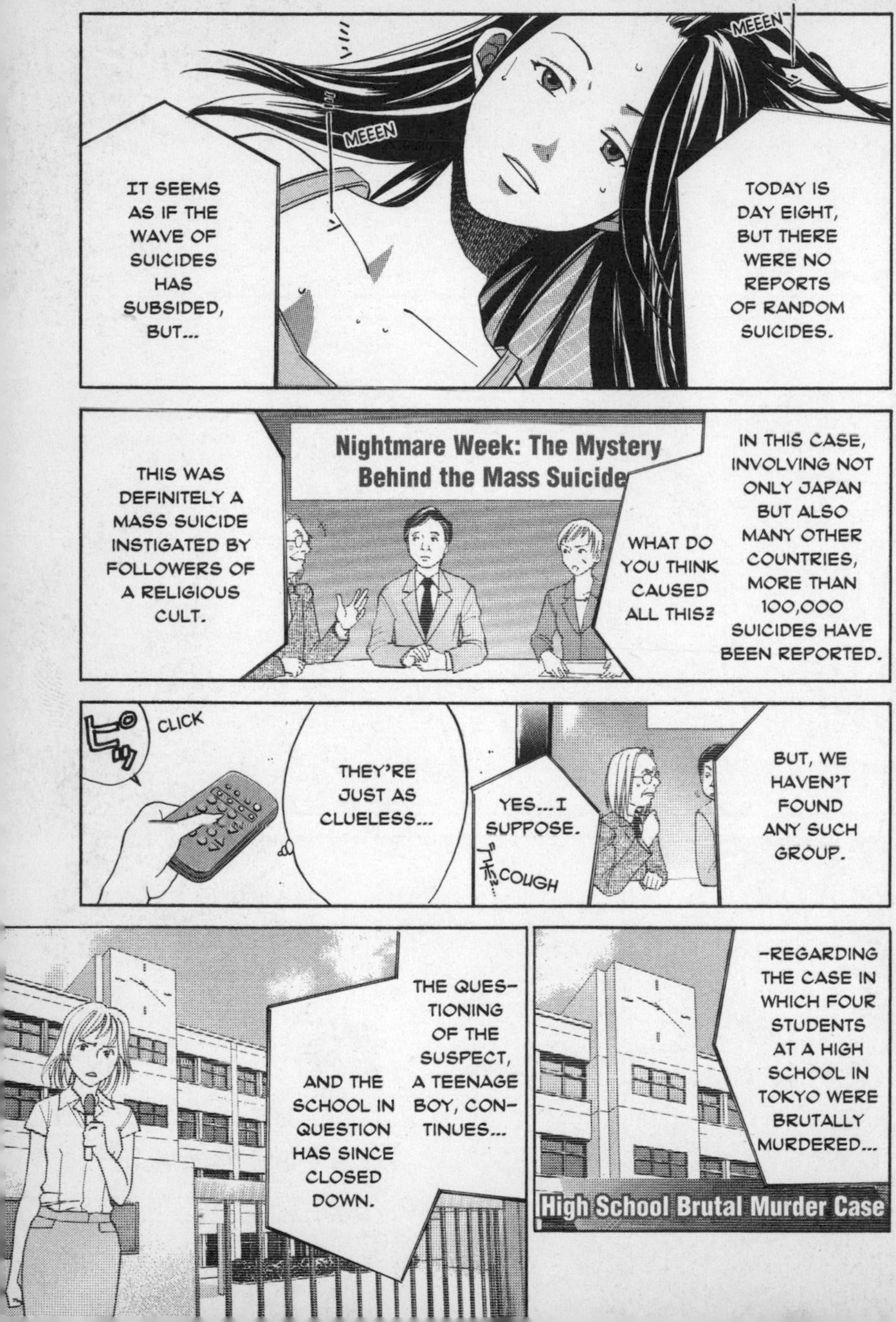
MEEEN
TODAY IS DAY EIGHT, BUT THERE WERE NO REPORTS OF RANDOM SUICIDES.
MEEEN
IT SEEMS AS IF THE WAVE OF SUICIDES HAS SUBSIDED, BUT...
IN THIS CASE, INVOLVING NOT ONLY JAPAN BUT ALSO MANY OTHER COUNTRIES, MORE THAN 100,000 SUICIDES HAVE BEEN REPORTED.
Nightmare Week: The Mystery Behind the Mass Suicide
WHAT DO YOU THINK CAUSED ALL THIS?
THIS WAS DEFINITELY A MASS SUICIDE INSTIGATED BY FOLLOWERS OF A RELIGIOUS CULT.
BUT, WE HAVEN'T FOUND ANY SUCH GROUP.
YES...I SUPPOSE.
COUGH
THEY'RE JUST AS CLUELESS...
CLICK
-REGARDING THE CASE IN WHICH FOUR STUDENTS AT A HIGH SCHOOL IN TOKYO WERE BRUTALLY MURDERED...
High School Brutal Murder Case
THE QUESTIONING OF THE SUSPECT, A TEENAGE BOY, CONTINUES...
AND THE SCHOOL IN QUESTION HAS SINCE CLOSED DOWN.

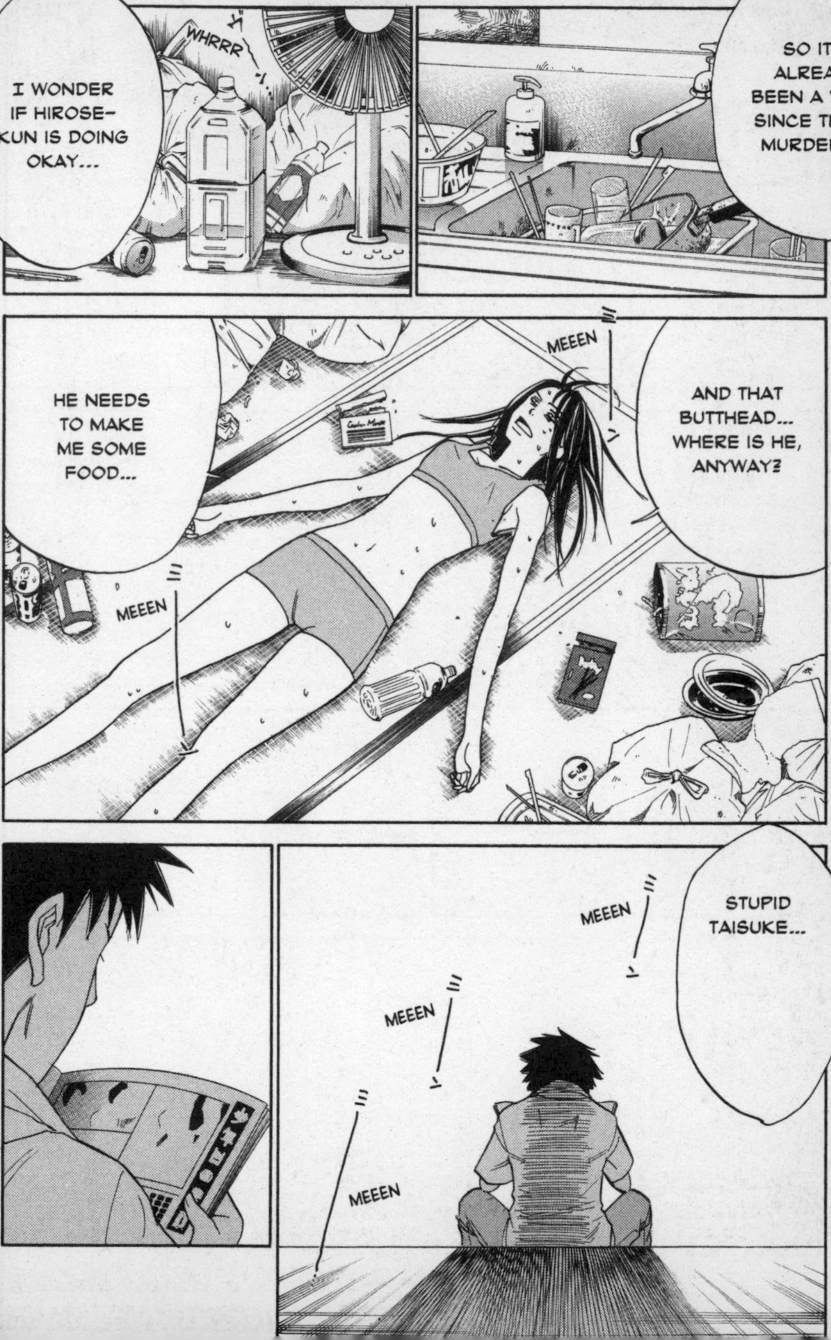
SO IT'S ALREADY BEEN A WEEK SINCE THOSE MURDERS...
WHRRR
I WONDER IF HIROSE-KUN IS DOING OKAY...
AND THAT BUTTHEAD... WHERE IS HE, ANYWAY?
MEEEN
HE NEEDS TO MAKE ME SOME FOOD...
MEEEN
STUPID TAISUKE...
MEEEN
MEEEN
MEEEN

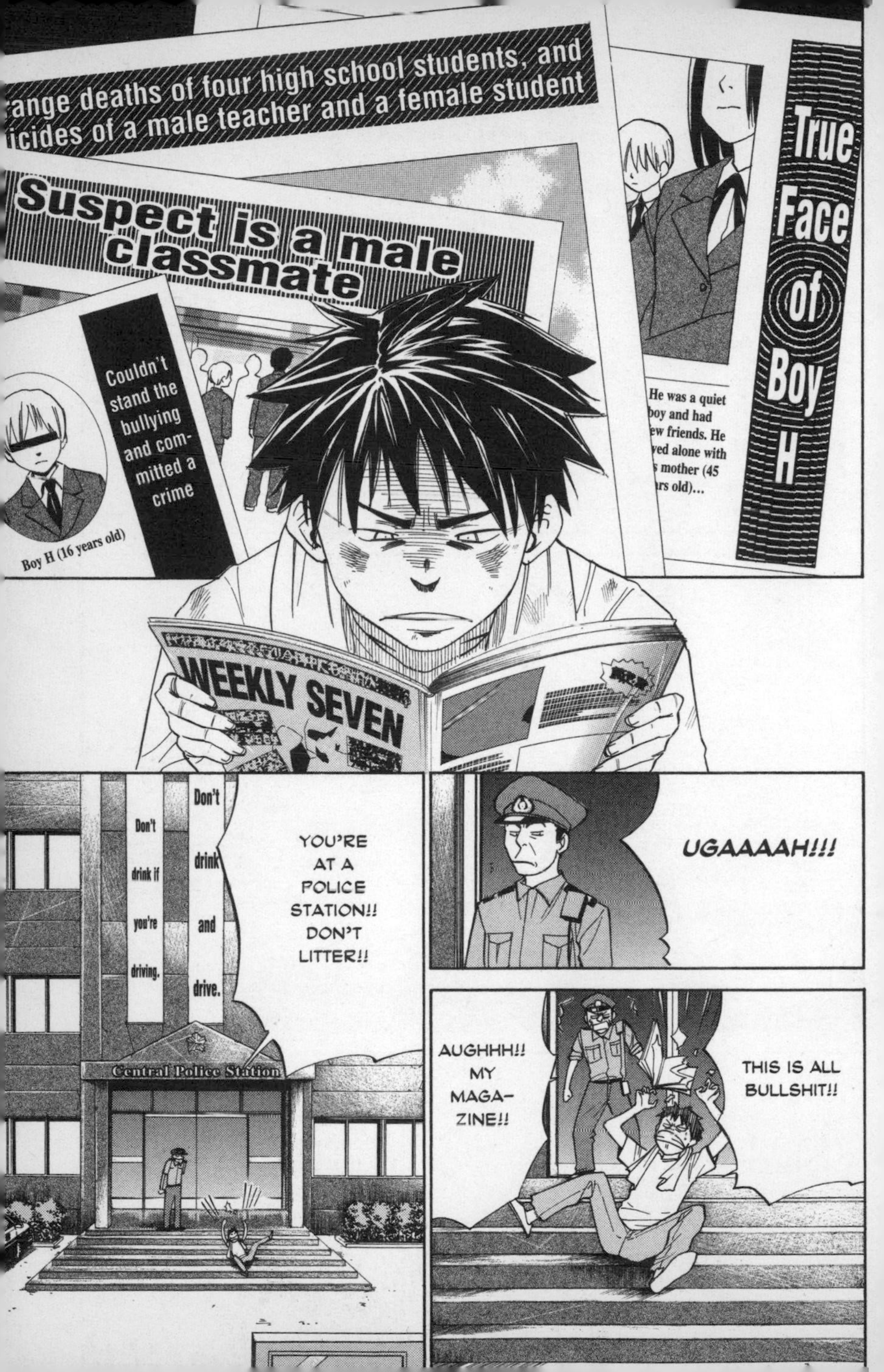
True Face of Boy H
He was a quiet boy and had ew friends. He ved alone with s mother (45 rs old)…
ange deaths of four high school students, and icides of a male teacher and a female student
Suspect is a male classmate
Couldn't stand the bullying and com-mitted a crime
Boy H (16 years old)
WEEKLY SEVEN
UGAAAAH!!!
THIS IS ALL BULLSHIT!!
AUGHHH!! MY MAGA-ZINE!!
YOU'RE AT A POLICE STATION!! DON'T LITTER!!
Don't drink and drive.
Don't drink if you're driving.
Central Police Station

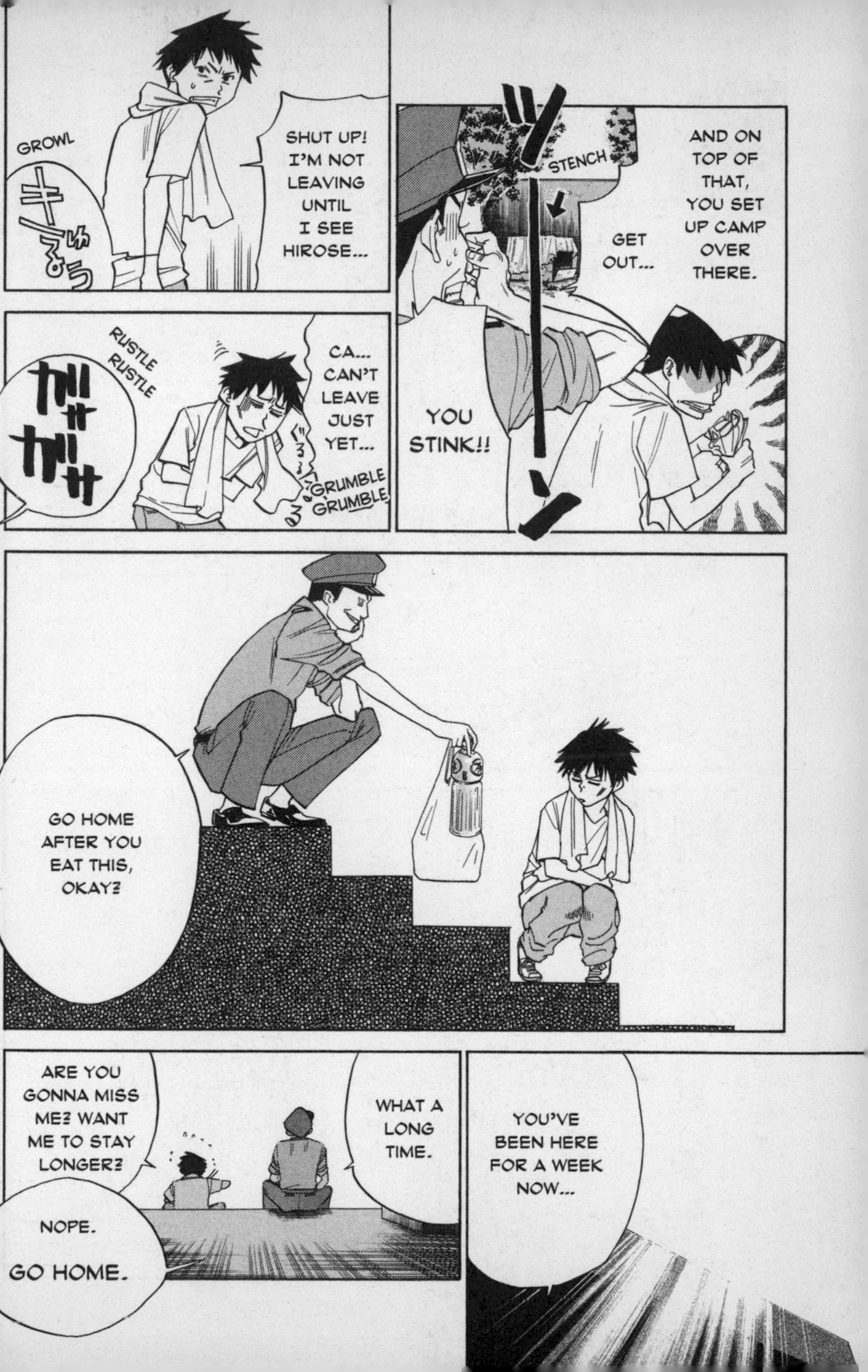
AND ON TOP OF THAT, YOU SET UP CAMP OVER THERE.
STENCH
GET OUT...
YOU STINK!!
SHUT UP! I'M NOT LEAVING UNTIL I SEE HIROSE...
GROWL
CA... CAN'T LEAVE JUST YET...
RUSTLE RUSTLE
GRUMBLE GRUMBLE
GO HOME AFTER YOU EAT THIS, OKAY?
YOU'VE BEEN HERE FOR A WEEK NOW...
WHAT A LONG TIME.
ARE YOU GONNA MISS ME? WANT ME TO STAY LONGER?
NOPE.
GO HOME.

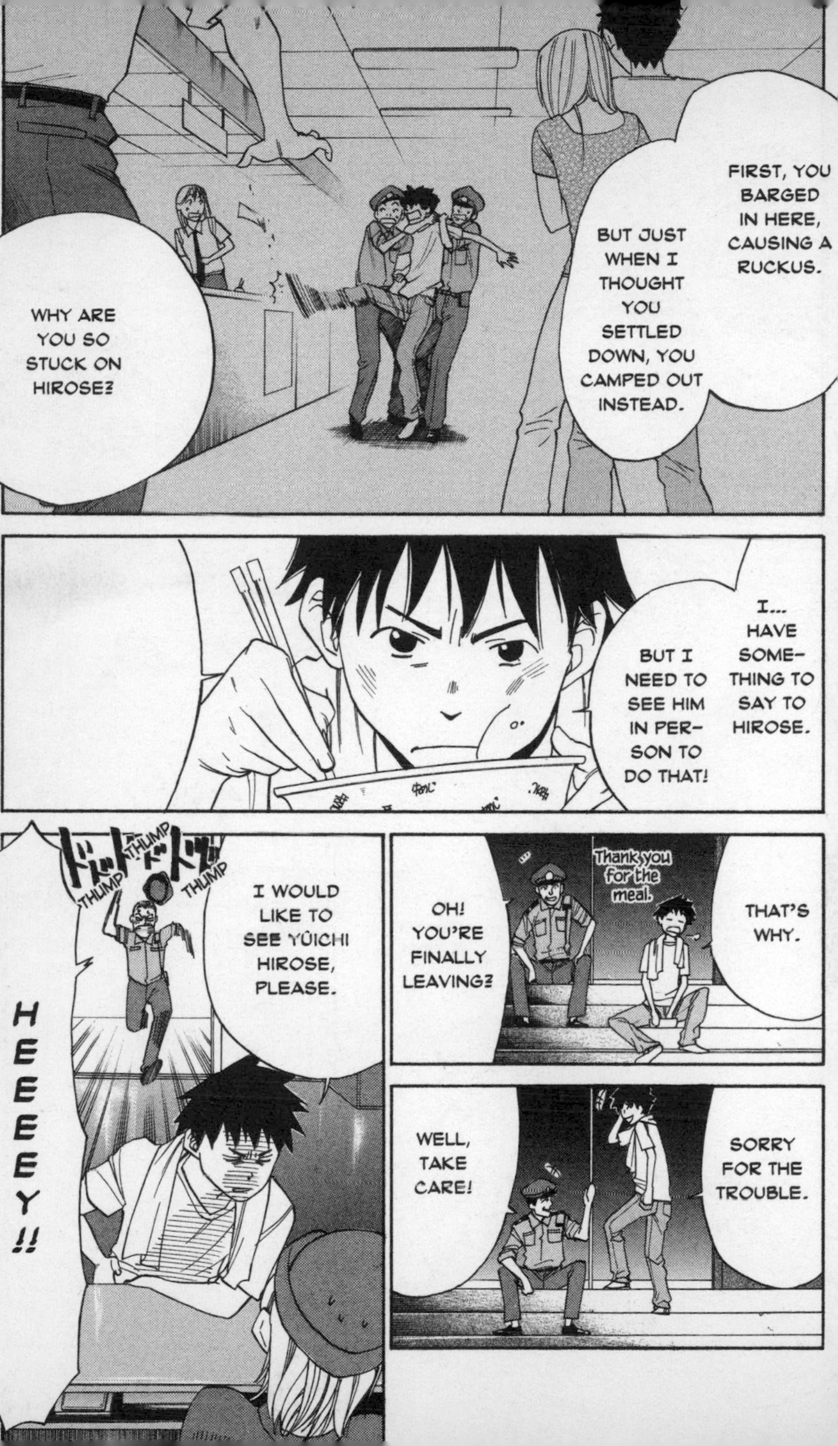
FIRST, YOU BARGED IN HERE, CAUSING A RUCKUS.
BUT JUST WHEN I THOUGHT YOU SETTLED DOWN, YOU CAMPED OUT INSTEAD.
WHY ARE YOU SO STUCK ON HIROSE?
I... HAVE SOME-THING TO SAY TO HIROSE.
BUT I NEED TO SEE HIM IN PER-SON TO DO THAT!
THAT'S WHY.
Thank you for the meal.
OH! YOU'RE FINALLY LEAVING?
SORRY FOR THE TROUBLE.
WELL, TAKE CARE!
I WOULD LIKE TO SEE YÛICHI HIROSE, PLEASE.
THUMP THUMP THUMP THUMP
HEEEEEY!!

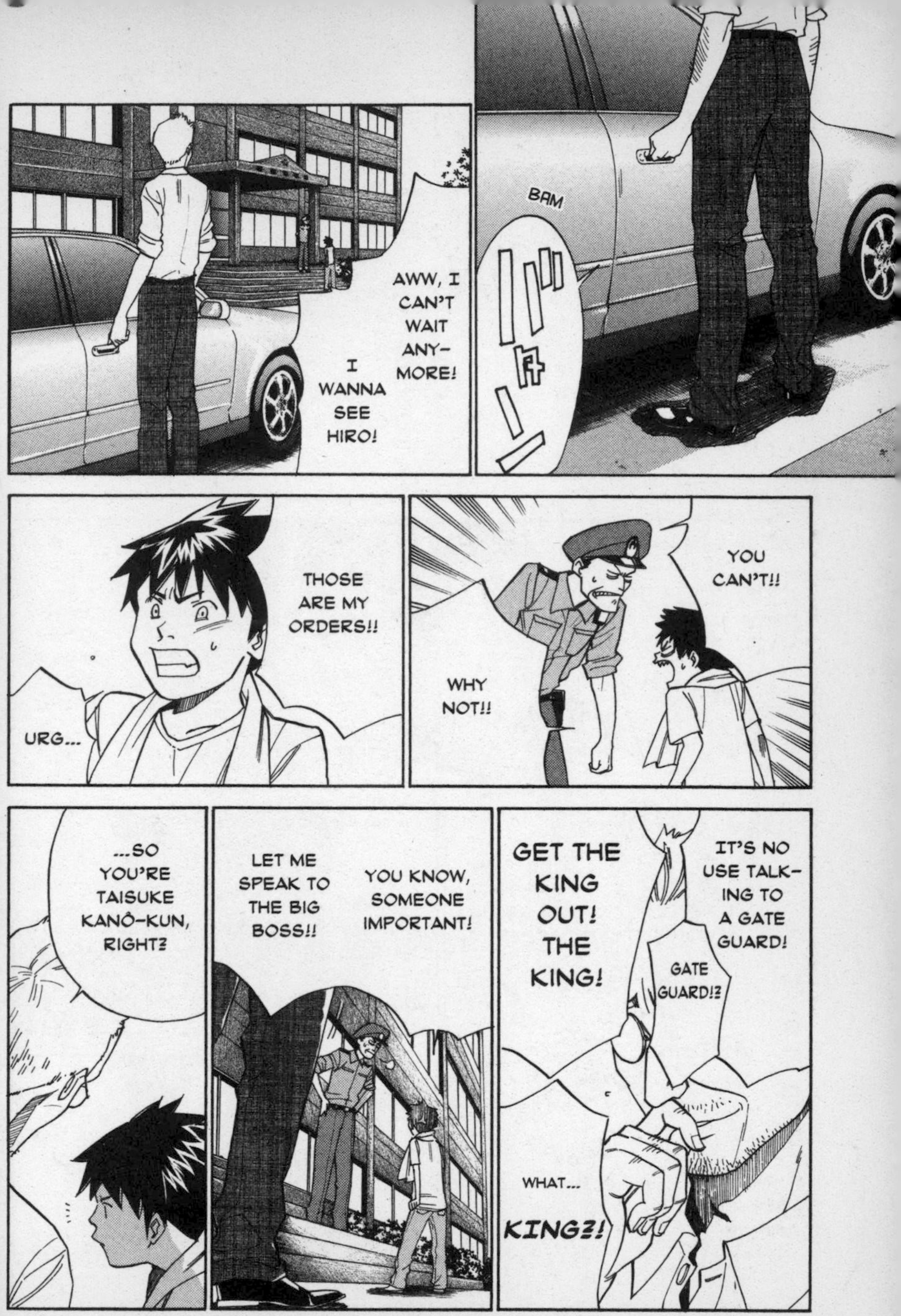
BAM
AWW, I CAN'T WAIT ANY-MORE!
I WANNA SEE HIRO!
YOU CAN'T!!
WHY NOT!!
THOSE ARE MY ORDERS!!
URG...
IT'S NO USE TALK-ING TO A GATE GUARD!
GATE GUARD!?
GET THE KING OUT! THE KING!
WHAT...
KING?!
YOU KNOW, SOMEONE IMPORTANT!
LET ME SPEAK TO THE BIG BOSS!!
...SO YOU'RE TAISUKE KANÔ-KUN, RIGHT?

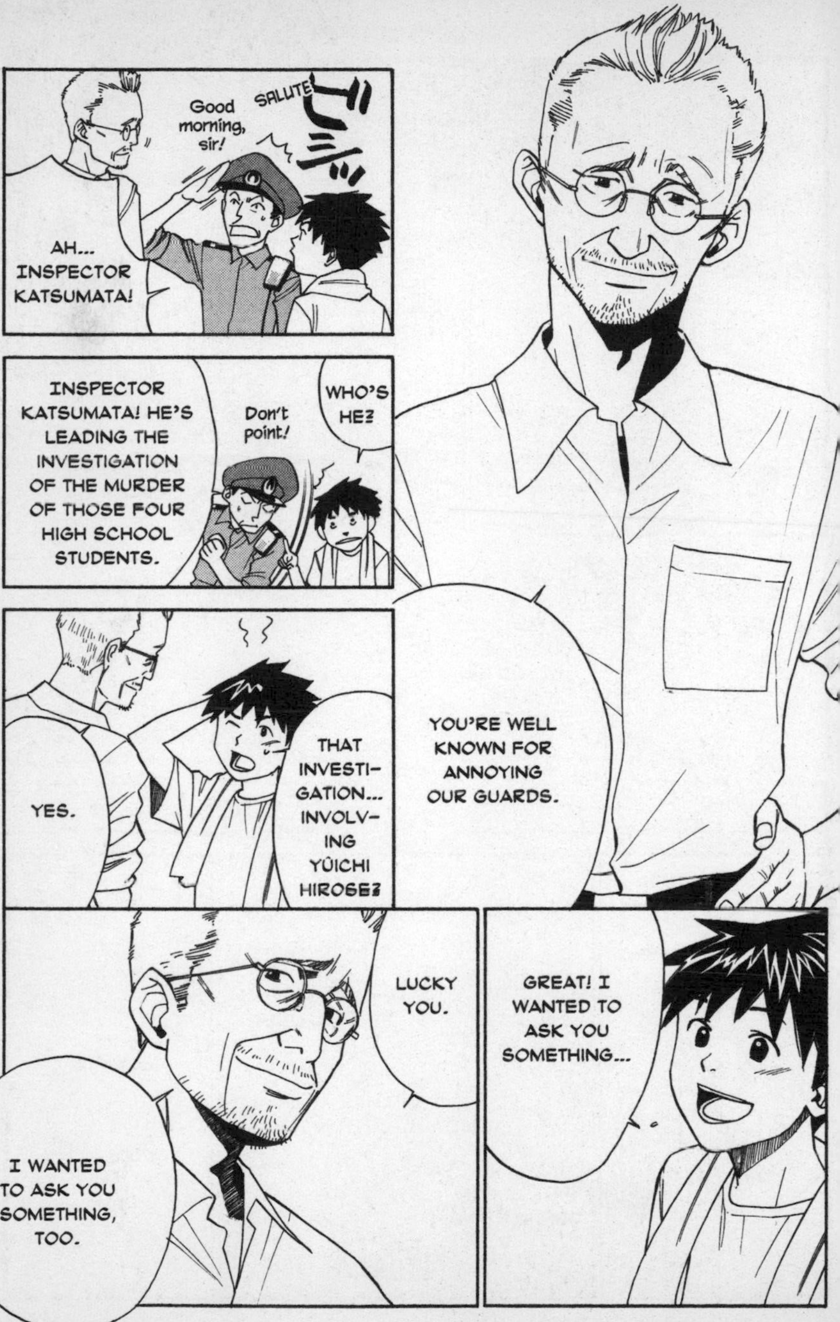
YOU'RE WELL KNOWN FOR ANNOYING OUR GUARDS.
SALUTE
Good morning, sir!
AH... INSPECTOR KATSUMATA!
WHO'S HE?
Don't point!
INSPECTOR KATSUMATA! HE'S LEADING THE INVESTIGATION OF THE MURDER OF THOSE FOUR HIGH SCHOOL STUDENTS.
THAT INVESTIGATION... INVOLVING YÛICHI HIROSE?
YES.
GREAT! I WANTED TO ASK YOU SOMETHING...
LUCKY YOU.
I WANTED TO ASK YOU SOMETHING, TOO.

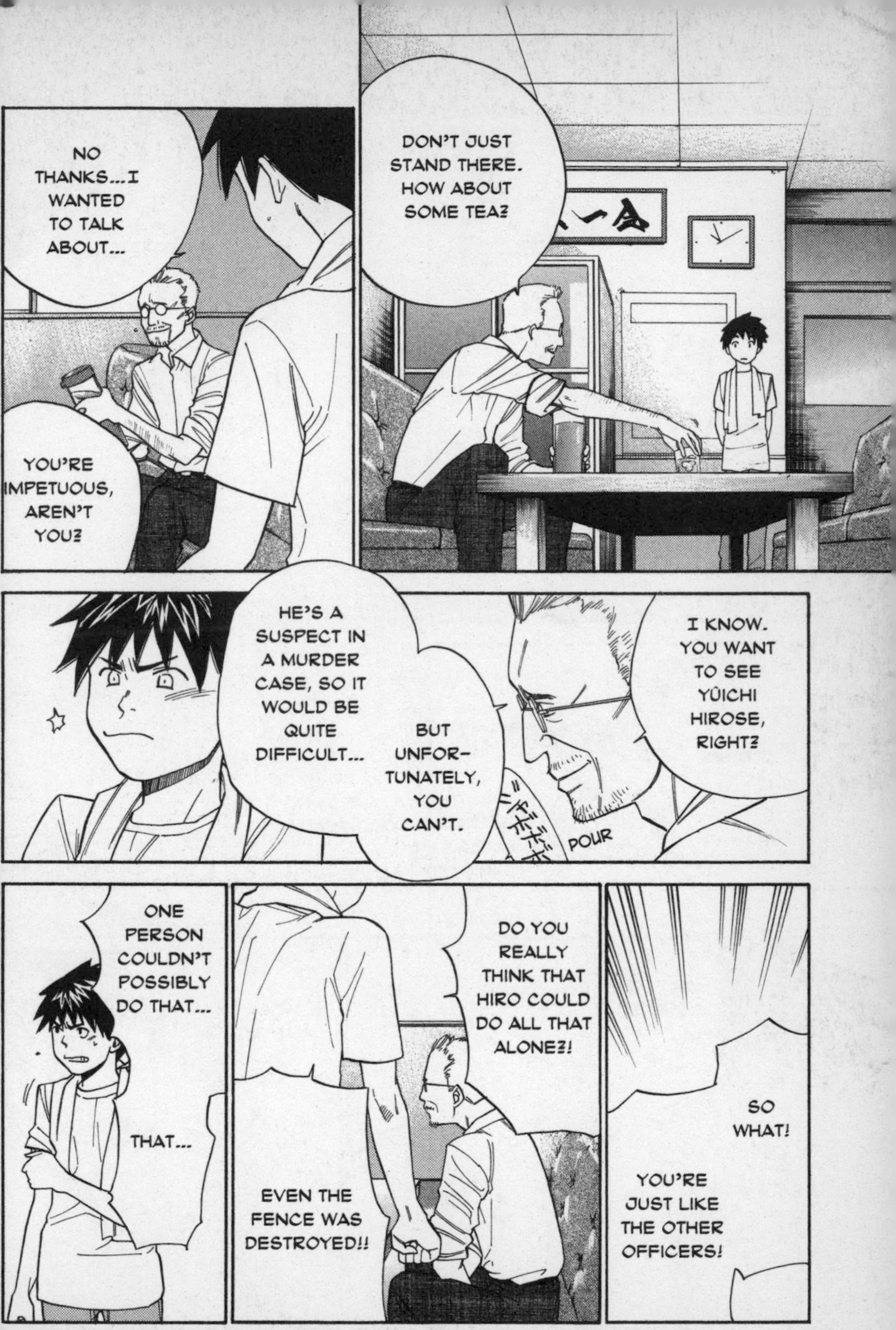
DON'T JUST STAND THERE. HOW ABOUT SOME TEA?
NO THANKS...I WANTED TO TALK ABOUT...
YOU'RE IMPETUOUS, AREN'T YOU?
I KNOW. YOU WANT TO SEE YÛICHI HIROSE, RIGHT?
POUR
BUT UNFORTUNATELY, YOU CAN'T.
HE'S A SUSPECT IN A MURDER CASE, SO IT WOULD BE QUITE DIFFICULT...
SO WHAT!
YOU'RE JUST LIKE THE OTHER OFFICERS!
DO YOU REALLY THINK THAT HIRO COULD DO ALL THAT ALONE?!
EVEN THE FENCE WAS DESTROYED!!
ONE PERSON COULDN'T POSSIBLY DO THAT...
THAT...

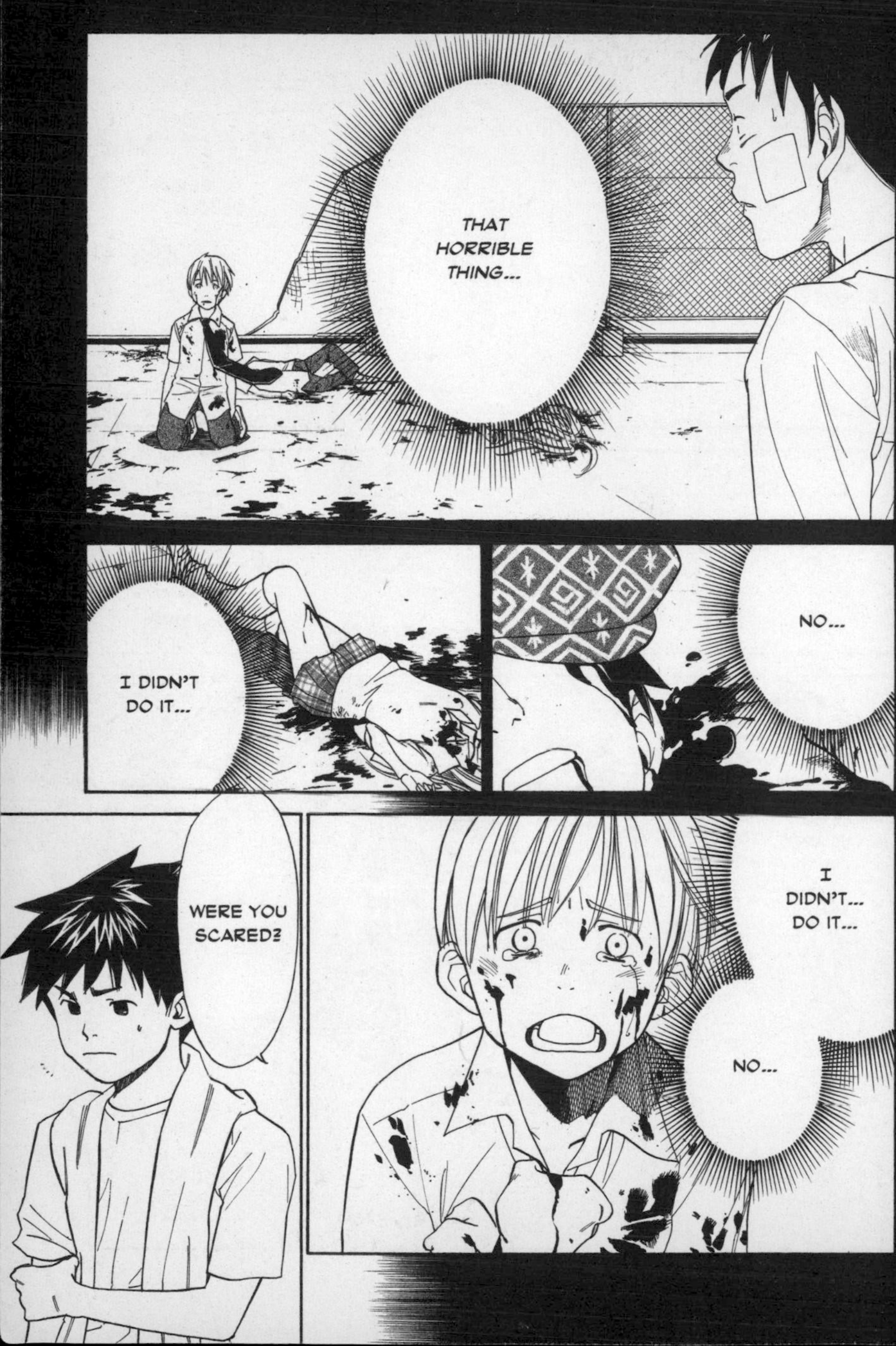
THAT HORRIBLE THING...
NO...
I DIDN'T DO IT...
I DIDN'T... DO IT...
NO...
WERE YOU SCARED?

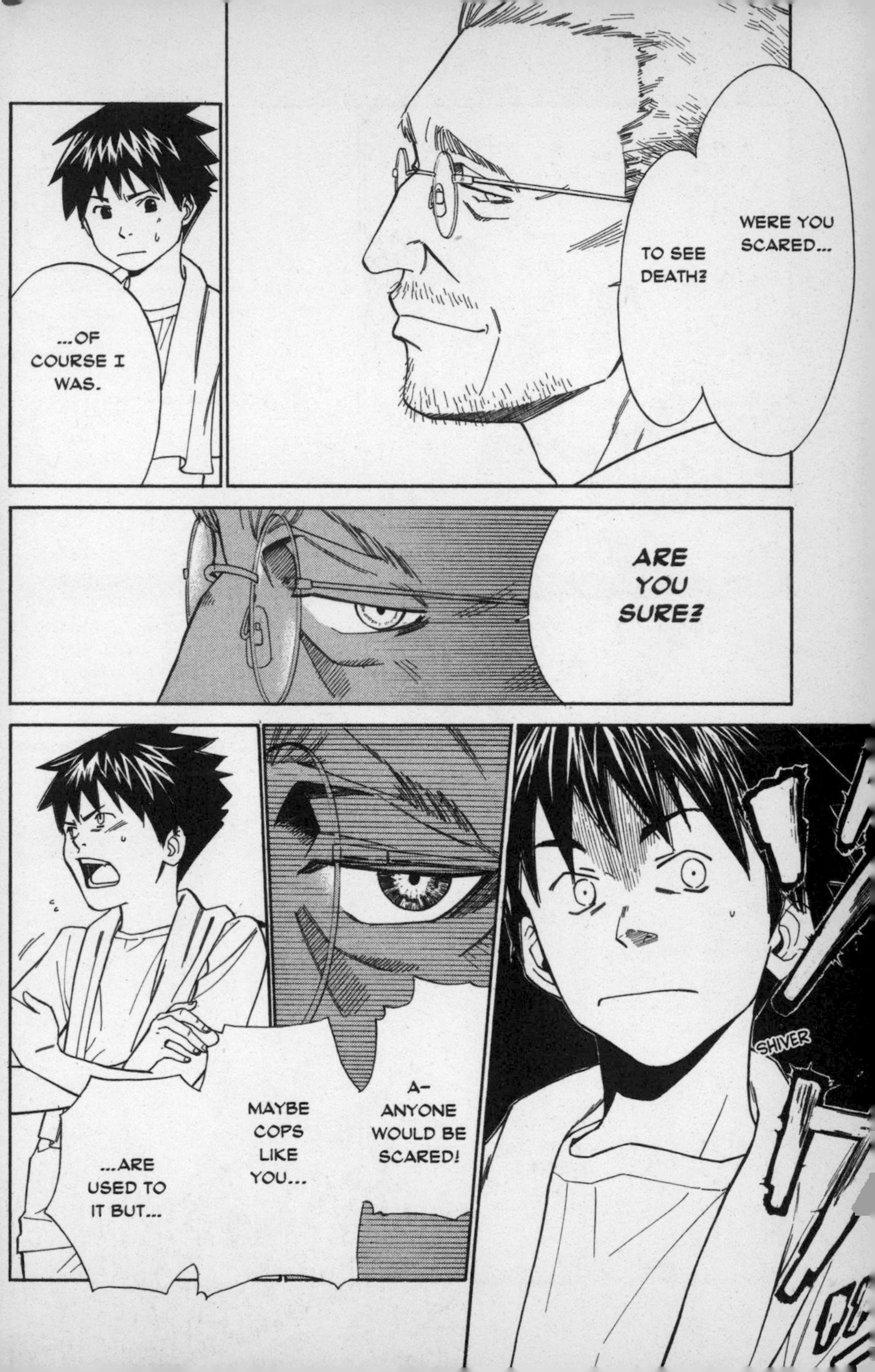
WERE YOU SCARED...
TO SEE DEATH?
...OF COURSE I WAS.
ARE YOU SURE?
SHIVER
A- ANYONE WOULD BE SCARED!
MAYBE COPS LIKE YOU...
...ARE USED TO IT BUT...

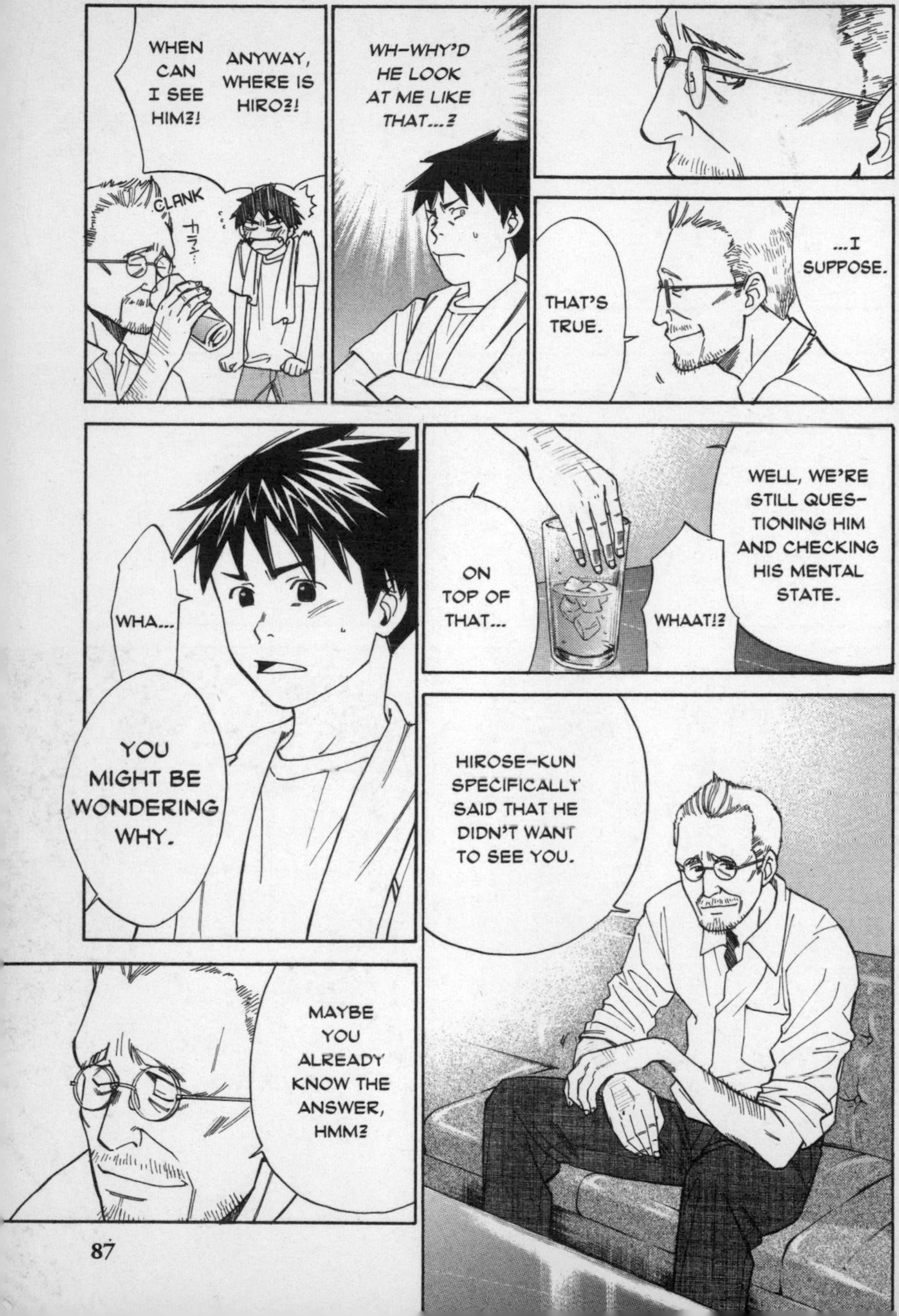
...I SUPPOSE.
THAT'S TRUE.
WH-WHY'D HE LOOK AT ME LIKE THAT...?
ANYWAY, WHERE IS HIRO?!
WHEN CAN I SEE HIM?!
CLANK
FIM...
WELL, WE'RE STILL QUES-TIONING HIM AND CHECKING HIS MENTAL STATE.
WHAAT!?
ON TOP OF THAT...
HIROSE-KUN SPECIFICALLY SAID THAT HE DIDN'T WANT TO SEE YOU.
WHA...
YOU MIGHT BE WONDERING WHY.
MAYBE YOU ALREADY KNOW THE ANSWER, HMM?

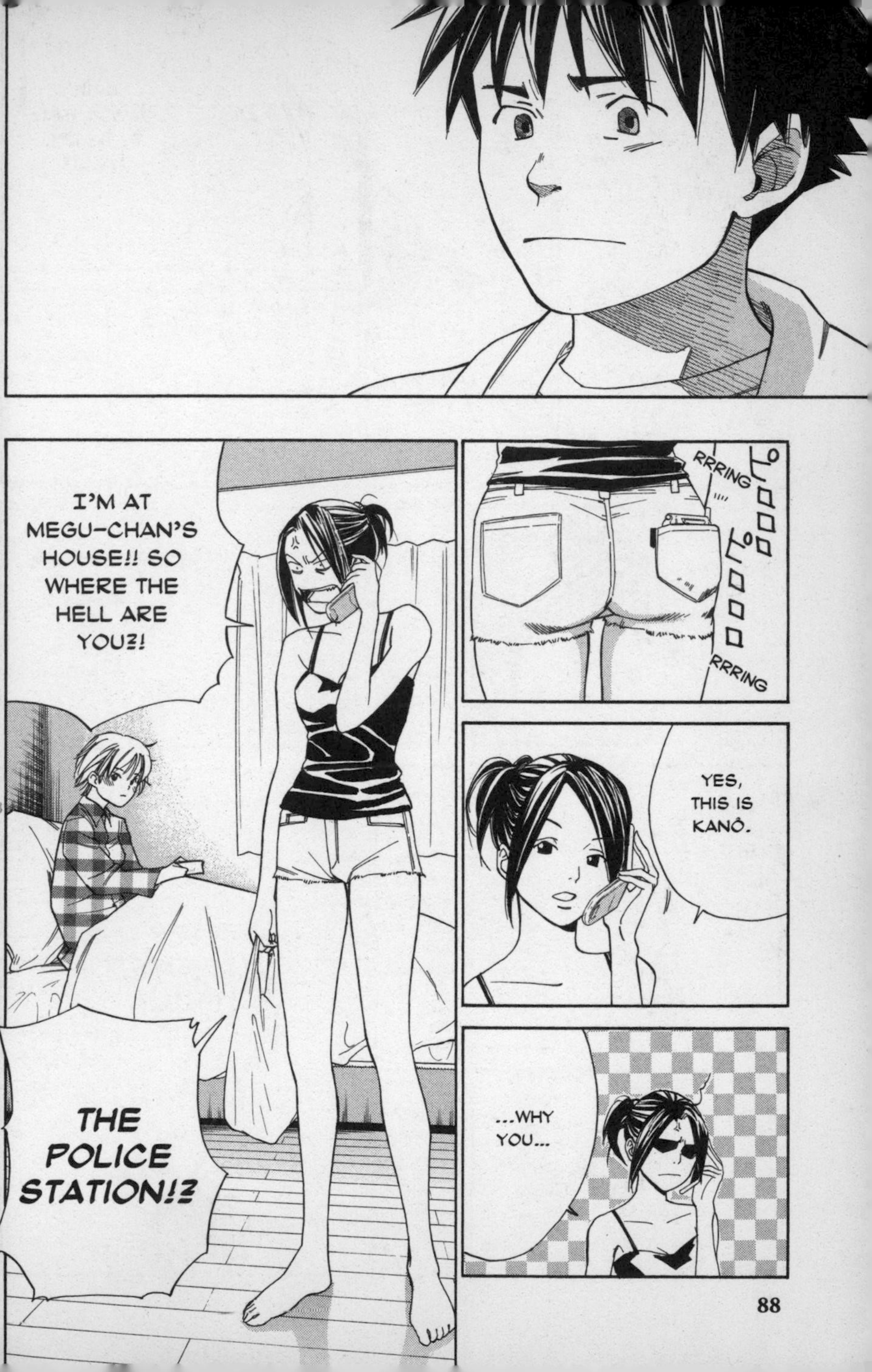
RRRING
RRRING
YES, THIS IS KANÔ.
...WHY YOU...
I'M AT MEGU-CHAN'S HOUSE!! SO WHERE THE HELL ARE YOU?!
THE POLICE STATION!?

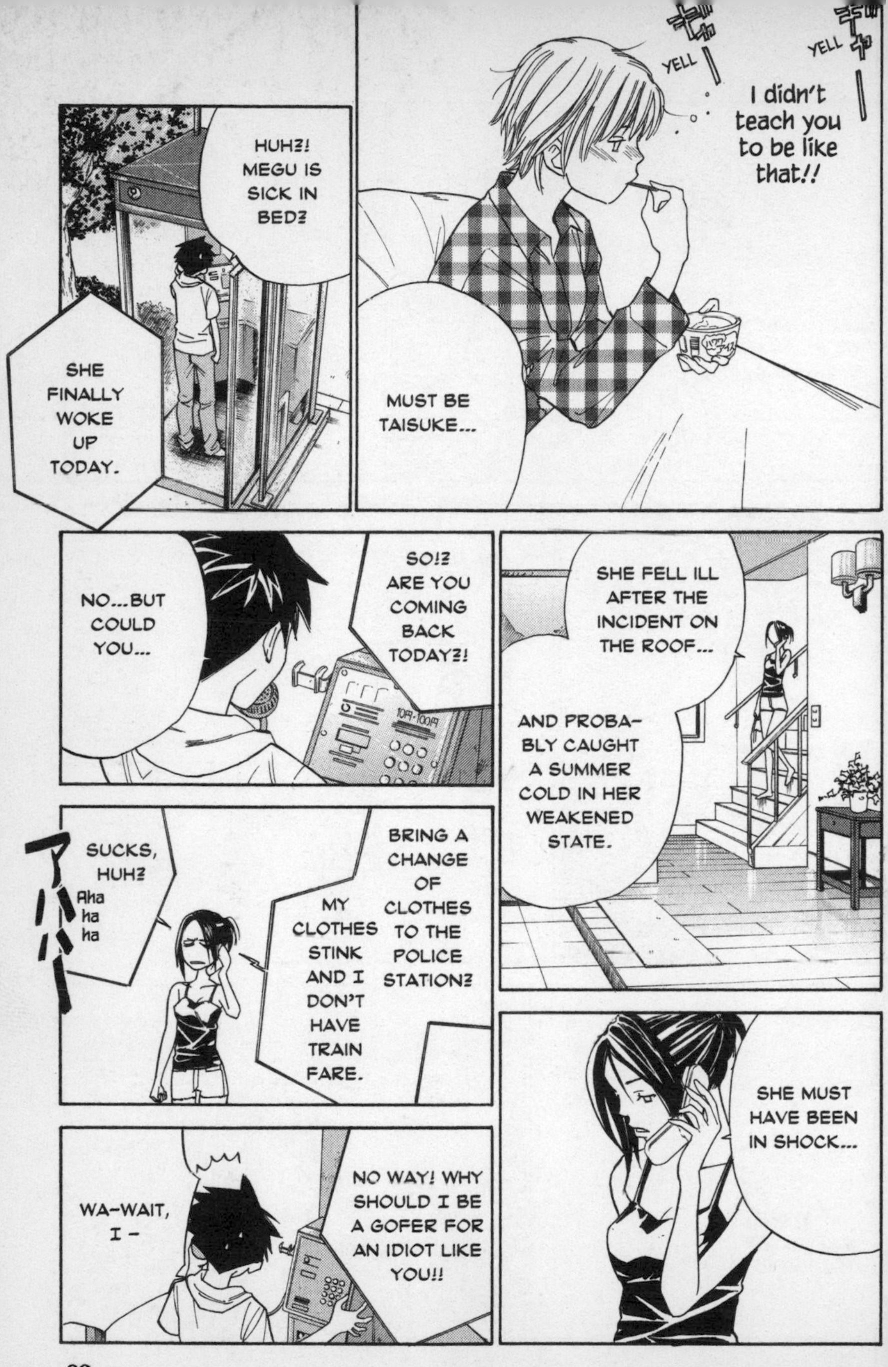
YELL
YELL
I didn't teach you to be like that!!
MUST BE TAISUKE...
HUH?! MEGU IS SICK IN BED?
SHE FINALLY WOKE UP TODAY.
SHE FELL ILL AFTER THE INCIDENT ON THE ROOF...
AND PROBABLY CAUGHT A SUMMER COLD IN HER WEAKENED STATE.
SHE MUST HAVE BEEN IN SHOCK...
SO!? ARE YOU COMING BACK TODAY?!
NO...BUT COULD YOU...
BRING A CHANGE OF CLOTHES TO THE POLICE STATION?
MY CLOTHES STINK AND I DON'T HAVE TRAIN FARE.
SUCKS, HUH?
Aha ha ha
NO WAY! WHY SHOULD I BE A GOFER FOR AN IDIOT LIKE YOU!!
WA-WAIT, I -

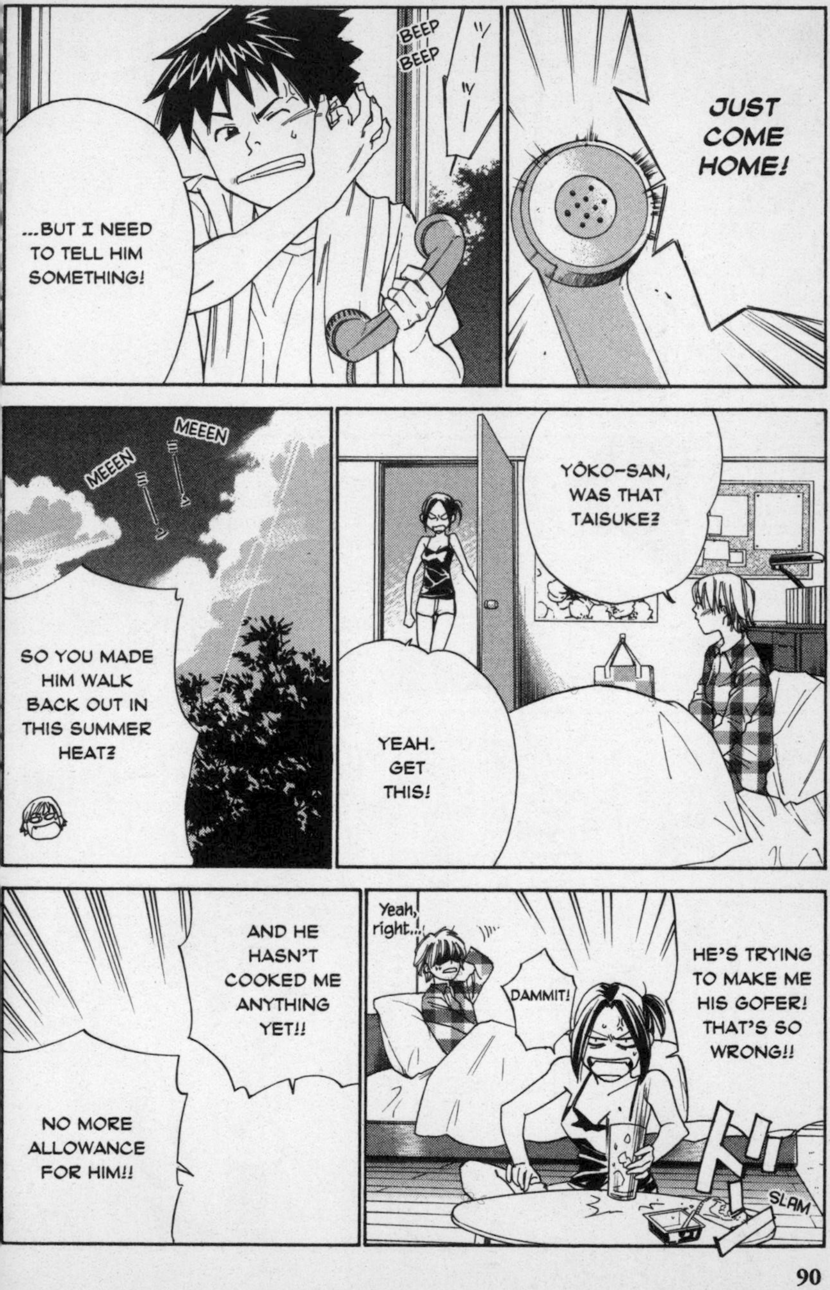
JUST COME HOME!
BEEP BEEP
...BUT I NEED TO TELL HIM SOMETHING!
YÔKO-SAN, WAS THAT TAISUKE?
YEAH. GET THIS!
MEEEN
MEEEN
SO YOU MADE HIM WALK BACK OUT IN THIS SUMMER HEAT?
HE'S TRYING TO MAKE ME HIS GOFER! THAT'S SO WRONG!!
Yeah, right...
DAMMIT!
SLAM
AND HE HASN'T COOKED ME ANYTHING YET!!
NO MORE ALLOWANCE FOR HIM!!

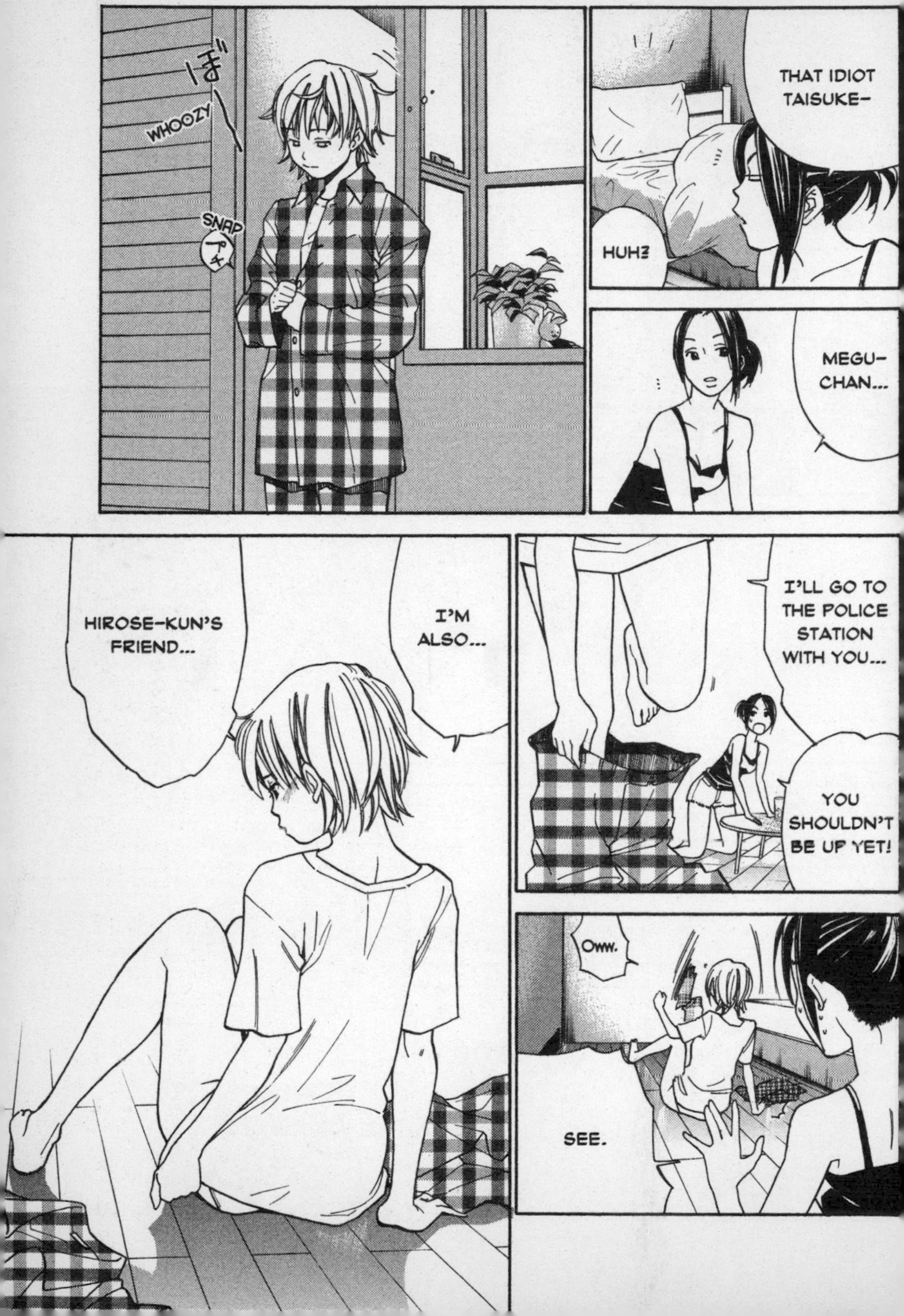
THAT IDIOT TAISUKE-
HUH?
MEGU-CHAN...
WHOOZY
SNAP
I'LL GO TO THE POLICE STATION WITH YOU...
YOU SHOULDN'T BE UP YET!
Oww.
SEE.
I'M ALSO...
HIROSE-KUN'S FRIEND...

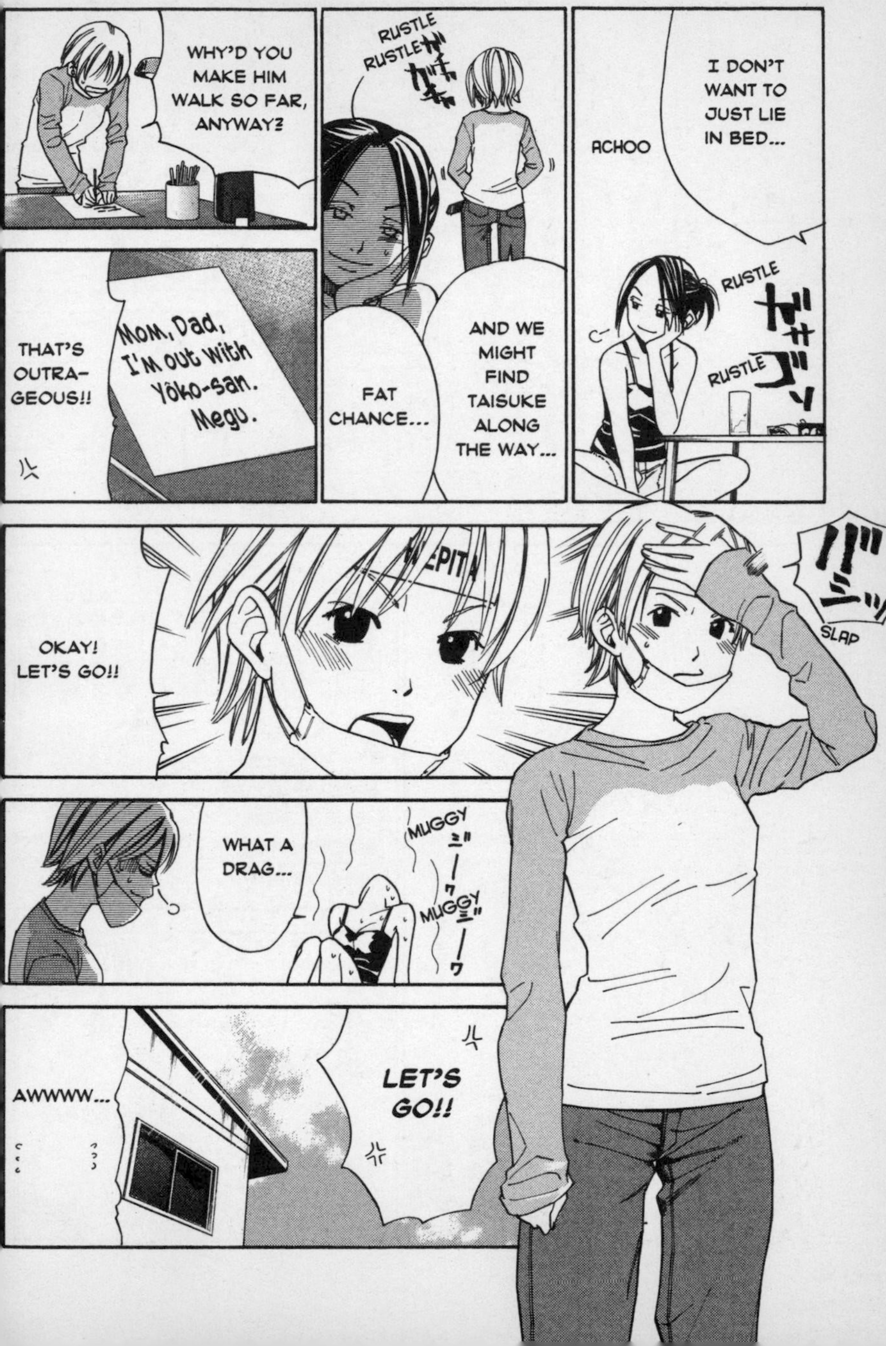

I DON'T WANT TO JUST LIE IN BED...
ACHOO
RUSTLE
RUSTLE
RUSTLE RUSTLE
AND WE MIGHT FIND TAISUKE ALONG THE WAY...
FAT CHANCE...
WHY'D YOU MAKE HIM WALK SO FAR, ANYWAY?
Mom, Dad, I'm out with Yôko-san. Megu.
THAT'S OUTRAGEOUS!!
SLAP
OKAY! LET'S GO!!
MUGGY
MUGGY
WHAT A DRAG...
LET'S GO!!
AWWWW...

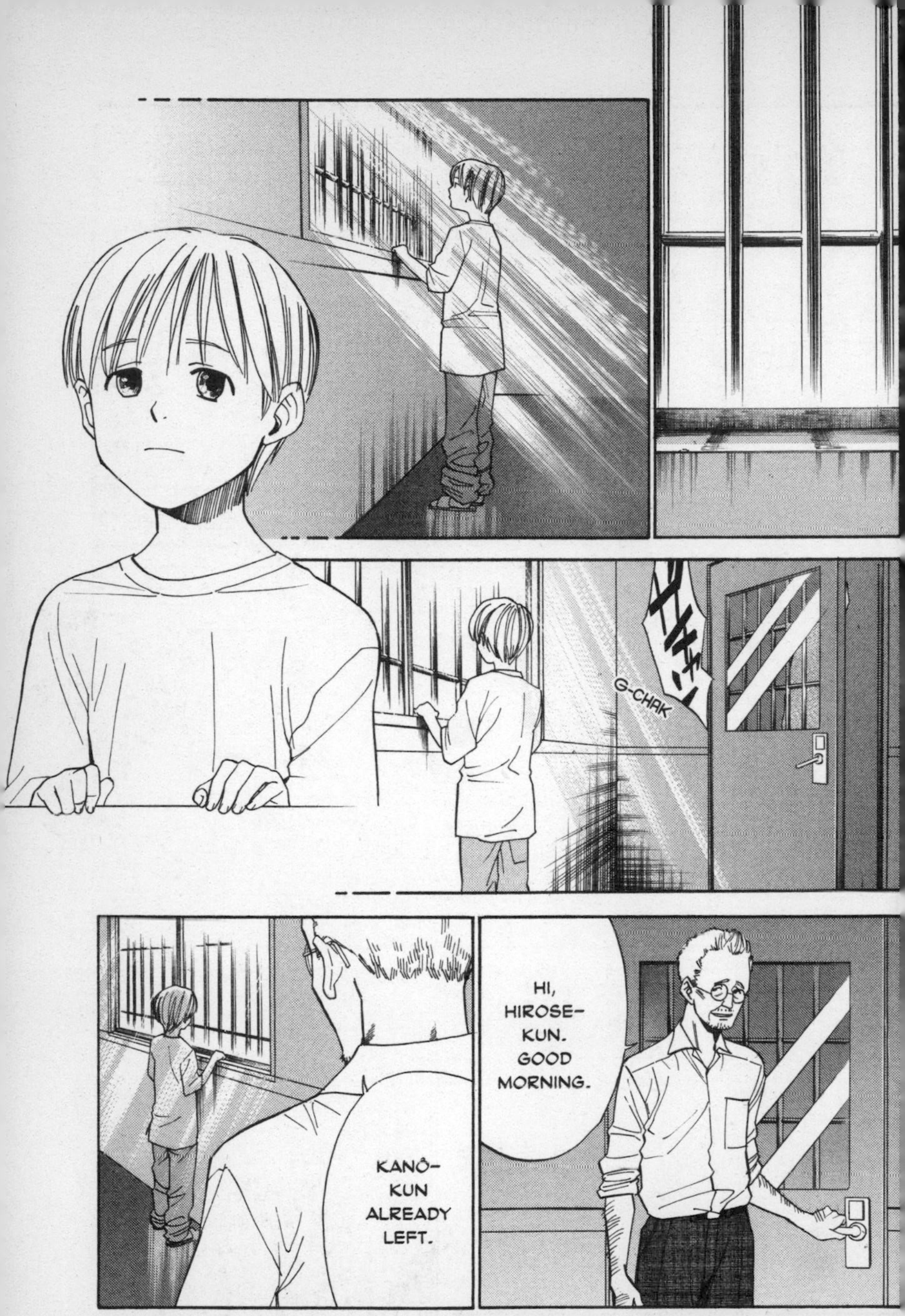
G-CHAK
HI, HIROSE-KUN. GOOD MORNING.
KANÔ-KUN ALREADY LEFT.

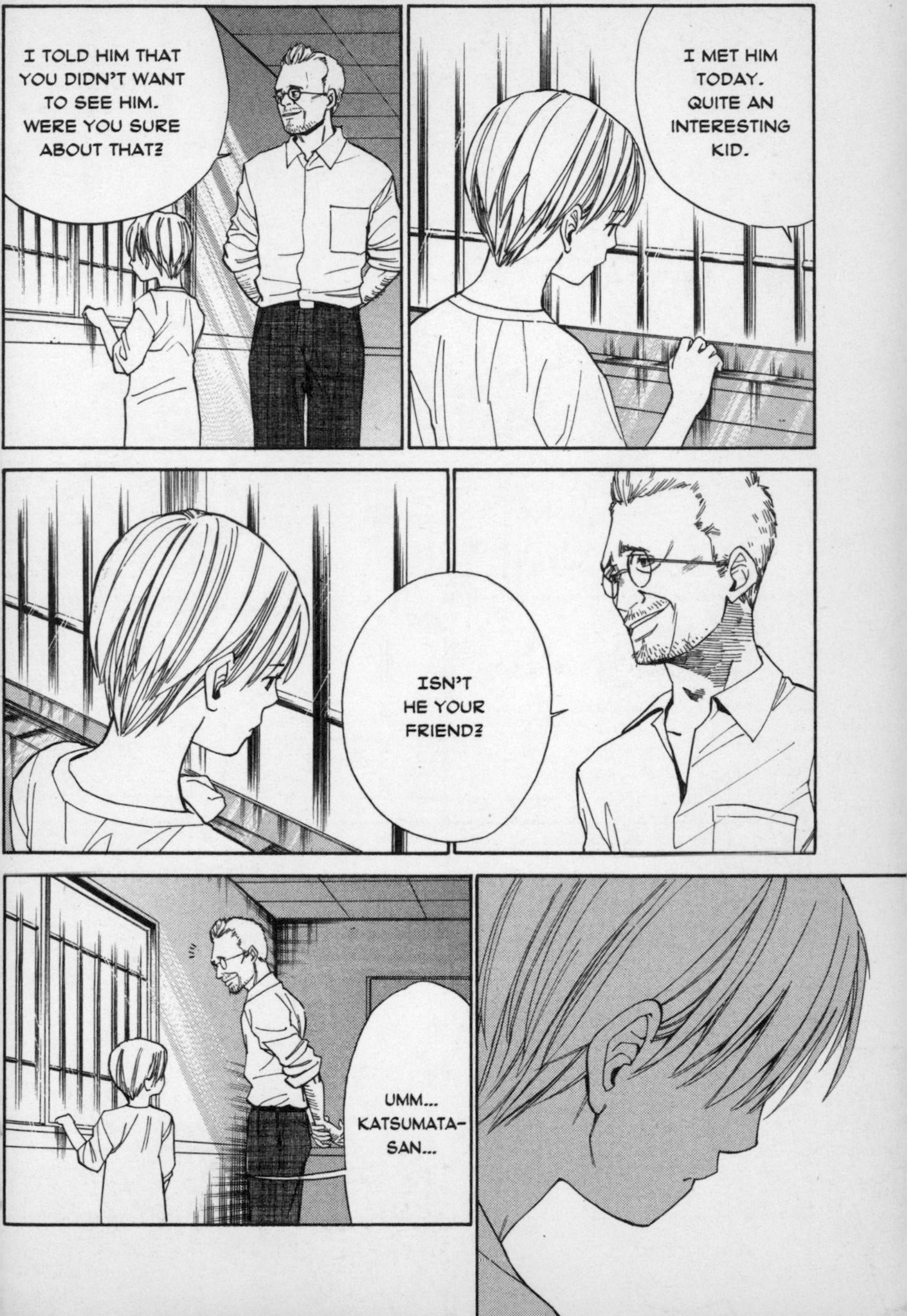
I MET HIM TODAY. QUITE AN INTERESTING KID.
I TOLD HIM THAT YOU DIDN'T WANT TO SEE HIM. WERE YOU SURE ABOUT THAT?
ISN'T HE YOUR FRIEND?
UMM... KATSUMATA-SAN...

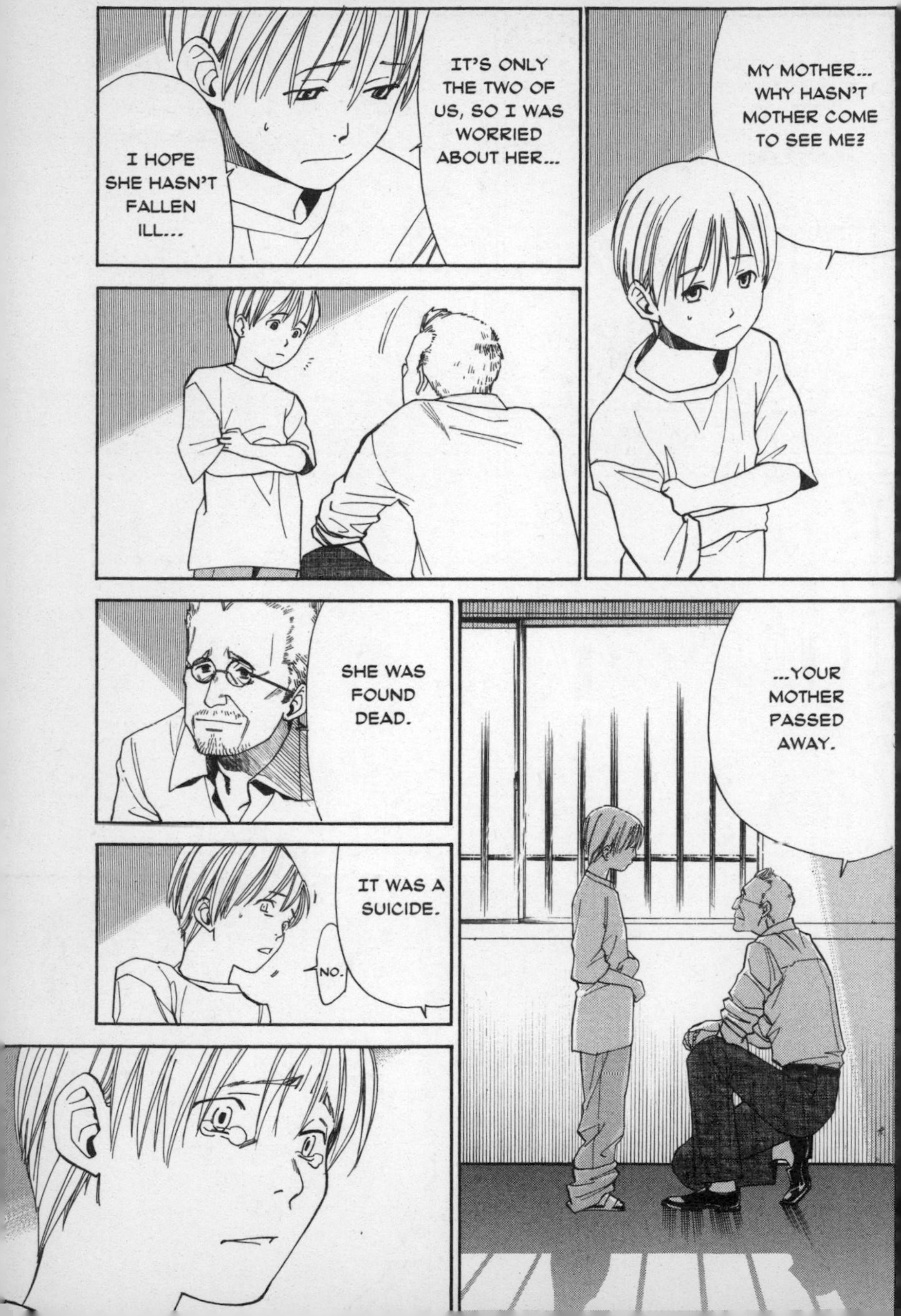
MY MOTHER... WHY HASN'T MOTHER COME TO SEE ME?
IT'S ONLY THE TWO OF US, SO I WAS WORRIED ABOUT HER...
I HOPE SHE HASN'T FALLEN ILL...
...YOUR MOTHER PASSED AWAY.
SHE WAS FOUND DEAD.
IT WAS A SUICIDE.
NO.

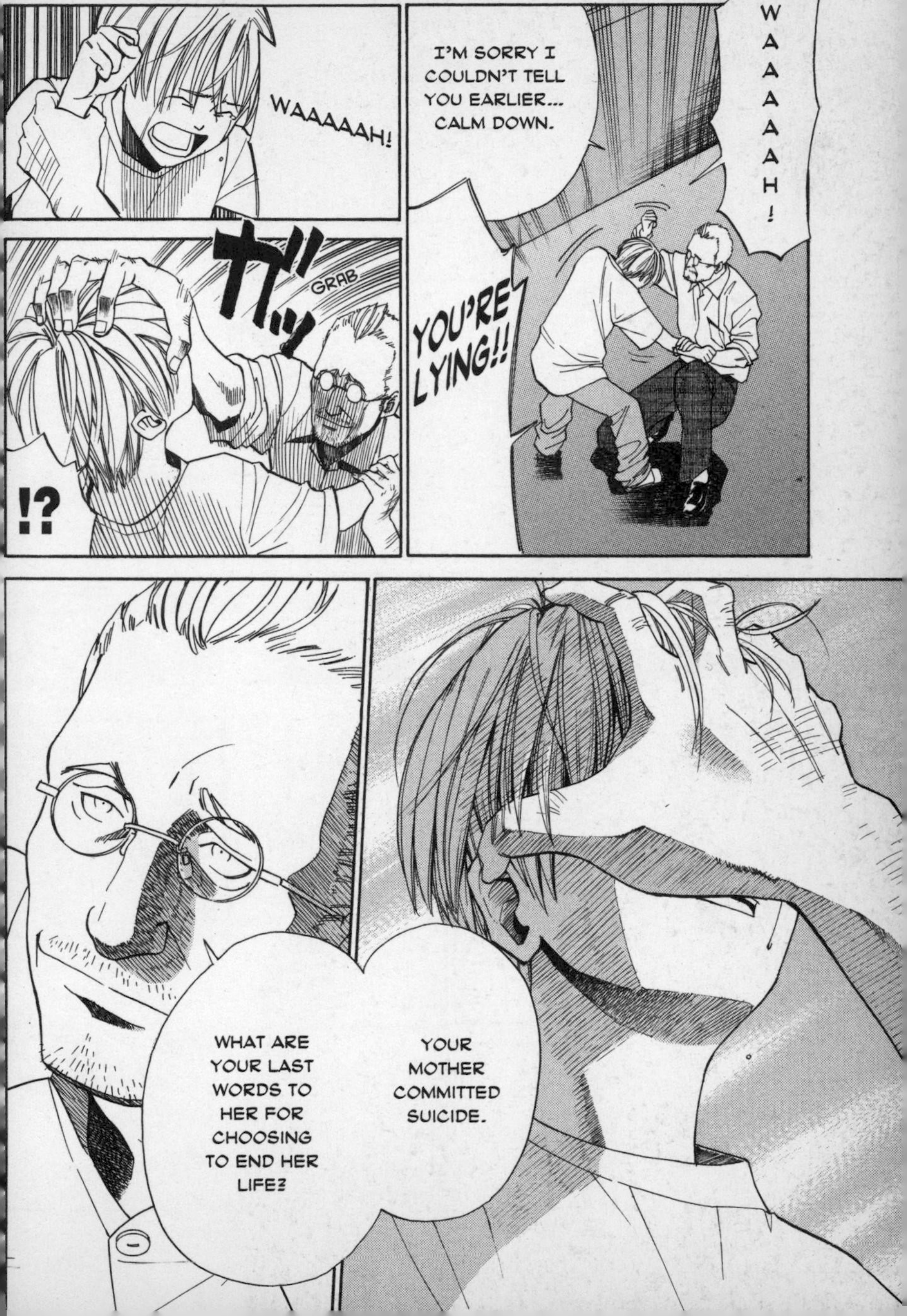
WAAAAAH!
I'M SORRY I COULDN'T TELL YOU EARLIER... CALM DOWN.
YOU'RE LYING!!
WAAAAAAH!
ガッ
GRAB
!?
YOUR MOTHER COMMITTED SUICIDE.
WHAT ARE YOUR LAST WORDS TO HER FOR CHOOSING TO END HER LIFE?

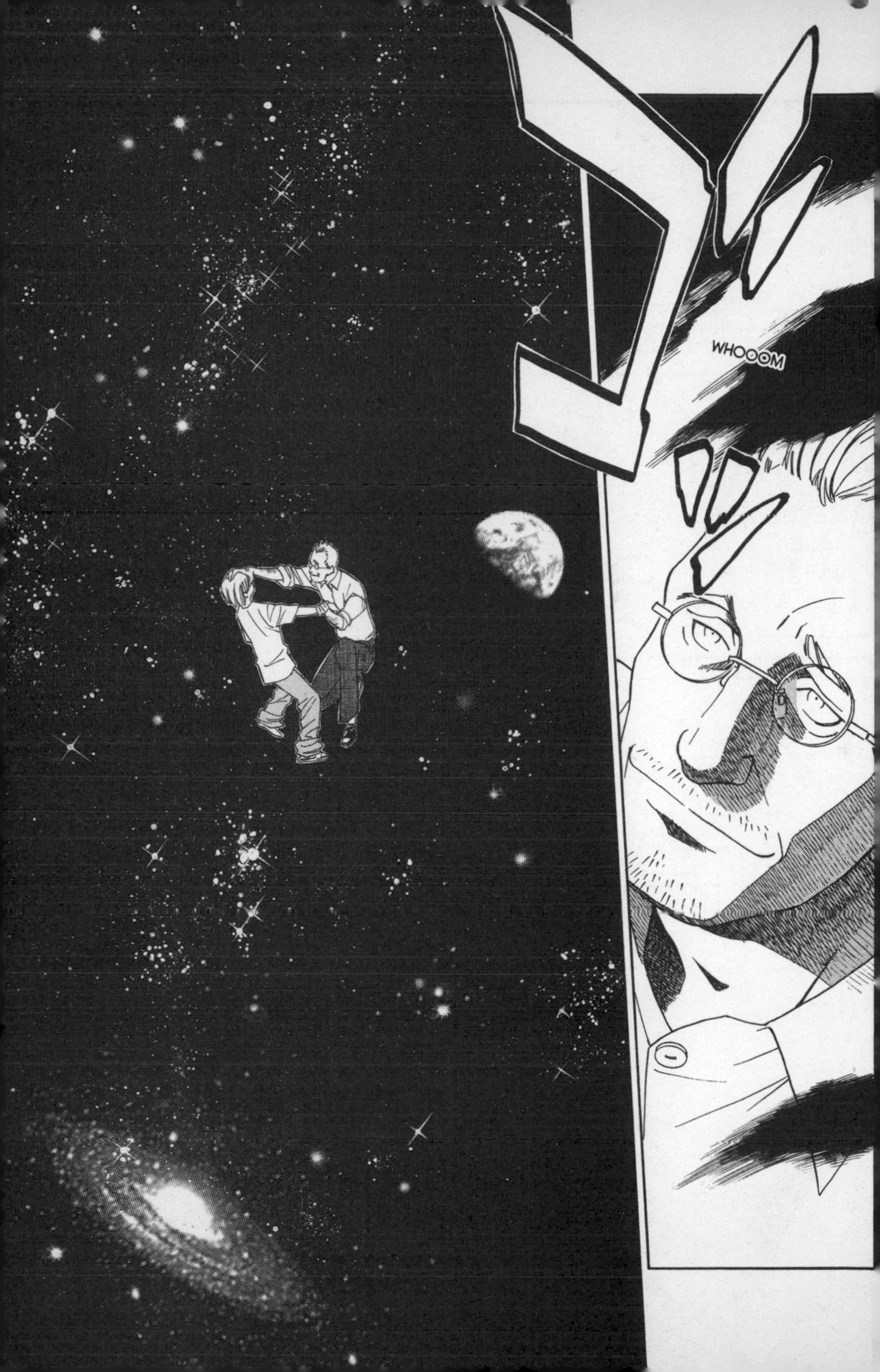
WHOOOM

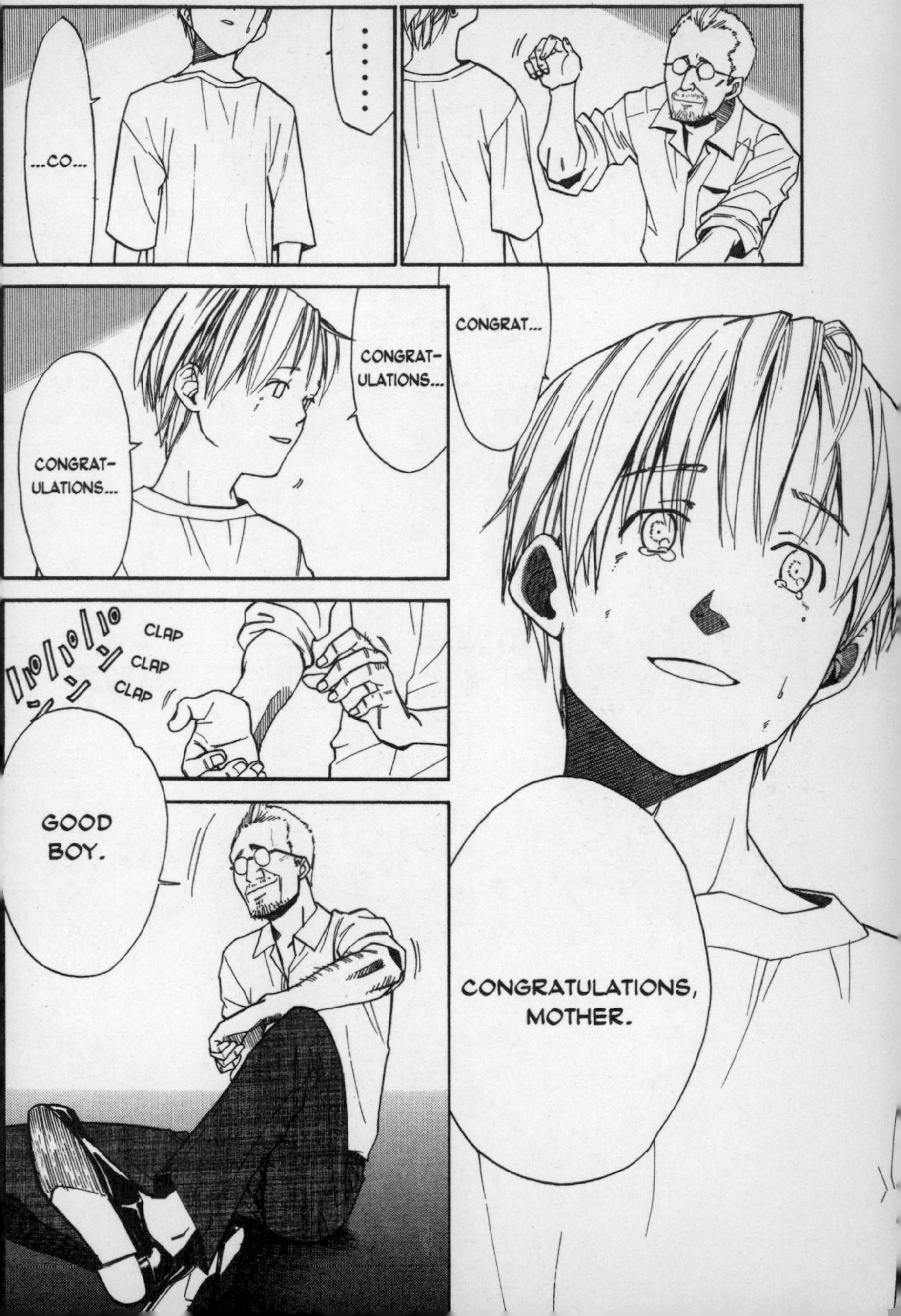
......
...CO...
CONGRAT...
CONGRATULATIONS, MOTHER.
CONGRAT-ULATIONS...
CONGRAT-ULATIONS...
CLAP CLAP CLAP
GOOD BOY.

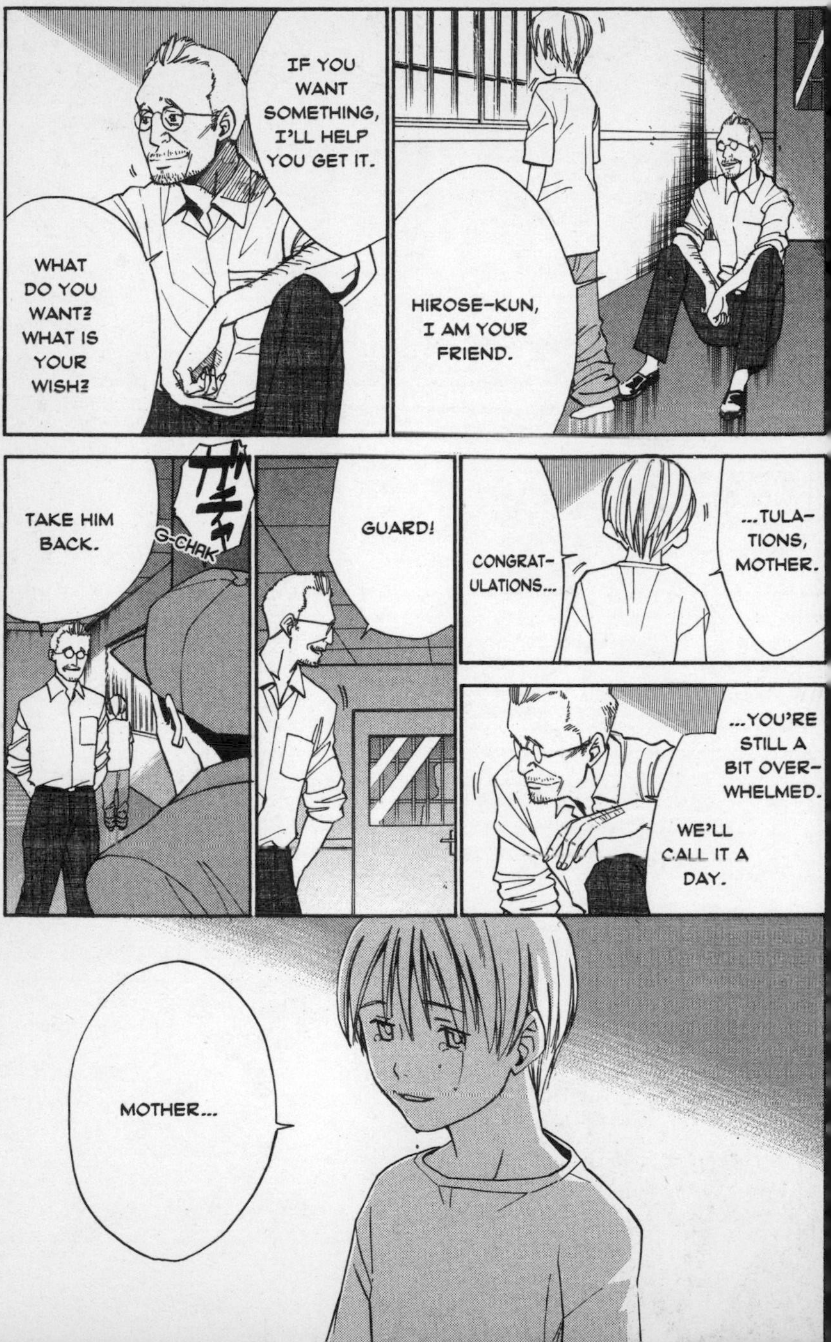
HIROSE-KUN, I AM YOUR FRIEND.
IF YOU WANT SOMETHING, I'LL HELP YOU GET IT.
WHAT DO YOU WANT? WHAT IS YOUR WISH?
...TULATIONS, MOTHER.
CONGRATULATIONS...
...YOU'RE STILL A BIT OVERWHELMED.
WE'LL CALL IT A DAY.
GUARD!
ガチャ
G-CHAK
TAKE HIM BACK.
MOTHER...

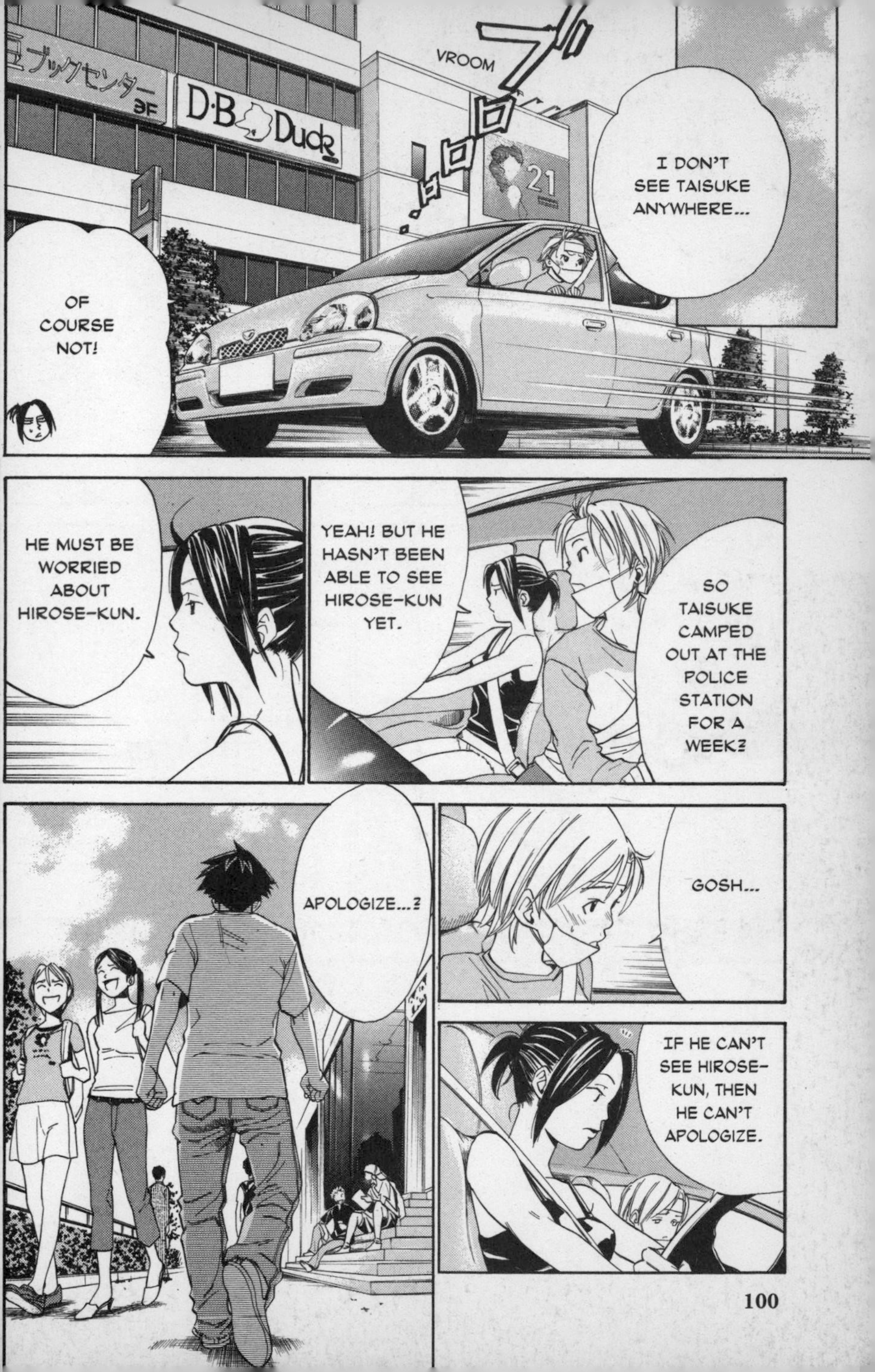
ブックセンター
3F
D·B Duck
21
VROOM
ブロロロ
I DON'T SEE TAISUKE ANYWHERE...
OF COURSE NOT!
SO TAISUKE CAMPED OUT AT THE POLICE STATION FOR A WEEK?
YEAH! BUT HE HASN'T BEEN ABLE TO SEE HIROSE-KUN YET.
HE MUST BE WORRIED ABOUT HIROSE-KUN.
GOSH...
IF HE CAN'T SEE HIROSE-KUN, THEN HE CAN'T APOLOGIZE.
APOLOGIZE...?

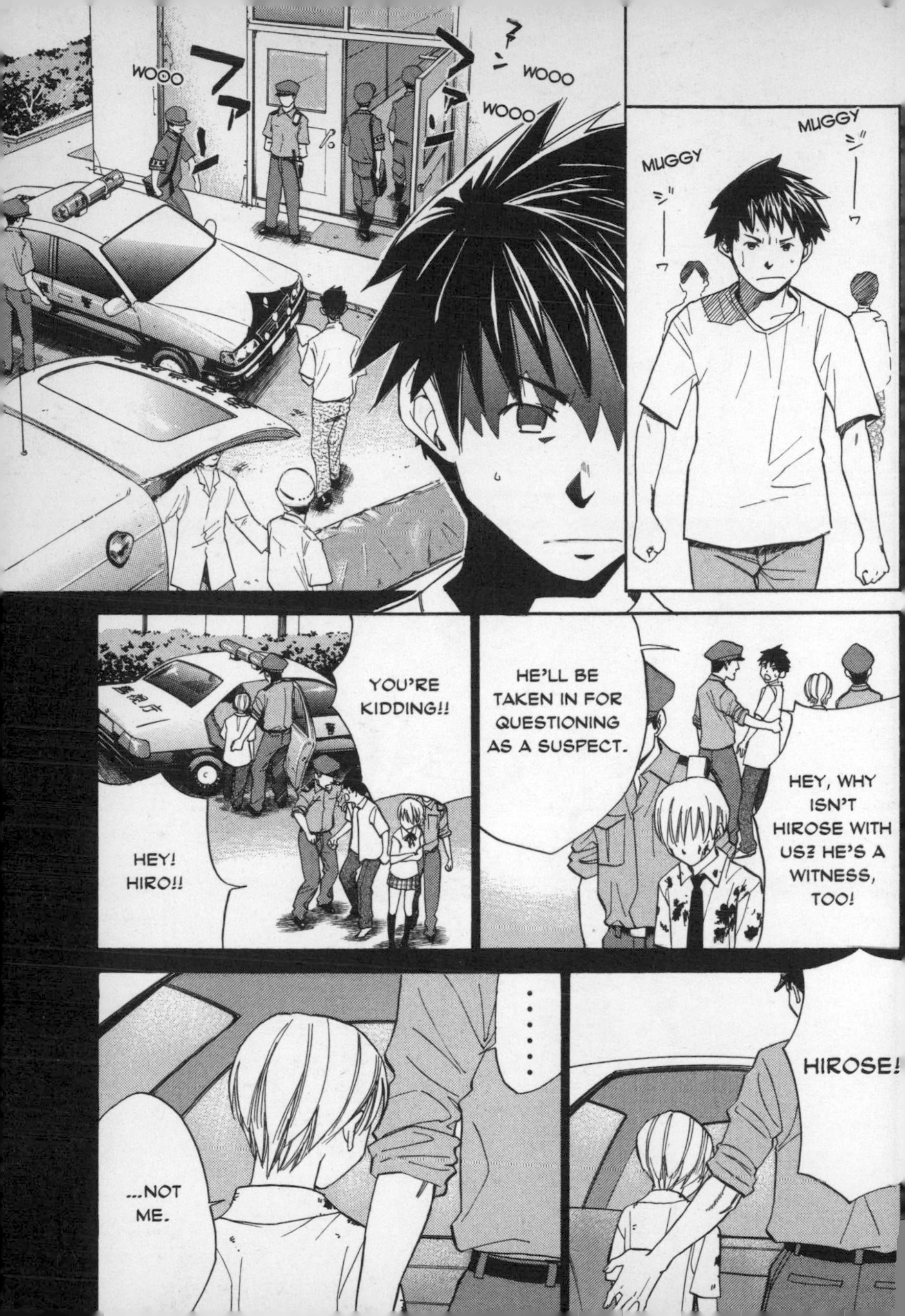
MUGGY
MUGGY
WOOO
WOOO
WOOO
HEY, WHY ISN'T HIROSE WITH US? HE'S A WITNESS, TOO!
HE'LL BE TAKEN IN FOR QUESTIONING AS A SUSPECT.
YOU'RE KIDDING!!
HEY! HIRO!!
HIROSE!
......
...NOT ME.

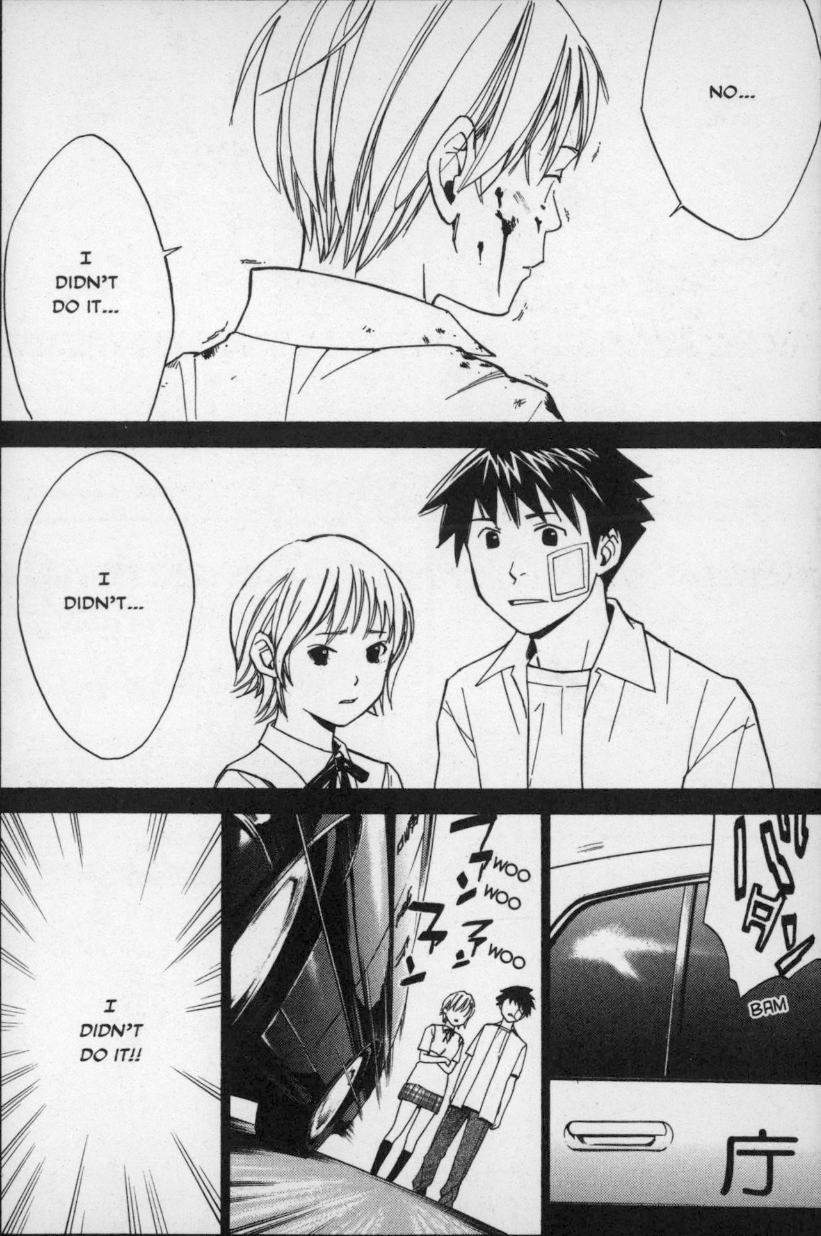
NO...
I DIDN'T DO IT...
I DIDN'T...
BAM
庁
WOO
WOO
WOO
I DIDN'T DO IT!!

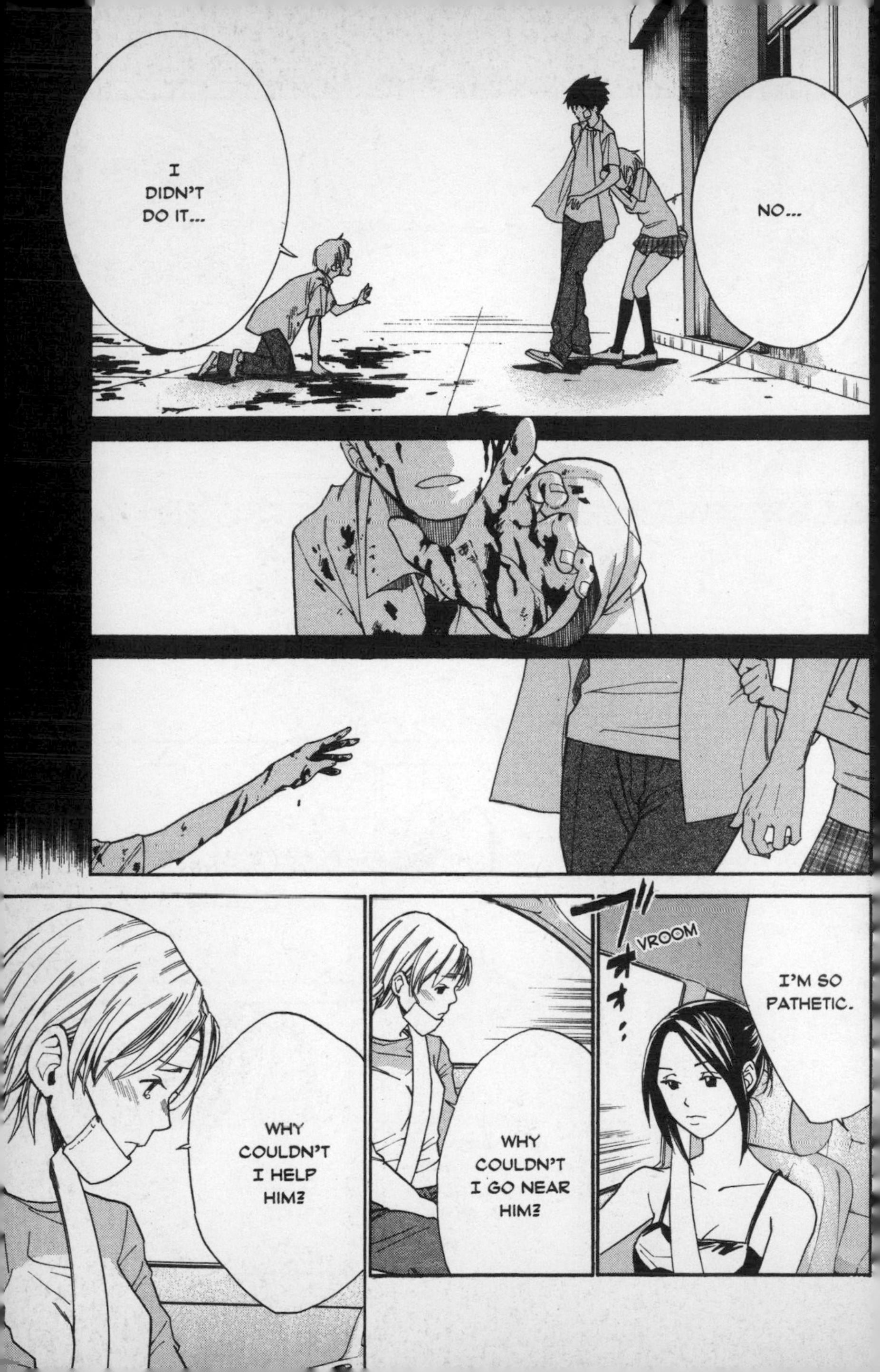
NO...
I DIDN'T DO IT...
VROOM
I'M SO PATHETIC.
WHY COULDN'T I GO NEAR HIM?
WHY COULDN'T I HELP HIM?

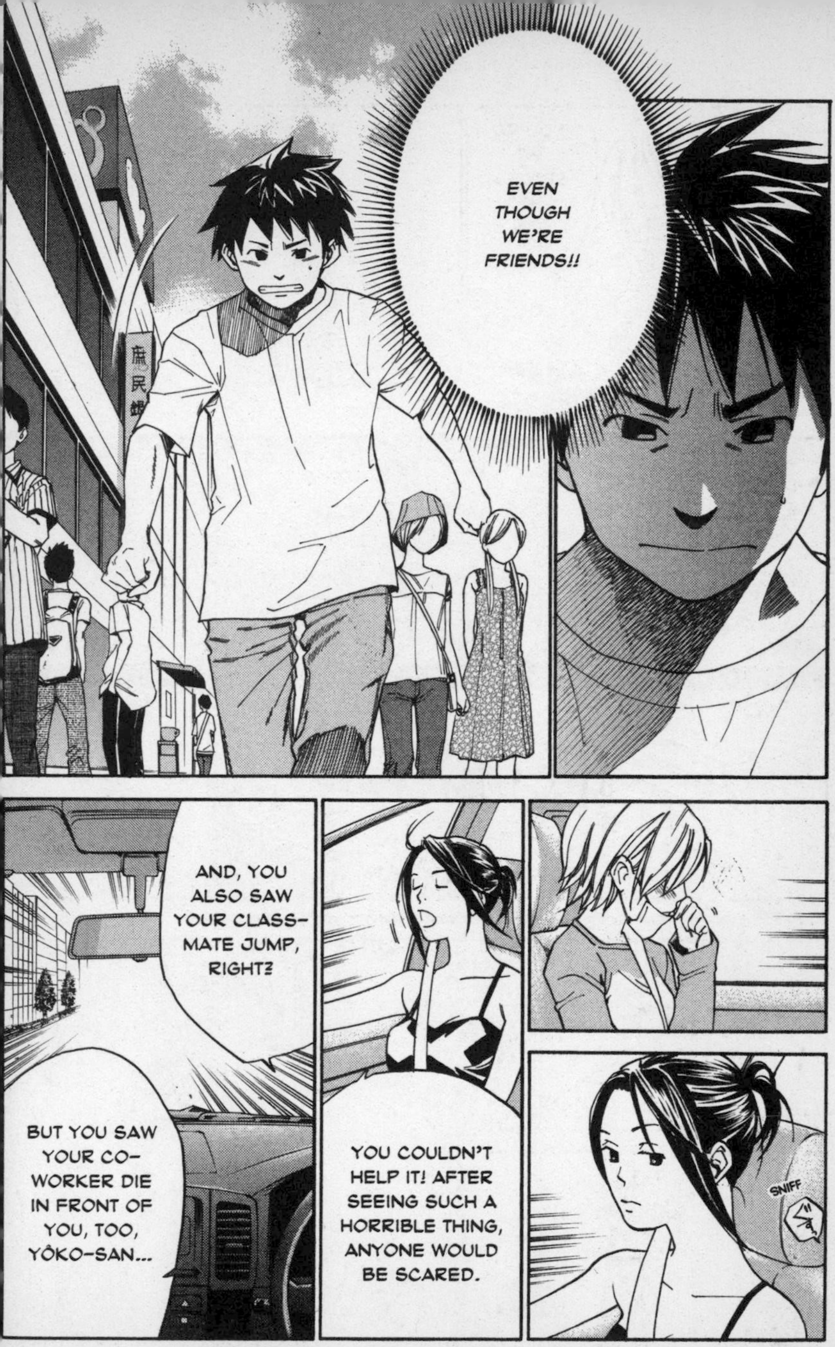
EVEN THOUGH WE'RE FRIENDS!!
SNIFF
YOU COULDN'T HELP IT! AFTER SEEING SUCH A HORRIBLE THING, ANYONE WOULD BE SCARED.
AND, YOU ALSO SAW YOUR CLASS-MATE JUMP, RIGHT?
BUT YOU SAW YOUR CO-WORKER DIE IN FRONT OF YOU, TOO, YÔKO-SAN...

YOU'RE SO STRONG, YŌKO-SAN.

BUT I'M SO WEAK.

. . . . . .

SKREECH

BRAKE

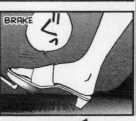

GRRROWL

GRRROWL

I'M STRONG, HUH...

ACTUALLY, I'M MORE HUNGRY THAN STRONG!

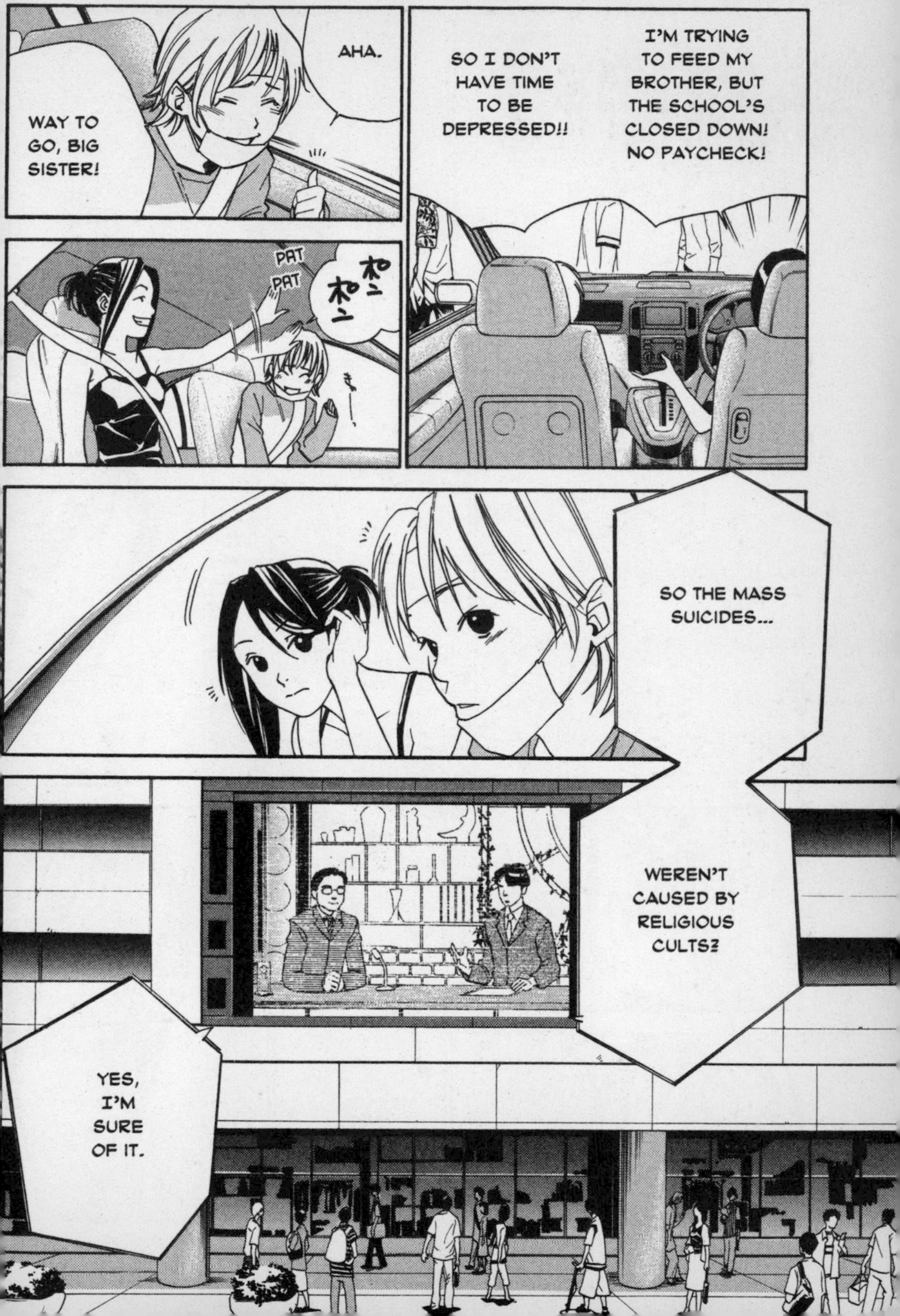

I'M TRYING TO FEED MY BROTHER, BUT THE SCHOOL'S CLOSED DOWN! NO PAYCHECK!
SO I DON'T HAVE TIME TO BE DEPRESSED!!
AHA.
WAY TO GO, BIG SISTER!
PAT PAT
ポン ポン
SO THE MASS SUICIDES...
WEREN'T CAUSED BY RELIGIOUS CULTS?
YES, I'M SURE OF IT.

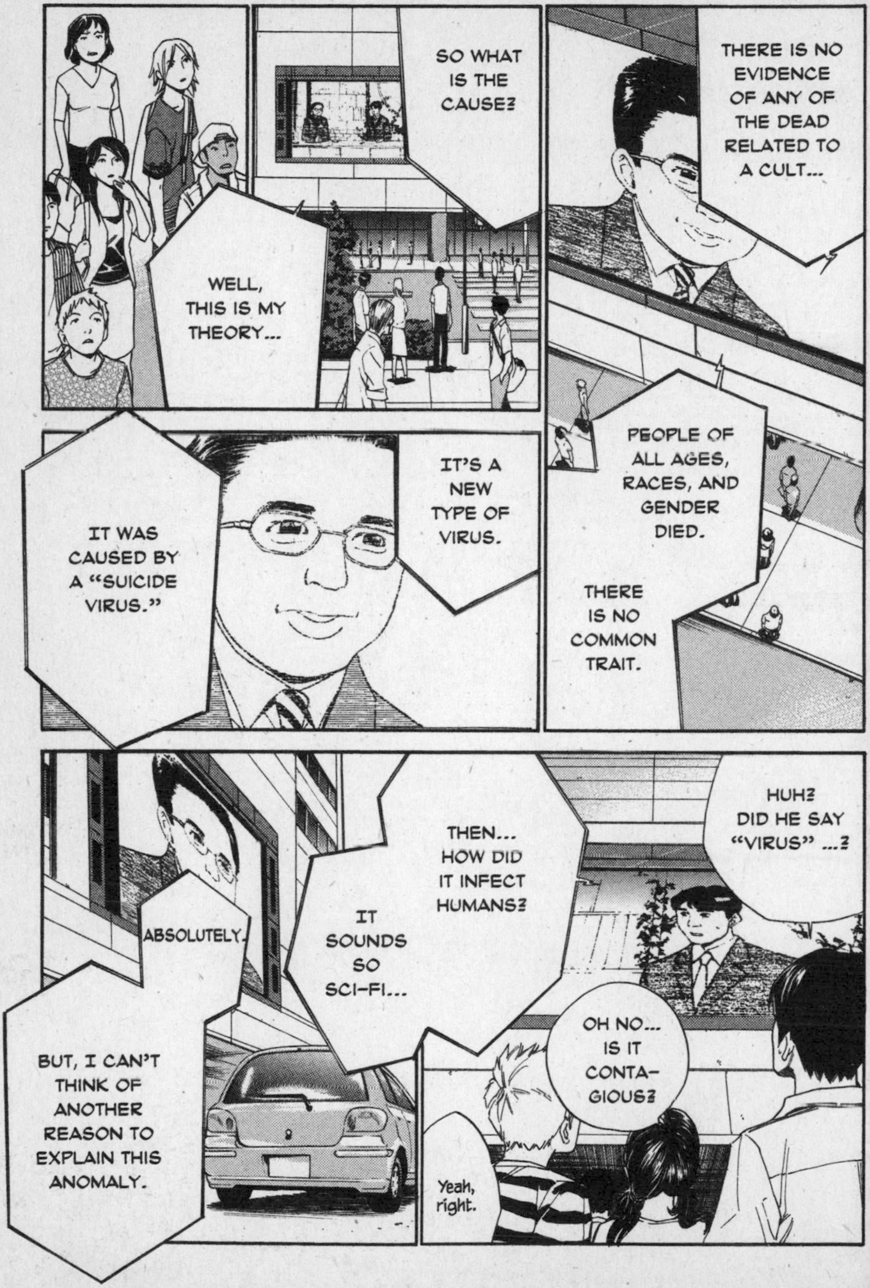
THERE IS NO EVIDENCE OF ANY OF THE DEAD RELATED TO A CULT...
PEOPLE OF ALL AGES, RACES, AND GENDER DIED.
THERE IS NO COMMON TRAIT.
SO WHAT IS THE CAUSE?
WELL, THIS IS MY THEORY...
IT WAS CAUSED BY A "SUICIDE VIRUS."
IT'S A NEW TYPE OF VIRUS.
HUH? DID HE SAY "VIRUS" ...?
OH NO... IS IT CONTAGIOUS?
Yeah, right.
THEN... HOW DID IT INFECT HUMANS?
IT SOUNDS SO SCI-FI...
ABSOLUTELY.
BUT, I CAN'T THINK OF ANOTHER REASON TO EXPLAIN THIS ANOMALY.

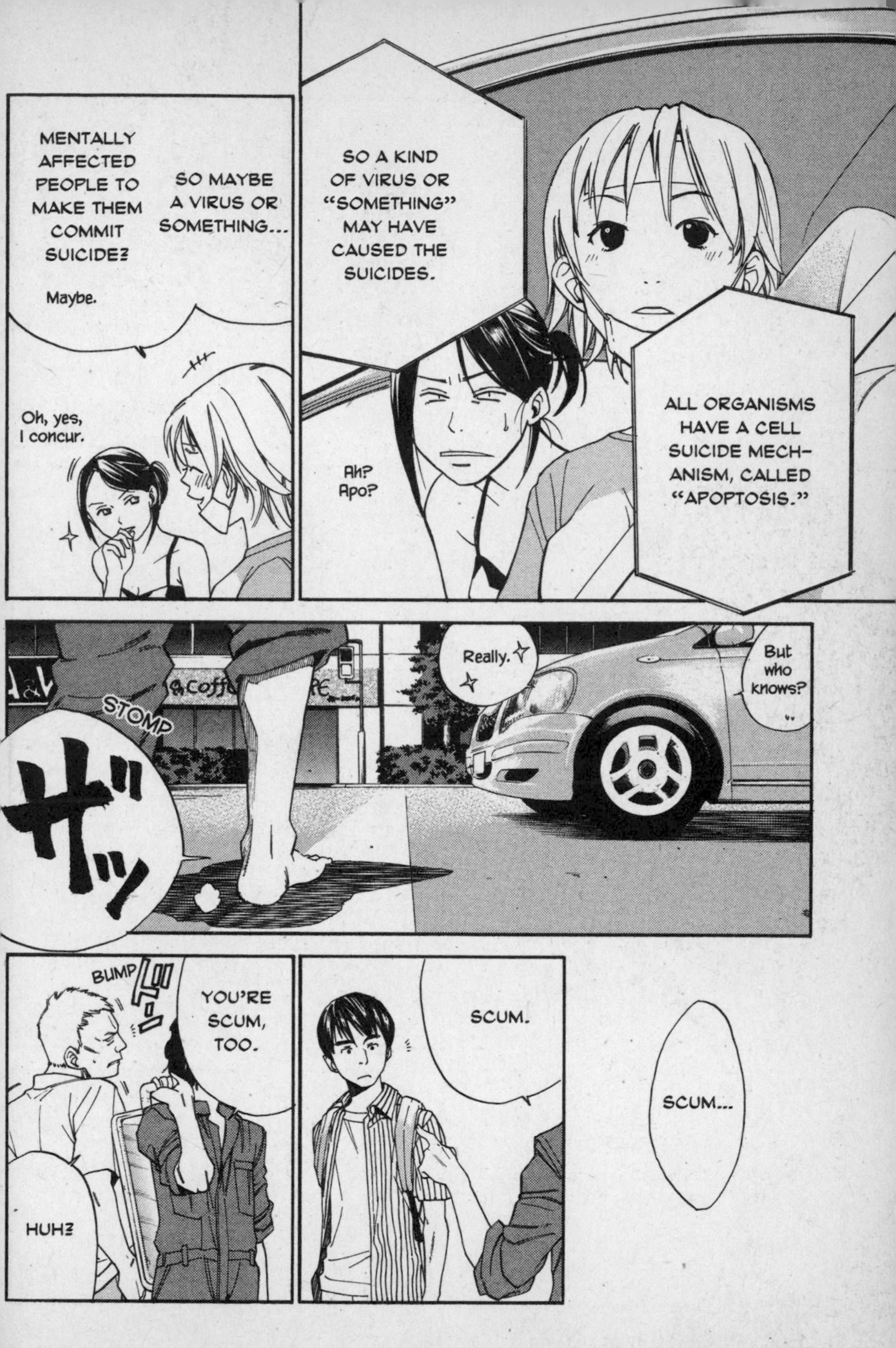
SO A KIND OF VIRUS OR "SOMETHING" MAY HAVE CAUSED THE SUICIDES.
ALL ORGANISMS HAVE A CELL SUICIDE MECH-ANISM, CALLED "APOPTOSIS."
Ah? Apo?
SO MAYBE A VIRUS OR SOMETHING...
MENTALLY AFFECTED PEOPLE TO MAKE THEM COMMIT SUICIDE?
Maybe.
Oh, yes, I concur.
But who knows?
Really.
STOMP
ザッ
SCUM...
SCUM.
BUMP
YOU'RE SCUM, TOO.
HUH?

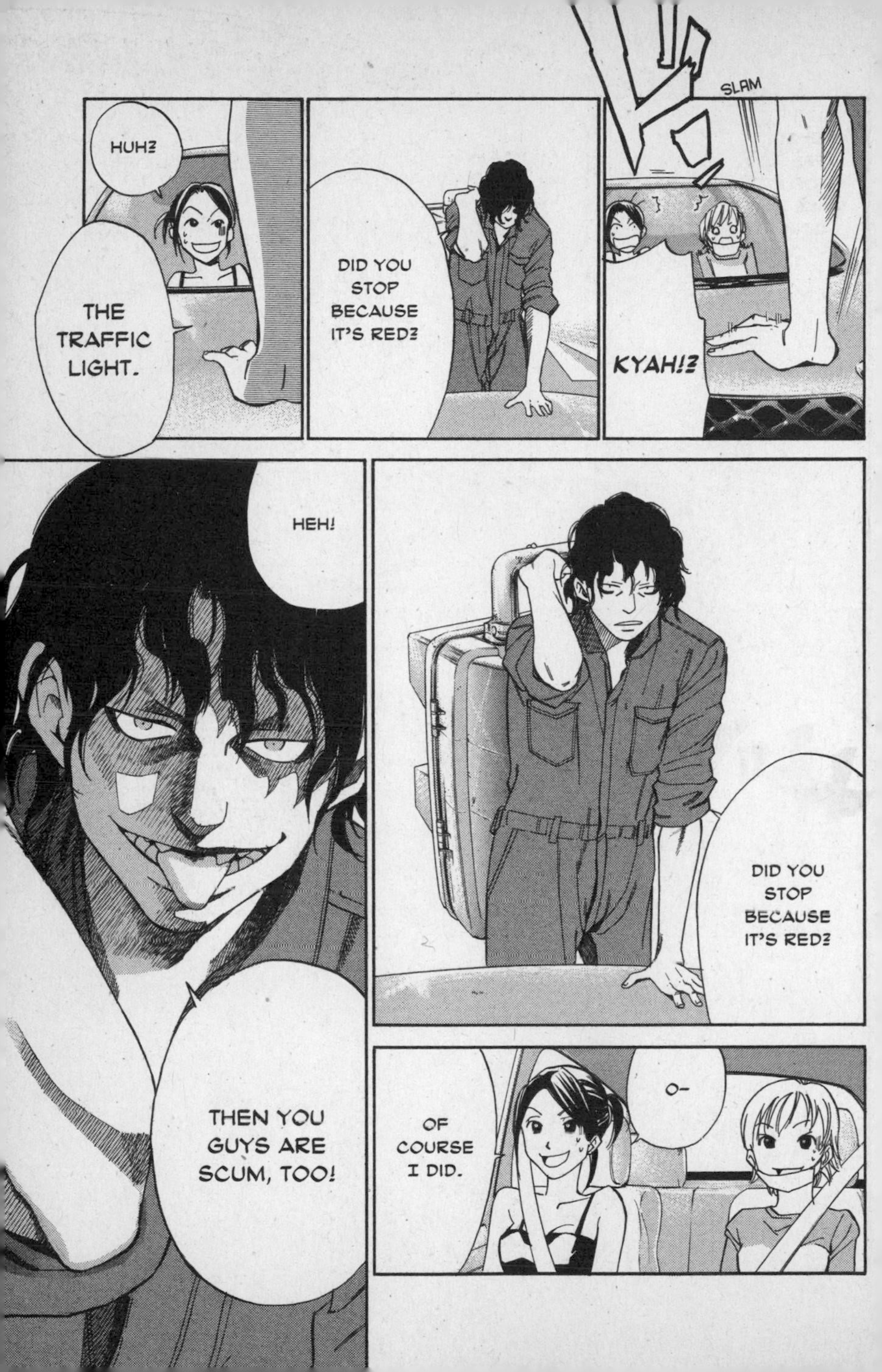
SLAM
KYAH!?
DID YOU STOP BECAUSE IT'S RED?
HUH?
THE TRAFFIC LIGHT.
DID YOU STOP BECAUSE IT'S RED?
O-
OF COURSE I DID.
HEH!
THEN YOU GUYS ARE SCUM, TOO!

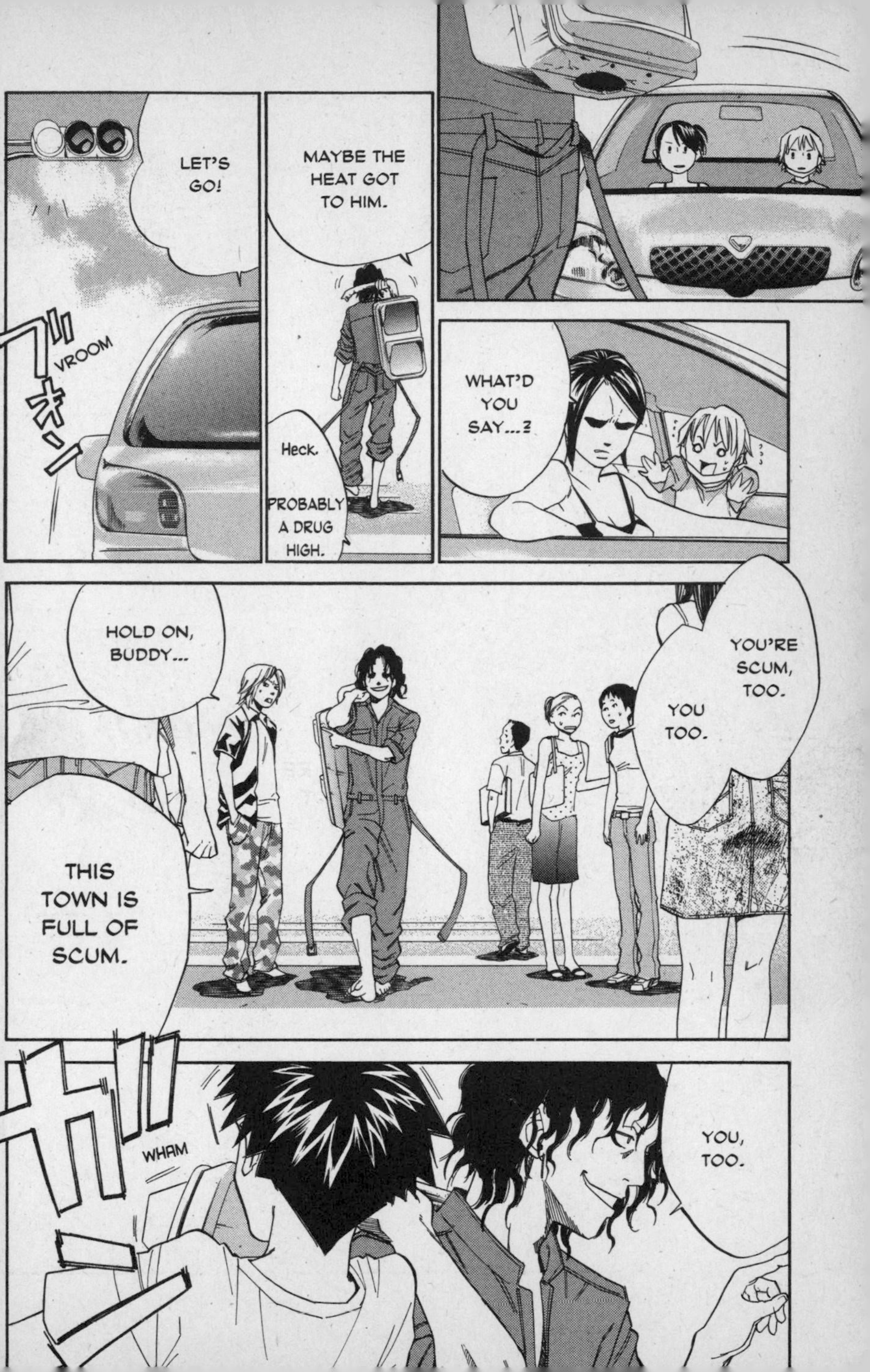
WHAT'D YOU SAY...?
MAYBE THE HEAT GOT TO HIM.
Heck.
PROBABLY A DRUG HIGH.
LET'S GO!
VROOM
YOU'RE SCUM, TOO.
YOU TOO.
HOLD ON, BUDDY...
THIS TOWN IS FULL OF SCUM.
YOU, TOO.
WHAM

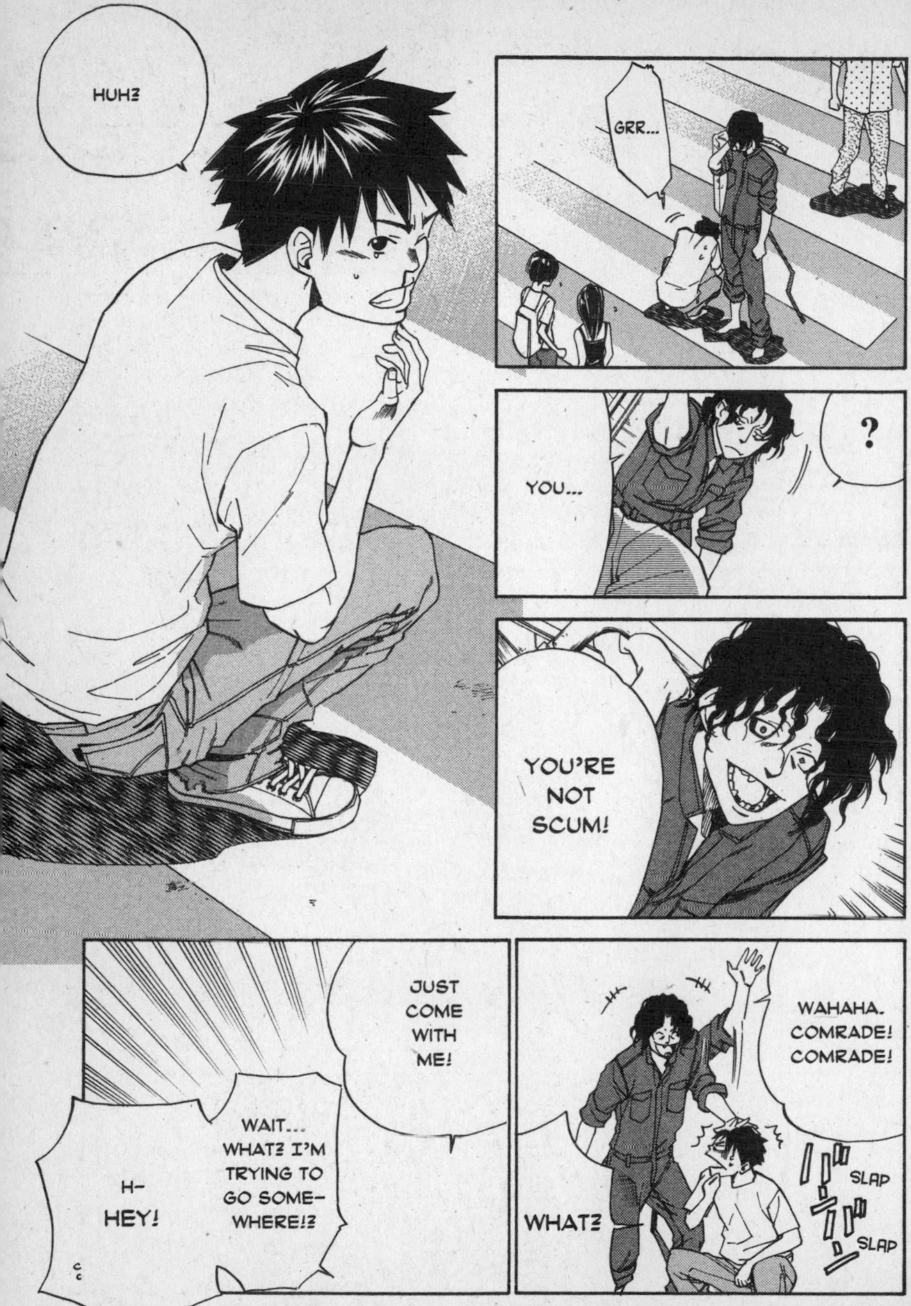
GRR...
?
YOU...
YOU'RE NOT SCUM!
HUH?
WAHAHA. COMRADE! COMRADE!
SLAP
SLAP
WHAT?
JUST COME WITH ME!
WAIT... WHAT? I'M TRYING TO GO SOMEWHERE!?
H-HEY!

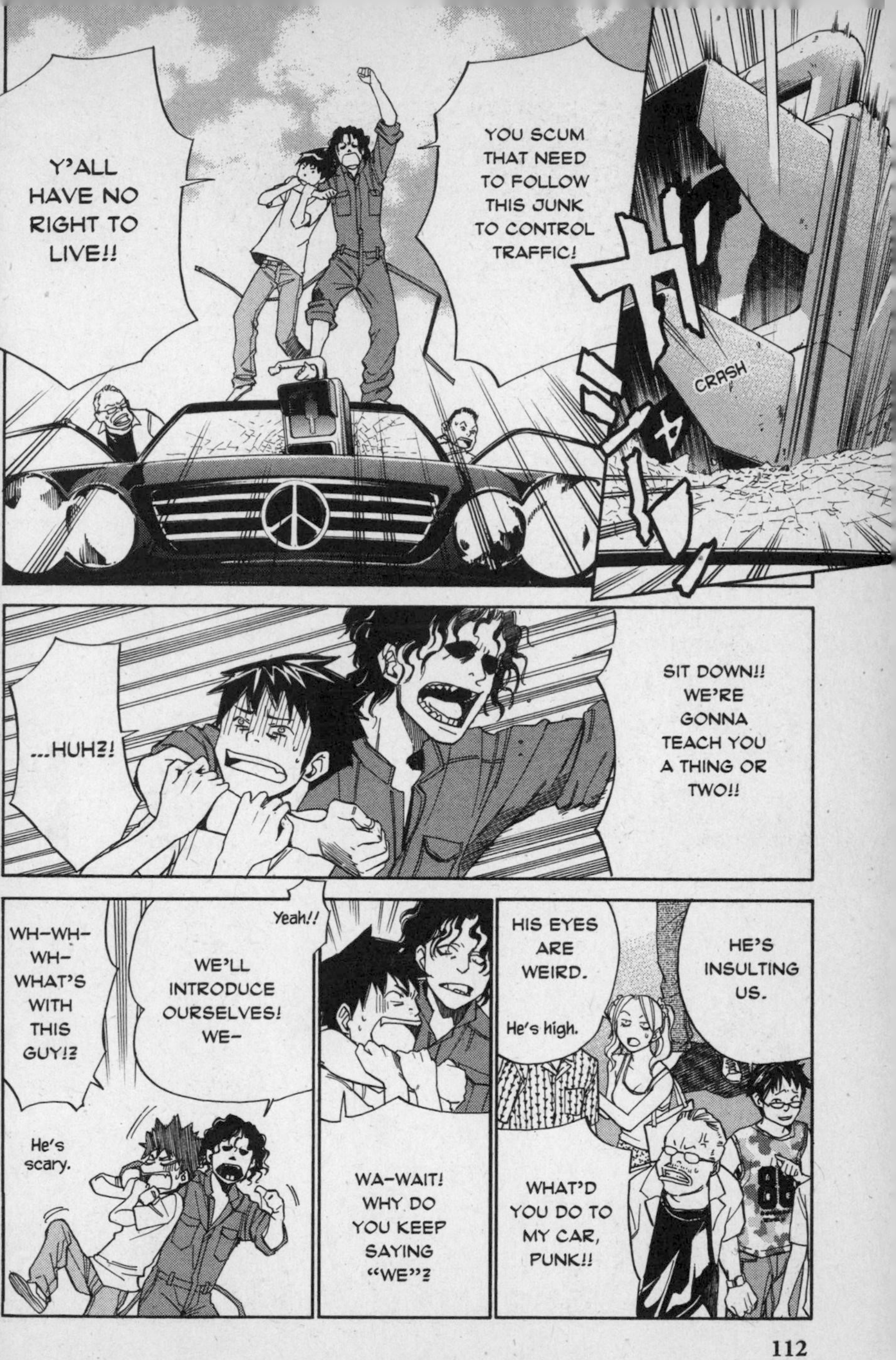
CRASH
YOU SCUM THAT NEED TO FOLLOW THIS JUNK TO CONTROL TRAFFIC!
Y'ALL HAVE NO RIGHT TO LIVE!!
SIT DOWN!! WE'RE GONNA TEACH YOU A THING OR TWO!!
...HUH?!
HE'S INSULTING US.
HIS EYES ARE WEIRD.
He's high.
WHAT'D YOU DO TO MY CAR, PUNK!!
WA-WAIT! WHY DO YOU KEEP SAYING "WE"?
Yeah!!
WE'LL INTRODUCE OURSELVES! WE-
WH-WH-WH-WHAT'S WITH THIS GUY!?
He's scary.

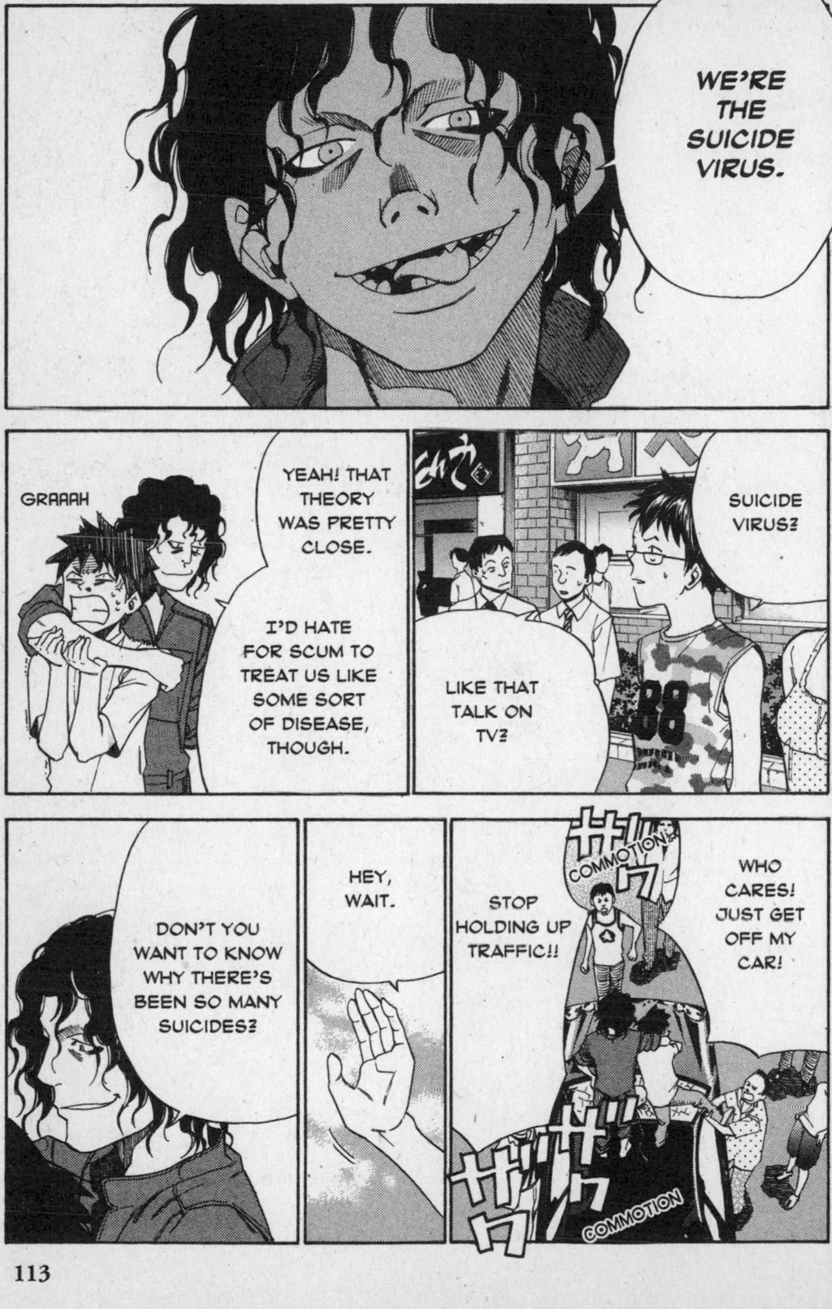
WE'RE THE SUICIDE VIRUS.
SUICIDE VIRUS?
LIKE THAT TALK ON TV?
YEAH! THAT THEORY WAS PRETTY CLOSE.
I'D HATE FOR SCUM TO TREAT US LIKE SOME SORT OF DISEASE, THOUGH.
GRAAAH
WHO CARES! JUST GET OFF MY CAR!
COMMOTION
STOP HOLDING UP TRAFFIC!!
COMMOTION
HEY, WAIT.
DON'T YOU WANT TO KNOW WHY THERE'S BEEN SO MANY SUICIDES?

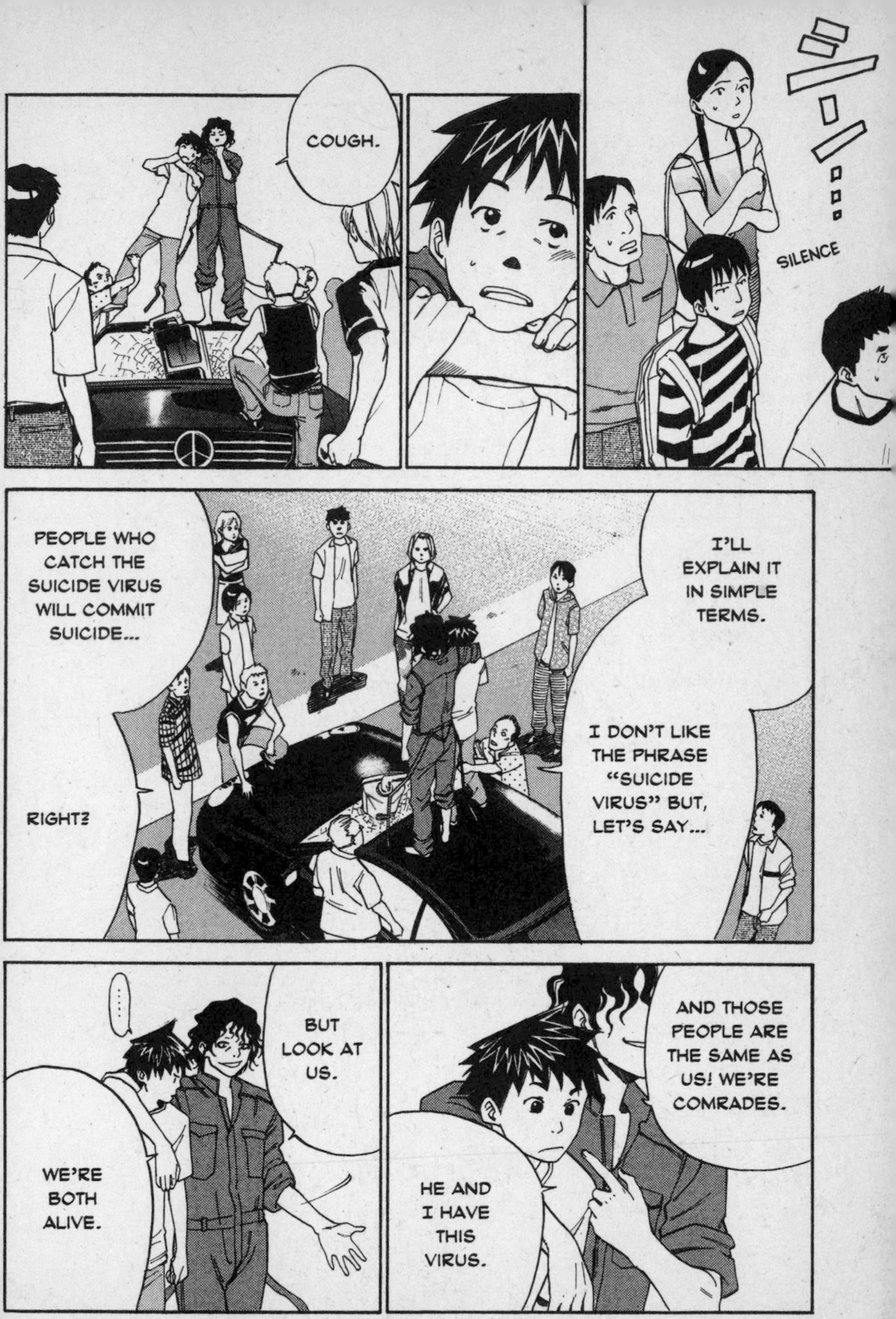
SILENCE
COUGH.
I'LL EXPLAIN IT IN SIMPLE TERMS.
I DON'T LIKE THE PHRASE "SUICIDE VIRUS" BUT, LET'S SAY...
PEOPLE WHO CATCH THE SUICIDE VIRUS WILL COMMIT SUICIDE...
RIGHT?
AND THOSE PEOPLE ARE THE SAME AS US! WE'RE COMRADES.
HE AND I HAVE THIS VIRUS.
BUT LOOK AT US.
.....
WE'RE BOTH ALIVE.

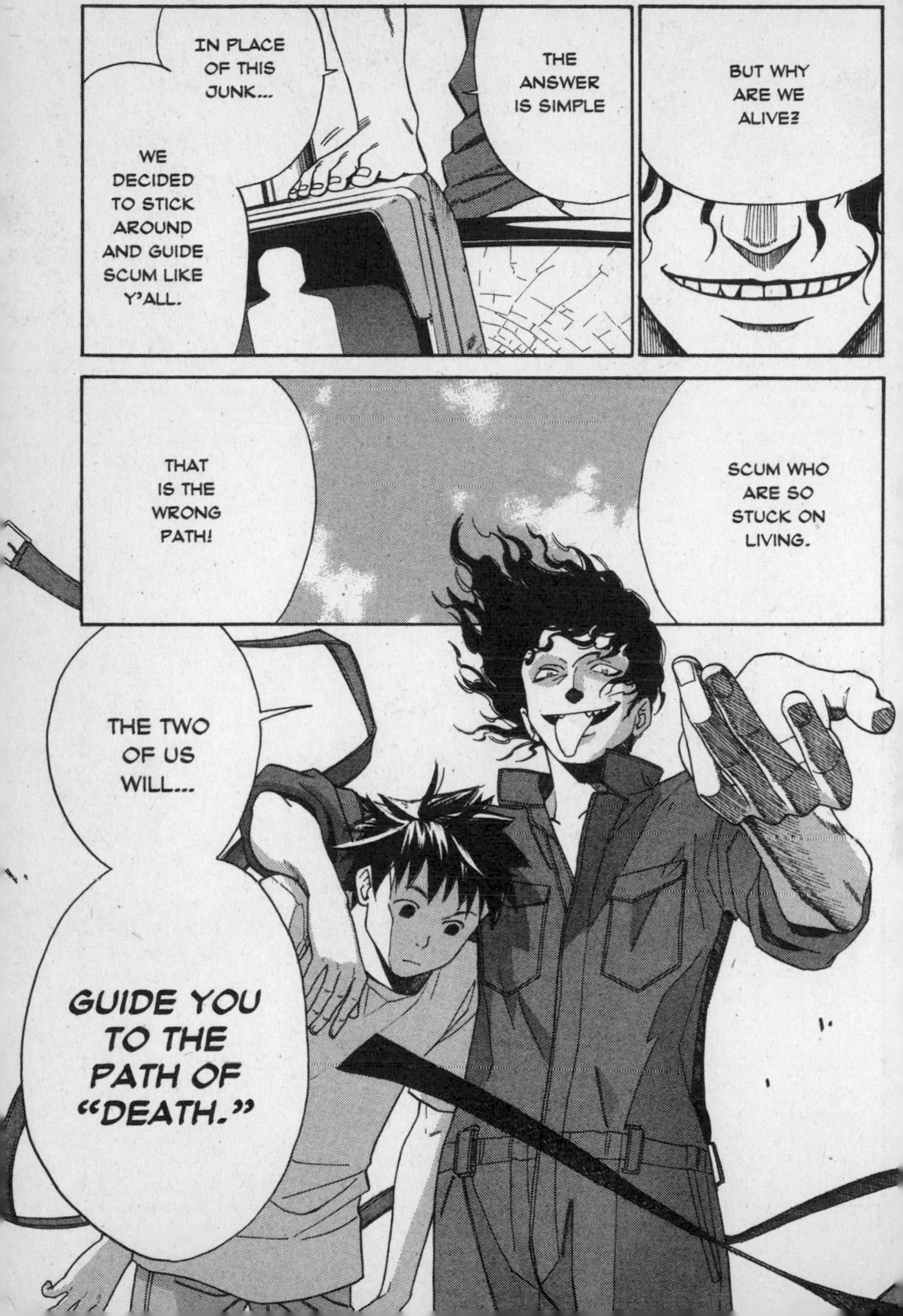
BUT WHY ARE WE ALIVE?
THE ANSWER IS SIMPLE
IN PLACE OF THIS JUNK...
WE DECIDED TO STICK AROUND AND GUIDE SCUM LIKE Y'ALL.
SCUM WHO ARE SO STUCK ON LIVING.
THAT IS THE WRONG PATH!
THE TWO OF US WILL...
GUIDE YOU TO THE PATH OF "DEATH."

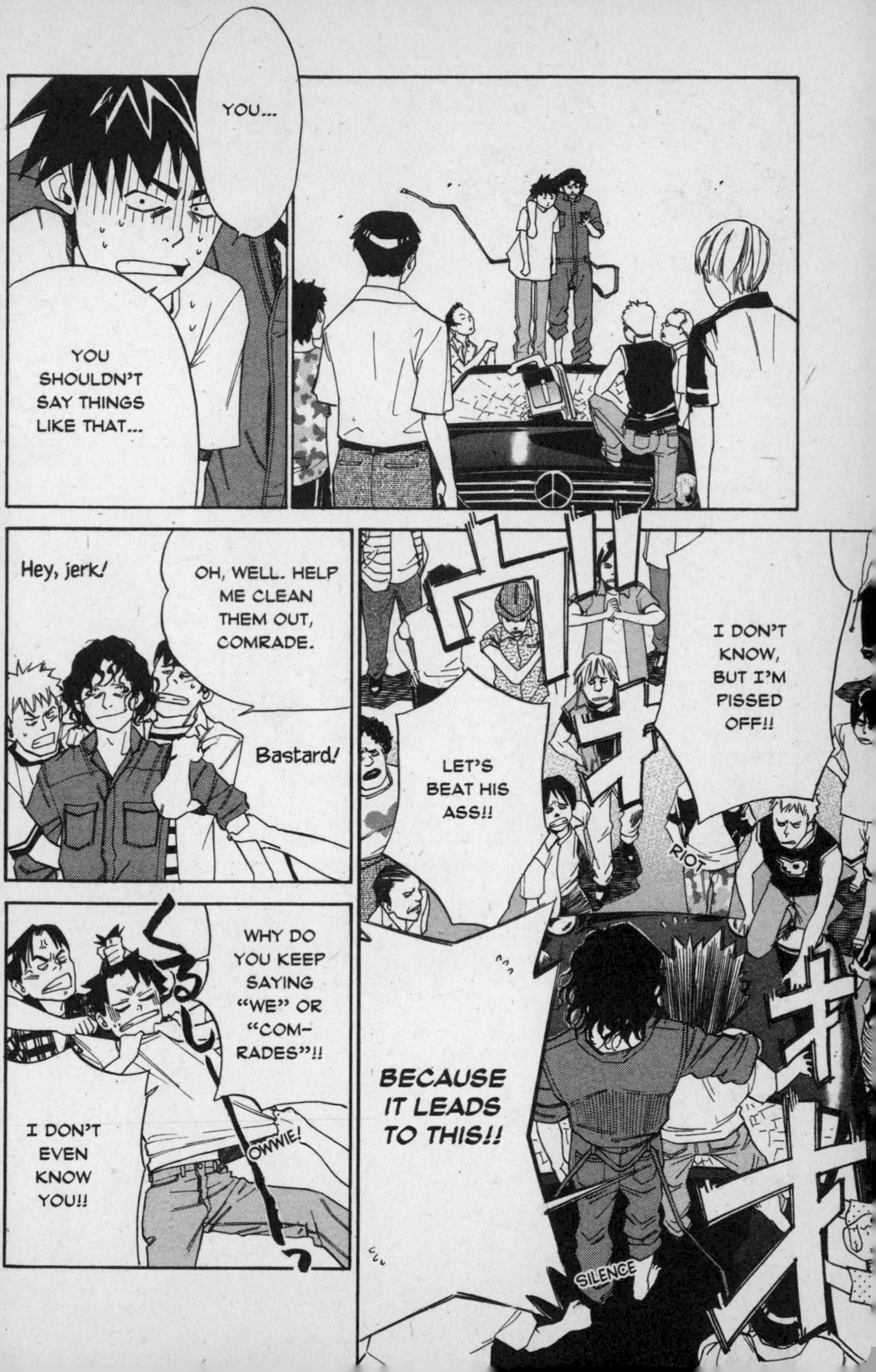
YOU...
YOU SHOULDN'T SAY THINGS LIKE THAT...
I DON'T KNOW, BUT I'M PISSED OFF!!
LET'S BEAT HIS ASS!!
RIOT
BECAUSE IT LEADS TO THIS!!
SILENCE
OH, WELL. HELP ME CLEAN THEM OUT, COMRADE.
Hey, jerk!
Bastard!
WHY DO YOU KEEP SAYING "WE" OR "COM-RADES"!!
I DON'T EVEN KNOW YOU!!
OWWIE!

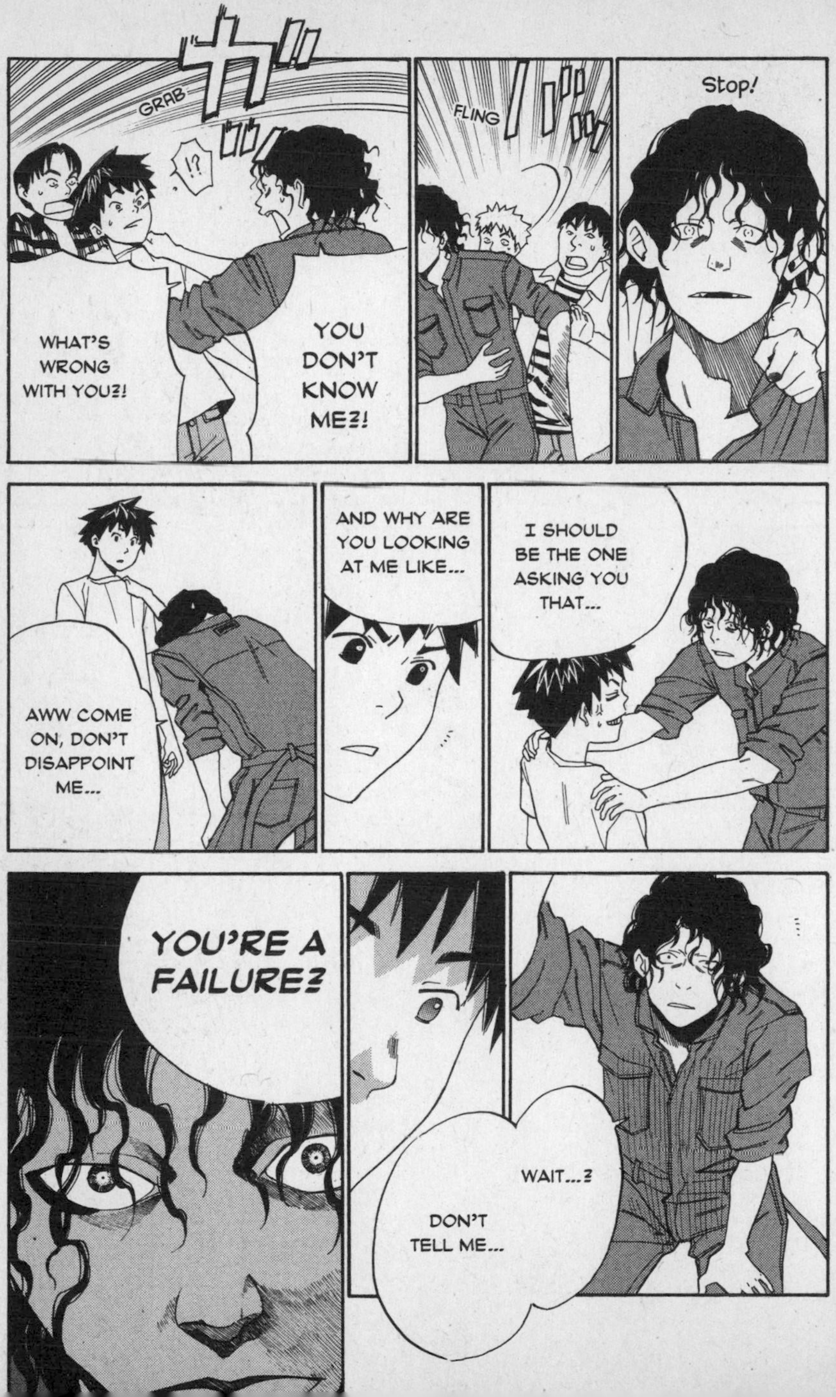
Stop!
FLING
GRAB
!?
YOU DON'T KNOW ME?!
WHAT'S WRONG WITH YOU?!
I SHOULD BE THE ONE ASKING YOU THAT...
AND WHY ARE YOU LOOKING AT ME LIKE...
AWW COME ON, DON'T DISAPPOINT ME...
WAIT...?
DON'T TELL ME...
YOU'RE A FAILURE?

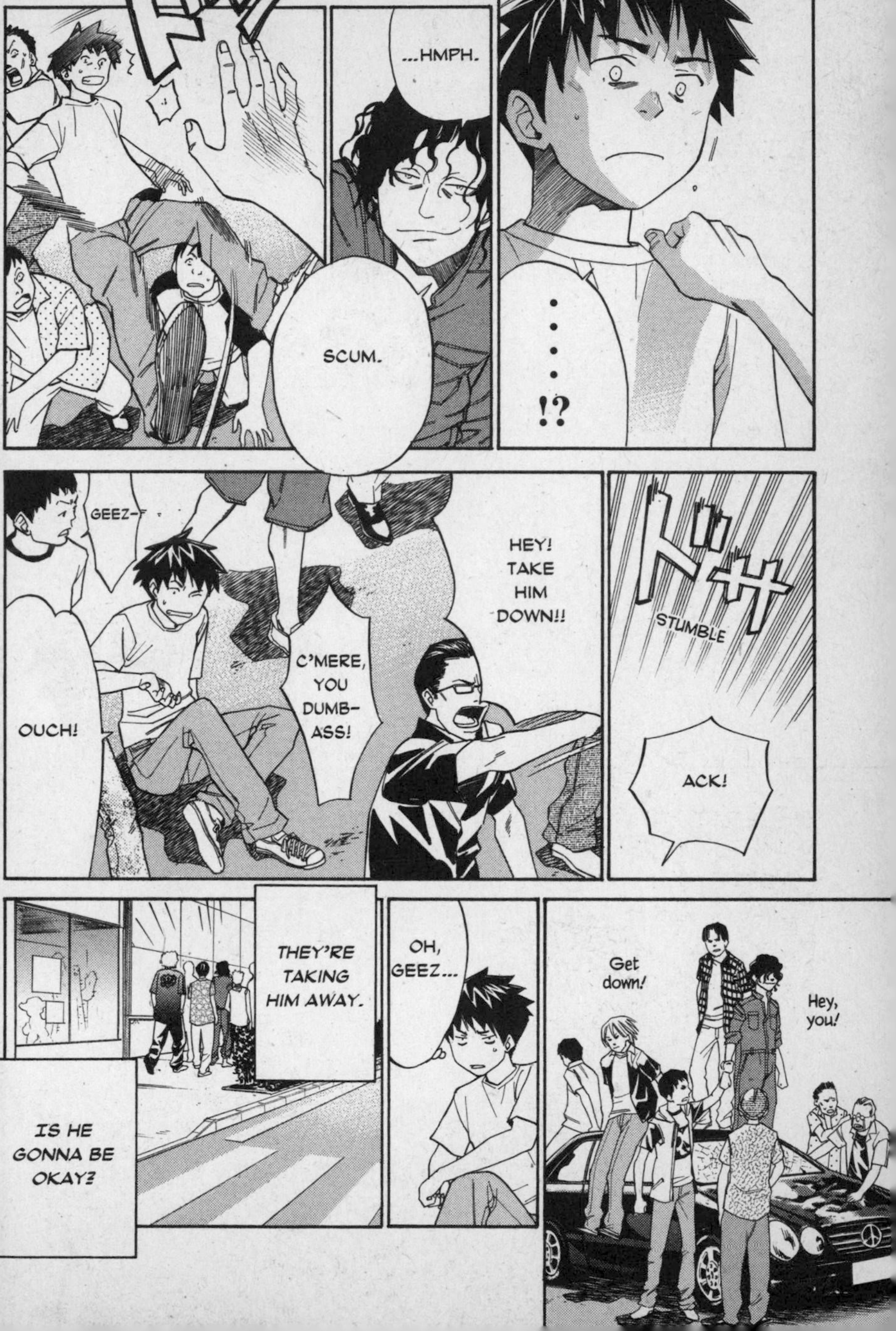
. . . .
!?
...HMPH.
SCUM.
PUSH
STUMBLE
ACK!
HEY! TAKE HIM DOWN!!
C'MERE, YOU DUMB-ASS!
GEEZ-
OUCH!
Hey, you!
Get down!
OH, GEEZ...
THEY'RE TAKING HIM AWAY.
IS HE GONNA BE OKAY?

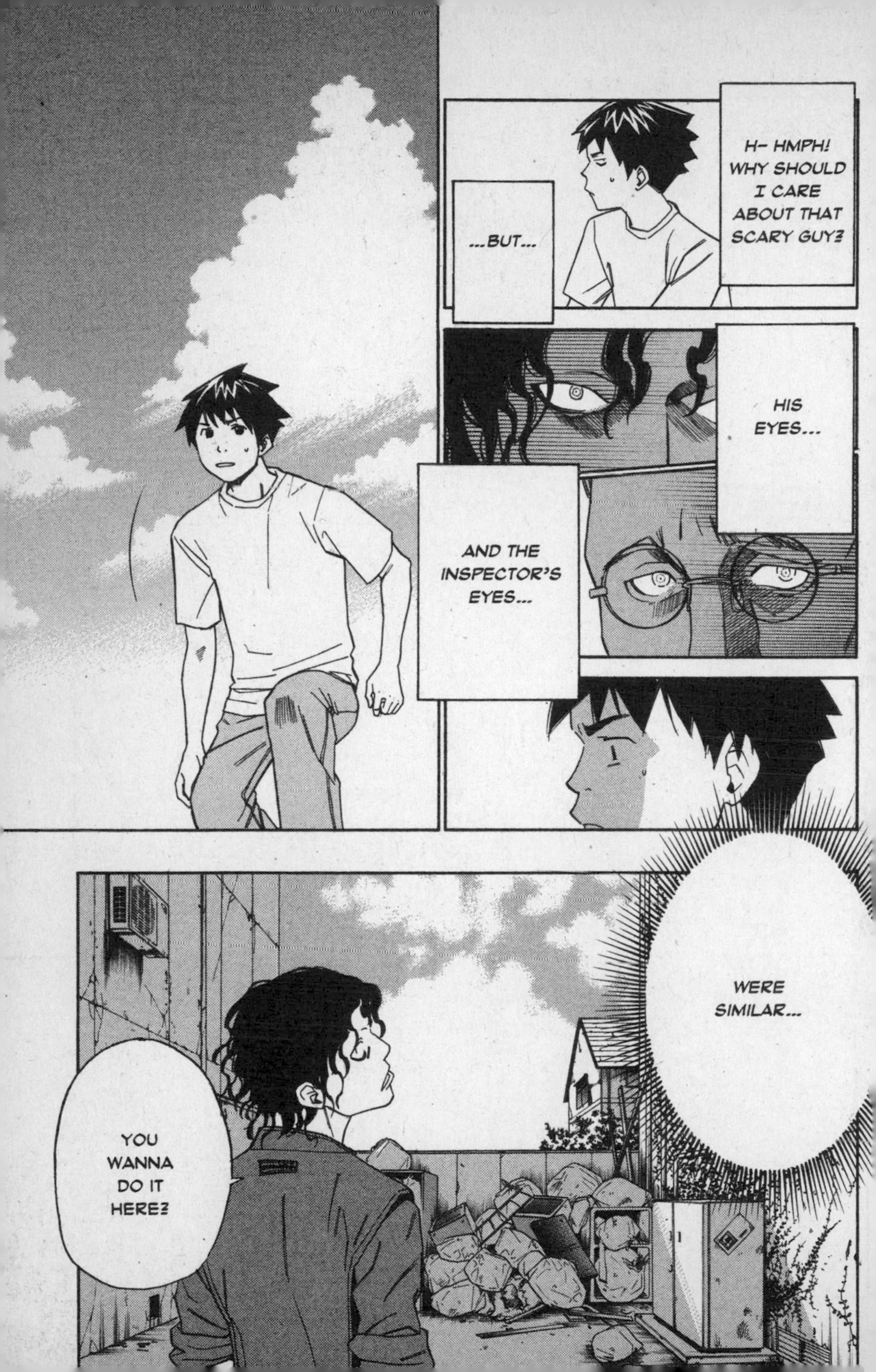
H- HMPH! WHY SHOULD I CARE ABOUT THAT SCARY GUY?
...BUT...
HIS EYES...
AND THE INSPECTOR'S EYES...
WERE SIMILAR...
YOU WANNA DO IT HERE?

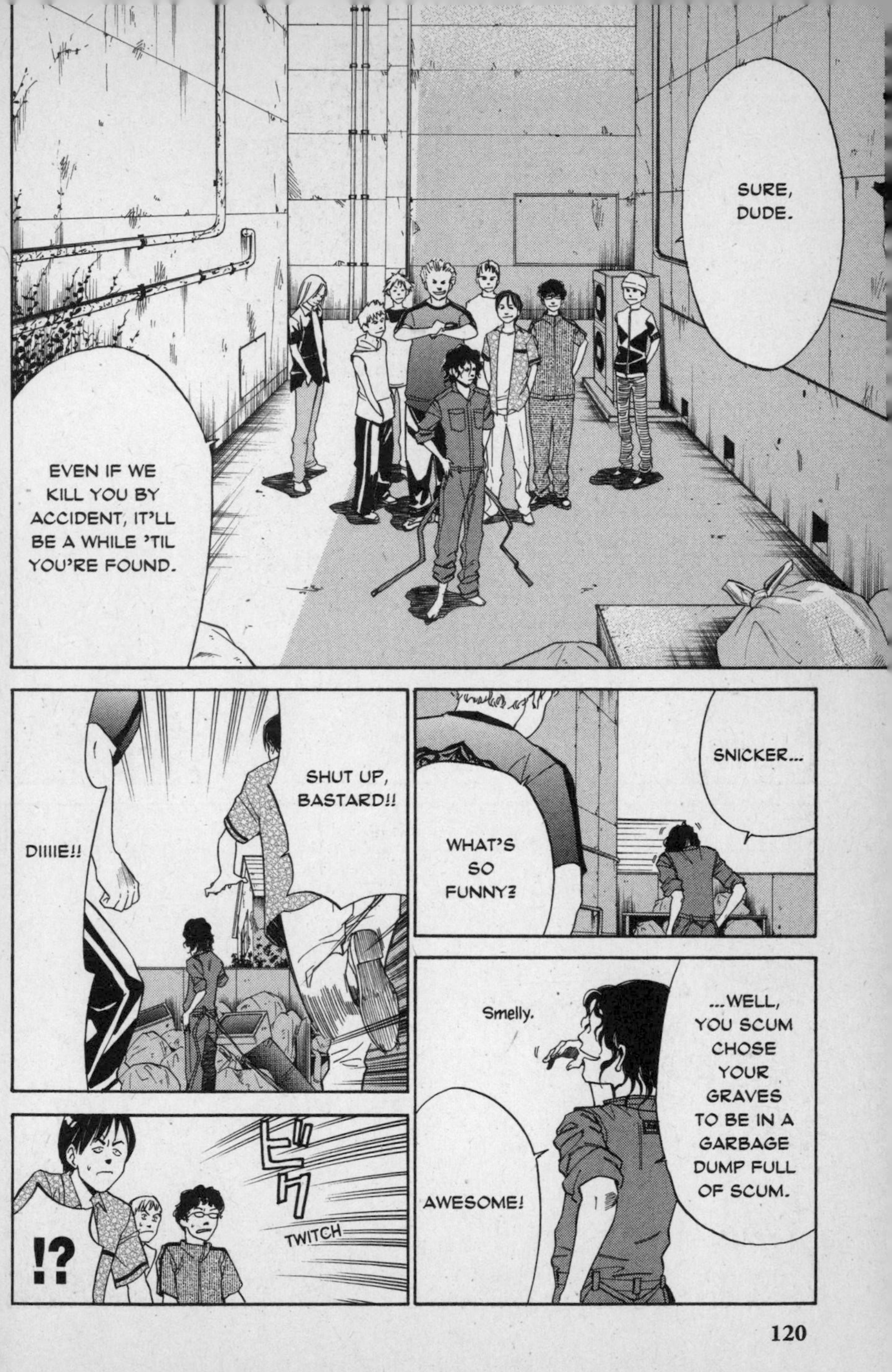
SURE, DUDE.
EVEN IF WE KILL YOU BY ACCIDENT, IT'LL BE A WHILE 'TIL YOU'RE FOUND.
SNICKER...
WHAT'S SO FUNNY?
...WELL, YOU SCUM CHOSE YOUR GRAVES TO BE IN A GARBAGE DUMP FULL OF SCUM.
Smelly.
AWESOME!
SHUT UP, BASTARD!!
DIIIIE!!
TWITCH
!?

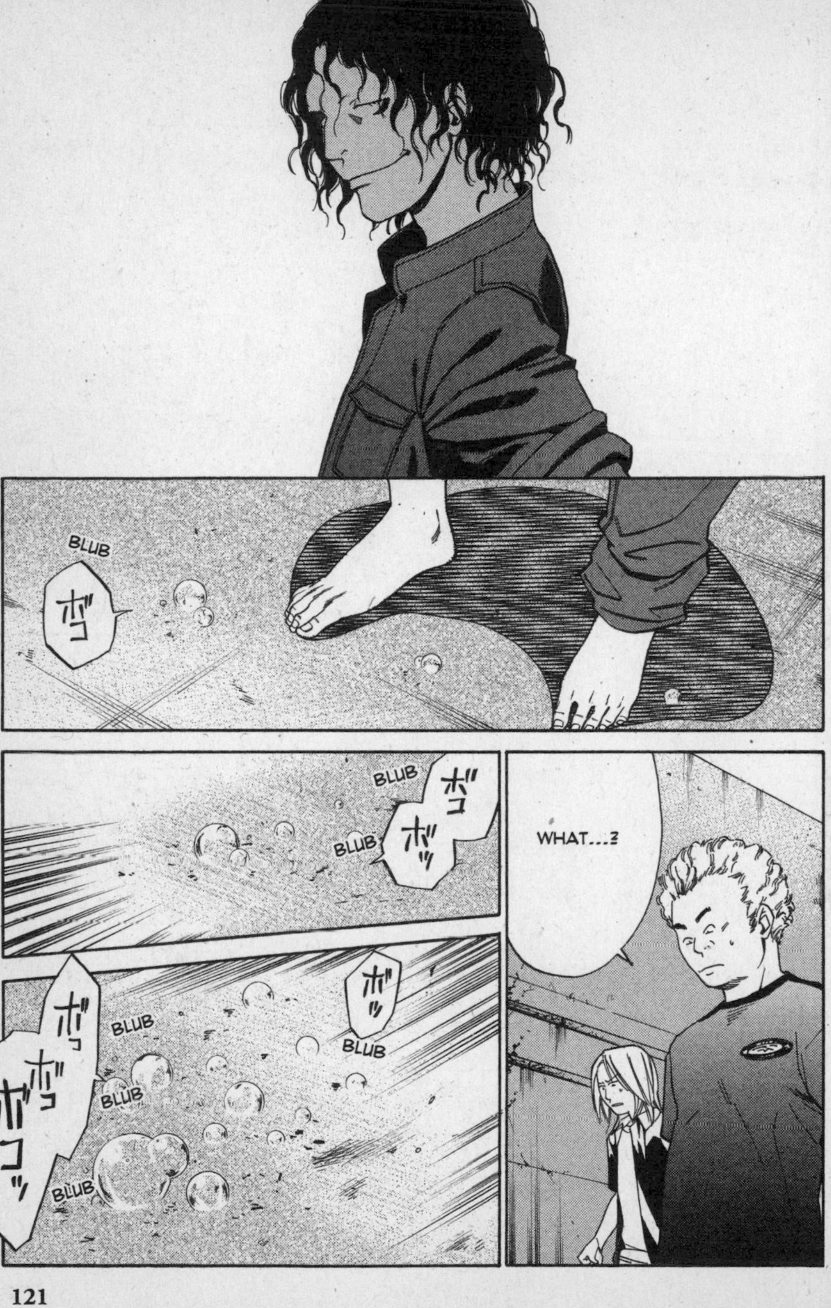
BLUB
ボコ
WHAT...?
ボコ
BLUB
ボッ
BLUB
ボッ
BLUB
ボコ
BLUB
ボコ
BLUB
ボコッ
BLUB

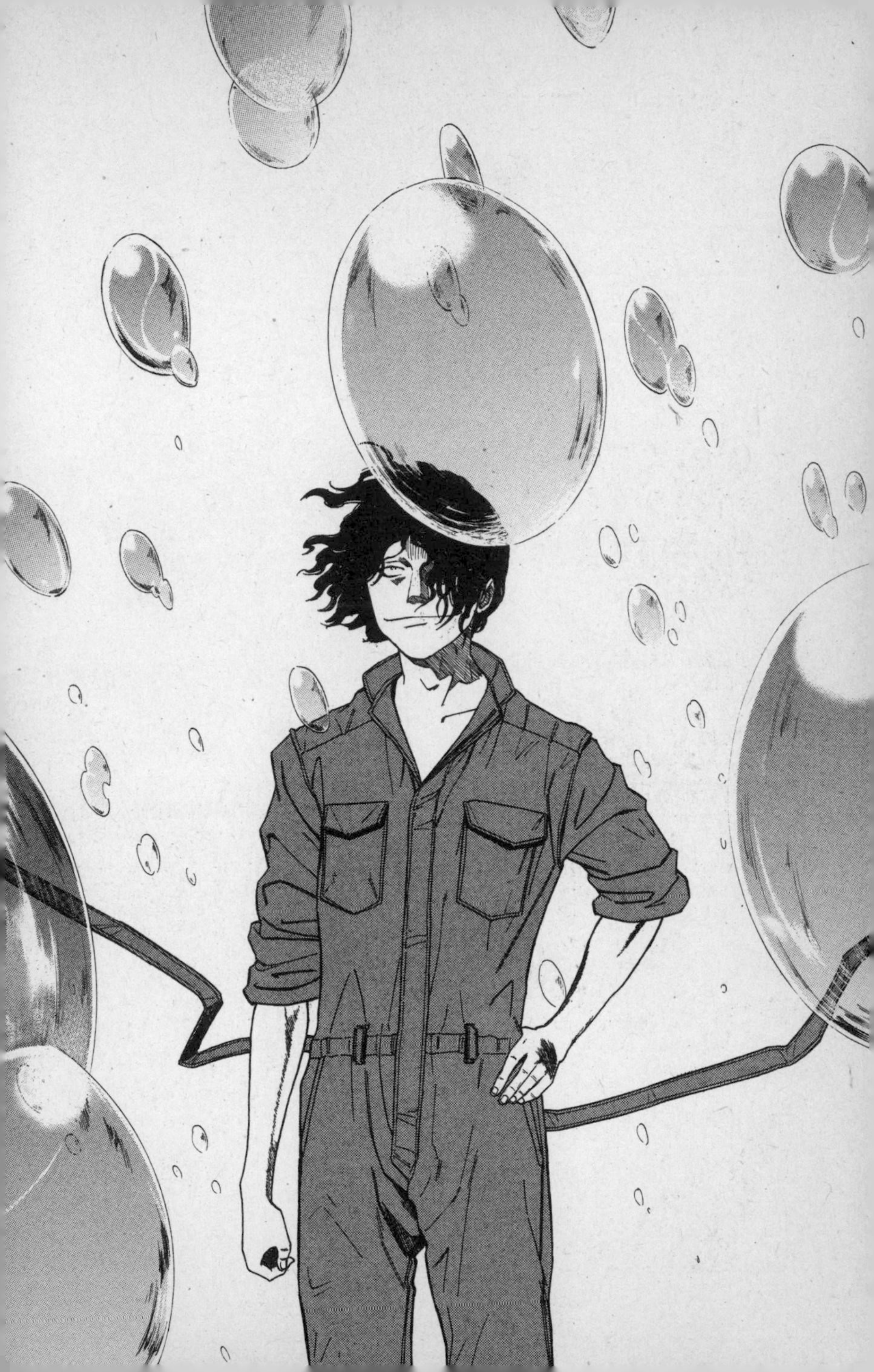

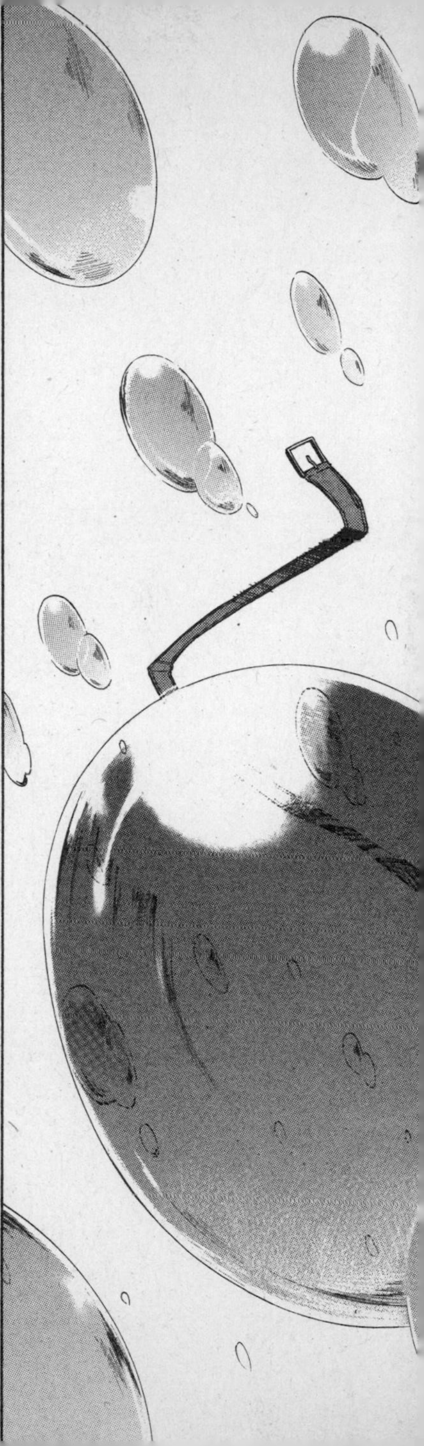

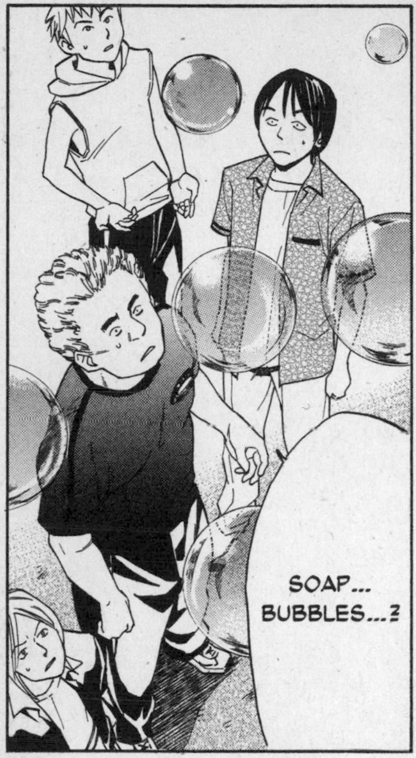
SOAP... BUBBLES...?

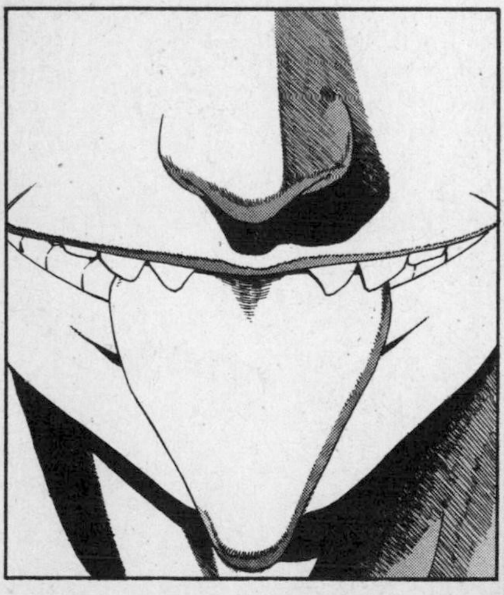

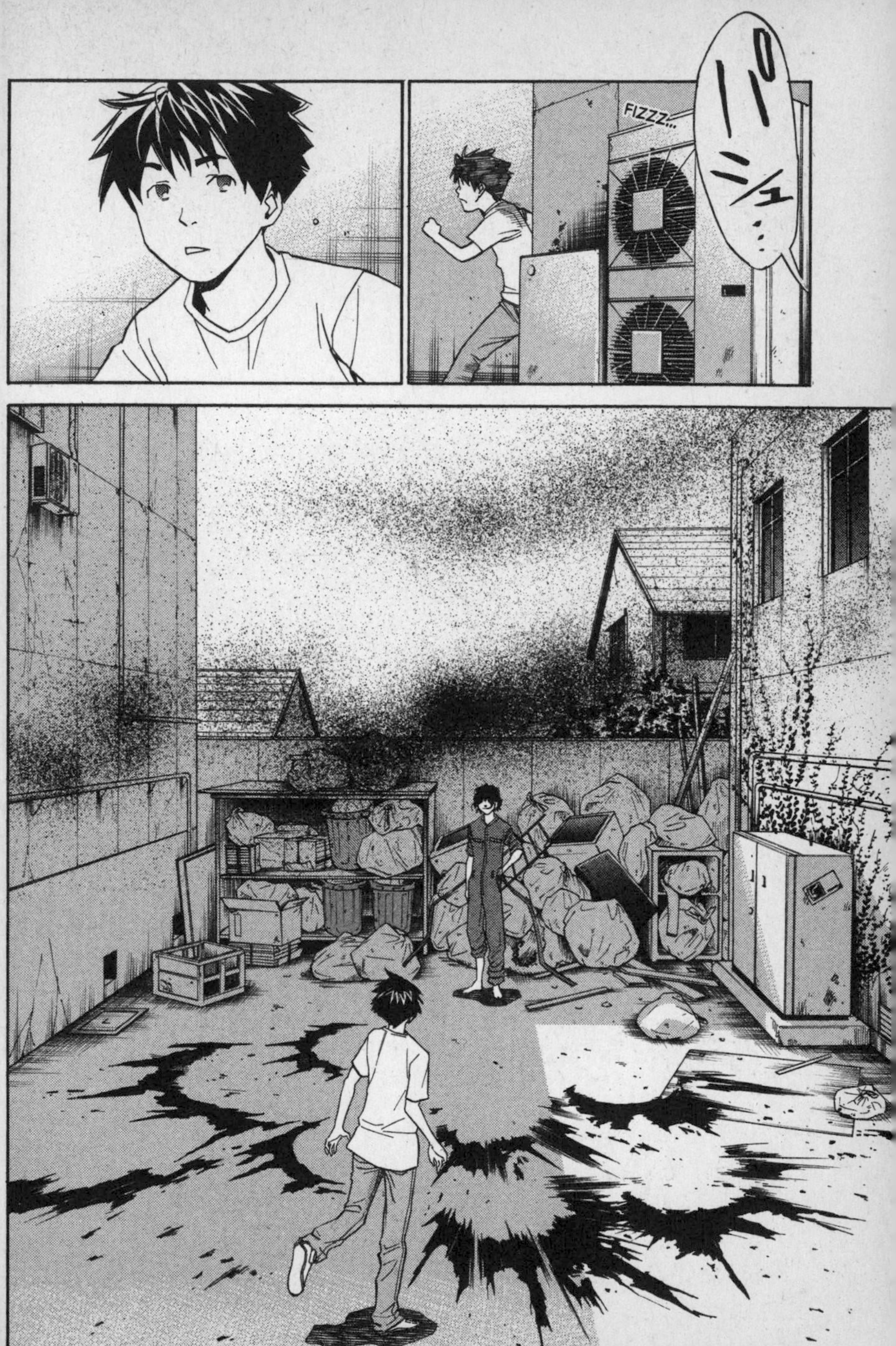
パシュ…
FIZZZ...

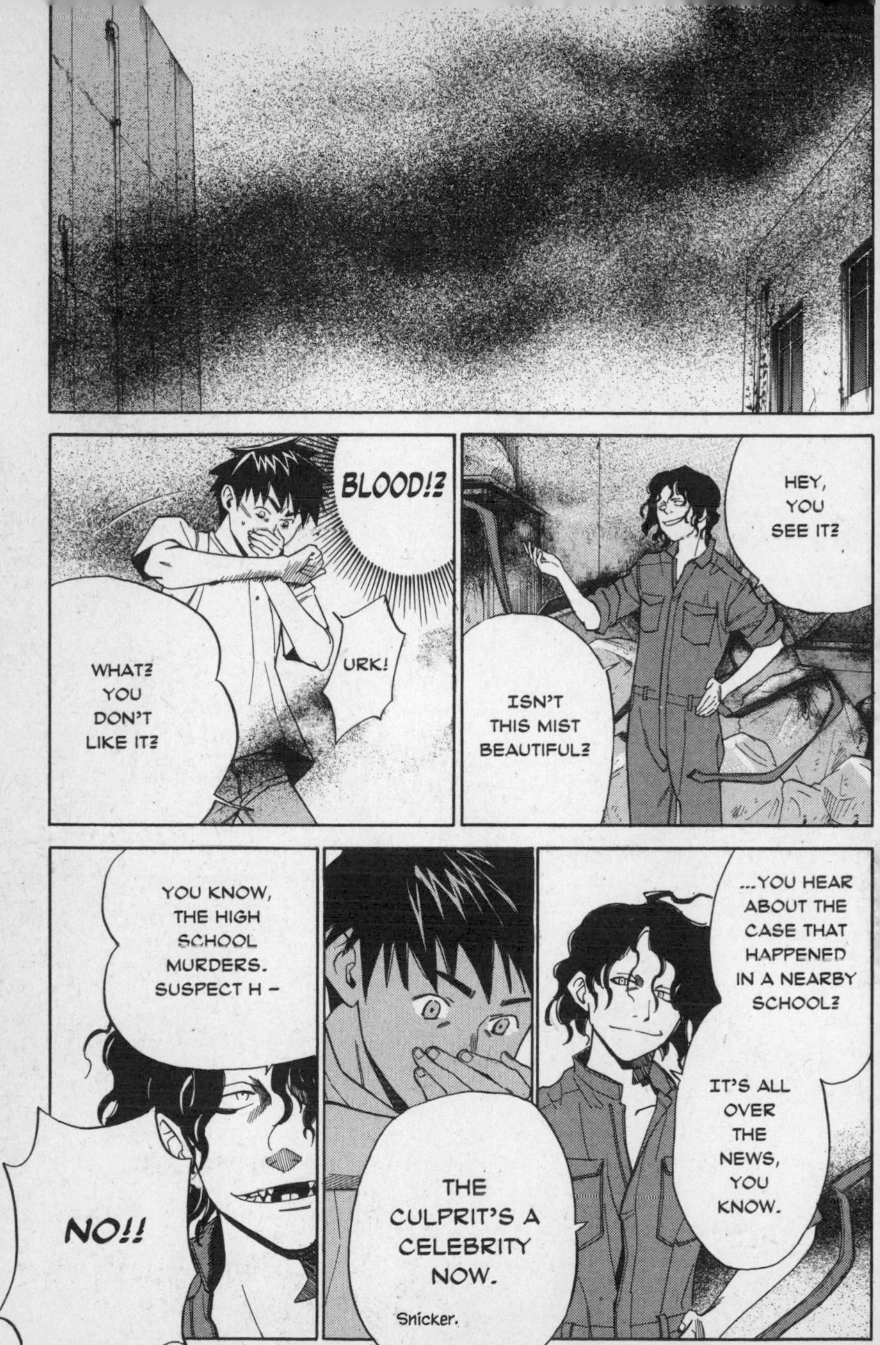
HEY, YOU SEE IT?
ISN'T THIS MIST BEAUTIFUL?
BLOOD!?
URK!
WHAT? YOU DON'T LIKE IT?
...YOU HEAR ABOUT THE CASE THAT HAPPENED IN A NEARBY SCHOOL?
IT'S ALL OVER THE NEWS, YOU KNOW.
THE CULPRIT'S A CELEBRITY NOW.
Snicker.
YOU KNOW, THE HIGH SCHOOL MURDERS. SUSPECT H –
NO!!

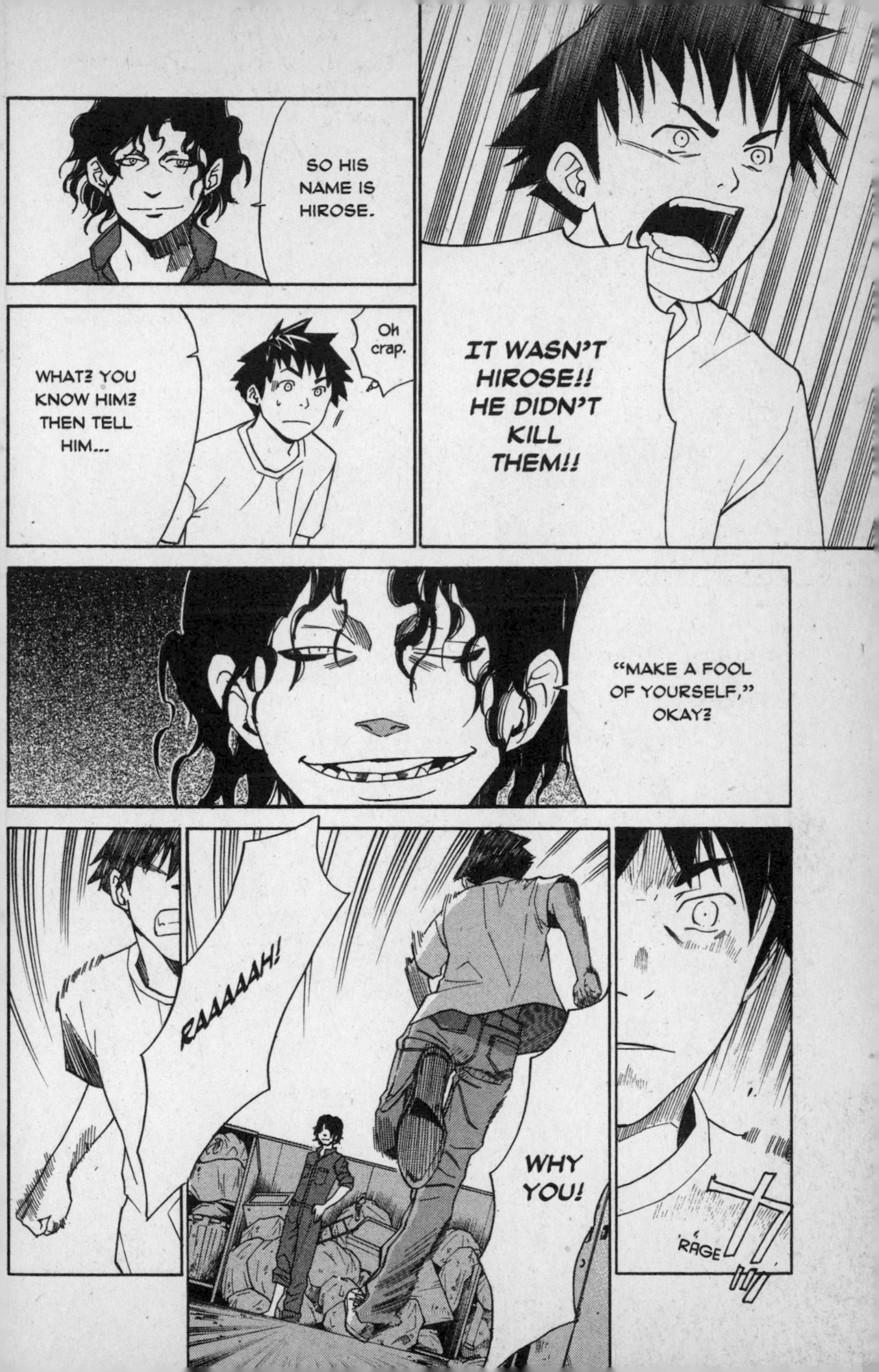
IT WASN'T HIROSE!! HE DIDN'T KILL THEM!!
SO HIS NAME IS HIROSE.
Oh crap.
WHAT? YOU KNOW HIM? THEN TELL HIM...
“MAKE A FOOL OF YOURSELF,” OKAY?
RAGE
WHY YOU!
RAAAAAH!

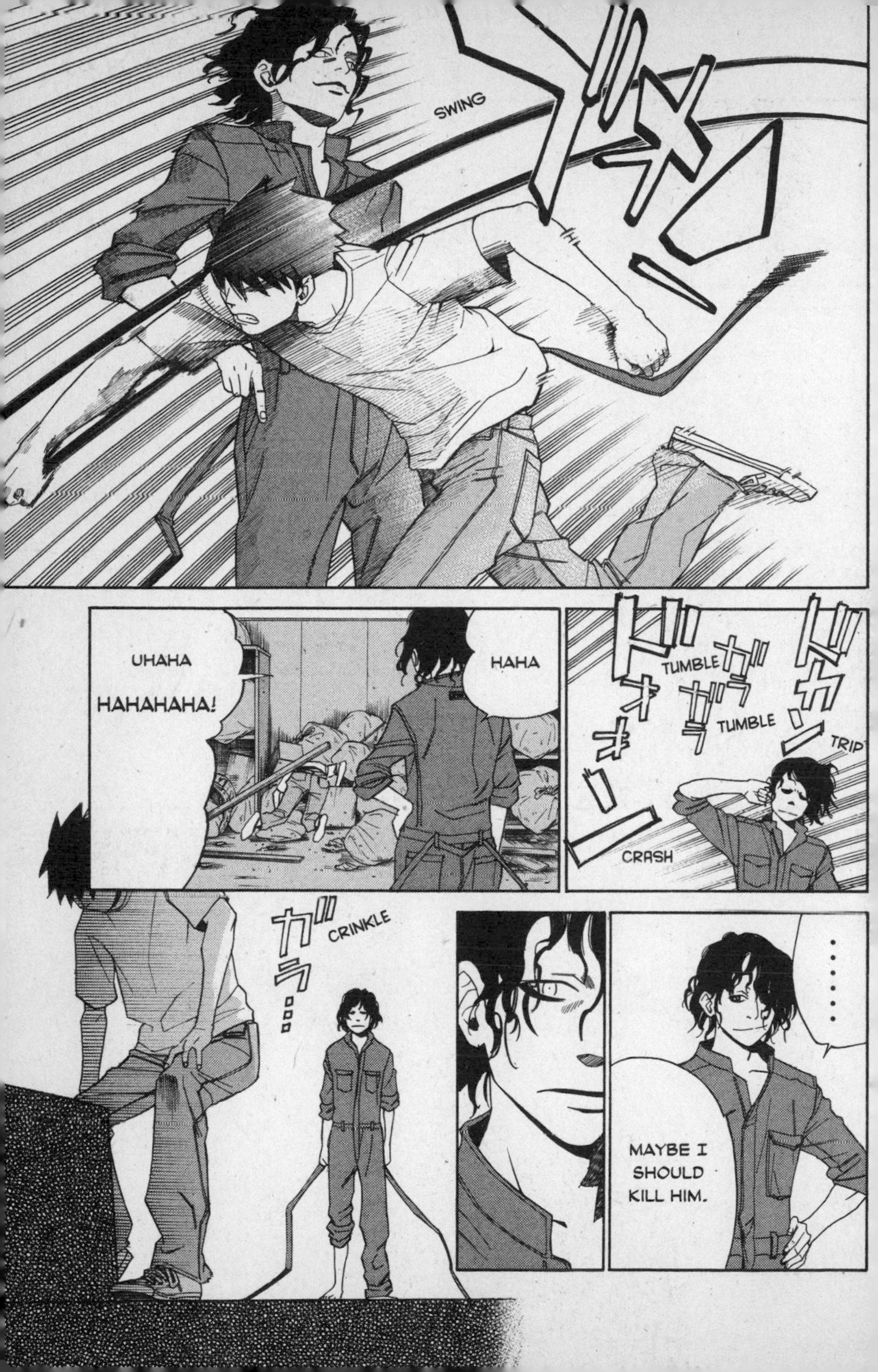
SWING
TUMBLE
TUMBLE
TRIP
CRASH
HAHA
UHAHA
HAHAHAHA!
......
MAYBE I SHOULD KILL HIM.
CRINKLE

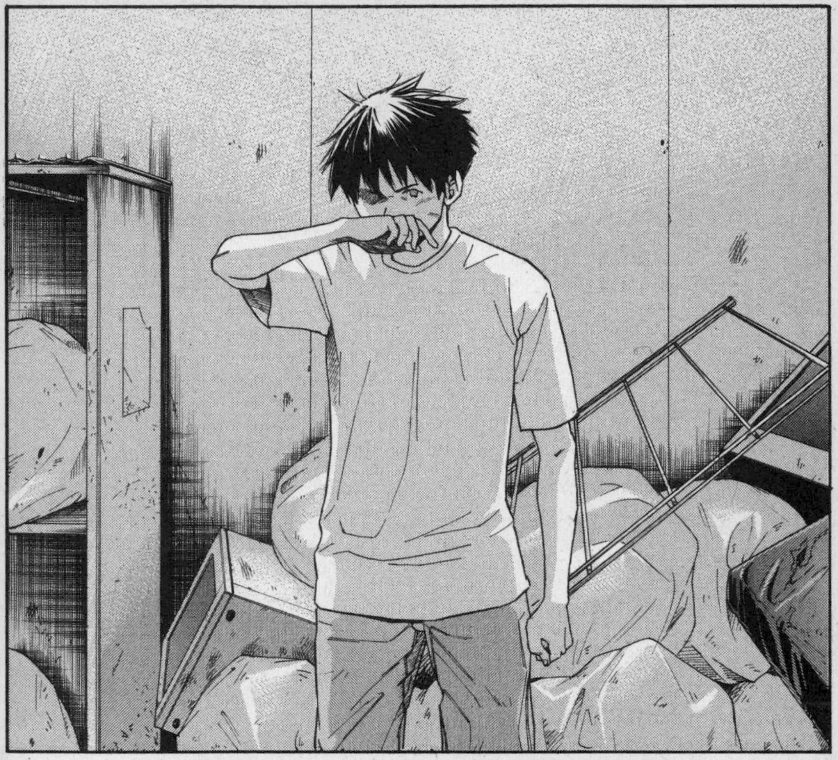
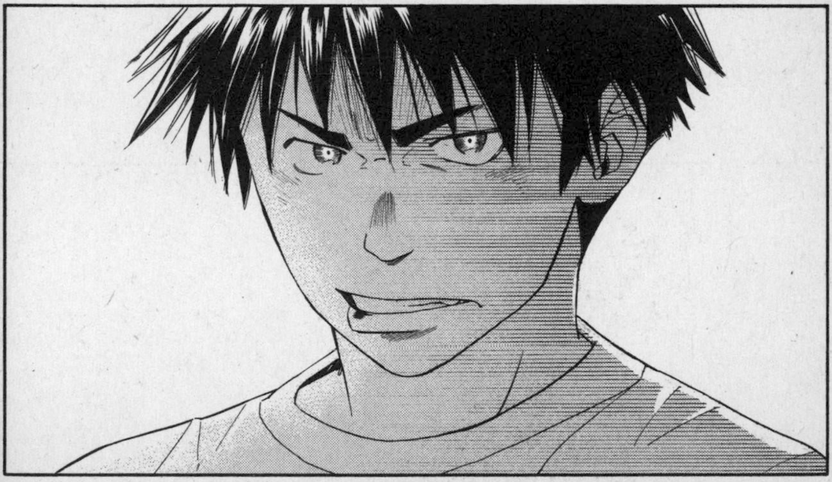

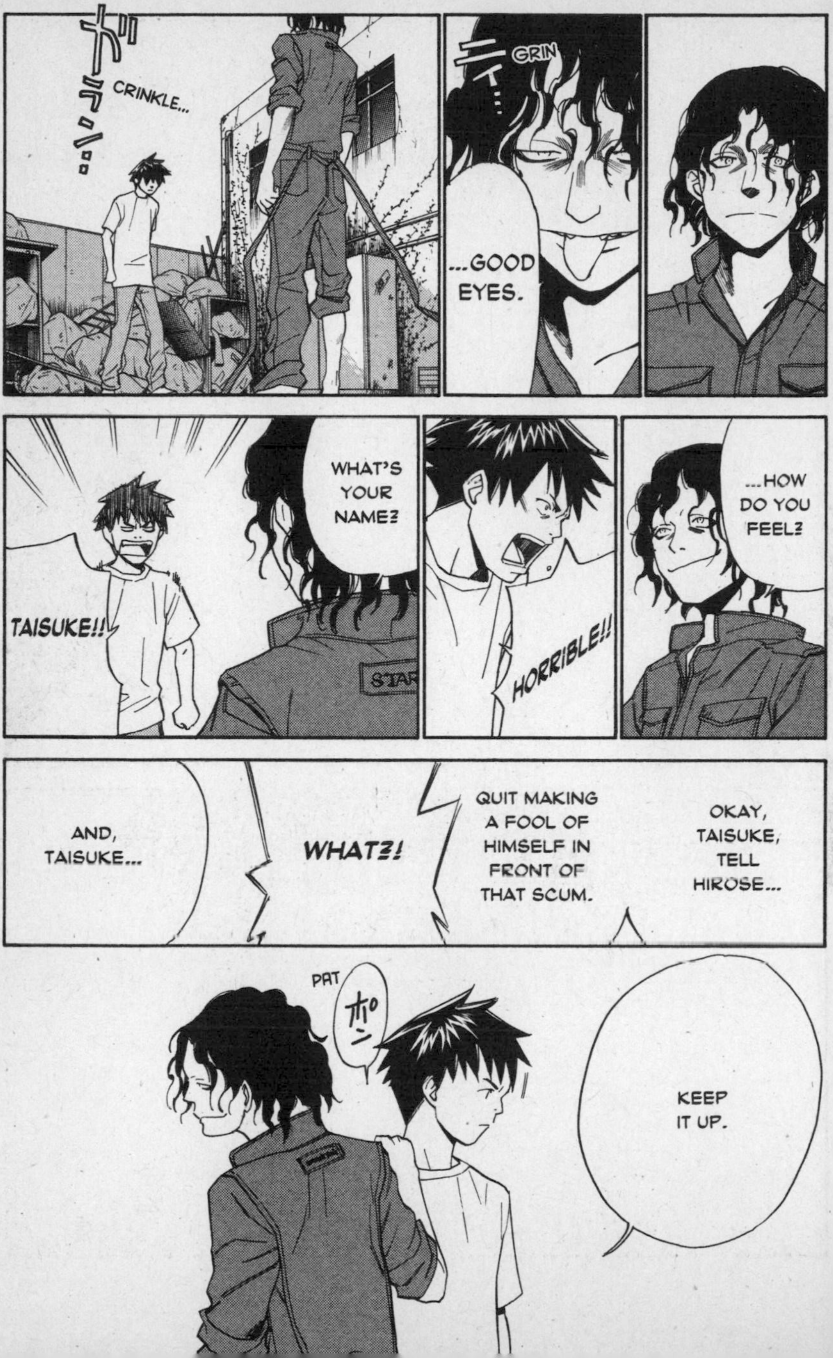
GRIN
...GOOD EYES.
CRINKLE...
...HOW DO YOU FEEL?
HORRIBLE!!
WHAT'S YOUR NAME?
TAISUKE!!
OKAY, TAISUKE, TELL HIROSE...
QUIT MAKING A FOOL OF HIMSELF IN FRONT OF THAT SCUM.
WHAT?!
AND, TAISUKE...
KEEP IT UP.
PAT

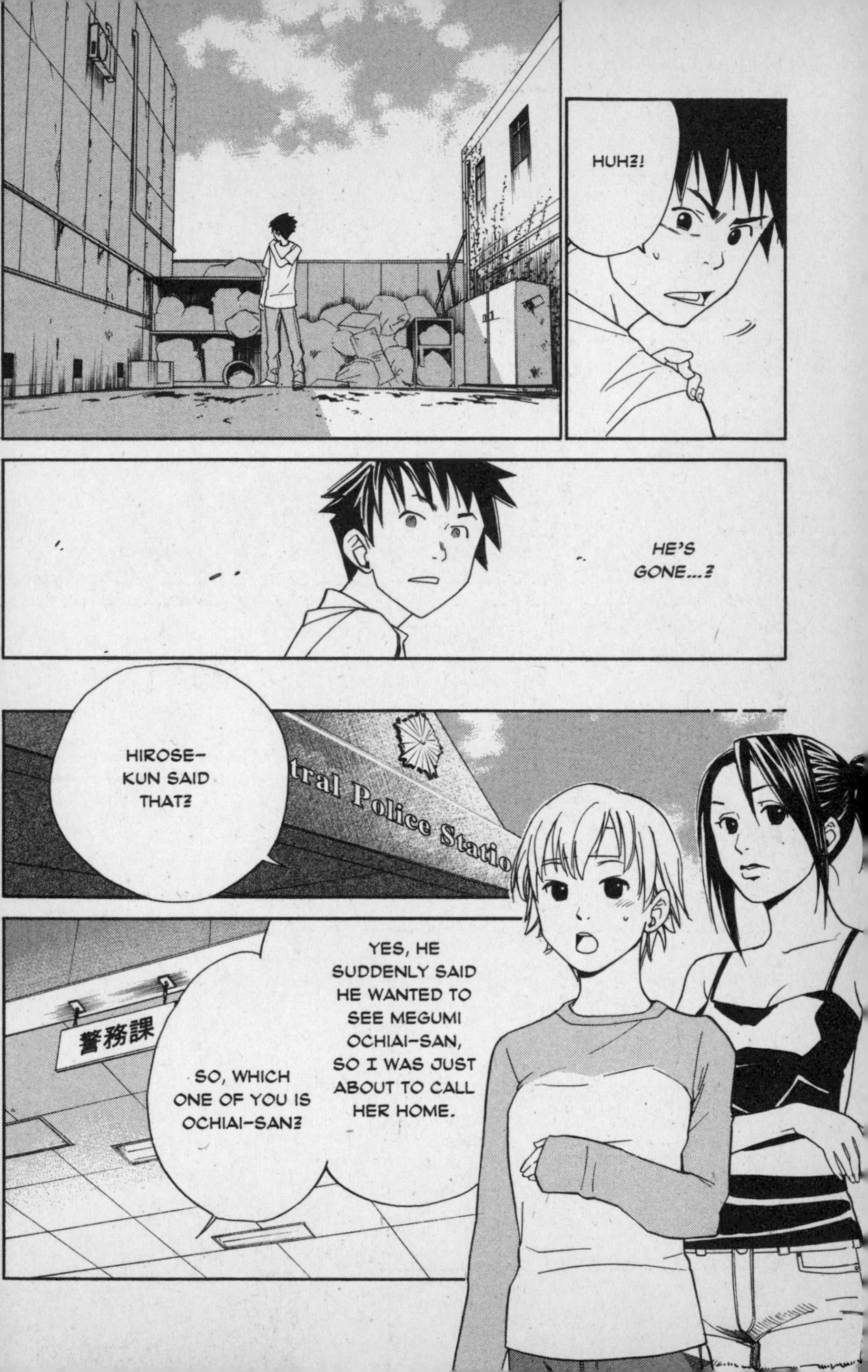
HUH?!
HE'S GONE...?
HIROSE-KUN SAID THAT?
tral Police Statio
YES, HE SUDDENLY SAID HE WANTED TO SEE MEGUMI OCHIAI-SAN, SO I WAS JUST ABOUT TO CALL HER HOME.
SO, WHICH ONE OF YOU IS OCHIAI-SAN?
警務課

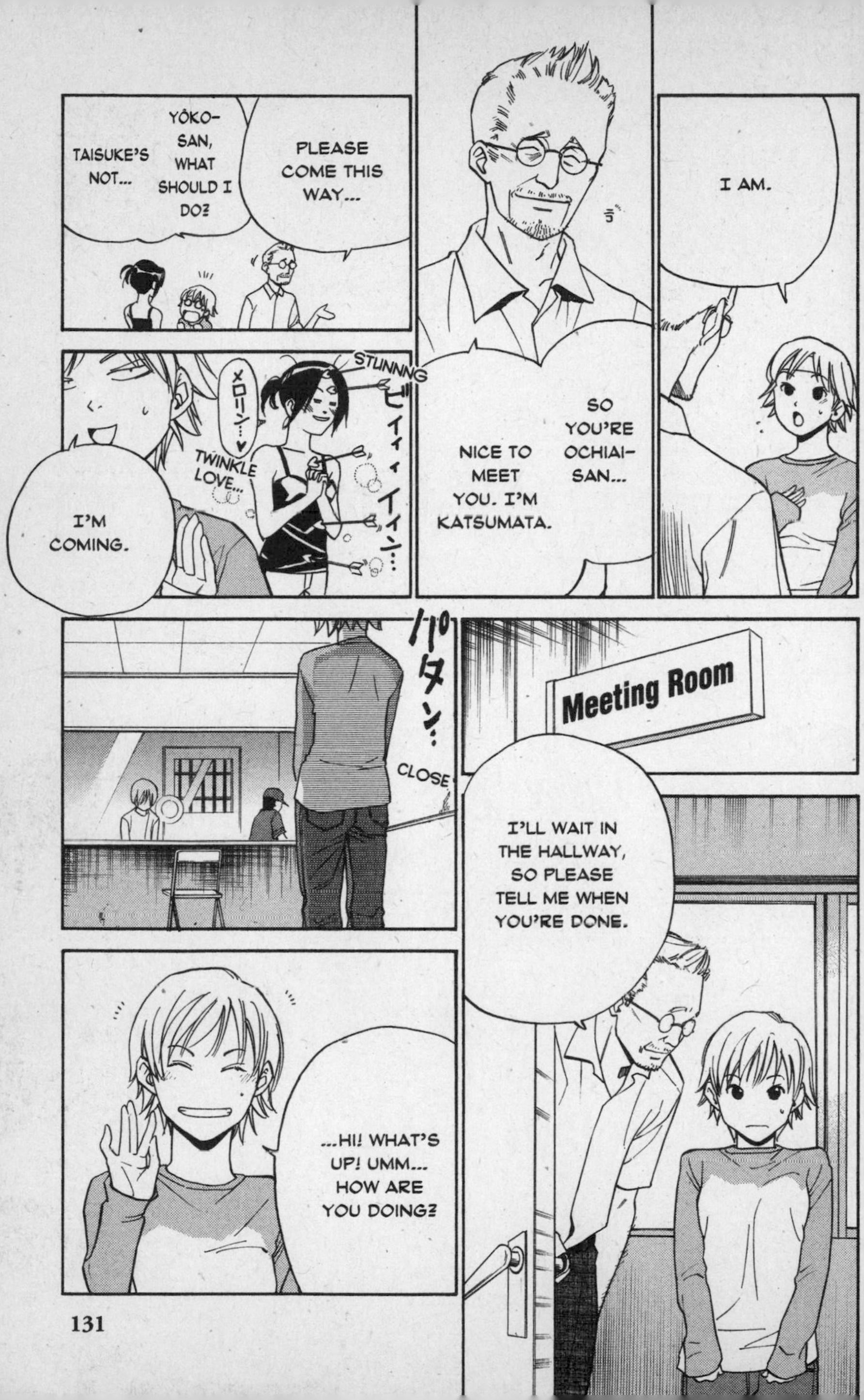
I AM.
SO YOU'RE OCHIAI-SAN...
NICE TO MEET YOU. I'M KATSUMATA.
PLEASE COME THIS WAY...
YÔKO-SAN, WHAT SHOULD I DO?
TAISUKE'S NOT...
STUNNNG
ビィィィイイン…
メロリン…♥
TWINKLE LOVE...
I'M COMING.
Meeting Room
I'LL WAIT IN THE HALLWAY, SO PLEASE TELL ME WHEN YOU'RE DONE.
パタン…
CLOSE
...HI! WHAT'S UP! UMM... HOW ARE YOU DOING?

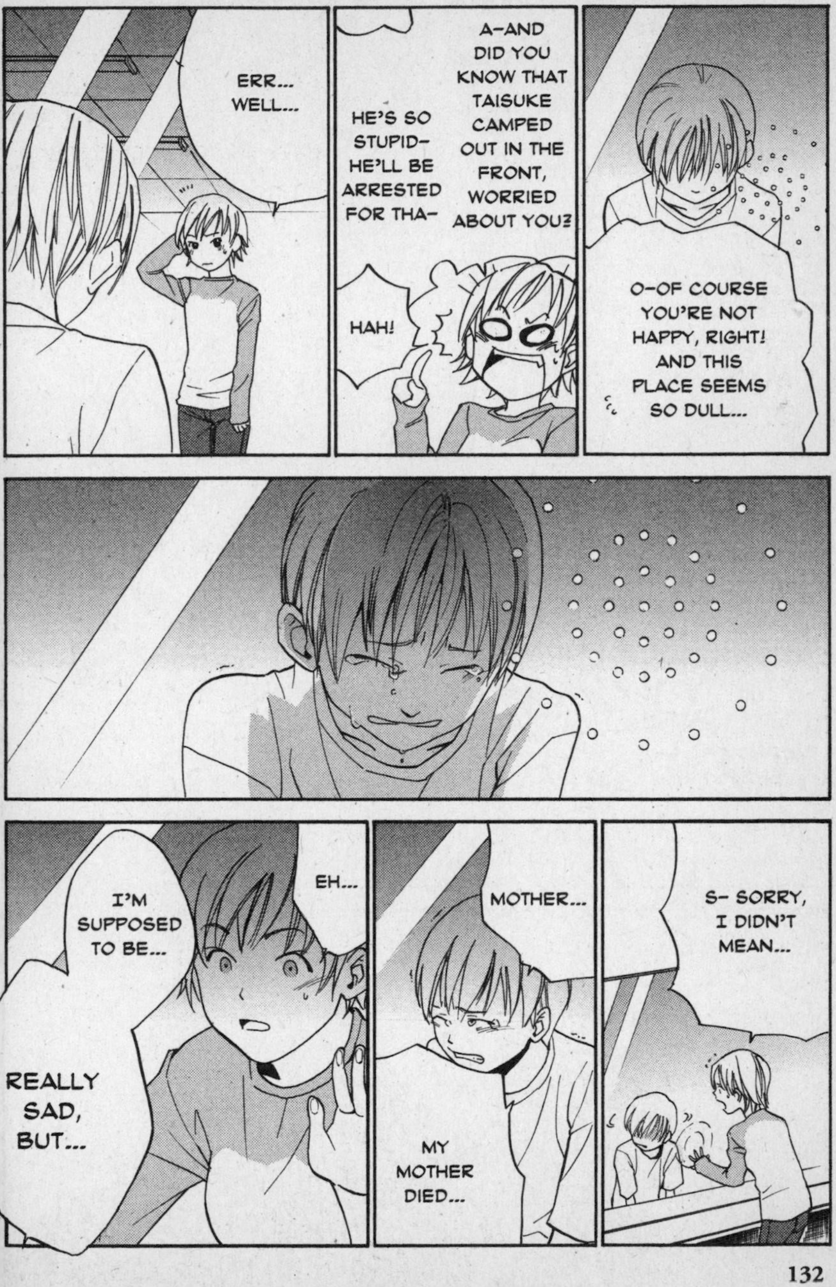
O-OF COURSE YOU'RE NOT HAPPY, RIGHT! AND THIS PLACE SEEMS SO DULL...
A-AND DID YOU KNOW THAT TAISUKE CAMPED OUT IN THE FRONT, WORRIED ABOUT YOU?
HE'S SO STUPID- HE'LL BE ARRESTED FOR THA-
HAH!
ERR... WELL...
S- SORRY, I DIDN'T MEAN...
MOTHER...
MY MOTHER DIED...
EH...
I'M SUPPOSED TO BE...
REALLY SAD, BUT...

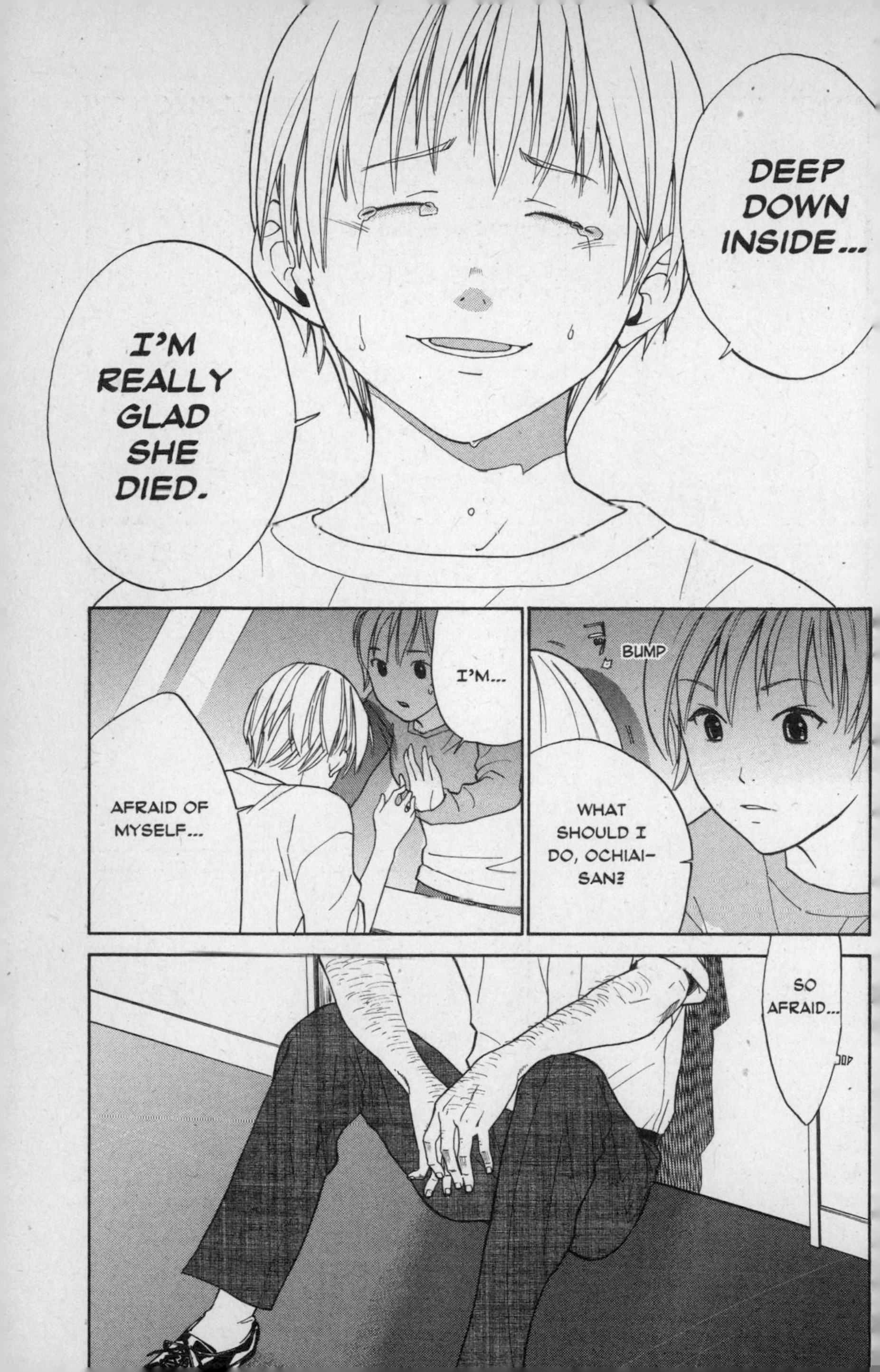
DEEP DOWN INSIDE...
I'M REALLY GLAD SHE DIED.
BUMP
WHAT SHOULD I DO, OCHIAI-SAN?
I'M...
AFRAID OF MYSELF...
SO AFRAID...

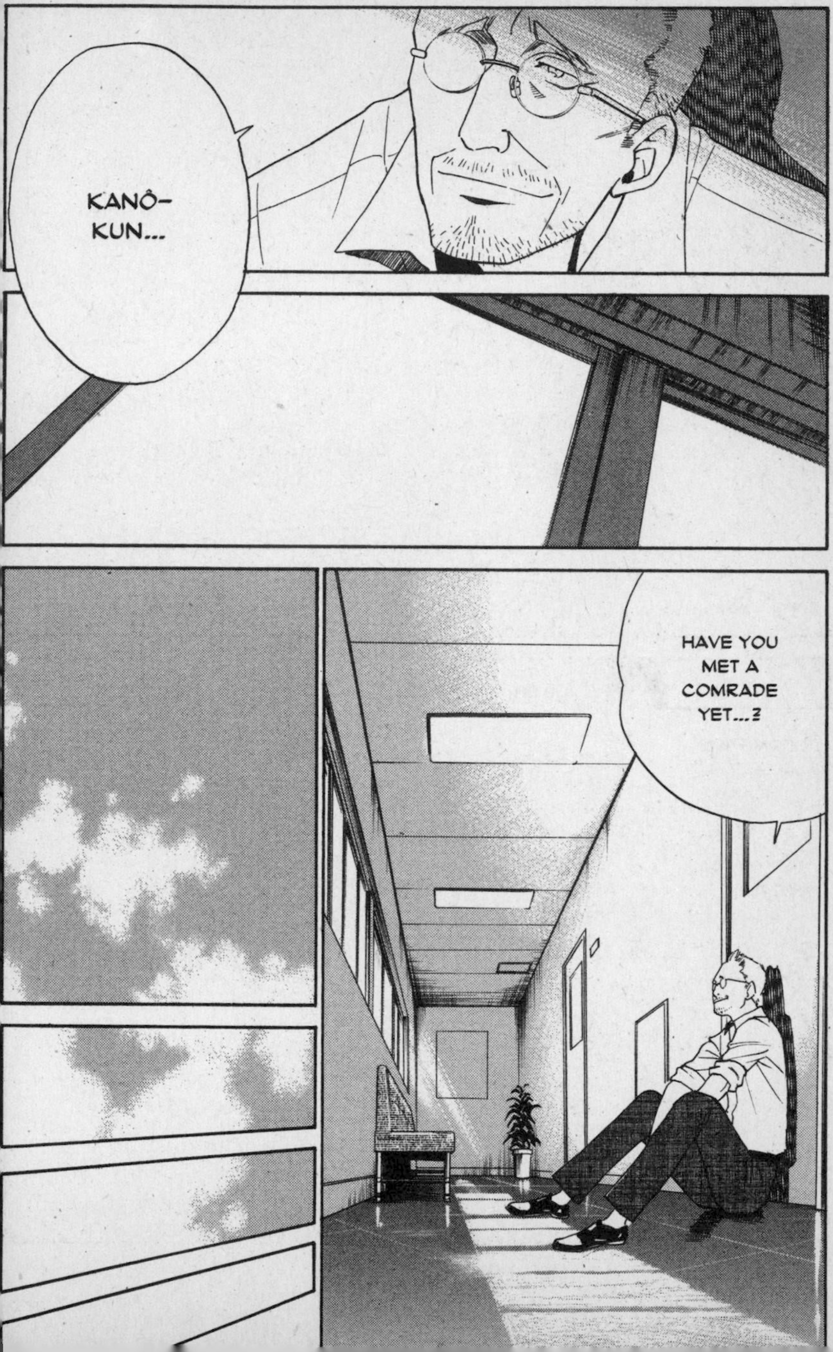
KANÔ-KUN...
HAVE YOU MET A COMRADE YET...?

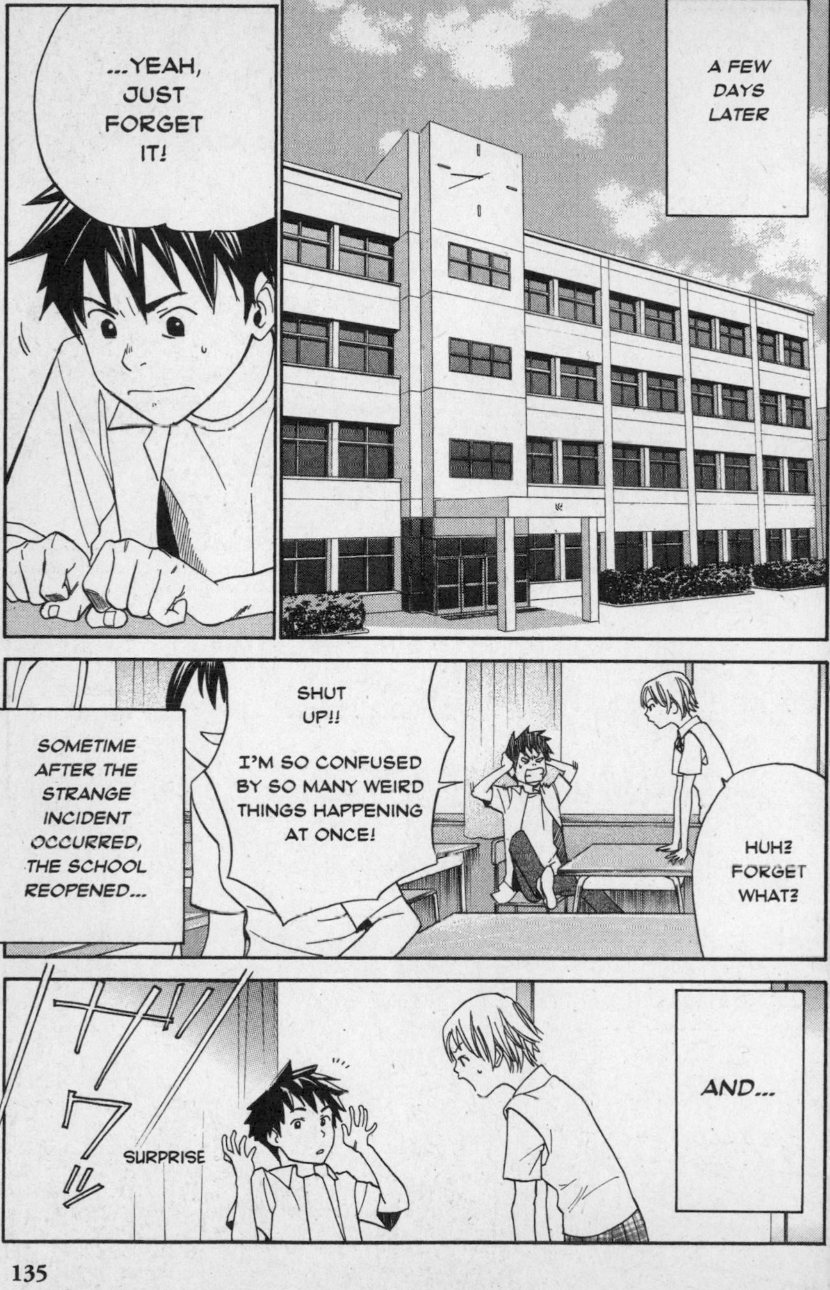
A FEW DAYS LATER
...YEAH, JUST FORGET IT!
HUH? FORGET WHAT?
SHUT UP!!
I'M SO CONFUSED BY SO MANY WEIRD THINGS HAPPENING AT ONCE!
SOMETIME AFTER THE STRANGE INCIDENT OCCURRED, THE SCHOOL REOPENED...
AND...
SURPRISE

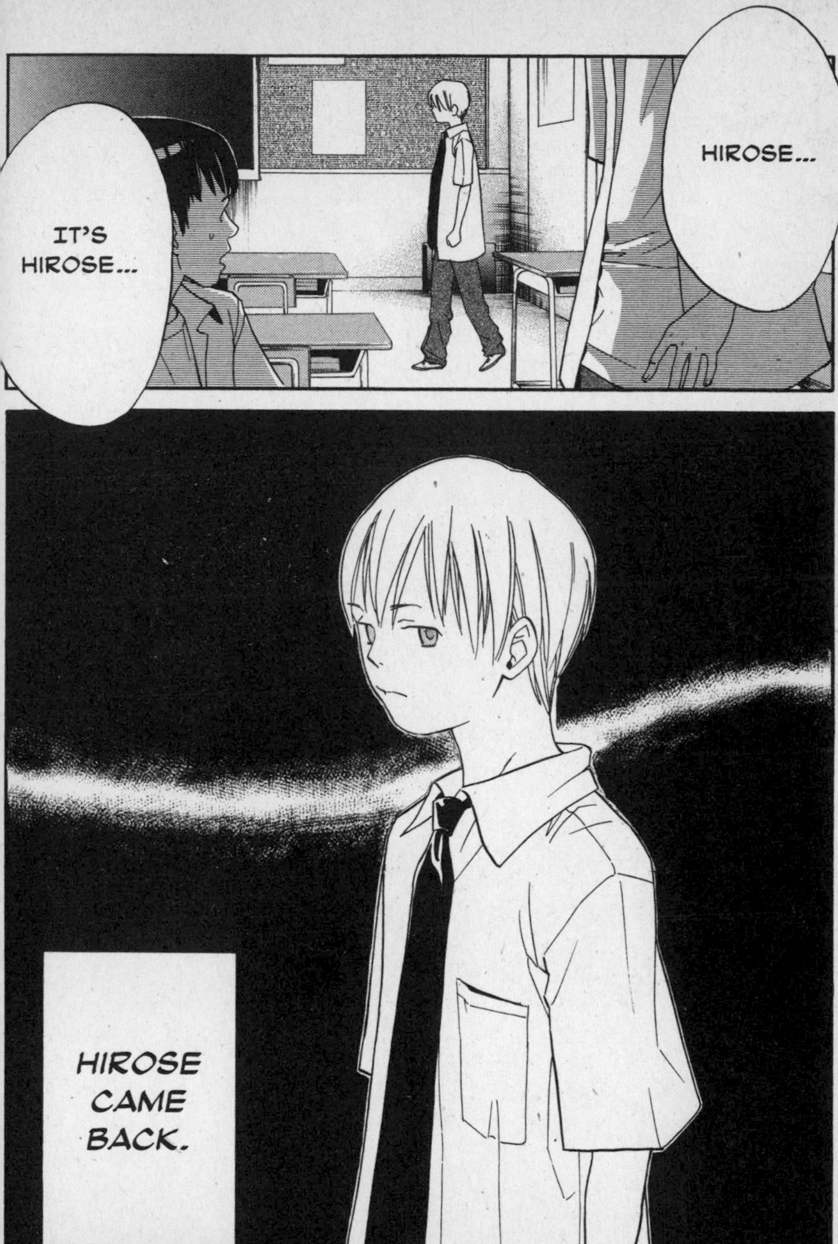
HIROSE...
IT'S HIROSE...
HIROSE CAME BACK.

Chapter 2/ End

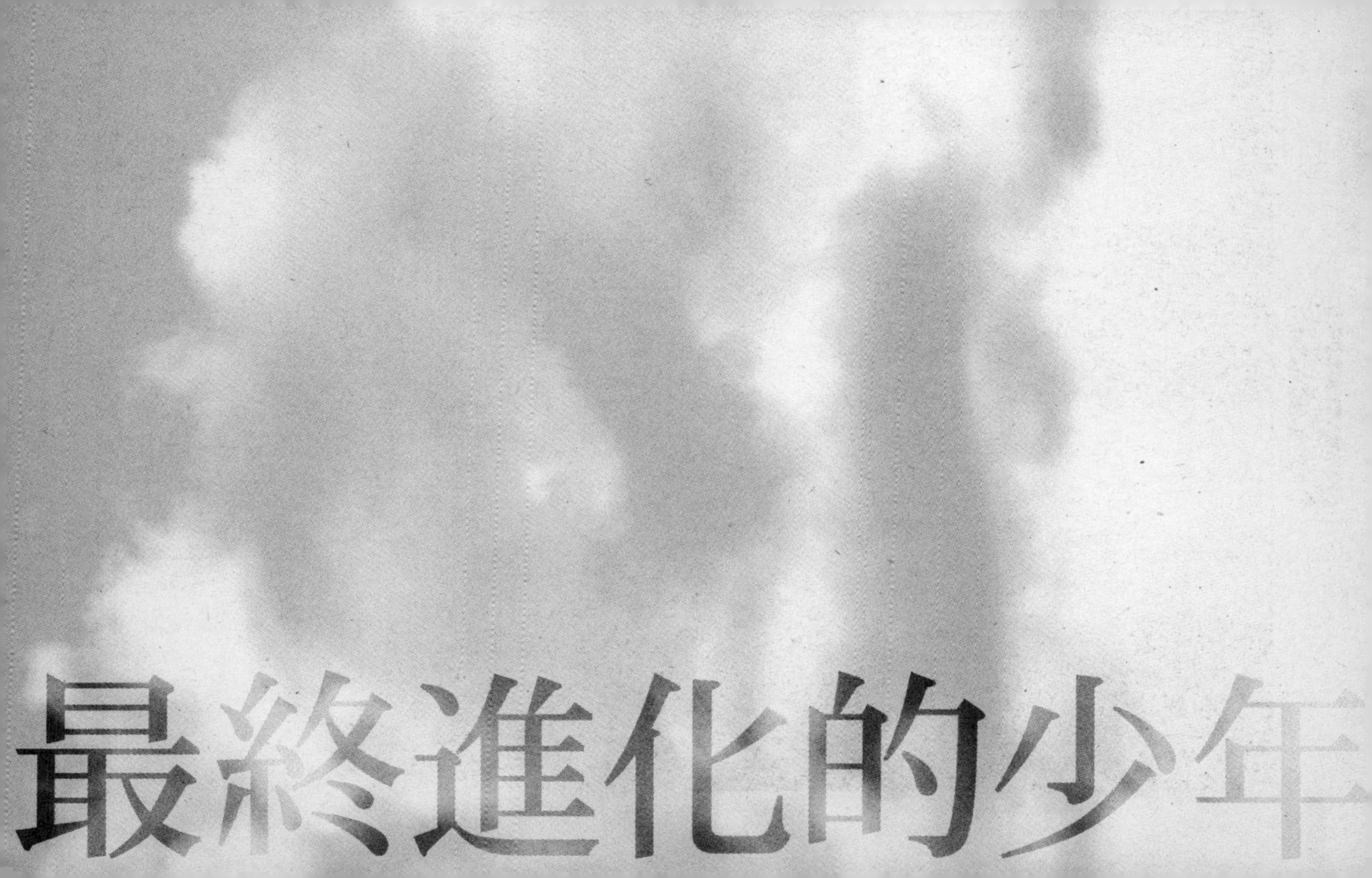
最終進化的少年

Alive

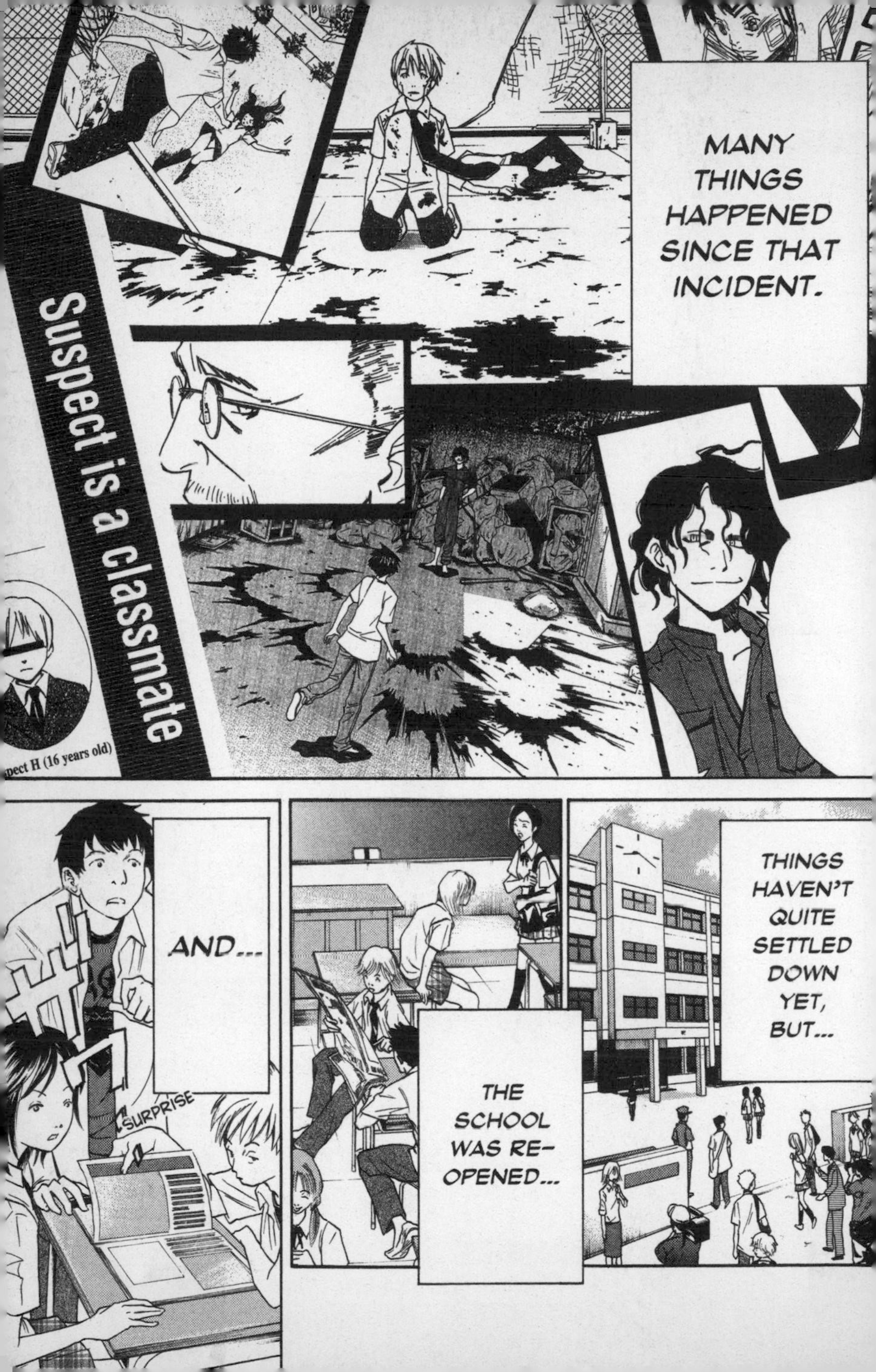
MANY THINGS HAPPENED SINCE THAT INCIDENT.
Suspect is a classmate
spect H (16 years old)
THINGS HAVEN'T QUITE SETTLED DOWN YET, BUT...
THE SCHOOL WAS RE-OPENED...
AND...
SURPRISE

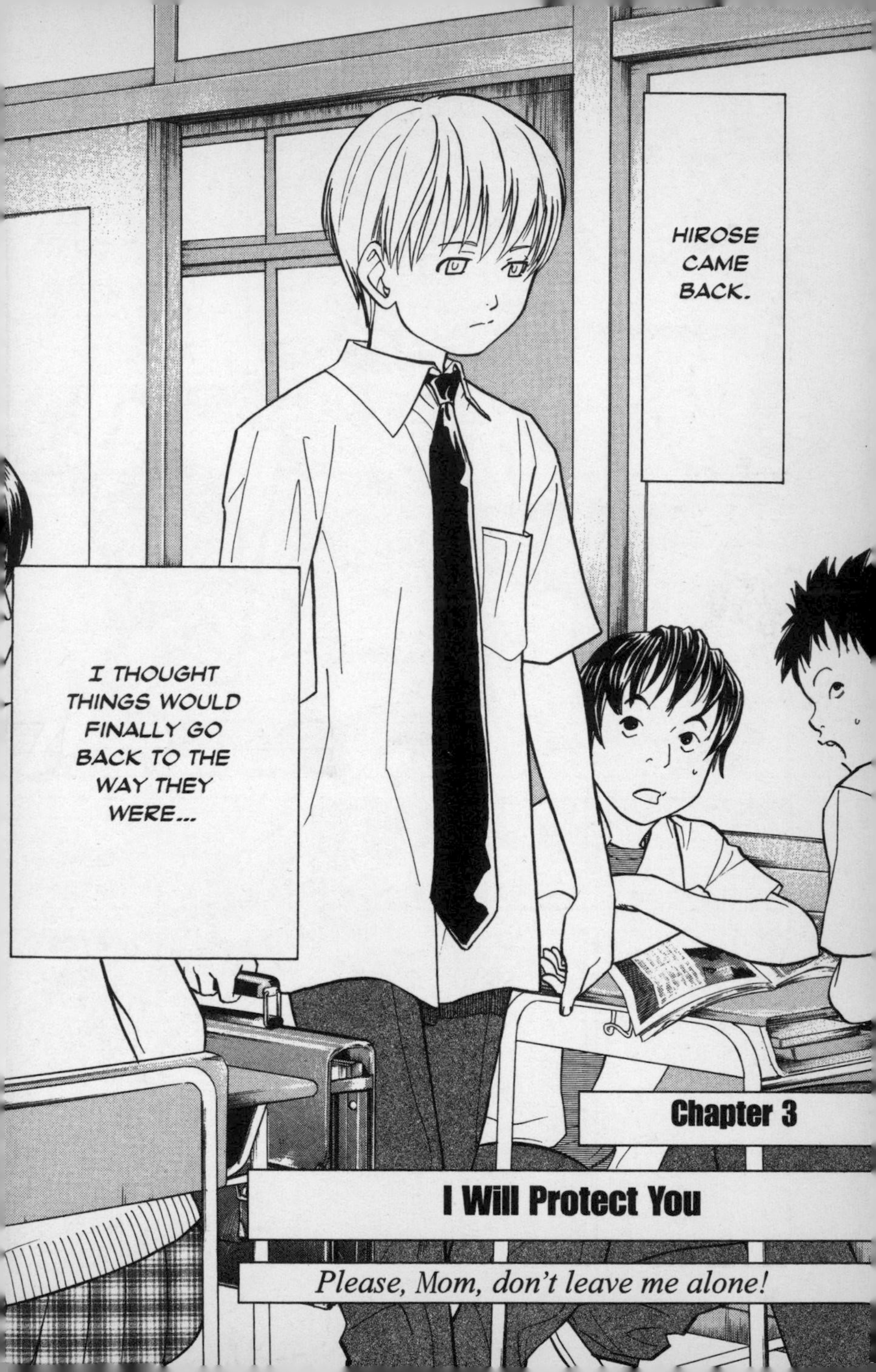
HIROSE CAME BACK.
I THOUGHT THINGS WOULD FINALLY GO BACK TO THE WAY THEY WERE...
Chapter 3
I Will Protect You
Please, Mom, don't leave me alone!

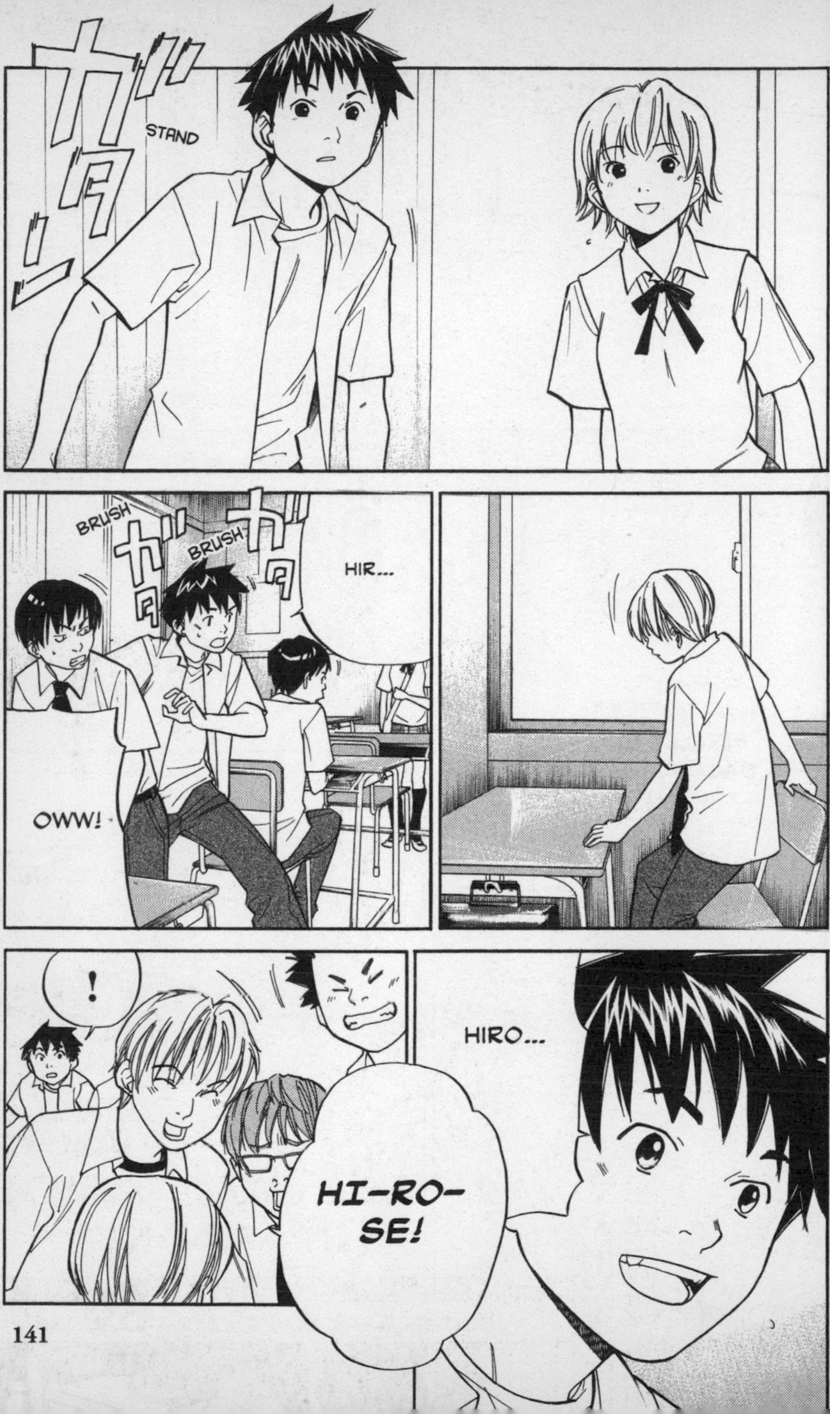
STAND
HIR...
BRUSH
BRUSH
OWW!
HIRO...
HI-RO-SE!
!

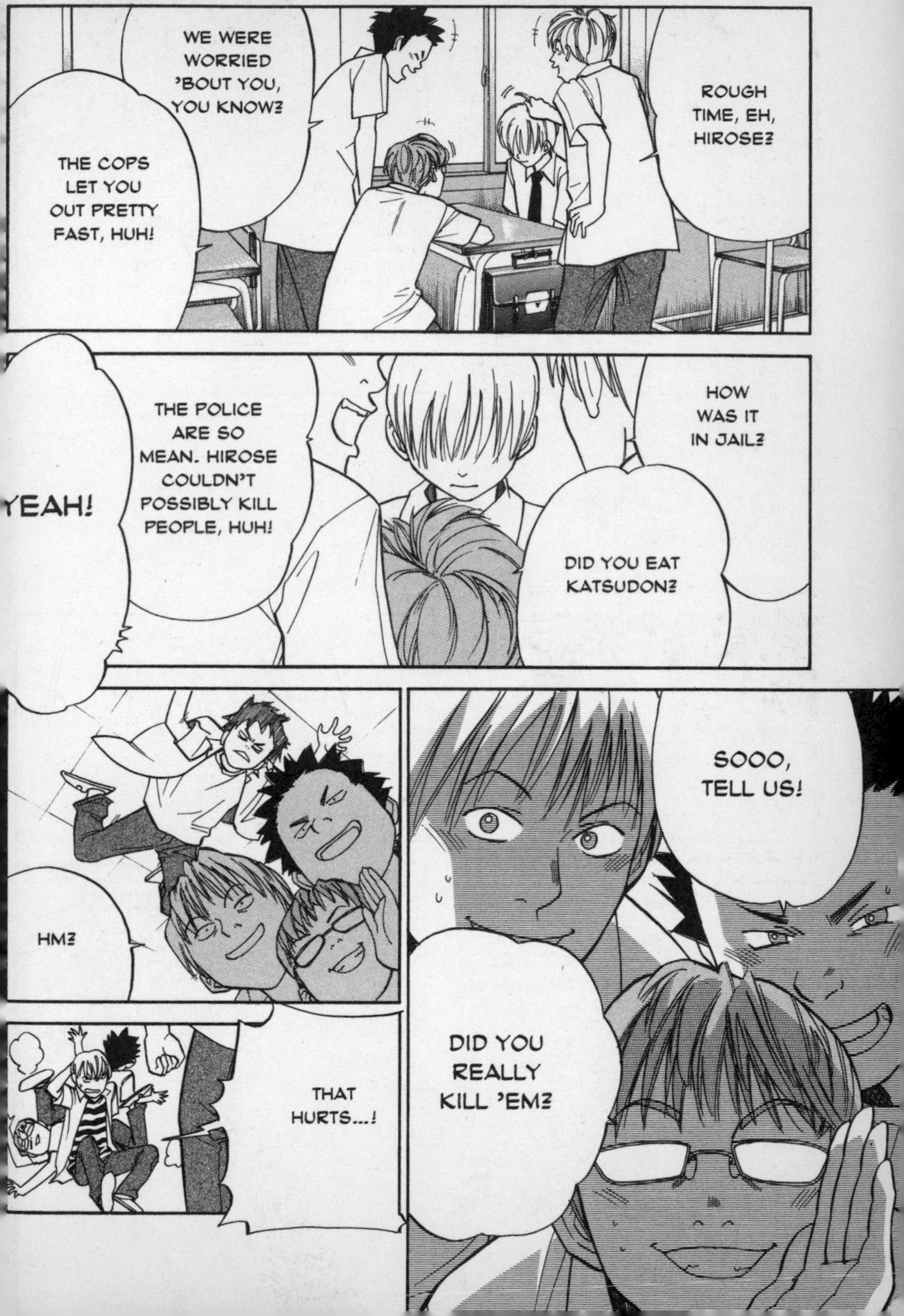
ROUGH TIME, EH, HIROSE?
WE WERE WORRIED 'BOUT YOU, YOU KNOW?
THE COPS LET YOU OUT PRETTY FAST, HUH!
HOW WAS IT IN JAIL?
DID YOU EAT KATSUDON?
THE POLICE ARE SO MEAN. HIROSE COULDN'T POSSIBLY KILL PEOPLE, HUH!
YEAH!
SOOO, TELL US!
DID YOU REALLY KILL 'EM?
HM?
THAT HURTS...!

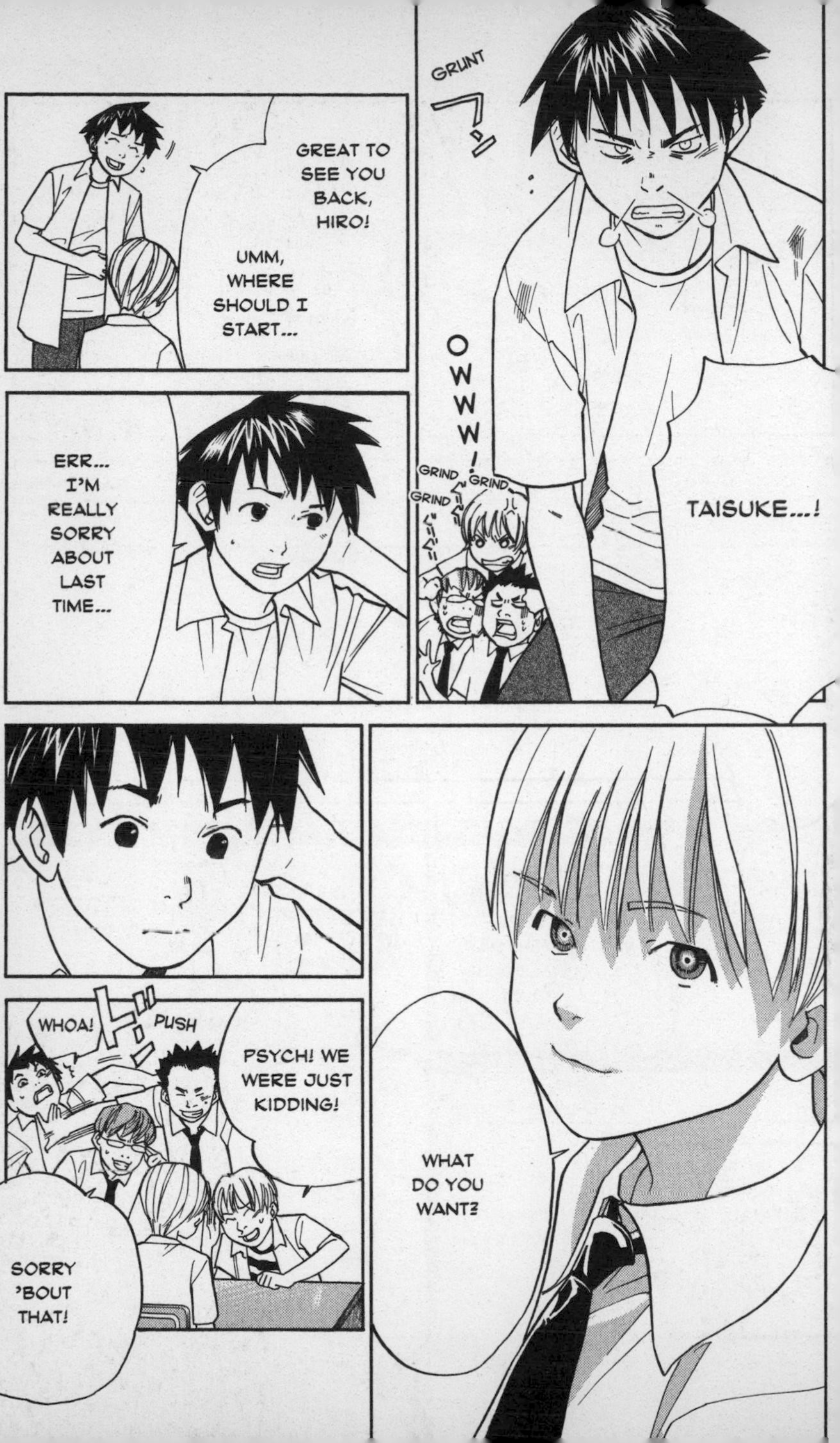
GRUNT
OWWW!
GRIND GRIND GRIND
TAISUKE...!
GREAT TO SEE YOU BACK, HIRO!
UMM, WHERE SHOULD I START...
ERR... I'M REALLY SORRY ABOUT LAST TIME...
WHAT DO YOU WANT?
PSYCH! WE WERE JUST KIDDING!
PUSH
WHOA!
SORRY 'BOUT THAT!

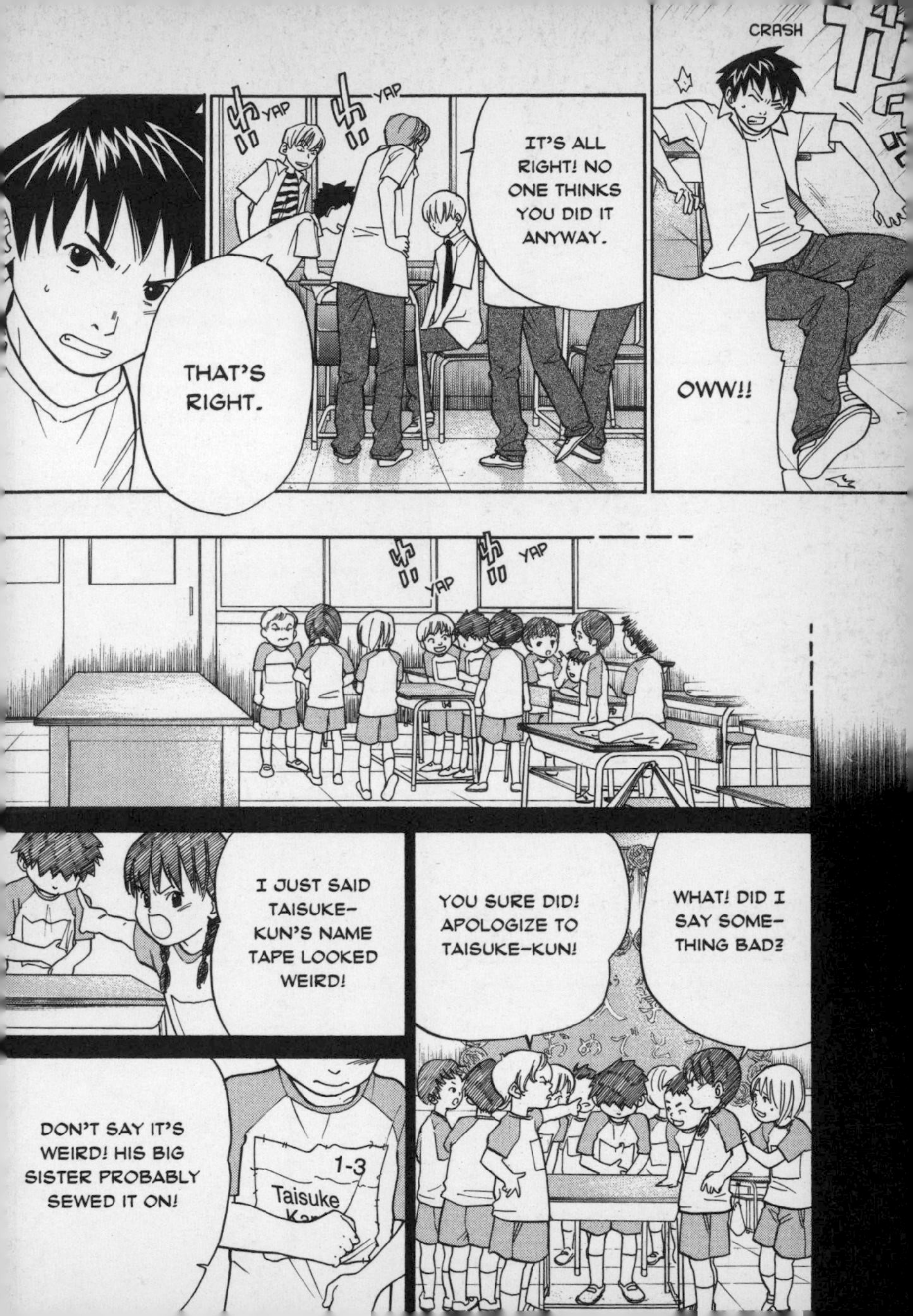
CRASH
OWW!!
YAP
YAP
IT'S ALL RIGHT! NO ONE THINKS YOU DID IT ANYWAY.
THAT'S RIGHT.
YAP
YAP
WHAT! DID I SAY SOME-THING BAD?
YOU SURE DID! APOLOGIZE TO TAISUKE-KUN!
I JUST SAID TAISUKE-KUN'S NAME TAPE LOOKED WEIRD!
DON'T SAY IT'S WEIRD! HIS BIG SISTER PROBABLY SEWED IT ON!
1-3
Taisuke

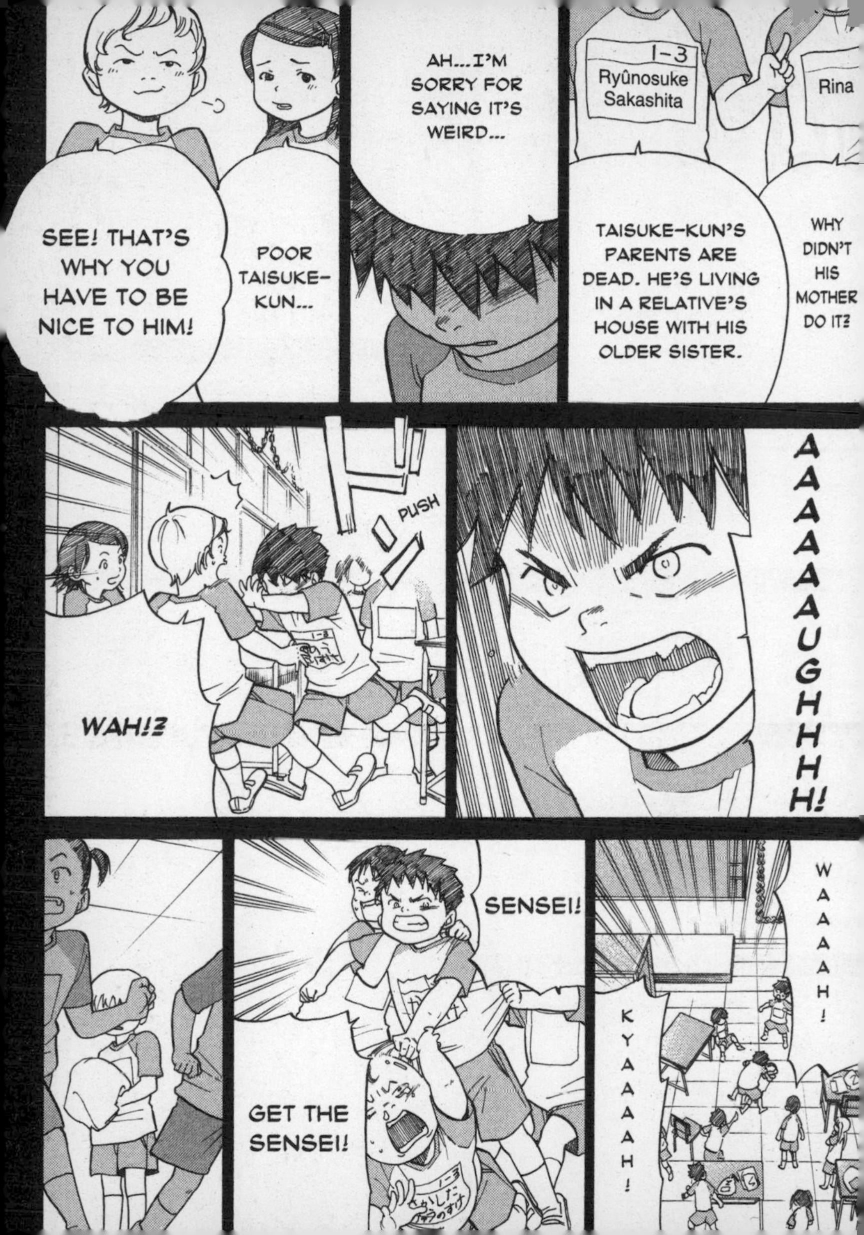
1-3
Ryûnosuke Sakashita
Rina
WHY DIDN'T HIS MOTHER DO IT?
TAISUKE-KUN'S PARENTS ARE DEAD. HE'S LIVING IN A RELATIVE'S HOUSE WITH HIS OLDER SISTER.
AH... I'M SORRY FOR SAYING IT'S WEIRD...
POOR TAISUKE-KUN...
SEE! THAT'S WHY YOU HAVE TO BE NICE TO HIM!
AAAAAAUGHHHH!
PUSH
WAH!?
WAAAAH!
KYAAAAH!
SENSEI!
GET THE SENSEI!

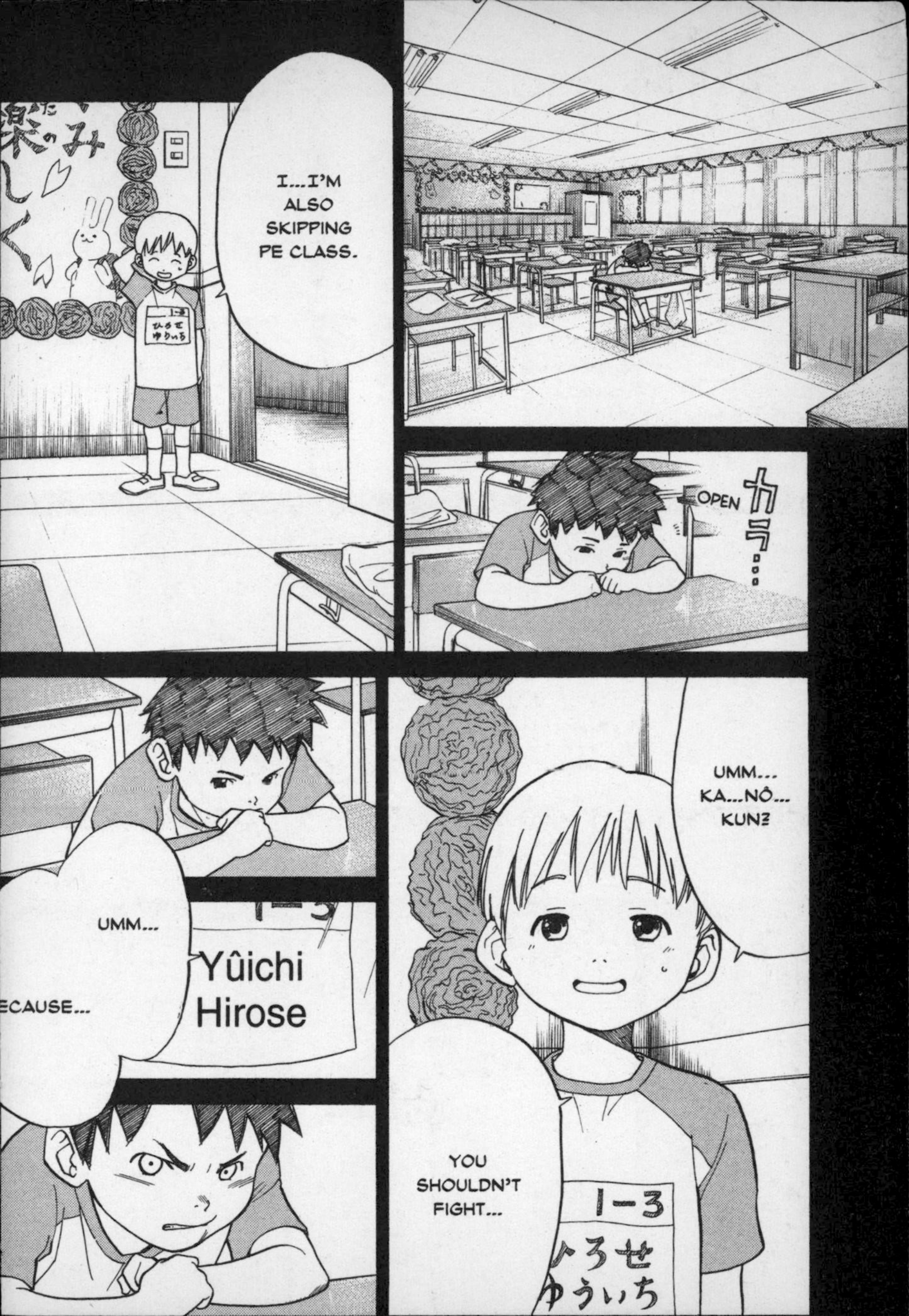
OPEN
カラ…
I...I'M ALSO SKIPPING PE CLASS.
UMM... KA...NÔ... KUN?
YOU SHOULDN'T FIGHT...
1−3
ひろせ
ゆういち
UMM...
1−3
Yûichi Hirose
ECAUSE...

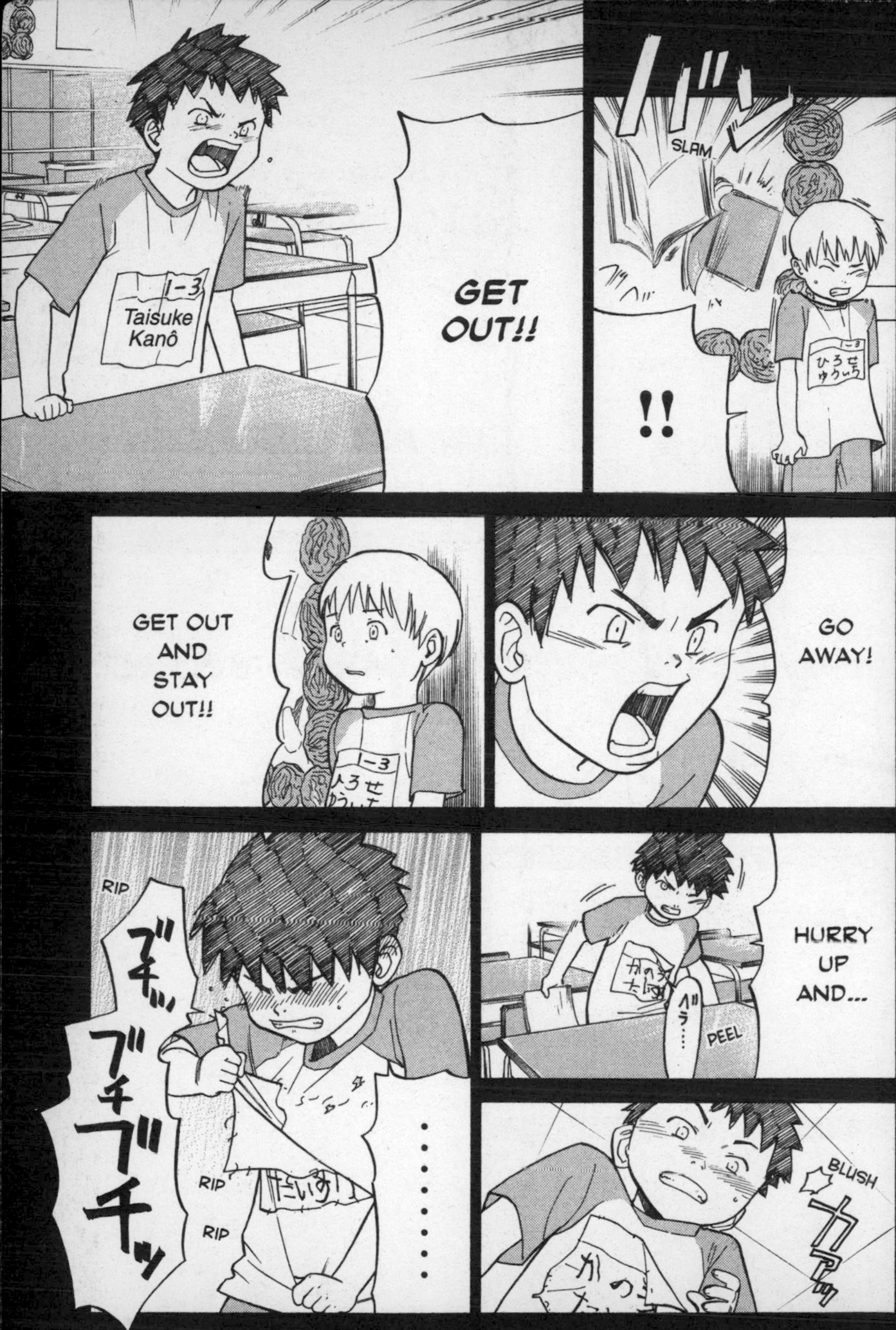
SLAM
!!
1-3
Taisuke Kanô
GET OUT!!
GO AWAY!
GET OUT AND STAY OUT!!
HURRY UP AND...
PEEL
BLUSH
RIP
RIP
RIP
......

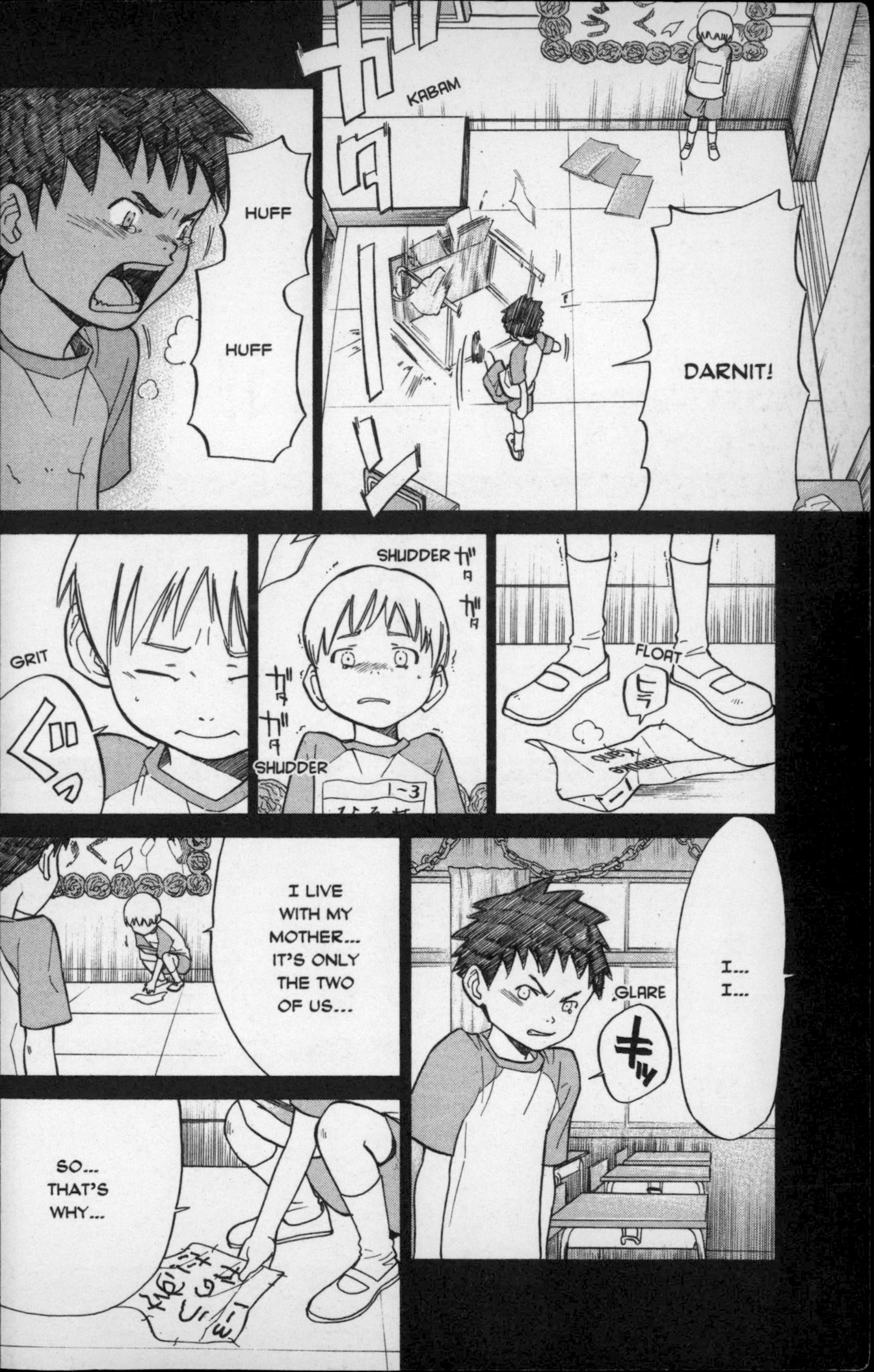
KABAM
DARNIT!
HUFF
HUFF
FLOAT
SHUDDER
SHUDDER
GRIT
I... I...
GLARE
I LIVE WITH MY MOTHER... IT'S ONLY THE TWO OF US...
SO... THAT'S WHY...

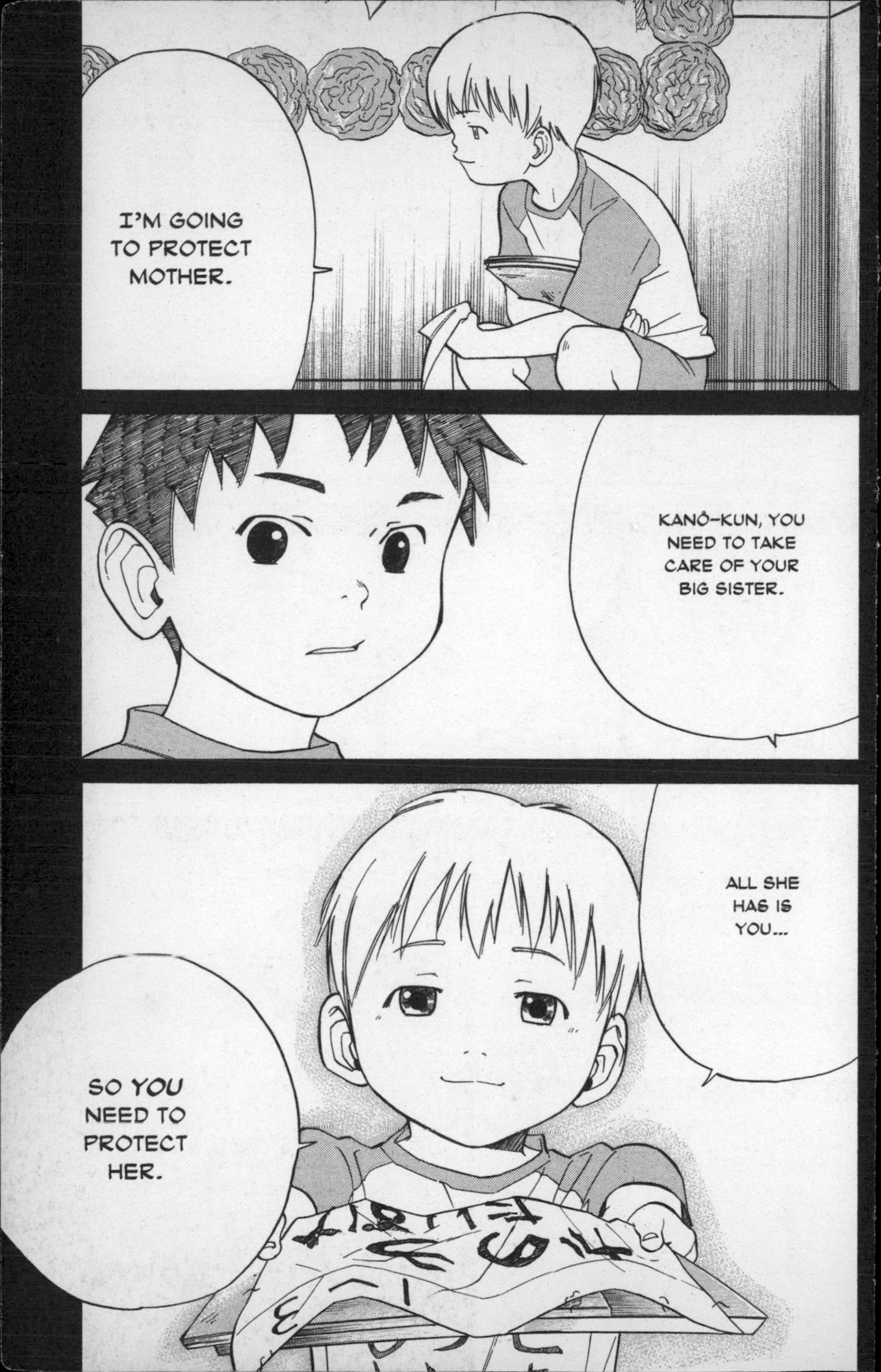
I'M GOING TO PROTECT MOTHER.
KANÔ-KUN, YOU NEED TO TAKE CARE OF YOUR BIG SISTER.
ALL SHE HAS IS YOU...
SO YOU NEED TO PROTECT HER.

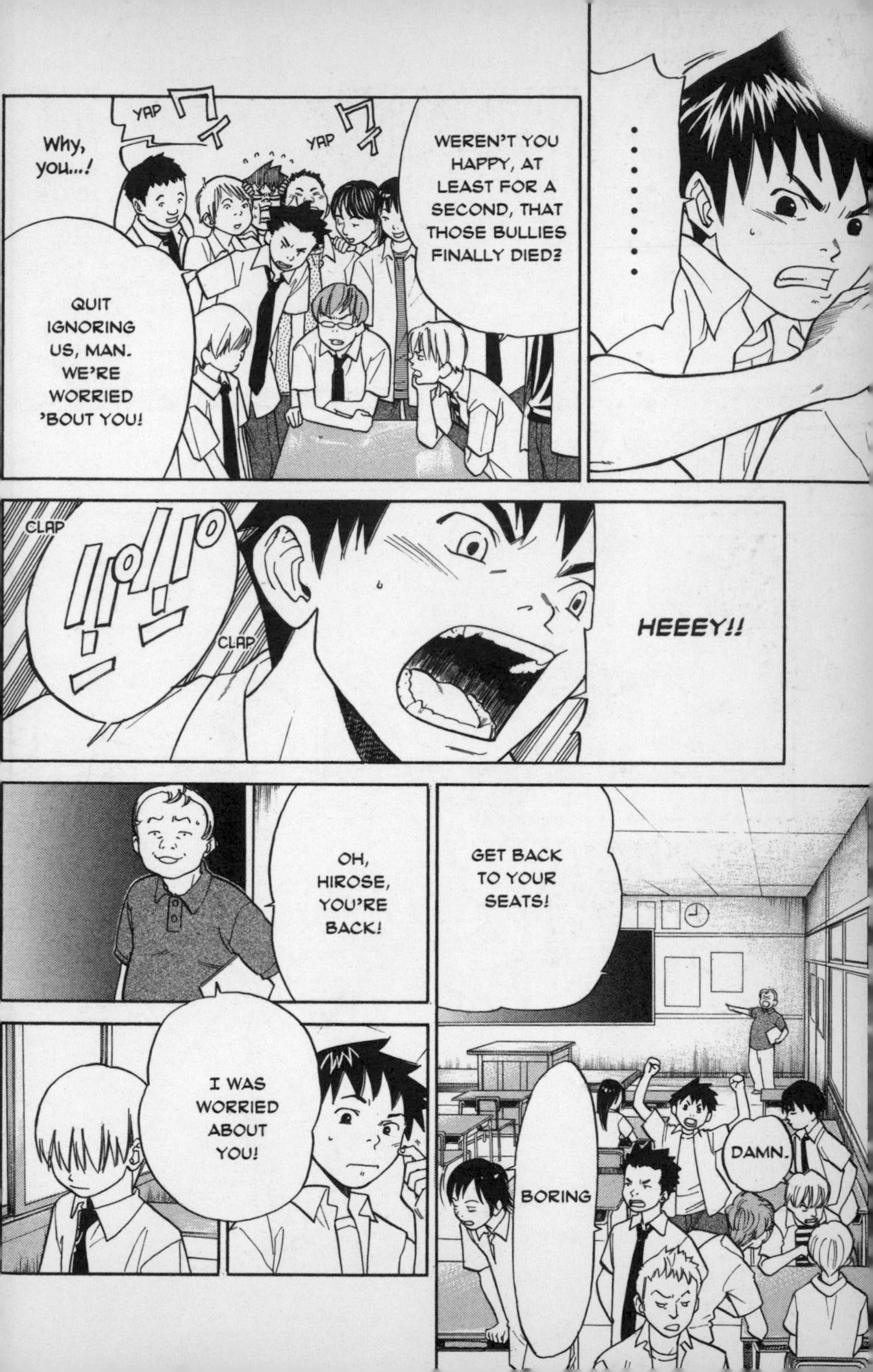
......
WEREN'T YOU HAPPY, AT LEAST FOR A SECOND, THAT THOSE BULLIES FINALLY DIED?
YAP
YAP
Why, you...!
QUIT IGNORING US, MAN. WE'RE WORRIED 'BOUT YOU!
HEEEY!!
CLAP
CLAP
GET BACK TO YOUR SEATS!
DAMN.
BORING
OH, HIROSE, YOU'RE BACK!
I WAS WORRIED ABOUT YOU!

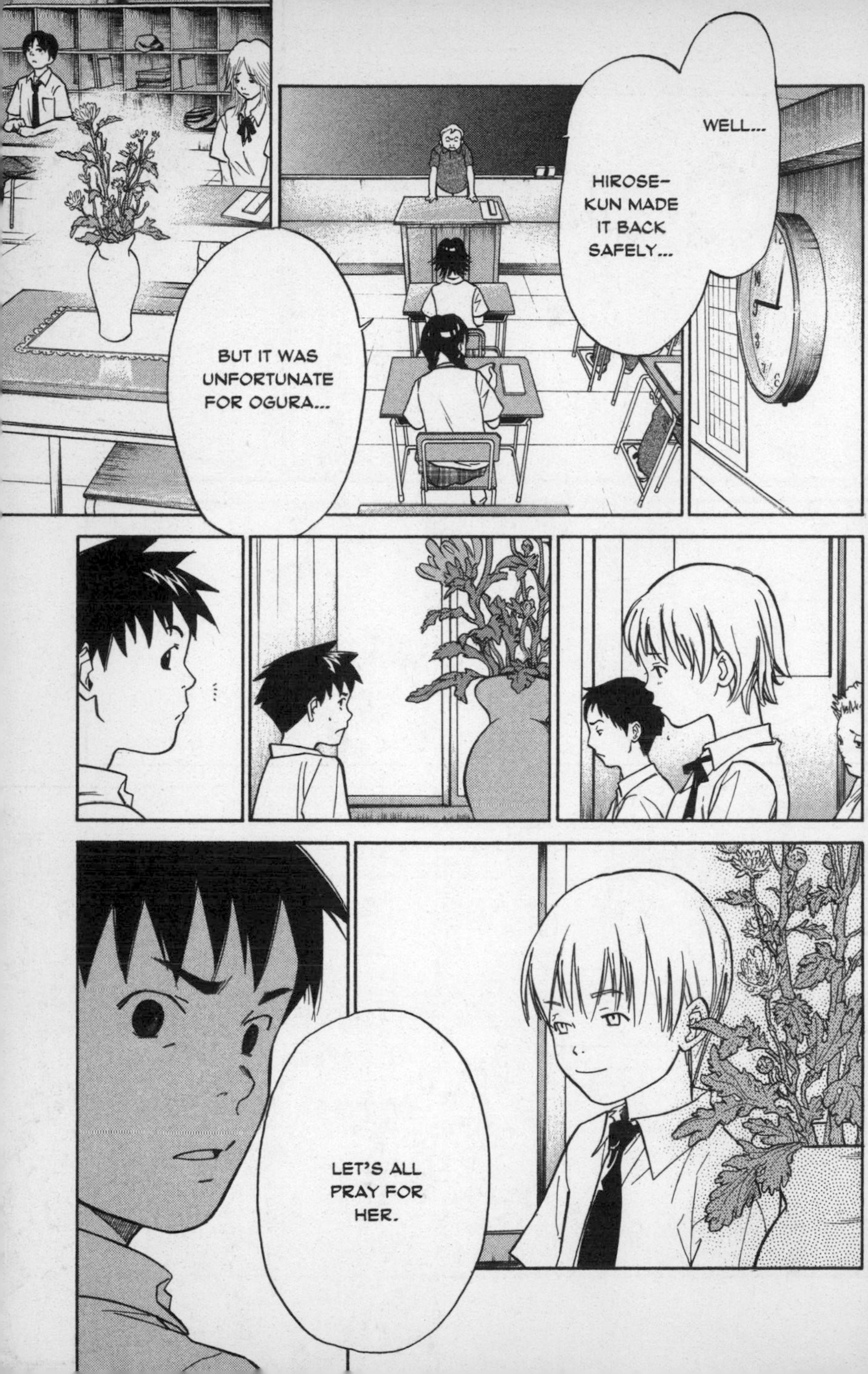
WELL...
HIROSE-KUN MADE IT BACK SAFELY...
BUT IT WAS UNFORTUNATE FOR OGURA...
LET'S ALL PRAY FOR HER.

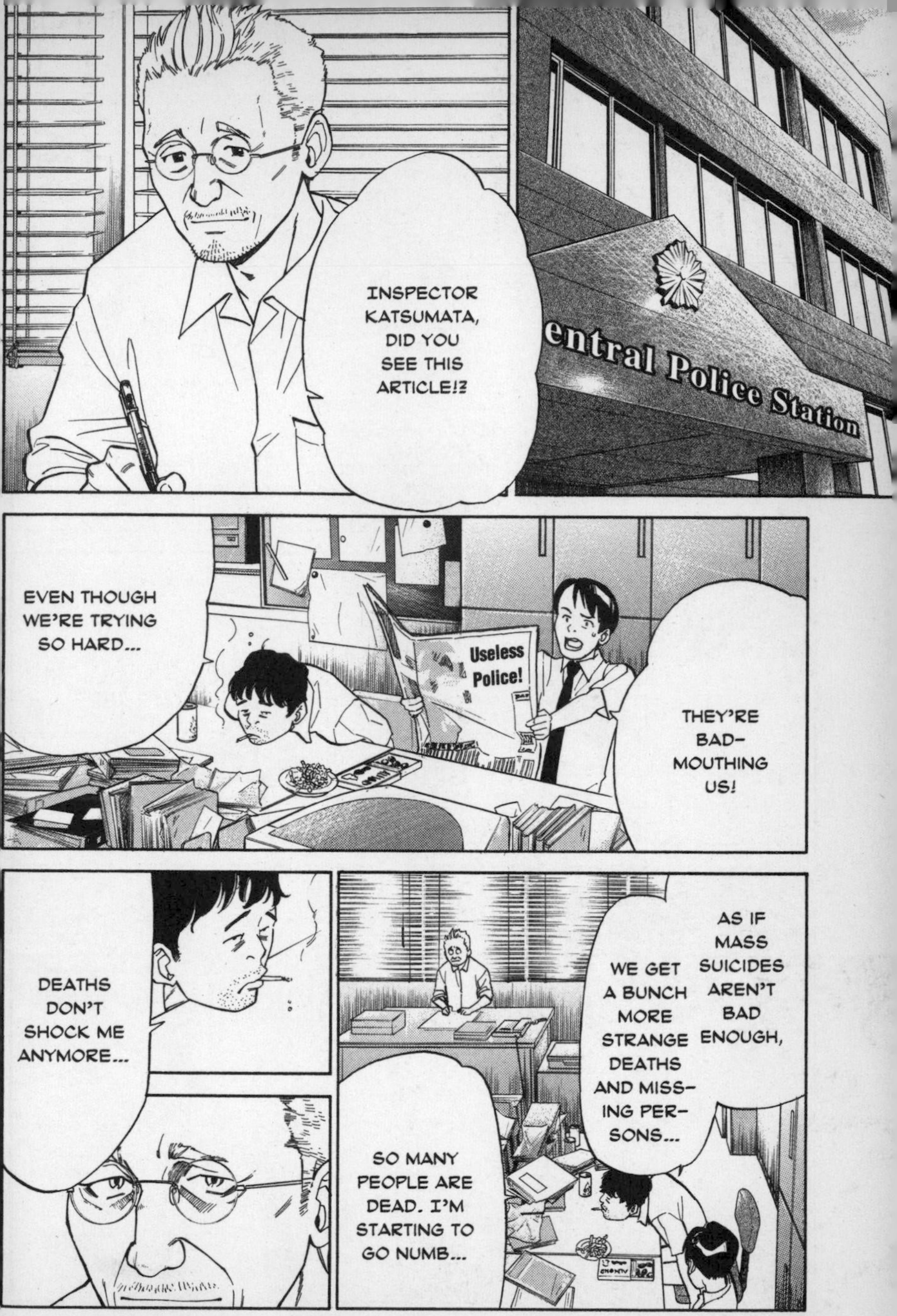
entral Police Station
INSPECTOR KATSUMATA, DID YOU SEE THIS ARTICLE!?
THEY'RE BAD-MOUTHING US!
Useless Police!
EVEN THOUGH WE'RE TRYING SO HARD...
AS IF MASS SUICIDES AREN'T BAD ENOUGH,
WE GET A BUNCH MORE STRANGE DEATHS AND MISSING PERSONS...
SO MANY PEOPLE ARE DEAD. I'M STARTING TO GO NUMB...
DEATHS DON'T SHOCK ME ANYMORE...

YOU'RE RIGHT ON, DUDE!

GRAB

WHO'RE YOU?

BLEAH

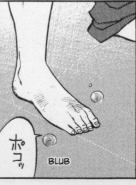

BLUB

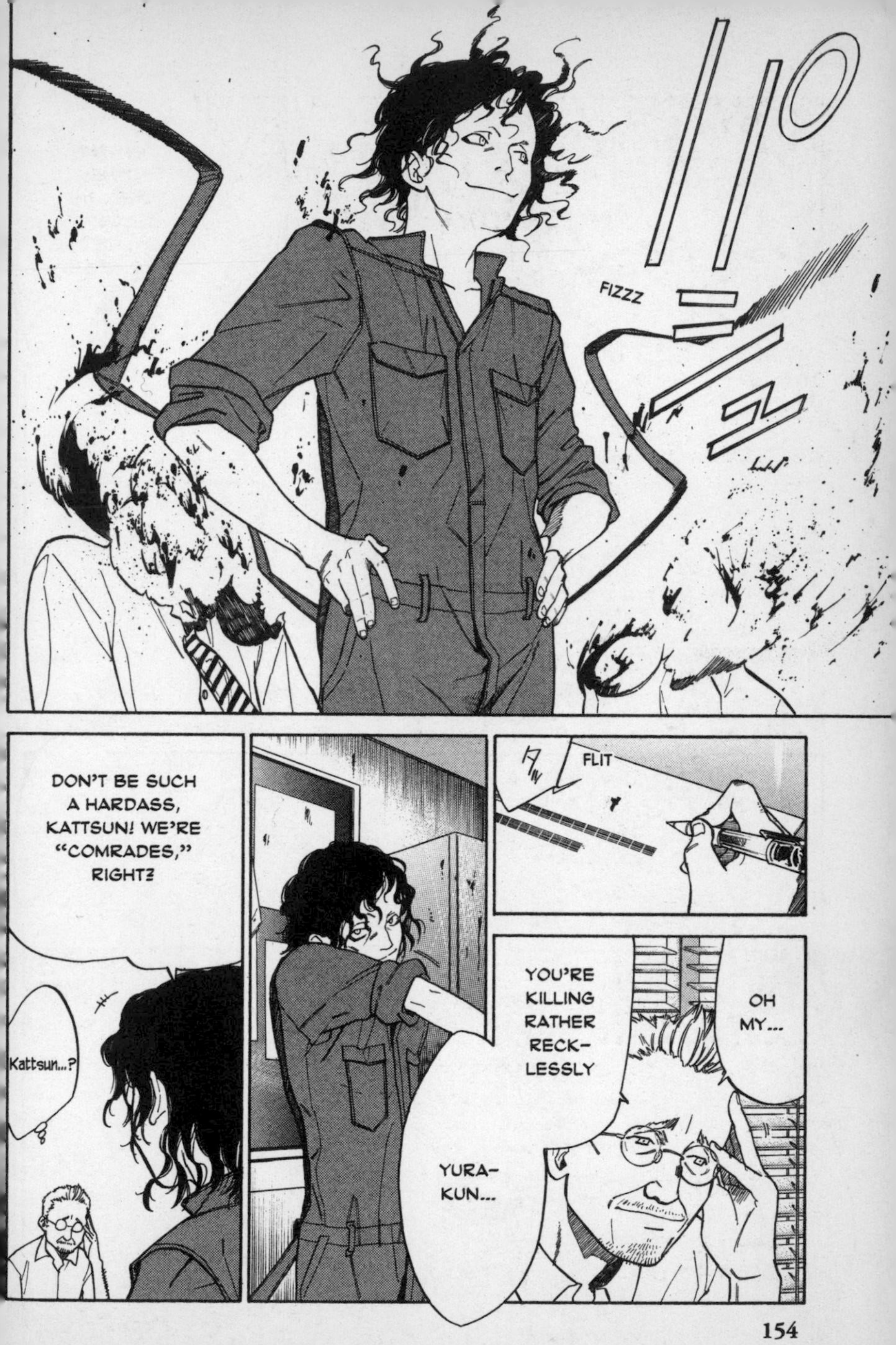
FIZZZ
FLIT
OH MY...
YOU'RE KILLING RATHER RECK-LESSLY
YURA-KUN...
DON'T BE SUCH A HARDASS, KATTSUN! WE'RE "COMRADES," RIGHT?
Kattsun...?

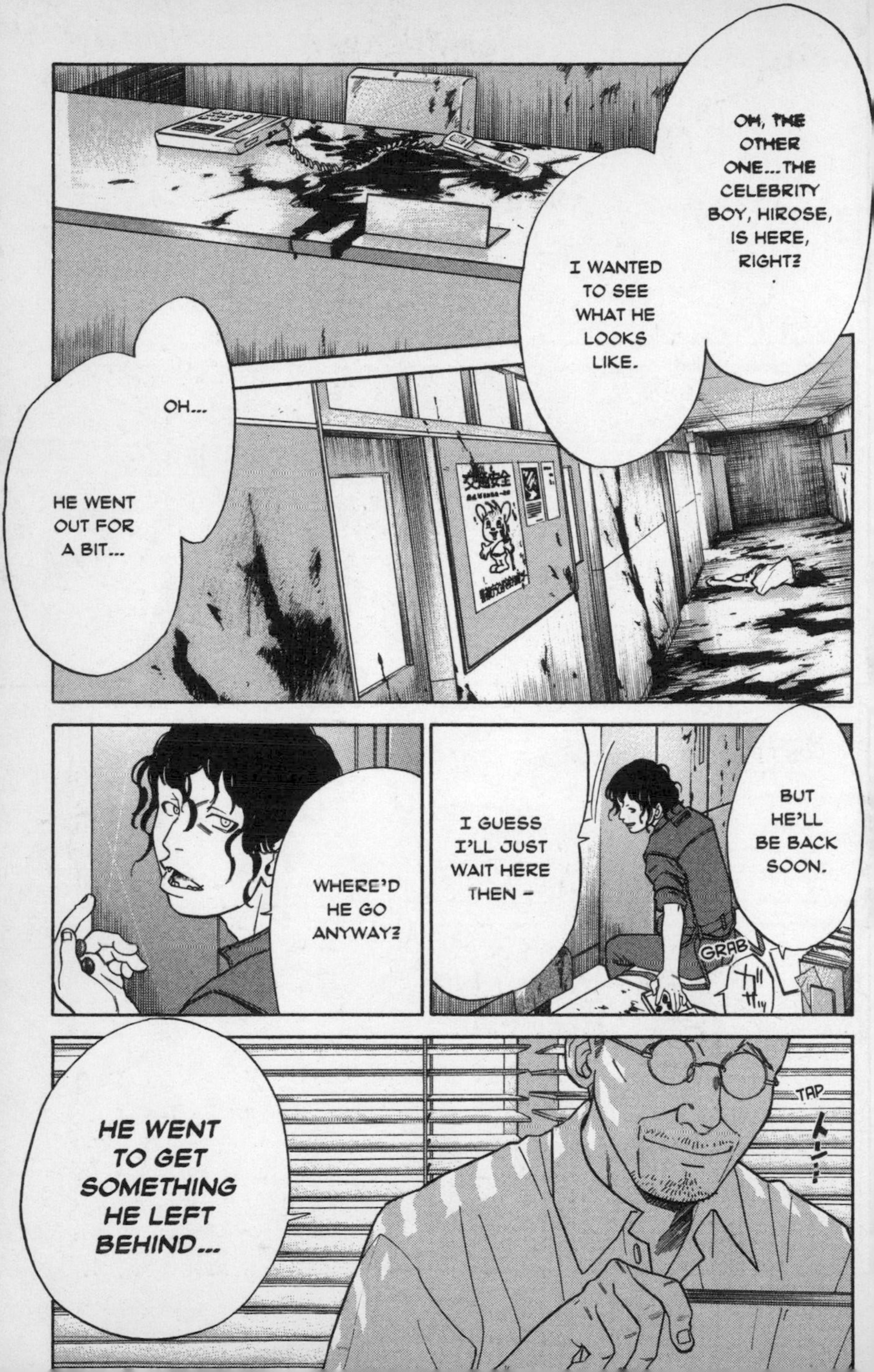
OH, THE OTHER ONE...THE CELEBRITY BOY, HIROSE, IS HERE, RIGHT?
I WANTED TO SEE WHAT HE LOOKS LIKE.
OH...
HE WENT OUT FOR A BIT...
BUT HE'LL BE BACK SOON.
I GUESS I'LL JUST WAIT HERE THEN –
GRAB
WHERE'D HE GO ANYWAY?
TAP
HE WENT TO GET SOMETHING HE LEFT BEHIND...

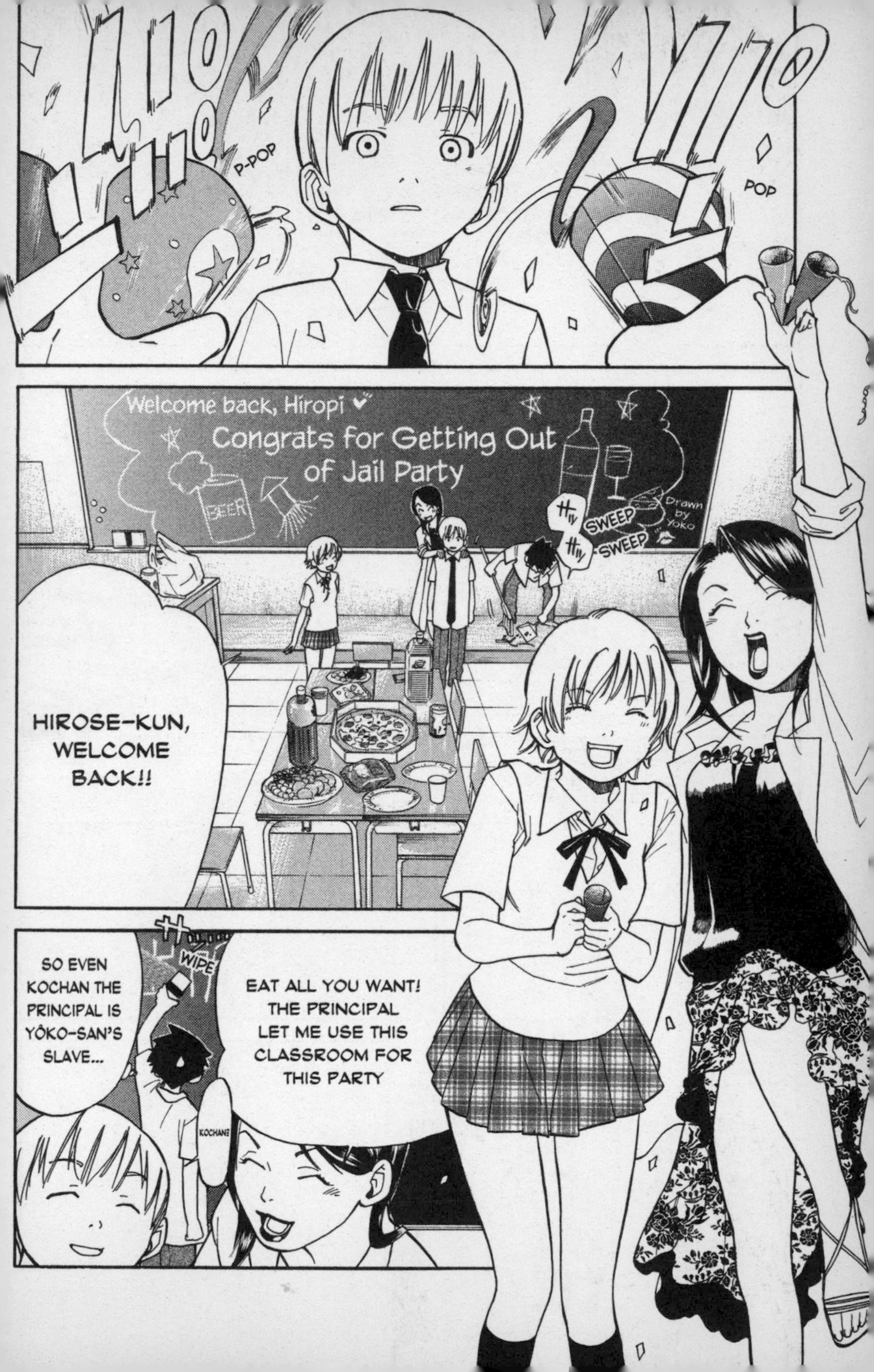

POP
P-POP
Welcome back, Hiropi
Congrats for Getting Out of Jail Party
BEER
Drawn by Yoko
SWEEP SWEEP
HIROSE-KUN, WELCOME BACK!!
EAT ALL YOU WANT! THE PRINCIPAL LET ME USE THIS CLASSROOM FOR THIS PARTY
KOCHAN?
WIPE
SO EVEN KOCHAN THE PRINCIPAL IS YÔKO-SAN'S SLAVE...

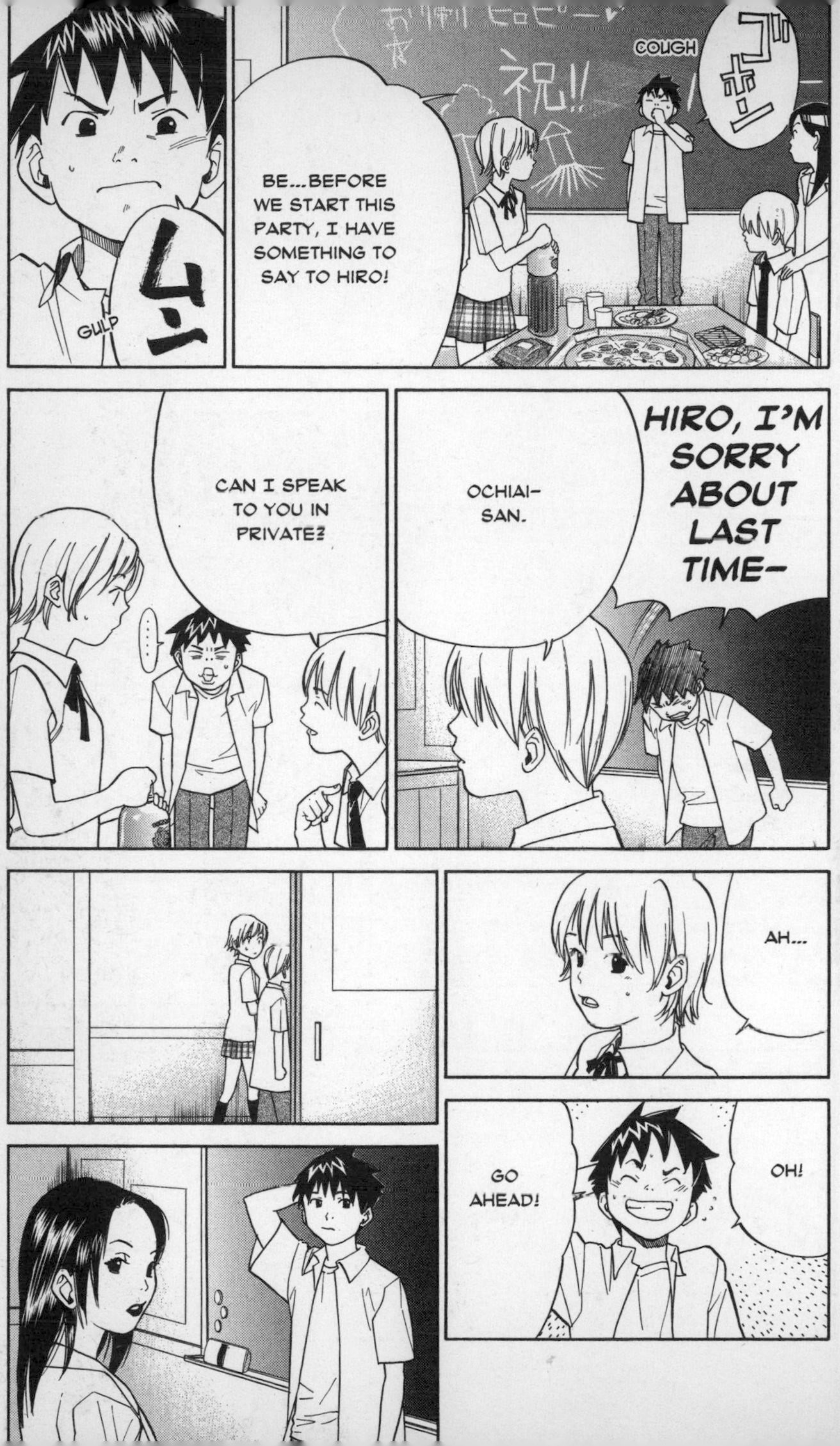
COUGH
BE...BEFORE WE START THIS PARTY, I HAVE SOMETHING TO SAY TO HIRO!
GULP
HIRO, I'M SORRY ABOUT LAST TIME—
OCHIAI-SAN.
CAN I SPEAK TO YOU IN PRIVATE?
......
AH...
OH!
GO AHEAD!

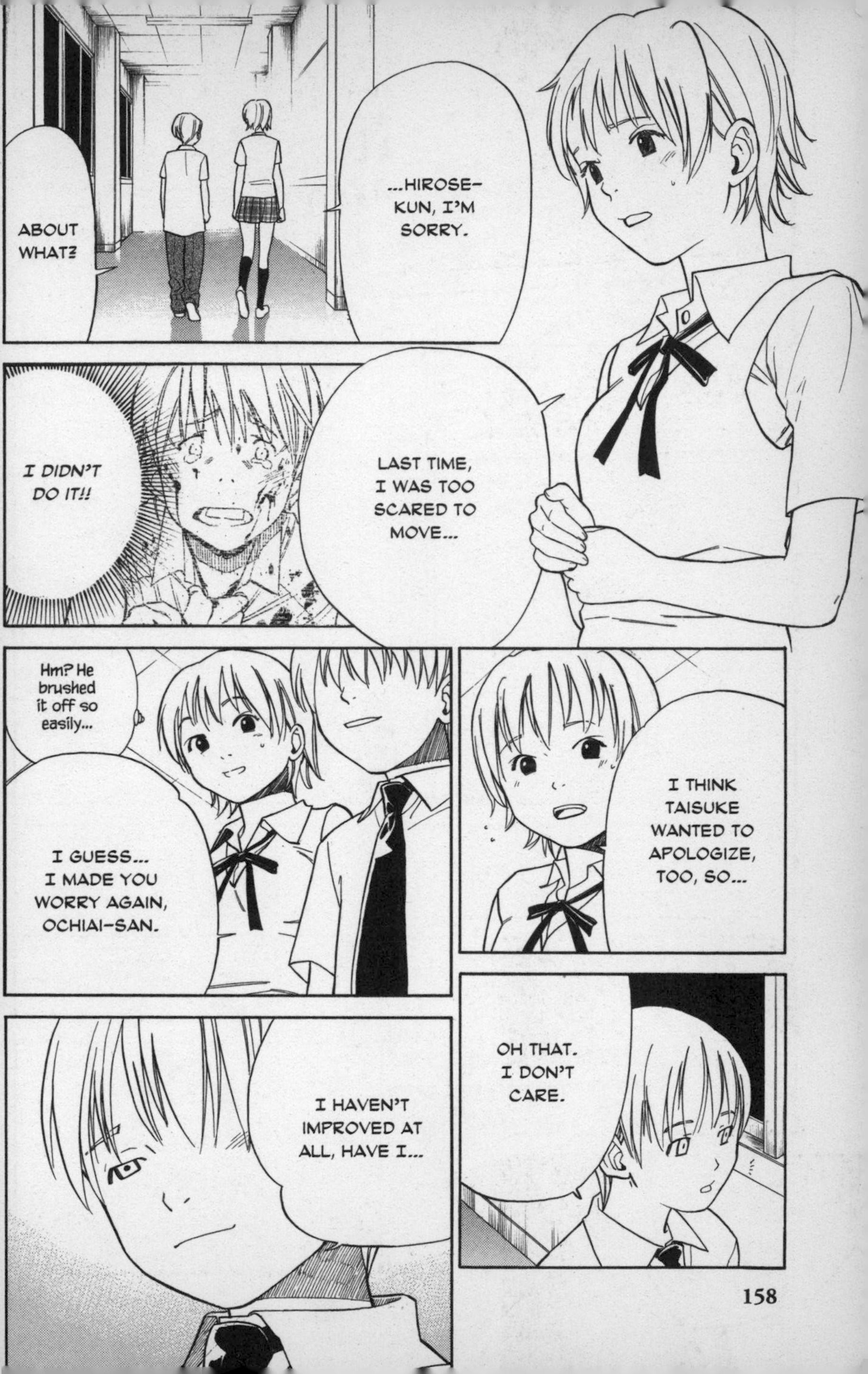
...HIROSE-KUN, I'M SORRY.
ABOUT WHAT?
I DIDN'T DO IT!!
LAST TIME, I WAS TOO SCARED TO MOVE...
I THINK TAISUKE WANTED TO APOLOGIZE, TOO, SO...
Hm? He brushed it off so easily...
I GUESS... I MADE YOU WORRY AGAIN, OCHIAI-SAN.
OH THAT. I DON'T CARE.
I HAVEN'T IMPROVED AT ALL, HAVE I...

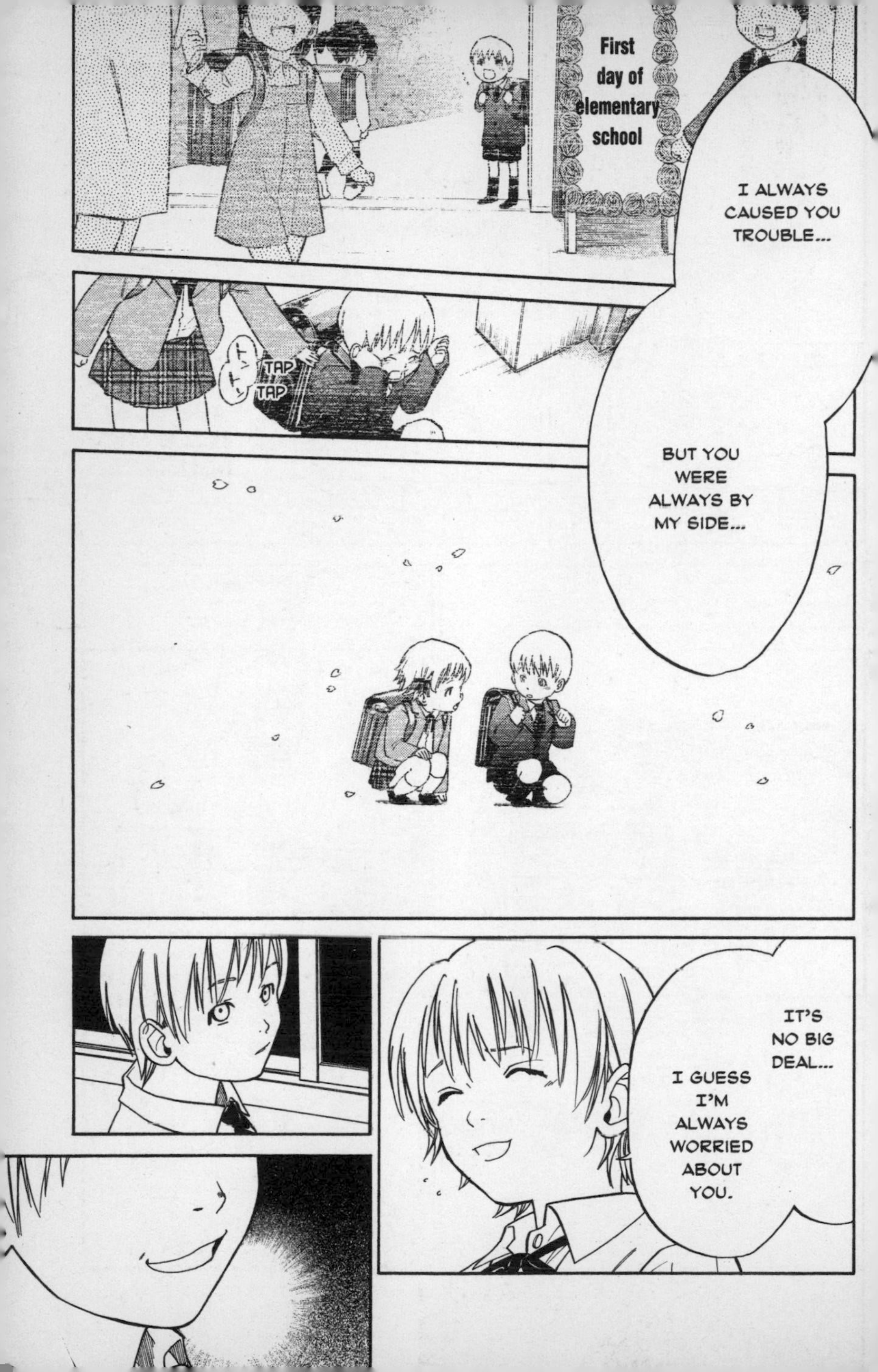
First day of elementary school
I ALWAYS CAUSED YOU TROUBLE...
TAP TAP
BUT YOU WERE ALWAYS BY MY SIDE...
IT'S NO BIG DEAL...
I GUESS I'M ALWAYS WORRIED ABOUT YOU.

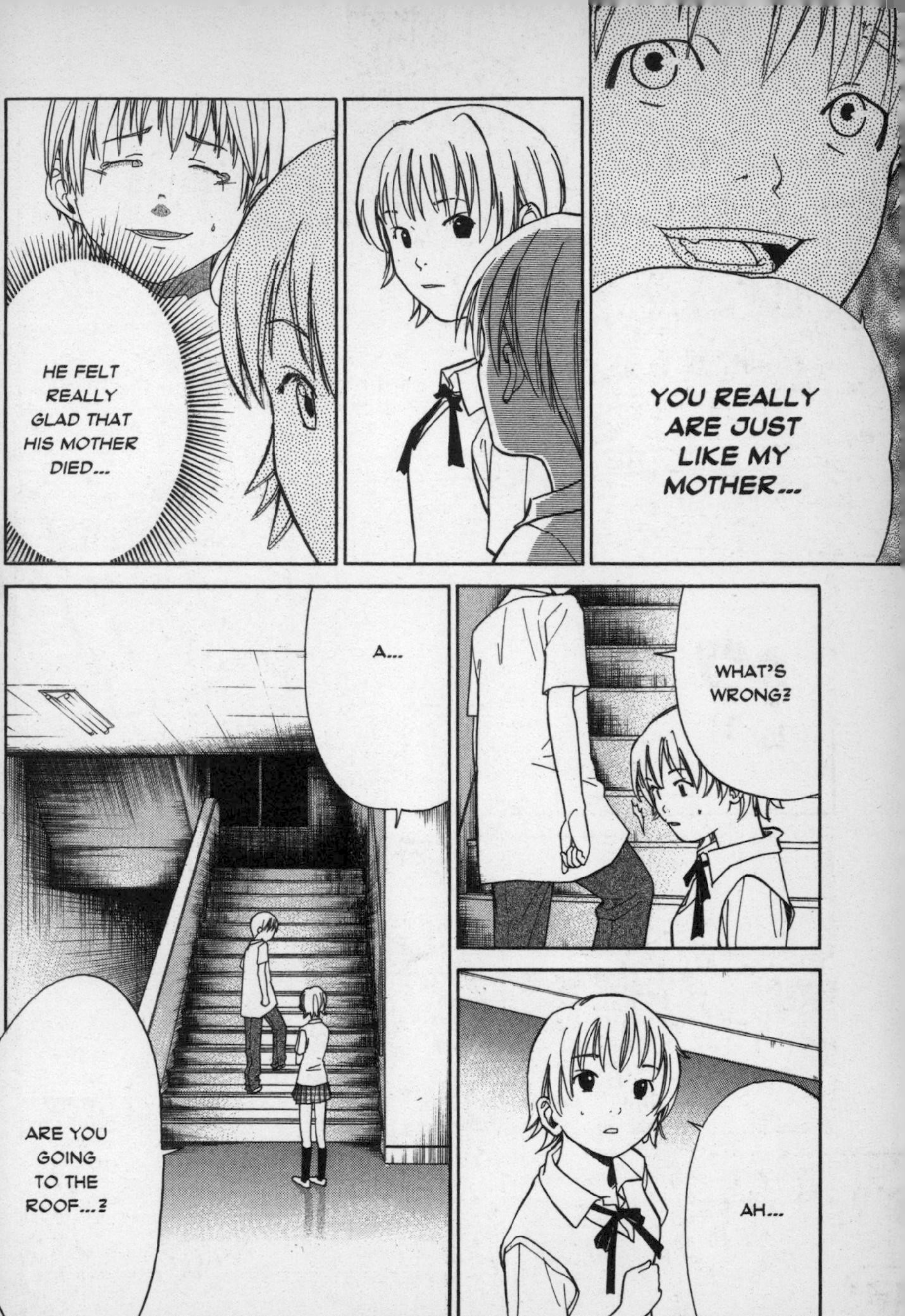
YOU REALLY ARE JUST LIKE MY MOTHER...
HE FELT REALLY GLAD THAT HIS MOTHER DIED...
WHAT'S WRONG?
AH...
A...
ARE YOU GOING TO THE ROOF...?

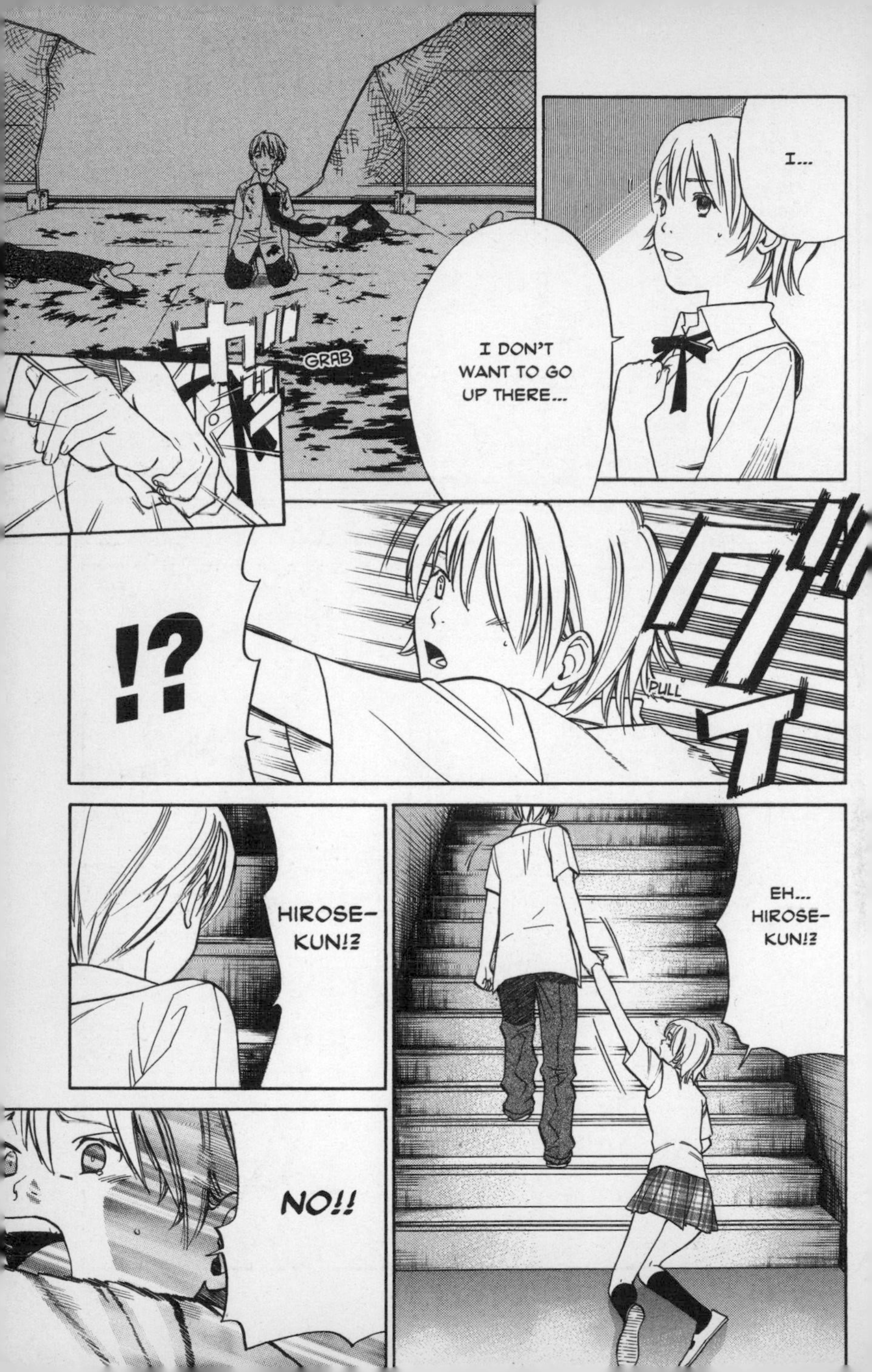
I...
I DON'T WANT TO GO UP THERE...
GRAB
PULL
!?
EH... HIROSE-KUN!?
HIROSE-KUN!?
NO!!

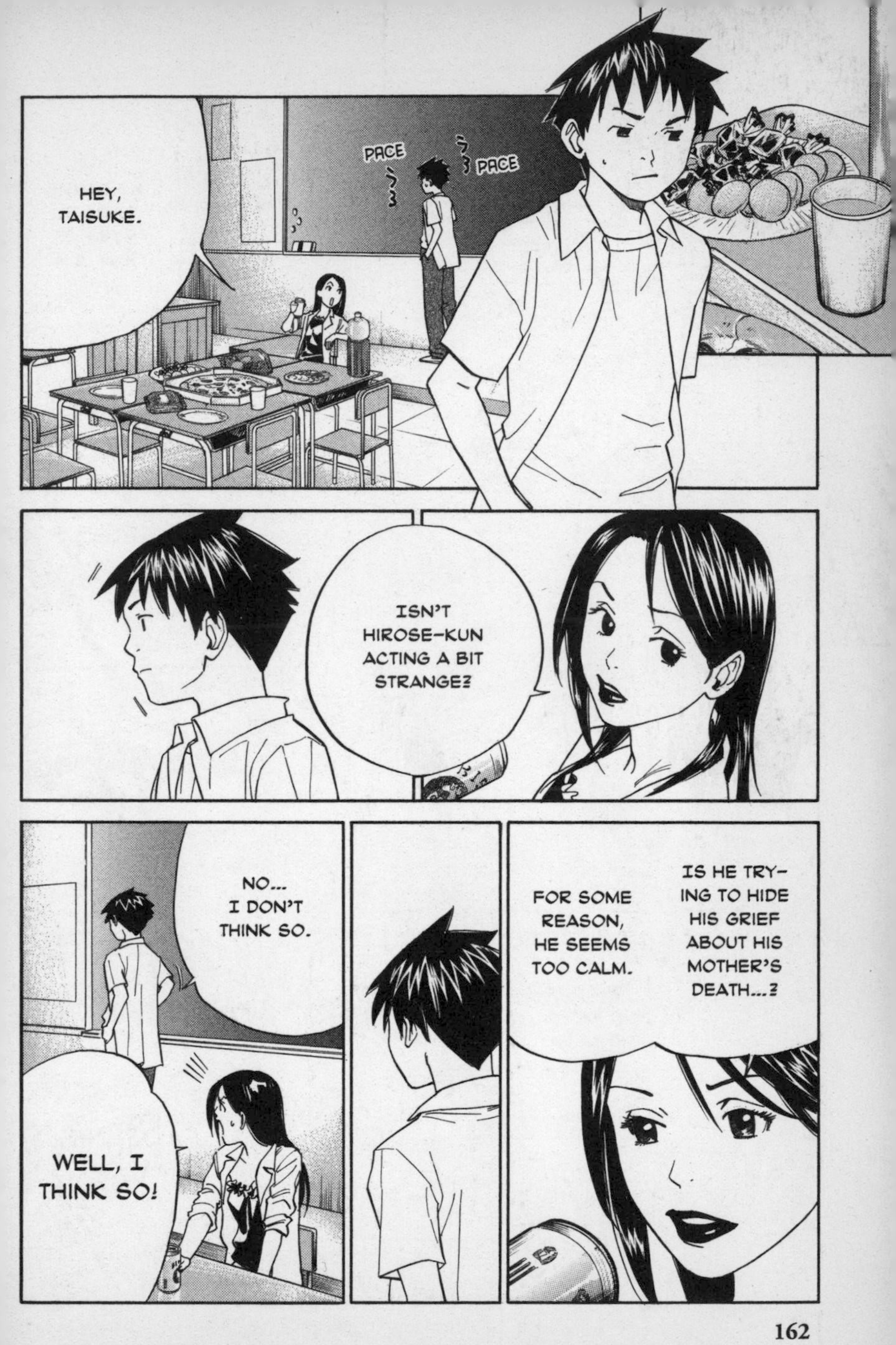
PACE
PACE
HEY, TAISUKE.
ISN'T HIROSE-KUN ACTING A BIT STRANGE?
FOR SOME REASON, HE SEEMS TOO CALM.
IS HE TRY-ING TO HIDE HIS GRIEF ABOUT HIS MOTHER'S DEATH...?
NO... I DON'T THINK SO.
WELL, I THINK SO!

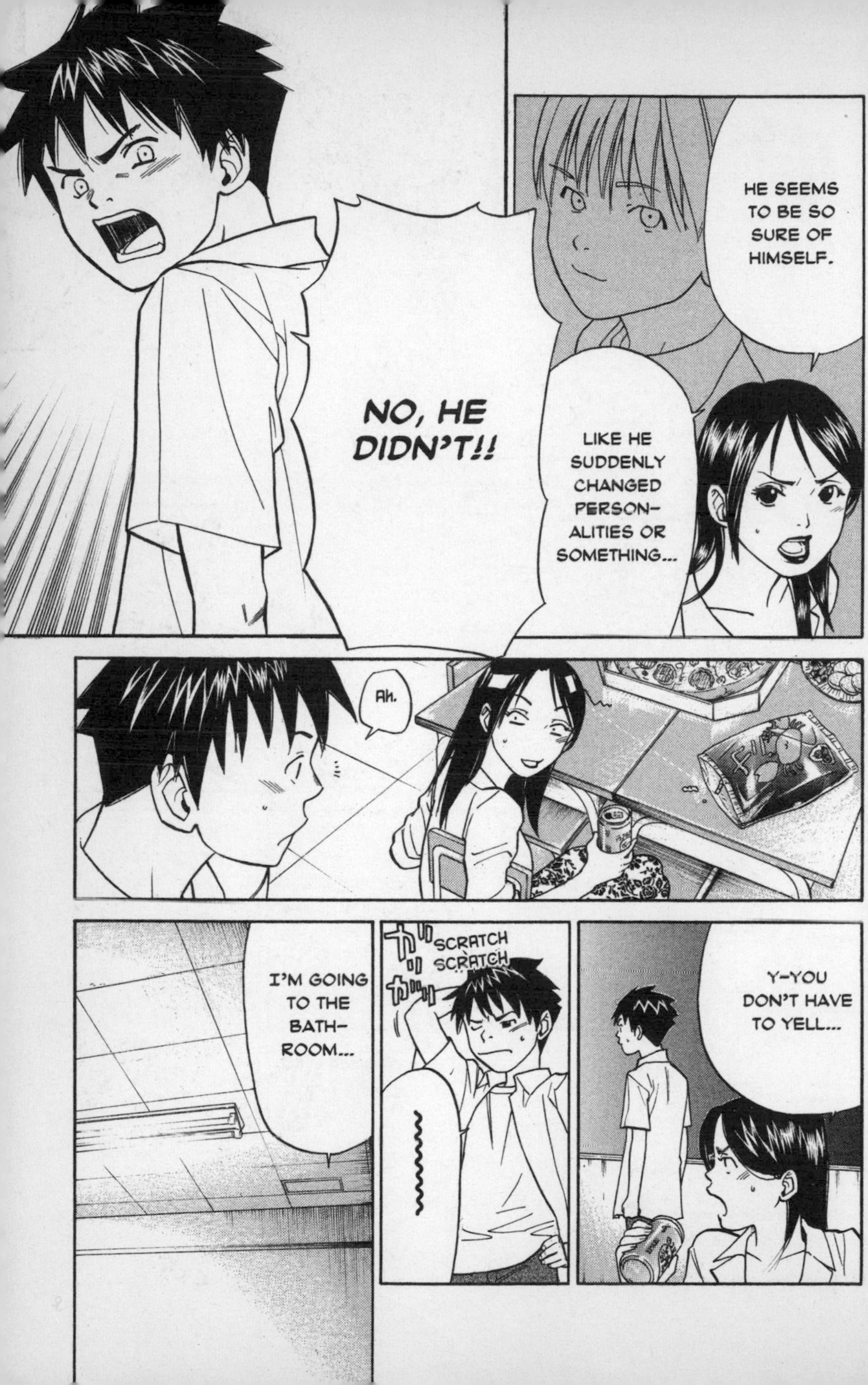
HE SEEMS TO BE SO SURE OF HIMSELF.
LIKE HE SUDDENLY CHANGED PERSON-ALITIES OR SOMETHING...
NO, HE DIDN'T!!
Ah.
Y-YOU DON'T HAVE TO YELL...
SCRATCH SCRATCH
I'M GOING TO THE BATH-ROOM...

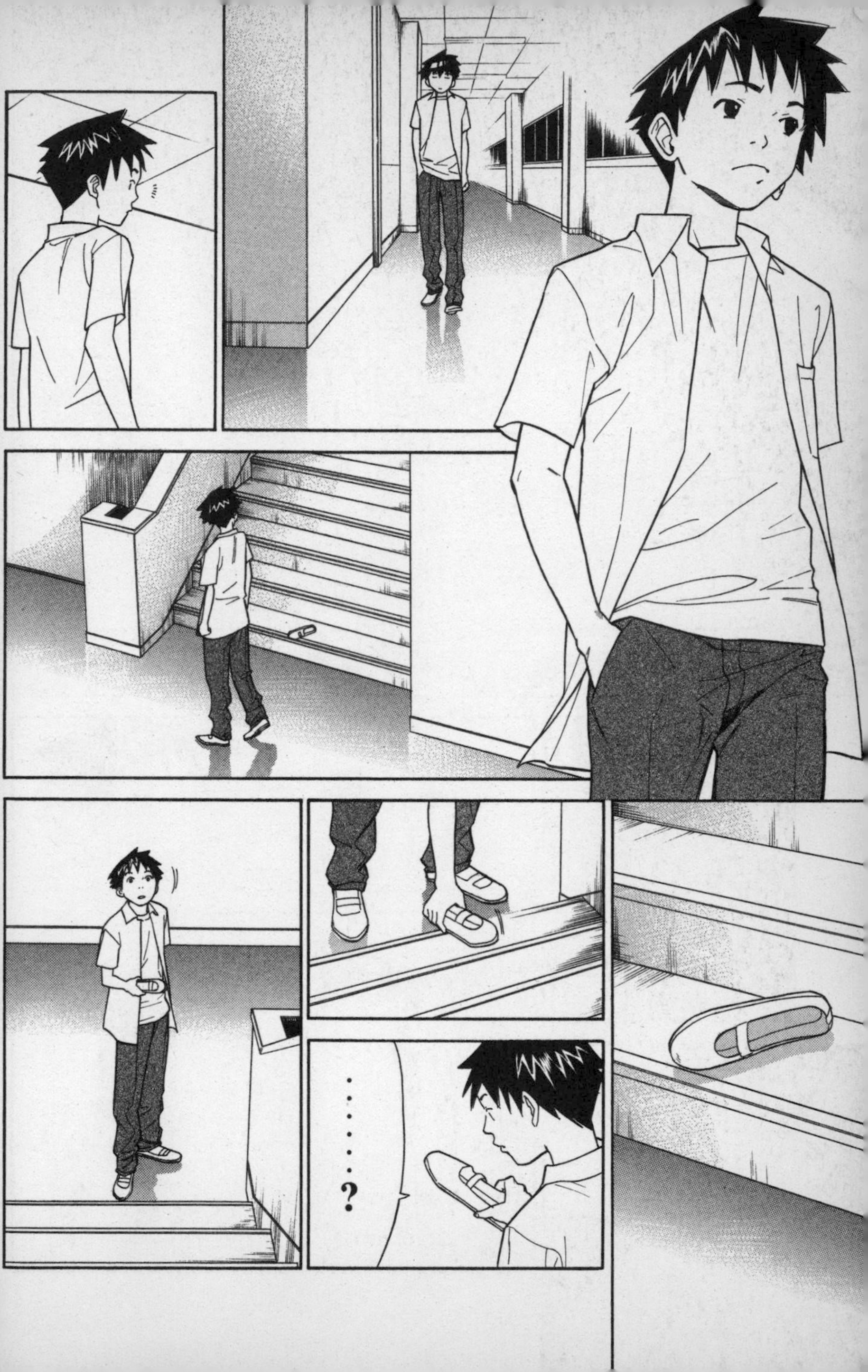
……?

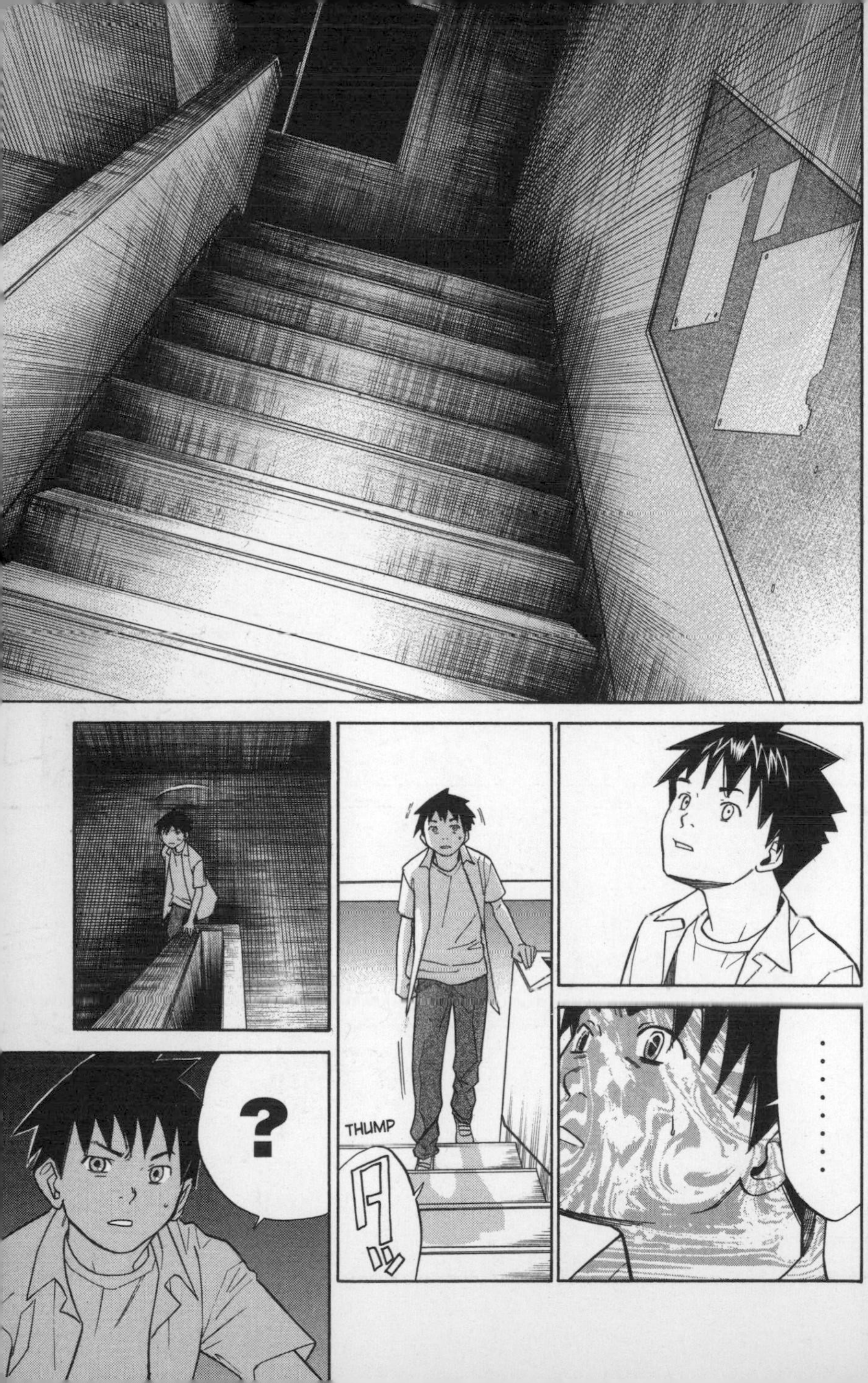

......
THUMP
?

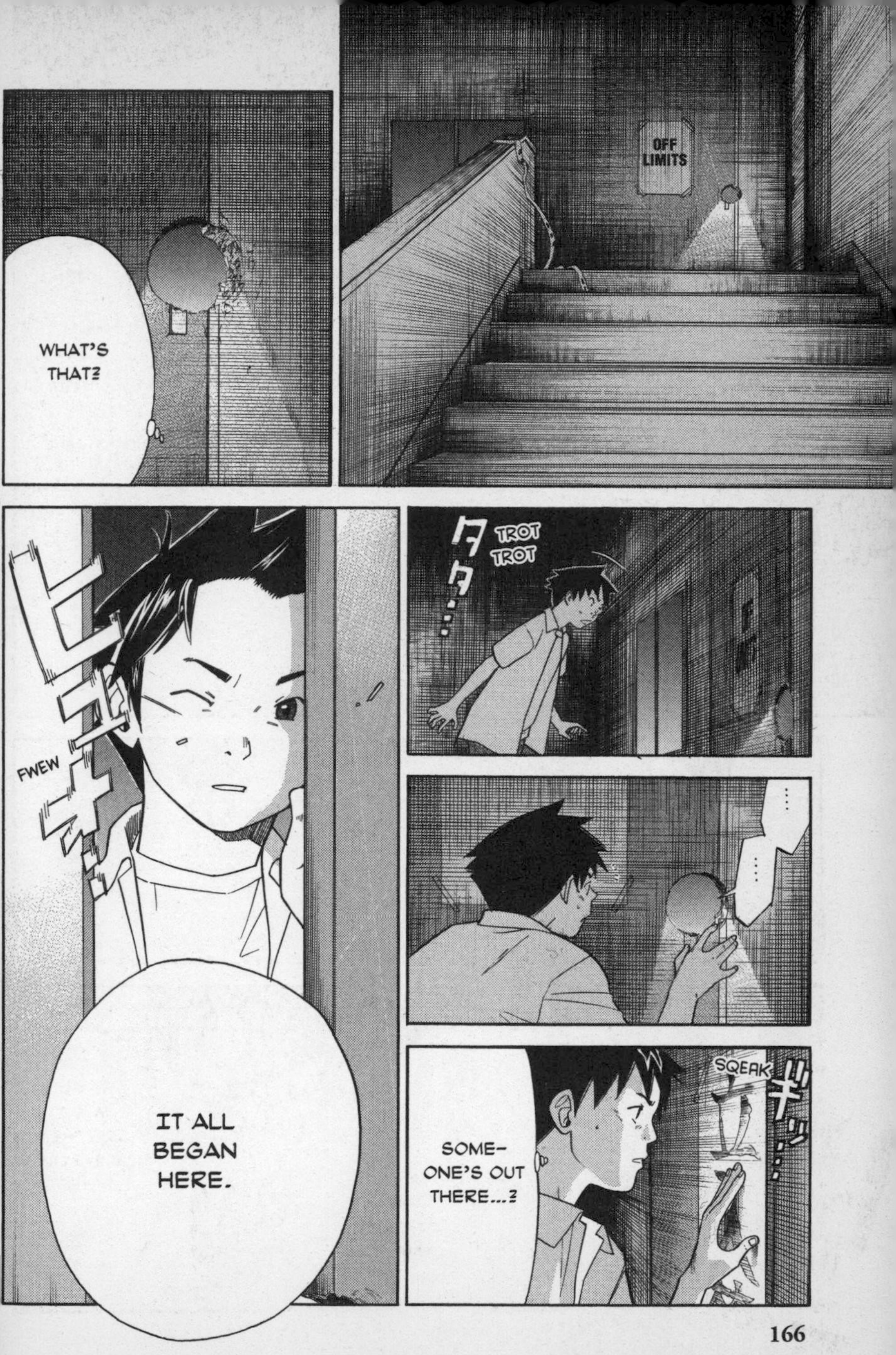
OFF LIMITS
WHAT'S THAT?
TROT TROT
......
......
SQEAK
SOME-ONE'S OUT THERE...?
FWEW
IT ALL BEGAN HERE.

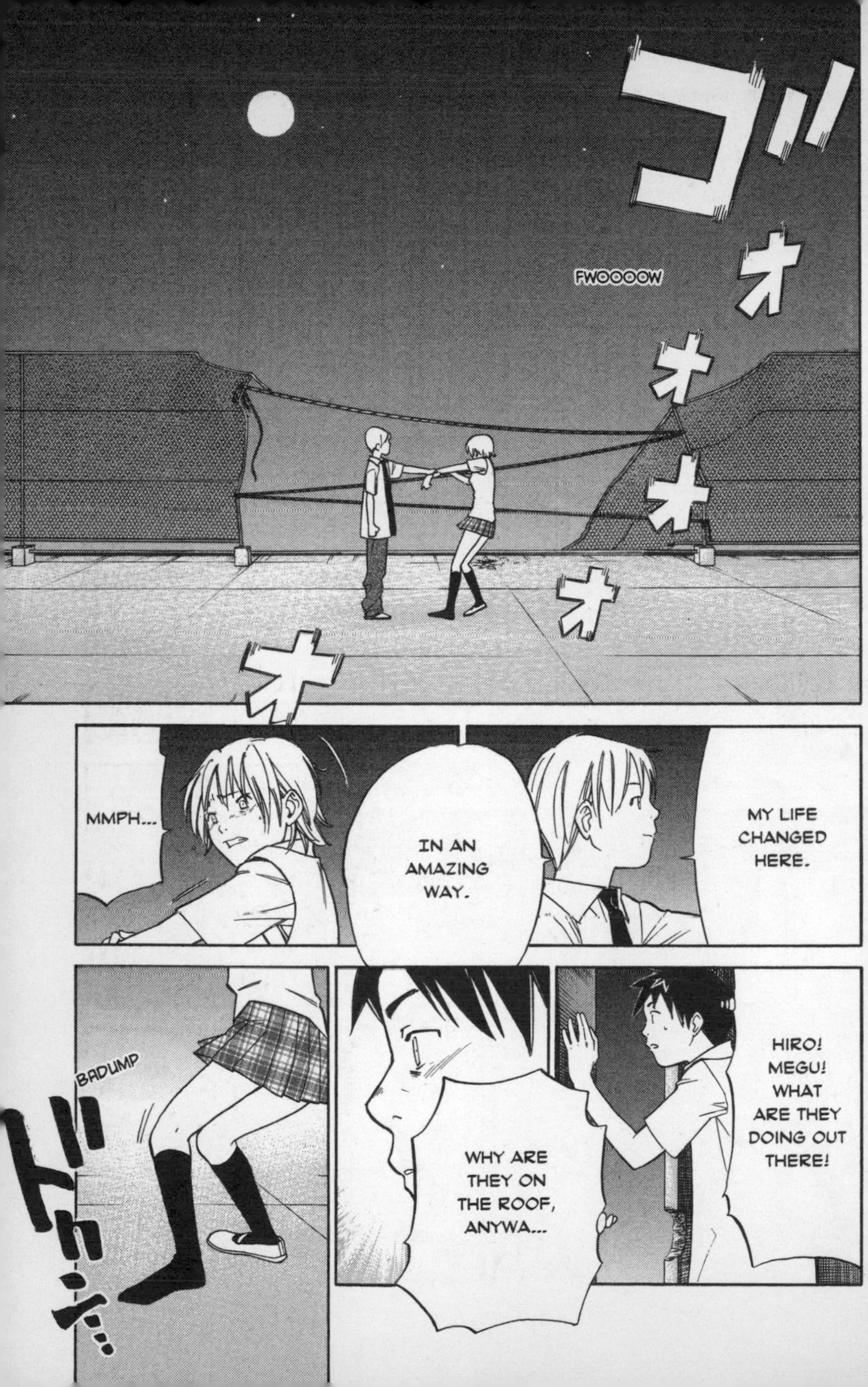
FWOOOOW
MY LIFE CHANGED HERE.
IN AN AMAZING WAY.
MMPH...
HIRO! MEGU! WHAT ARE THEY DOING OUT THERE!
WHY ARE THEY ON THE ROOF, ANYWA...
BADUMP

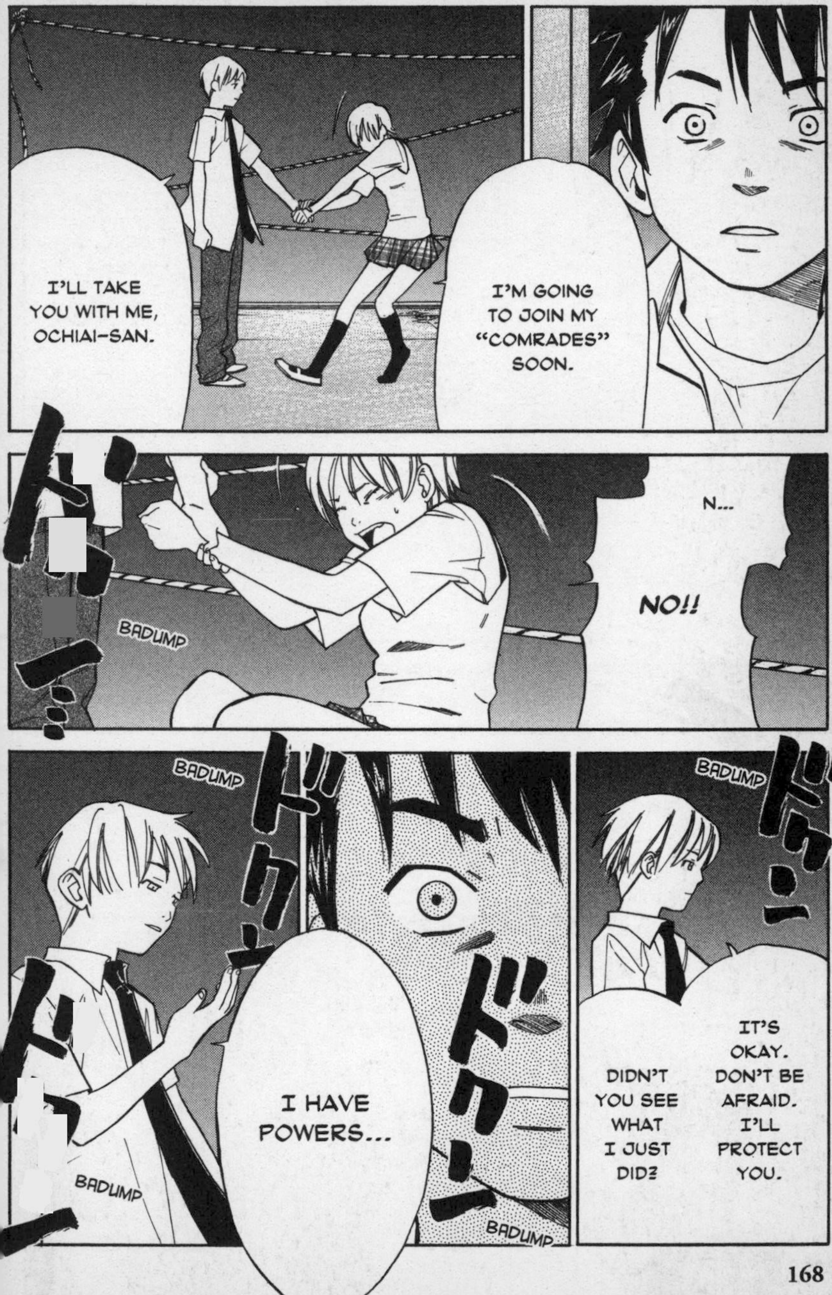
I'M GOING TO JOIN MY "COMRADES" SOON.
I'LL TAKE YOU WITH ME, OCHIAI-SAN.
N...
NO!!
BADUMP
BADUMP
IT'S OKAY. DON'T BE AFRAID. I'LL PROTECT YOU.
DIDN'T YOU SEE WHAT I JUST DID?
BADUMP
I HAVE POWERS...
BADUMP
BADUMP

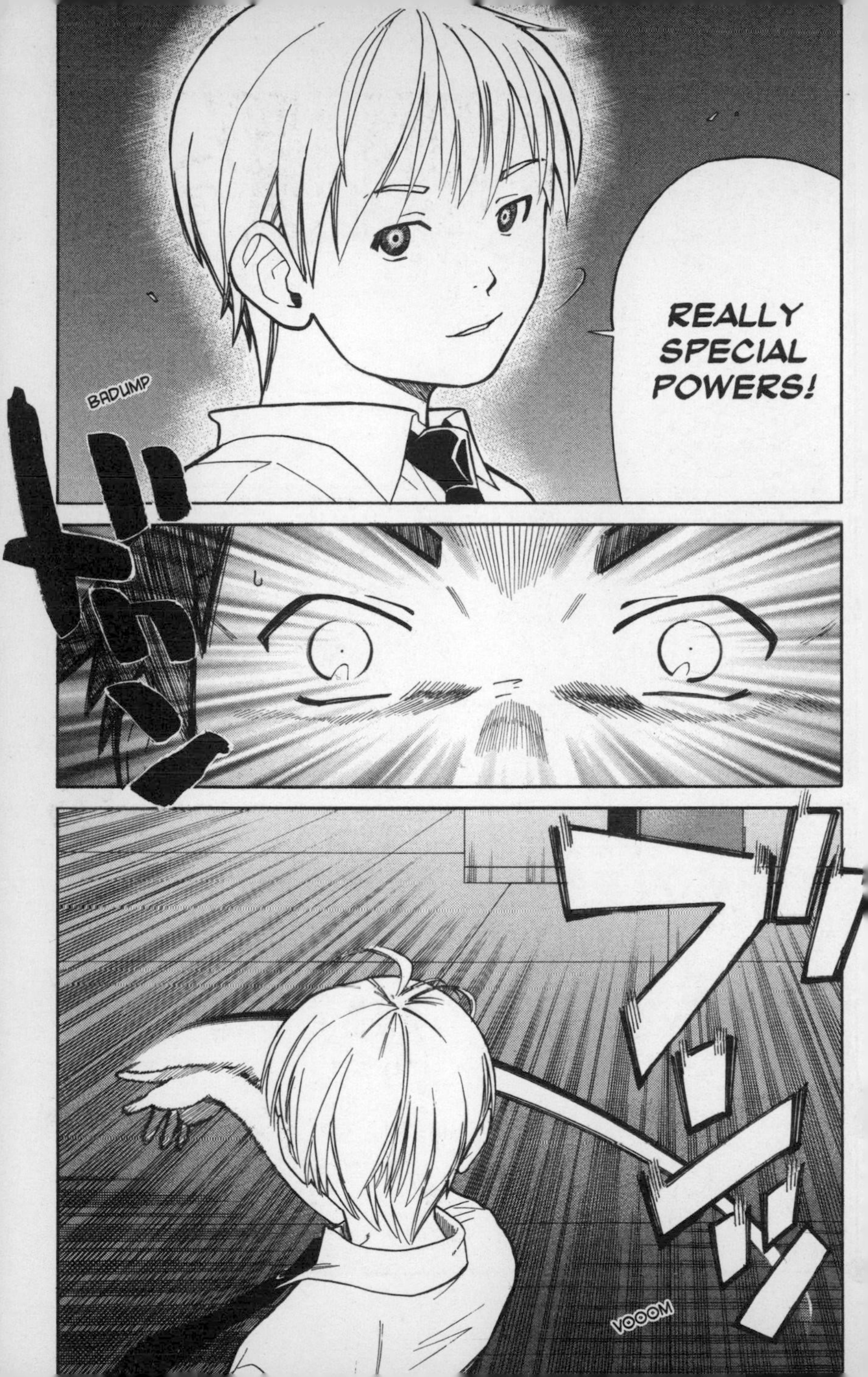
REALLY SPECIAL POWERS!
BADUMP
VOOOM

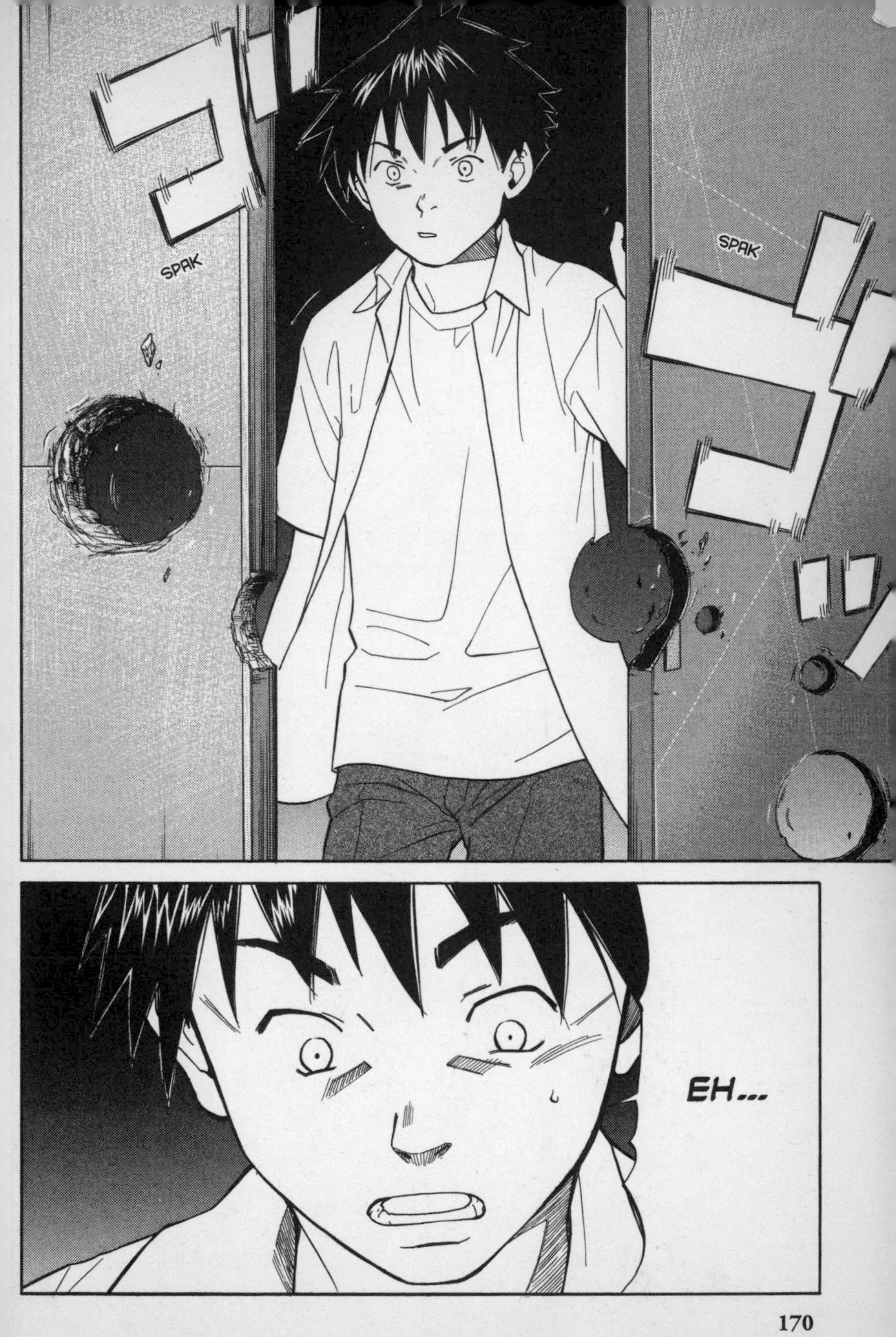
SPAK
SPAK
EH...

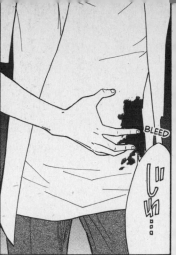

I CAN'T
CONTROL IT
WELL YET...

OH...
DID I
MISS?

TA....!?

BLEED

HNGHH...!

HNGH...

WOBBLE

WOBBLE

URRRGH...!

OW...

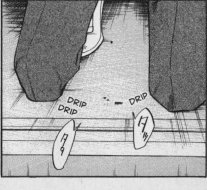

DRIP
DRIP

DRIP

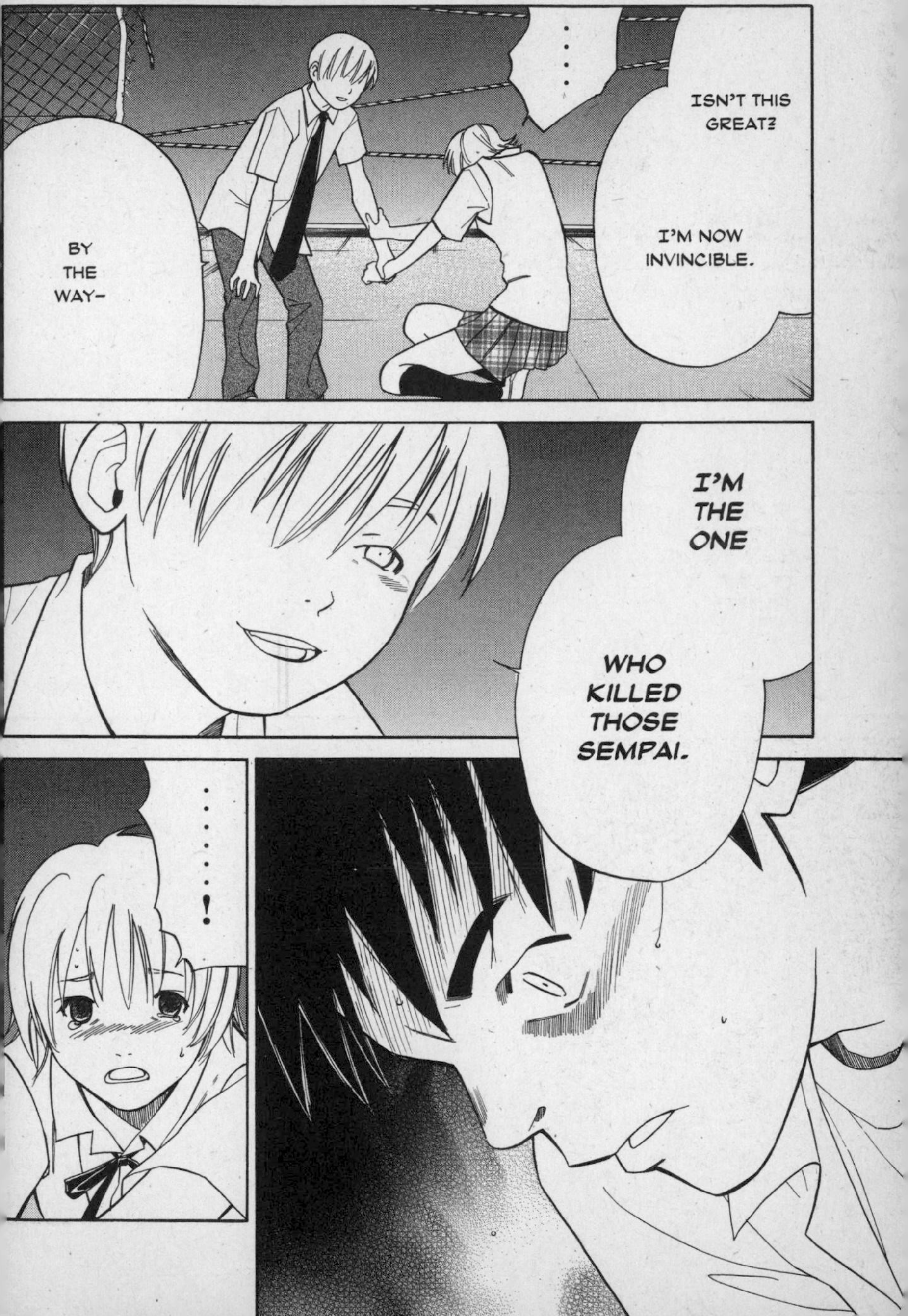
....
ISN'T THIS GREAT?
I'M NOW INVINCIBLE.
BY THE WAY-
I'M THE ONE
WHO KILLED THOSE SEMPAI.
.......!

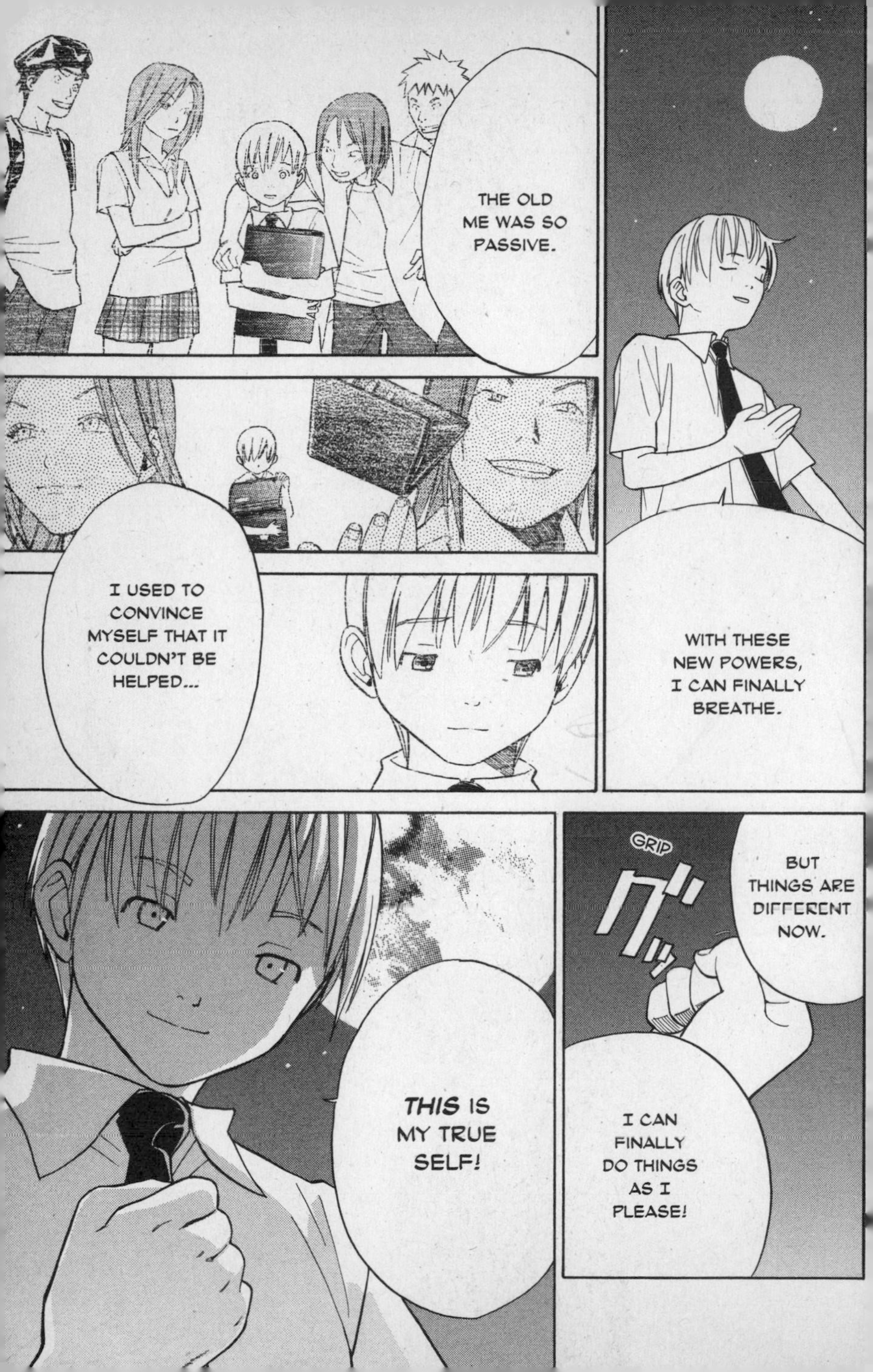
WITH THESE NEW POWERS, I CAN FINALLY BREATHE.
THE OLD ME WAS SO PASSIVE.
I USED TO CONVINCE MYSELF THAT IT COULDN'T BE HELPED...
BUT THINGS ARE DIFFERENT NOW.
GRIP
グッ
I CAN FINALLY DO THINGS AS I PLEASE!
THIS IS MY TRUE SELF!

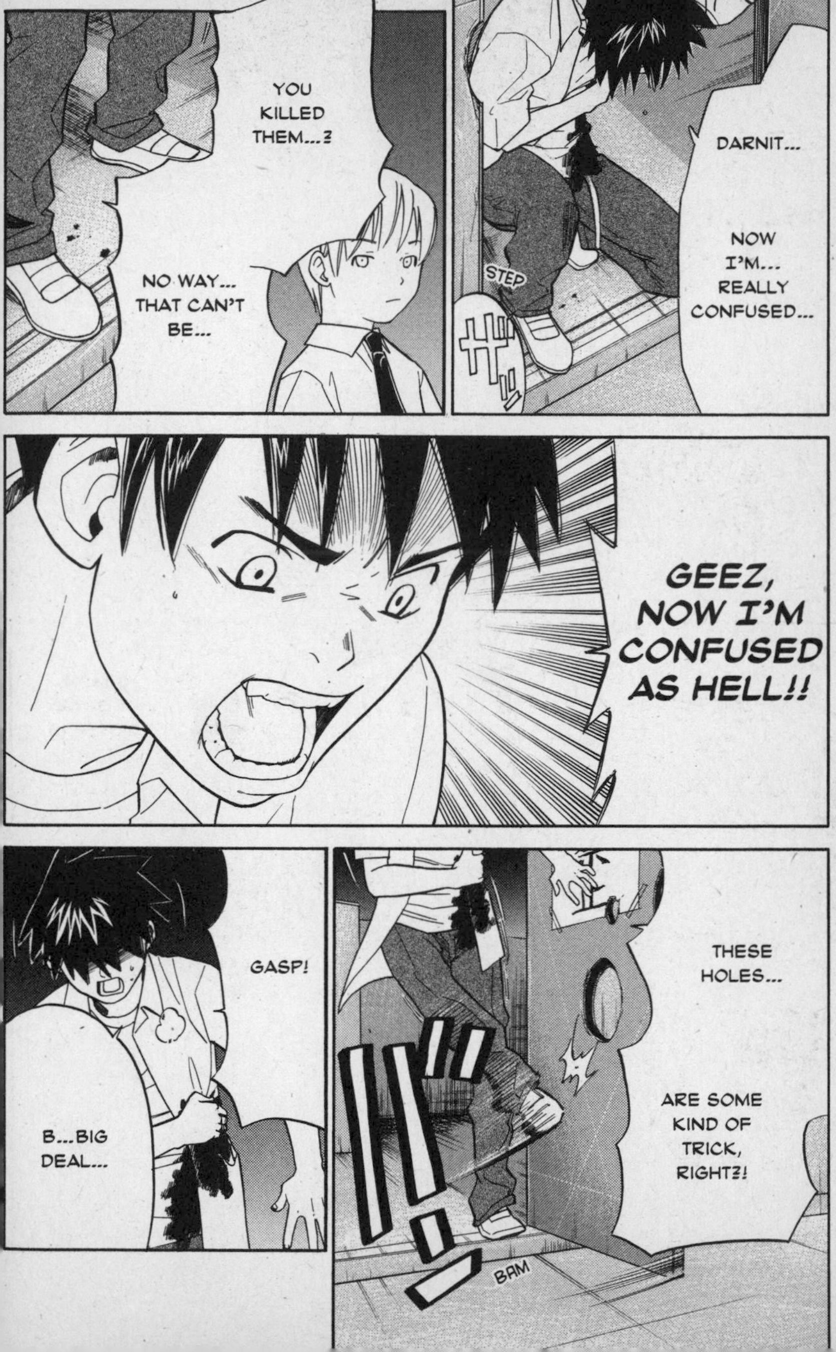
DARNIT...
NOW I'M... REALLY CONFUSED...
STEP
YOU KILLED THEM...?
NO WAY... THAT CAN'T BE...
GEEZ, NOW I'M CONFUSED AS HELL!!
THESE HOLES...
ARE SOME KIND OF TRICK, RIGHT?!
BAM
GASP!
B...BIG DEAL...

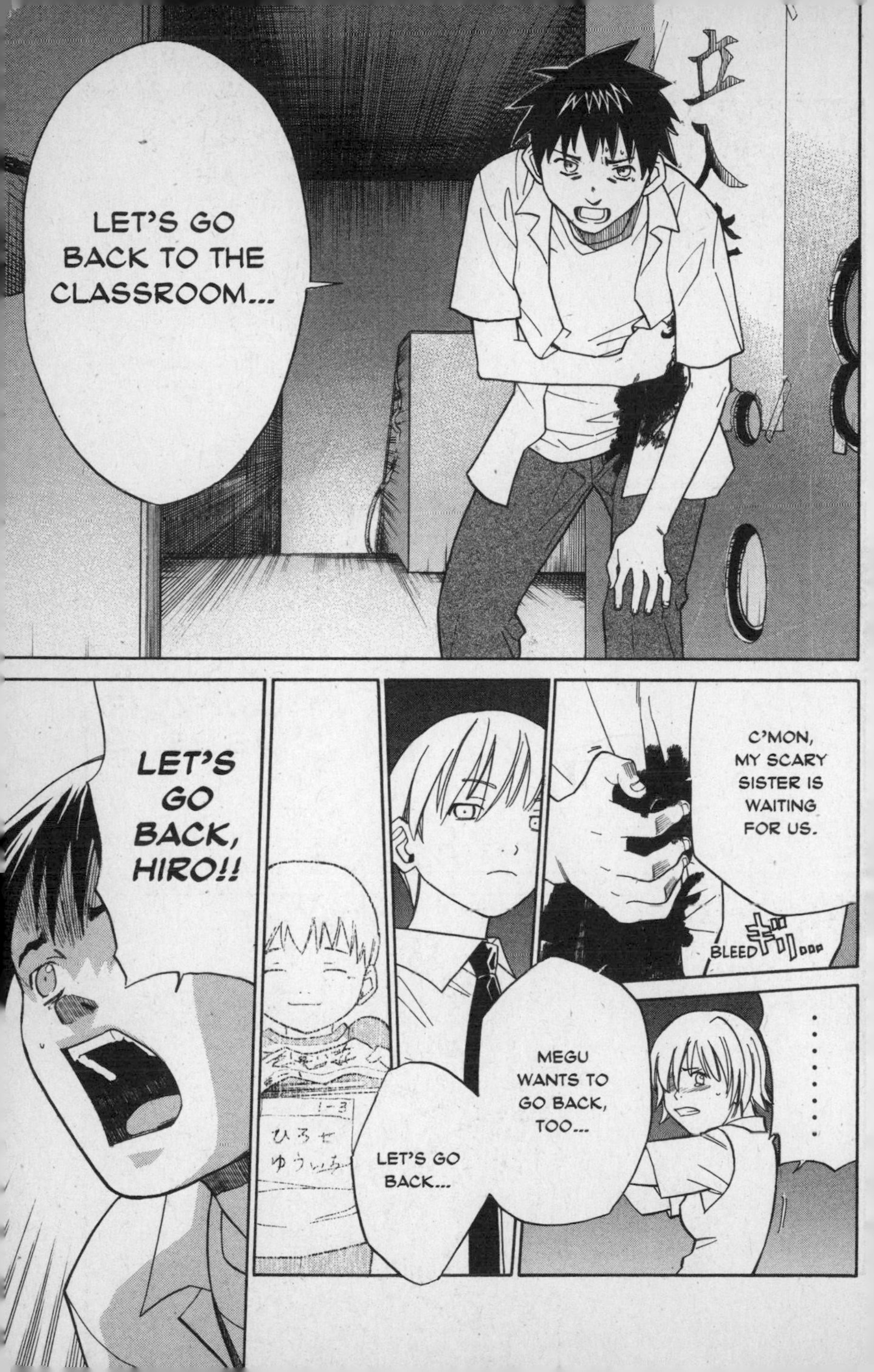
LET'S GO BACK TO THE CLASSROOM...
C'MON, MY SCARY SISTER IS WAITING FOR US.
BLEED ギリ...
......
MEGU WANTS TO GO BACK, TOO...
LET'S GO BACK...
LET'S GO BACK, HIRO!!

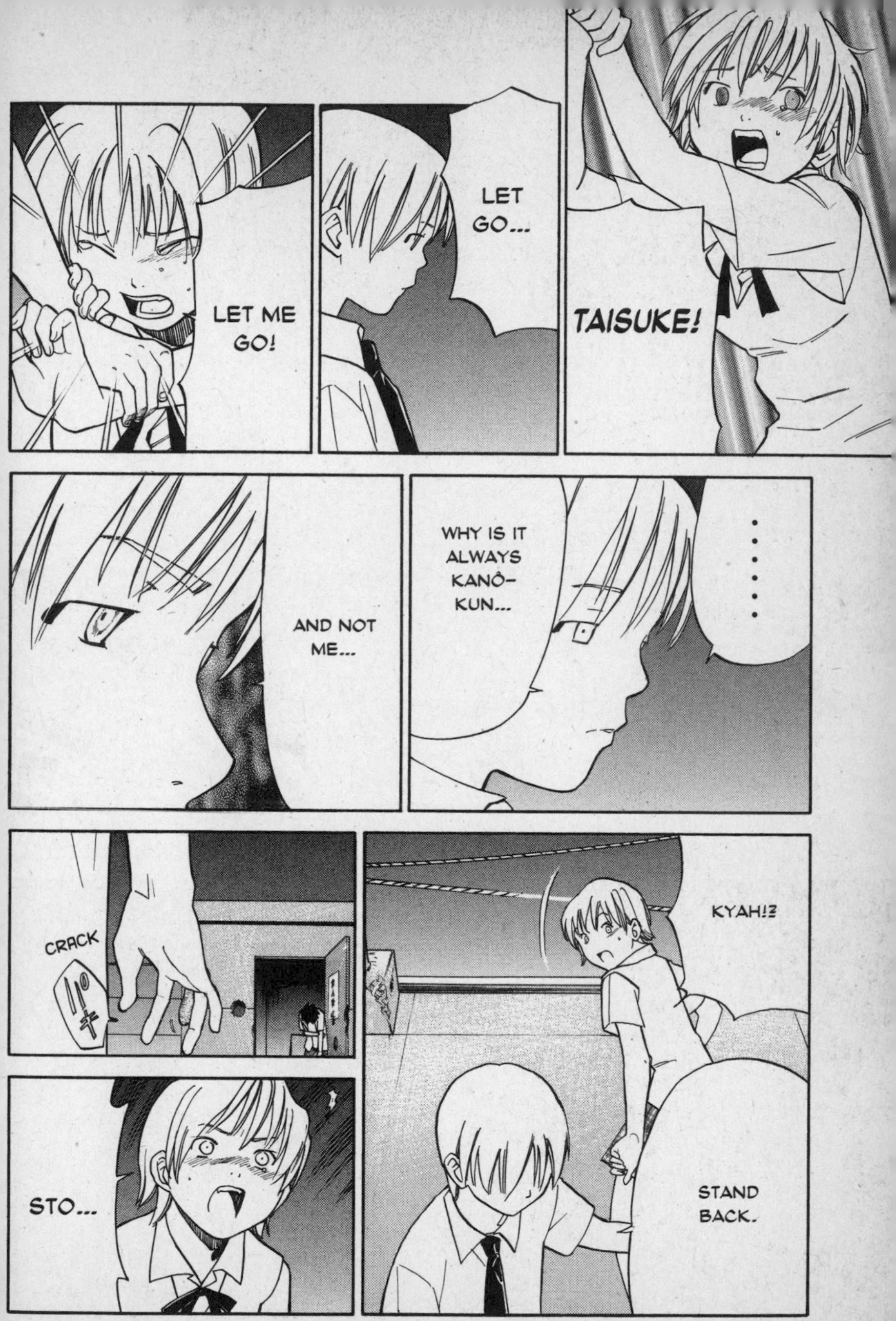
TAISUKE!
LET GO...
LET ME GO!
......
WHY IS IT ALWAYS KANÔ-KUN...
AND NOT ME...
KYAH!?
STAND BACK.
CRACK
パキ
STO...

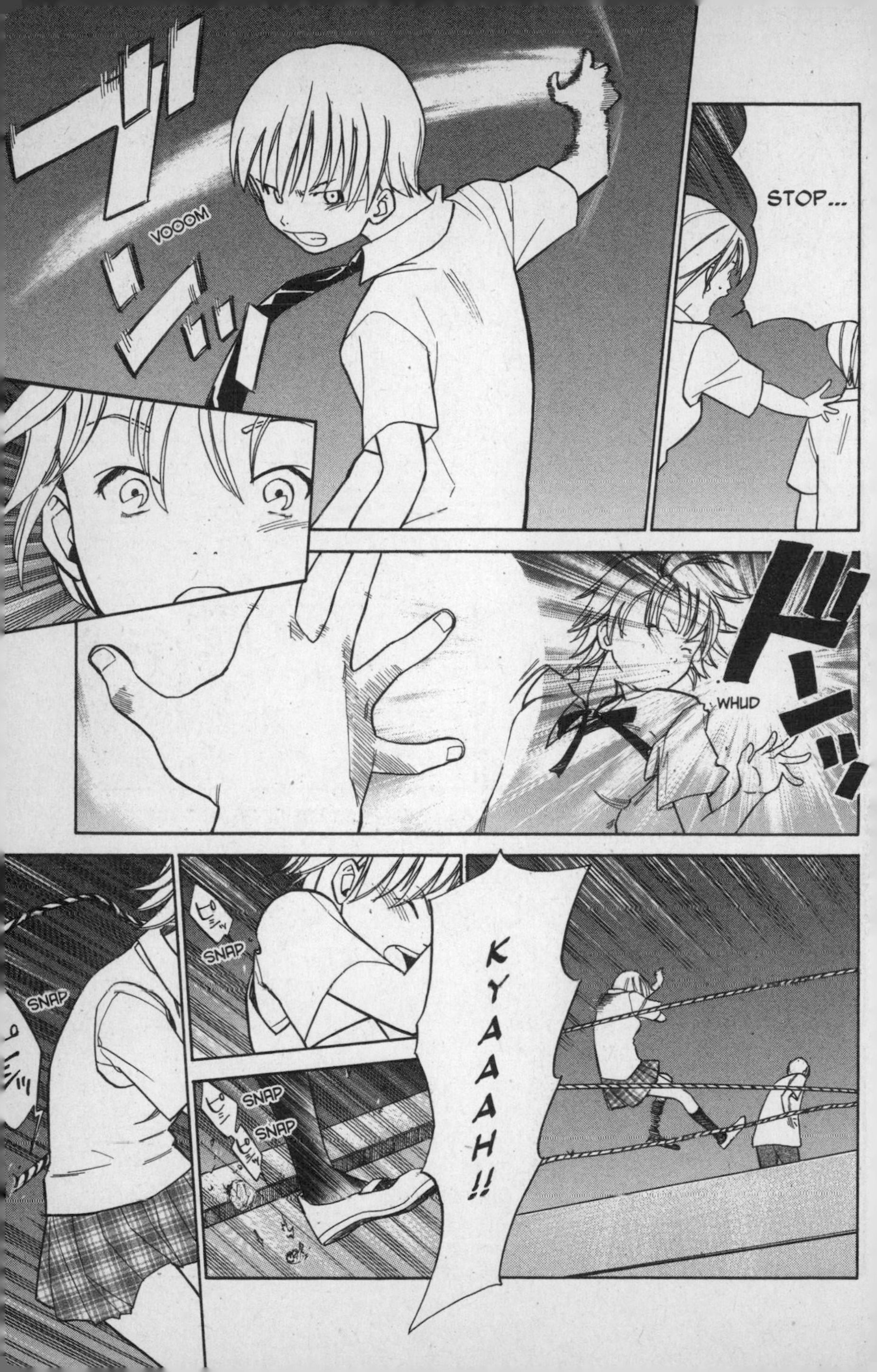
STOP...
VOOOM
WHUD
KYAAAH!!
SNAP
SNAP
SNAP
SNAP

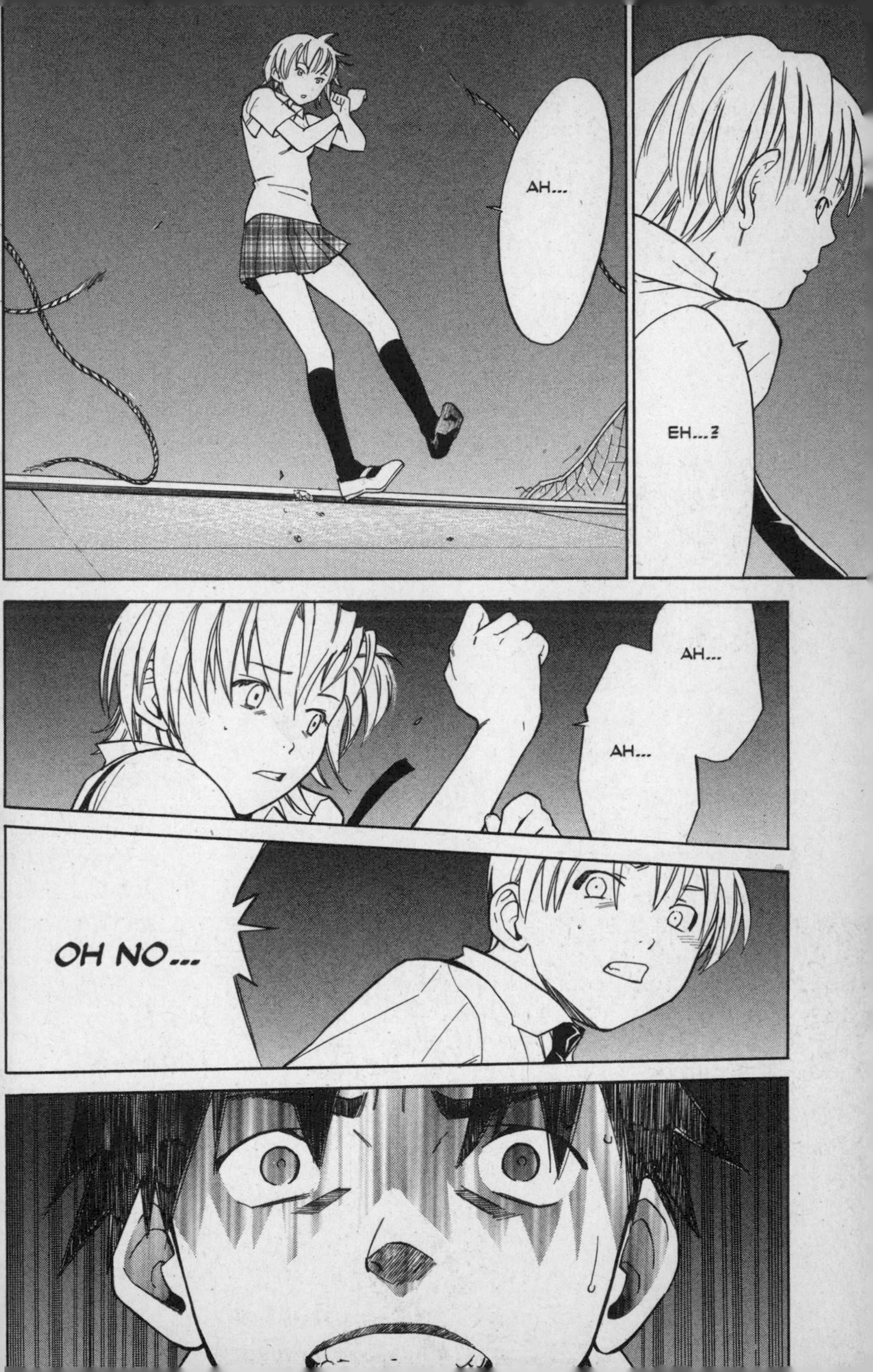
EH...?
AH...
AH...
AH...
OH NO...

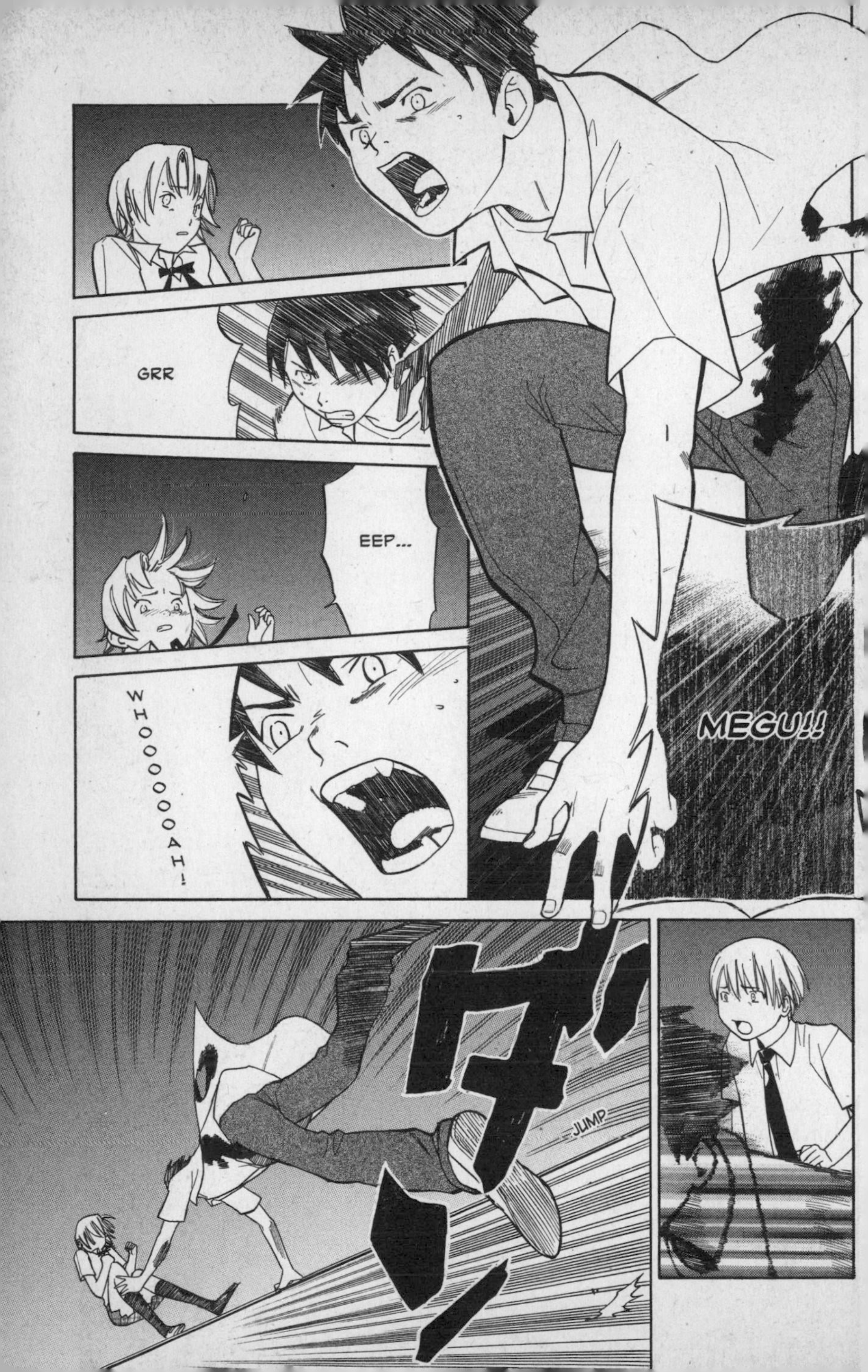
MEGU!!
GRR
EEP...
WHOOOOOOAH!
JUMP

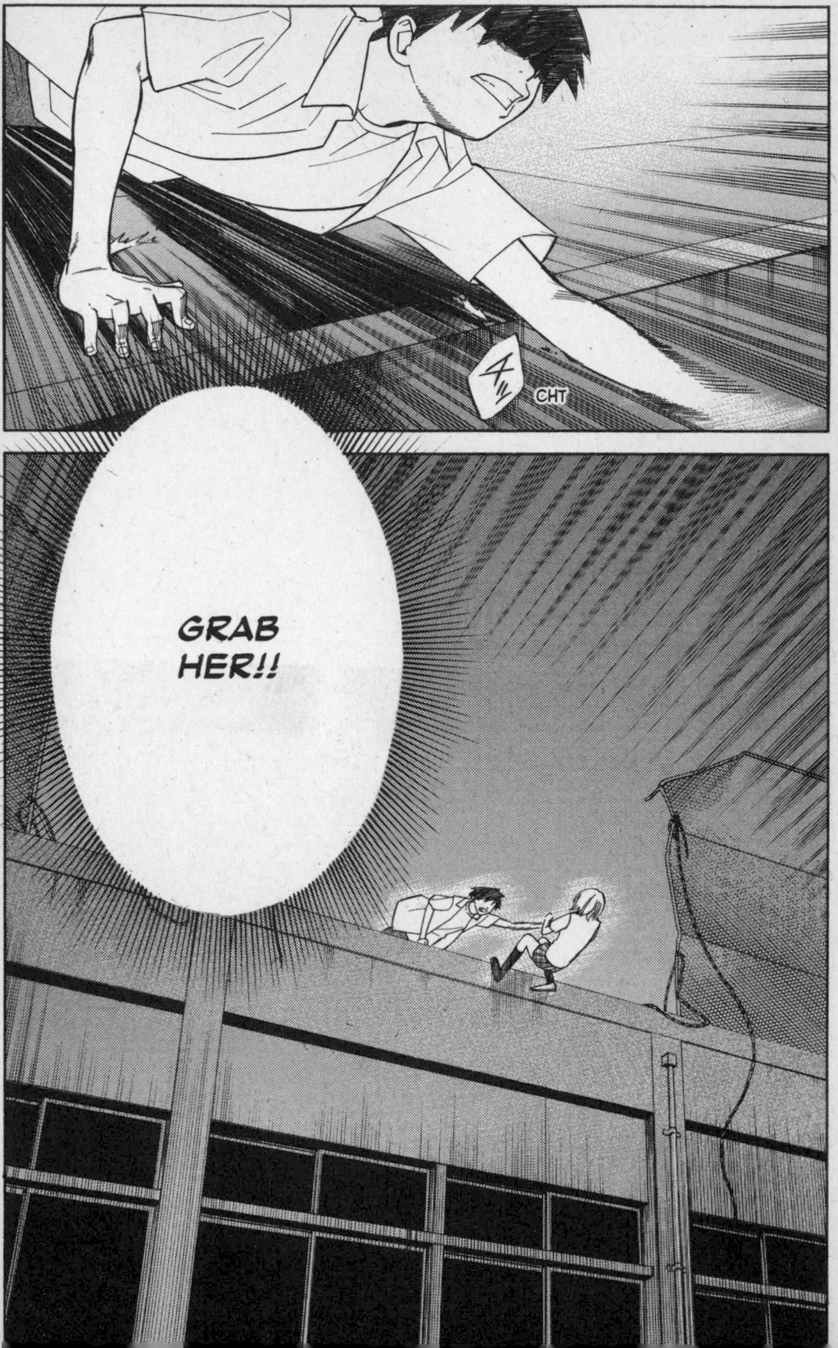
CHT
GRAB HER!!

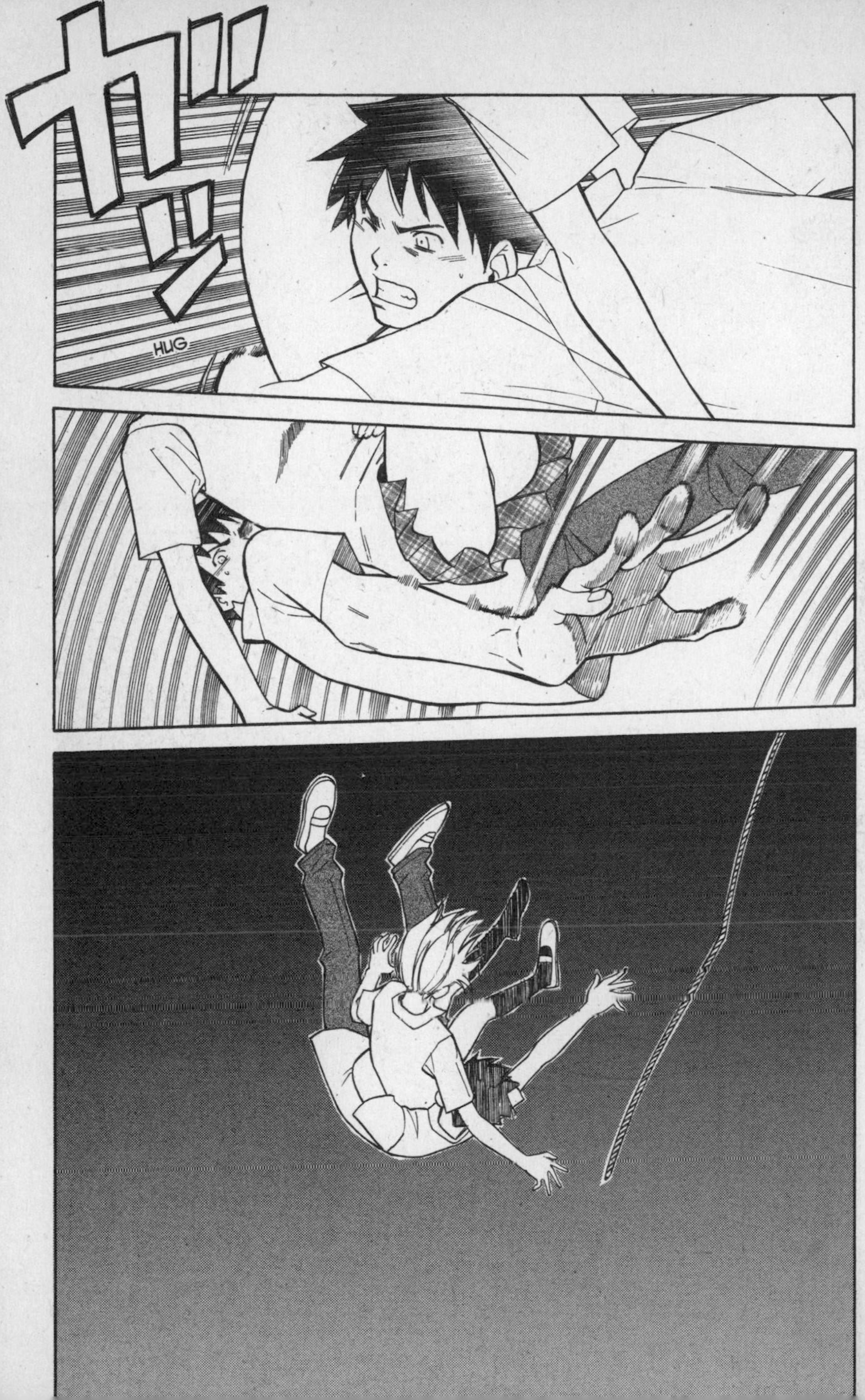
HUG

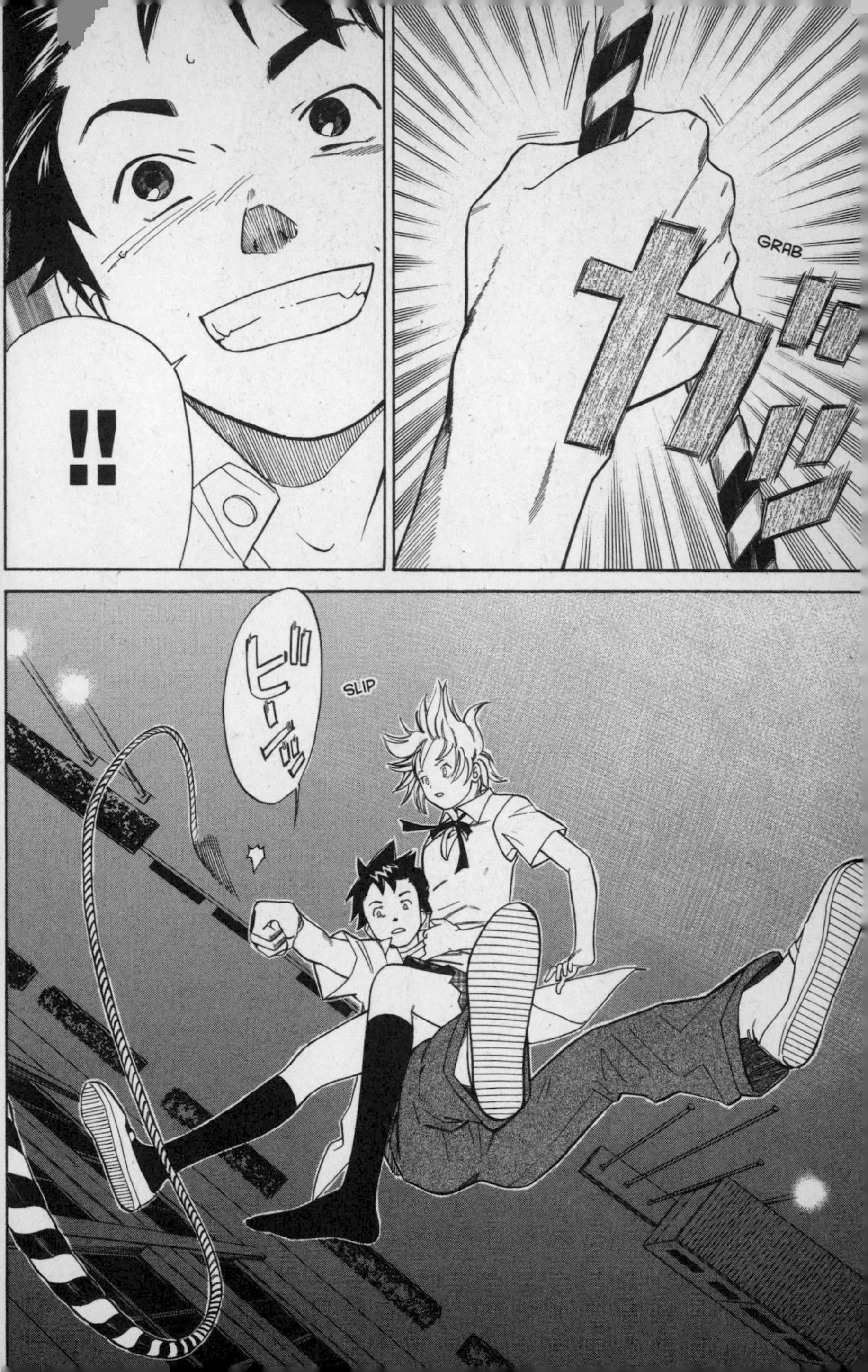

ガッ
GRAB
!!
SLIP

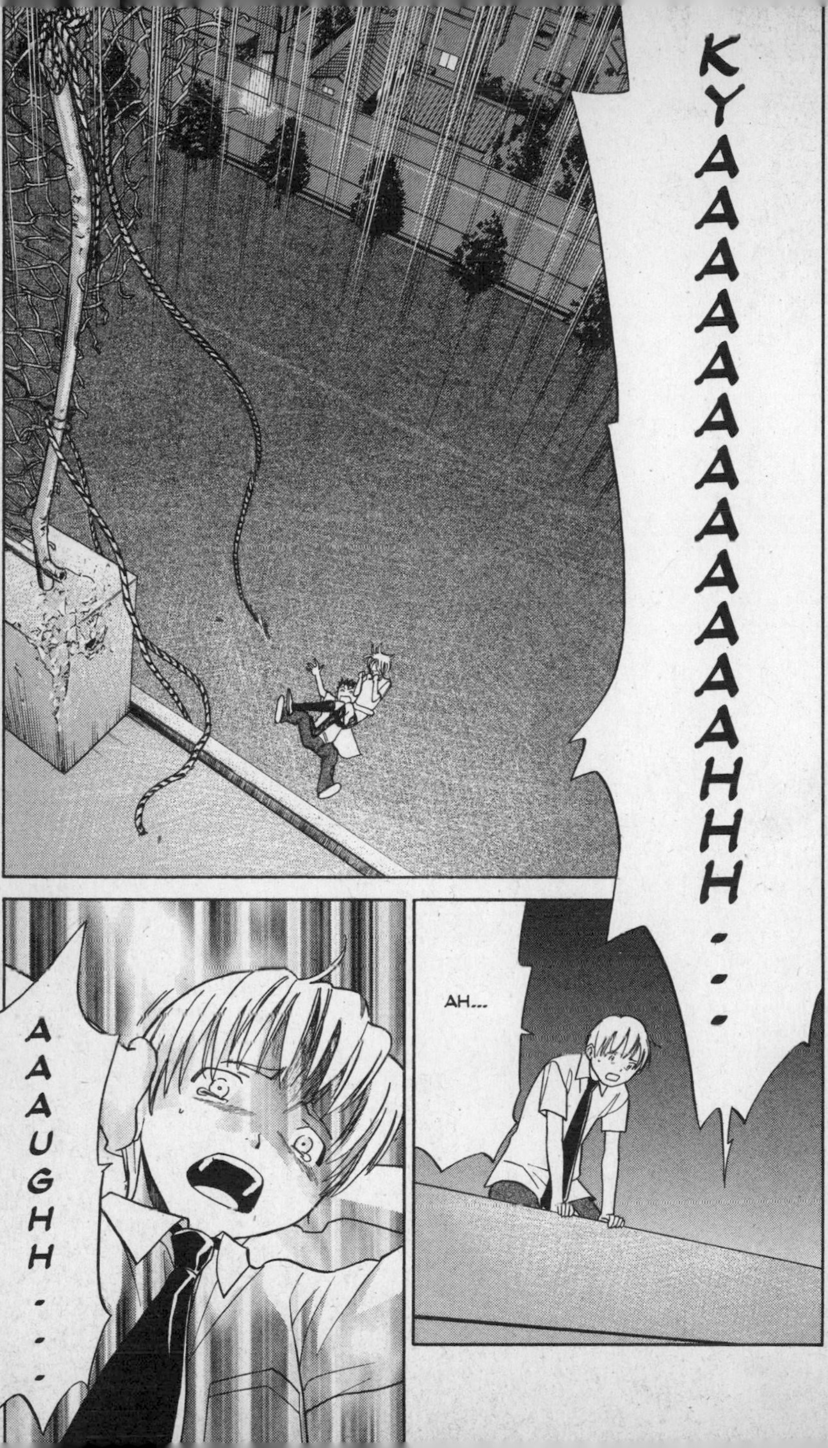
KYAAAAAAAAAAAAHHH...
AH...
AAAUGHH...

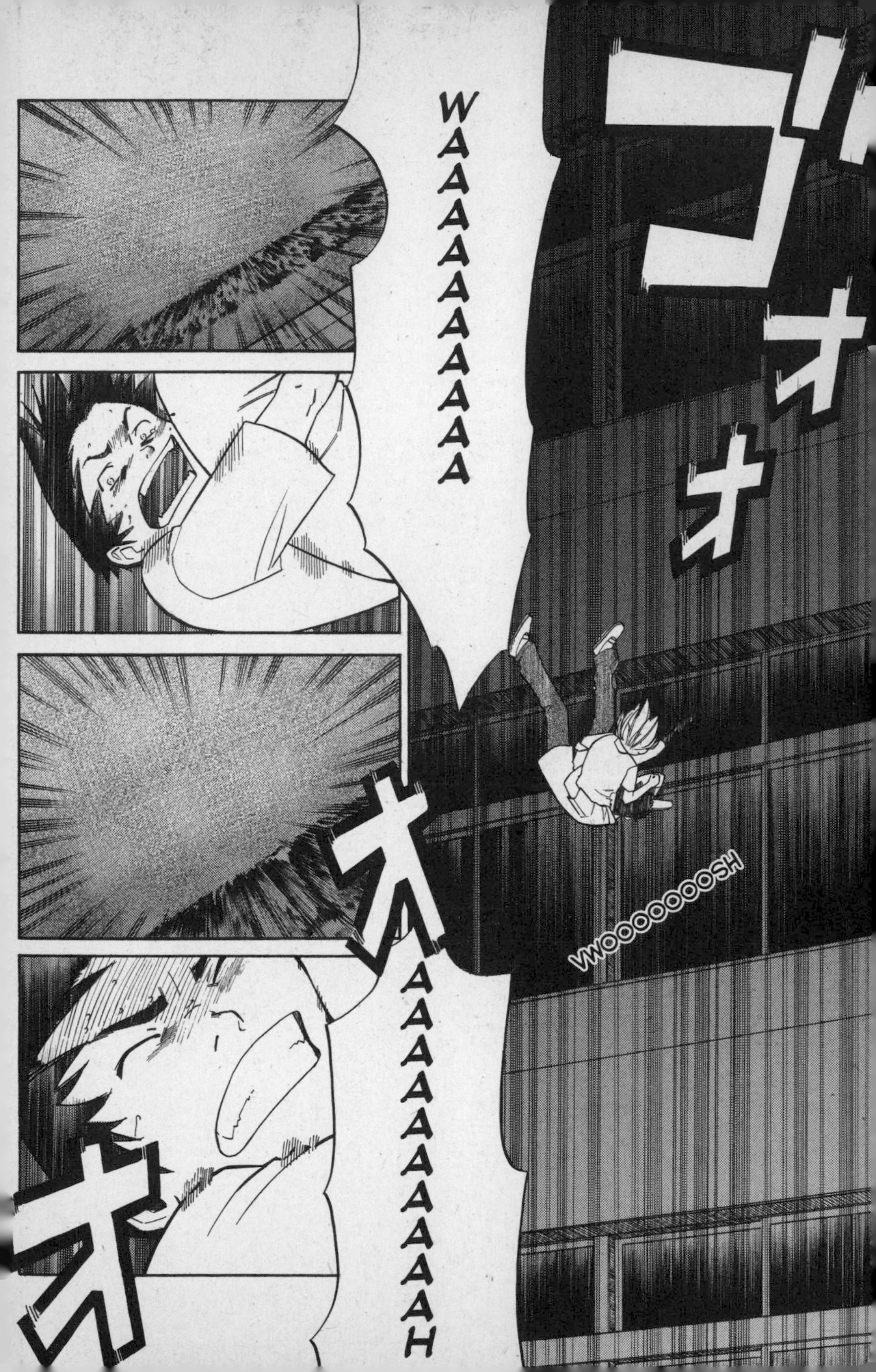
ゴォォオオ
WAAAAAAAAAAAA
AAAAAAAAAAAAH
VWOOOOOOOOSH

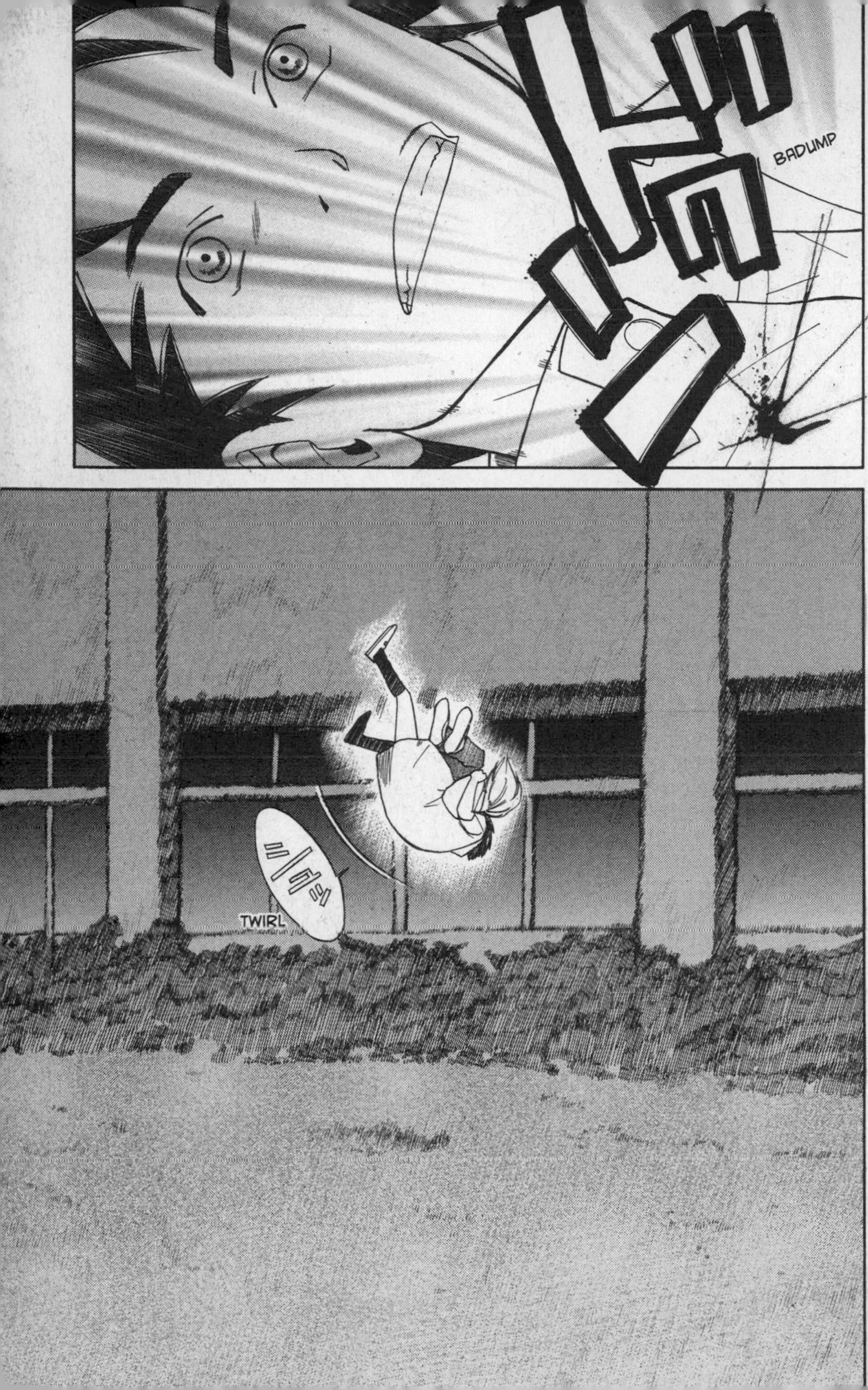
BADUMP
TWIRL

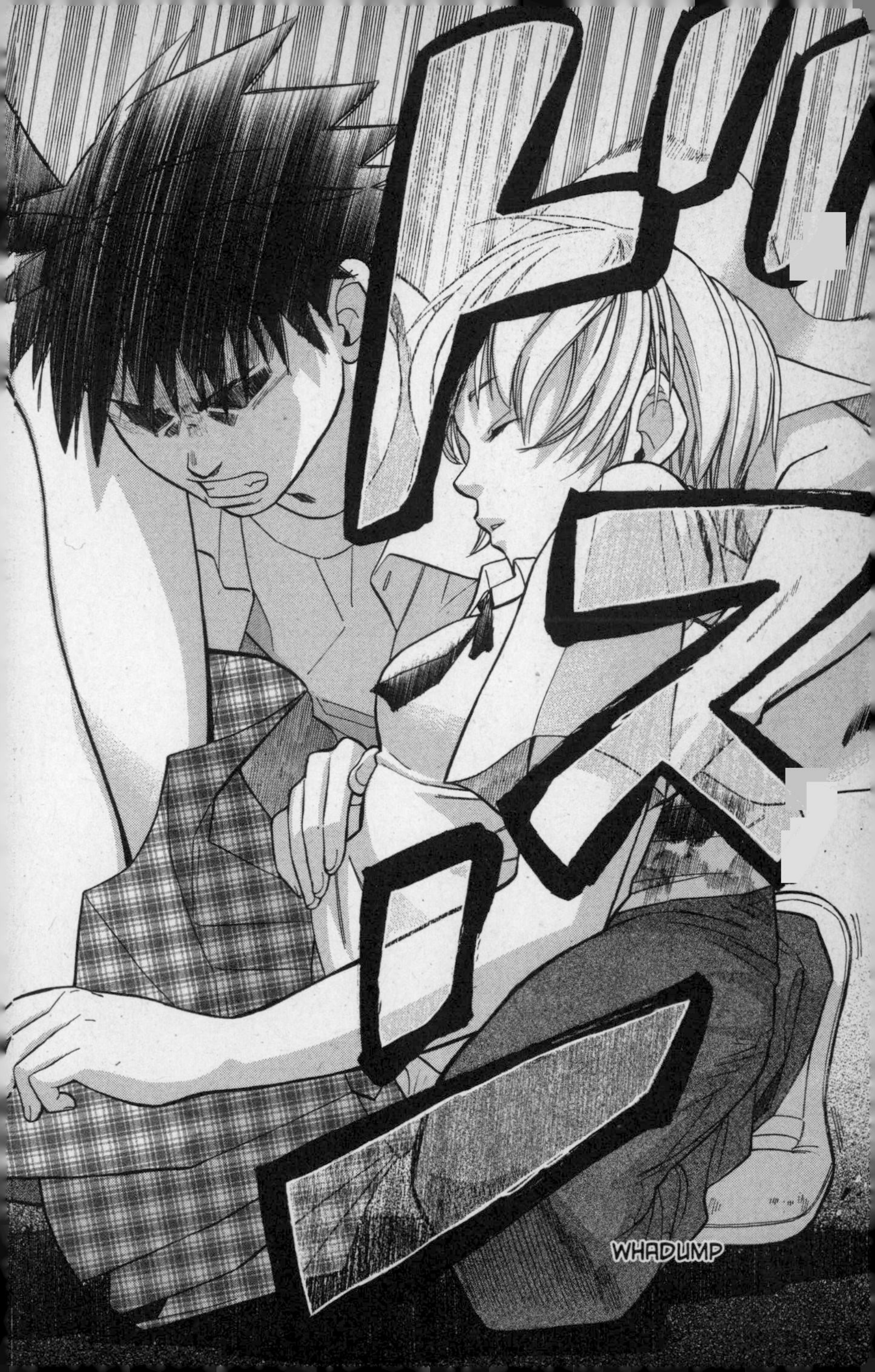
WHADUMP

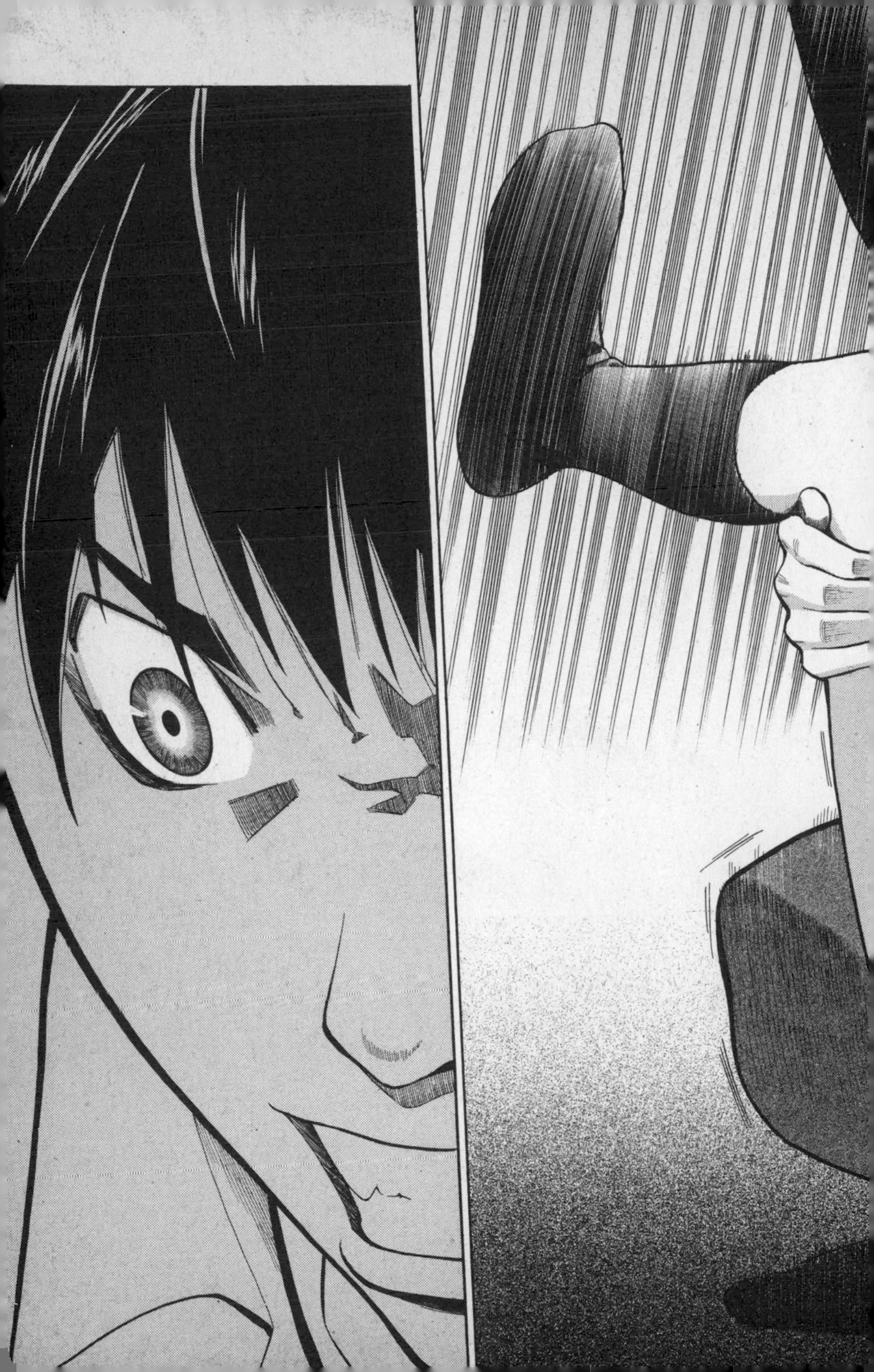

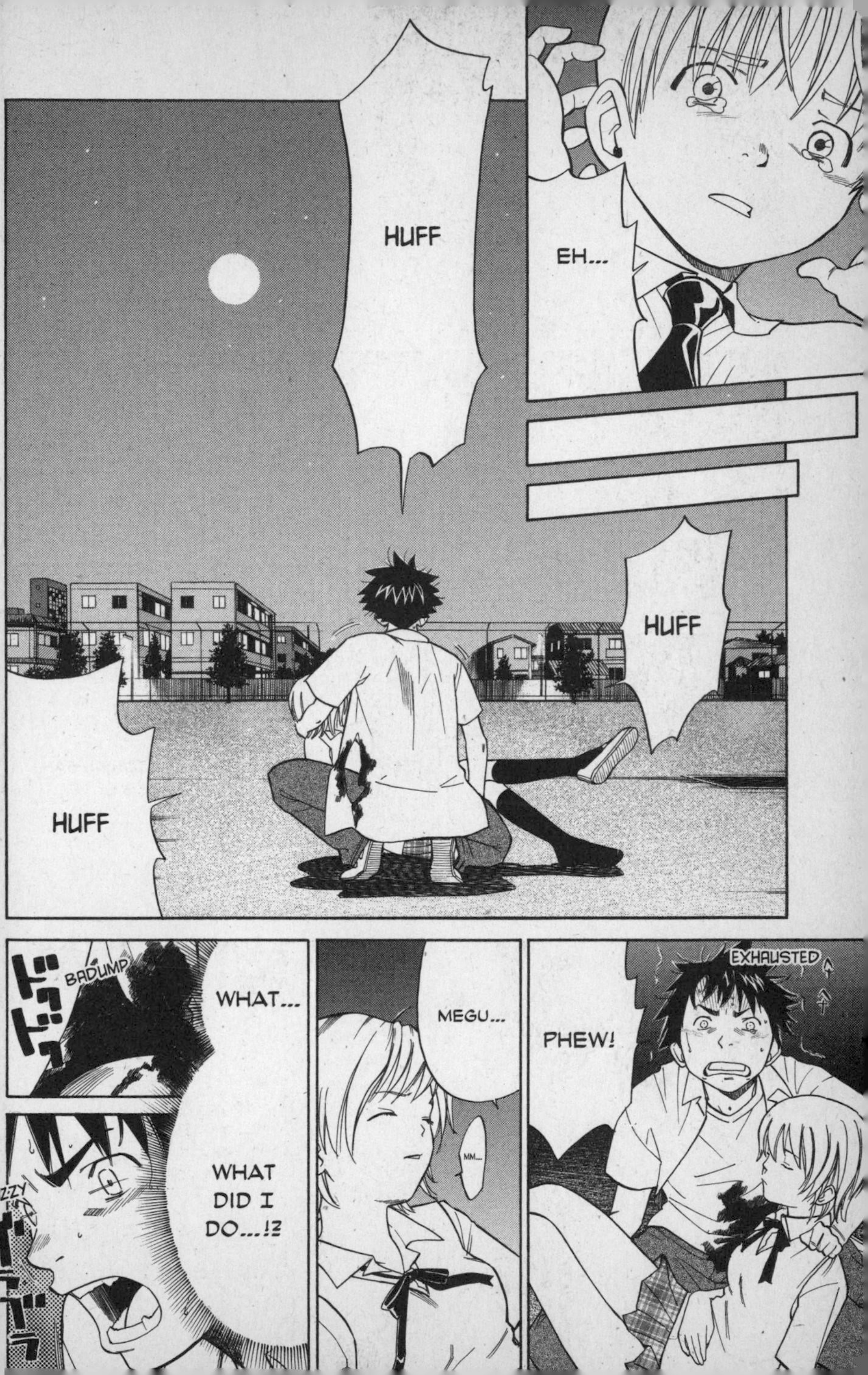
EH...
HUFF
HUFF
HUFF
EXHAUSTED
PHEW!
MEGU...
MM...
BADUMP
WHAT...
WHAT DID I DO...!?

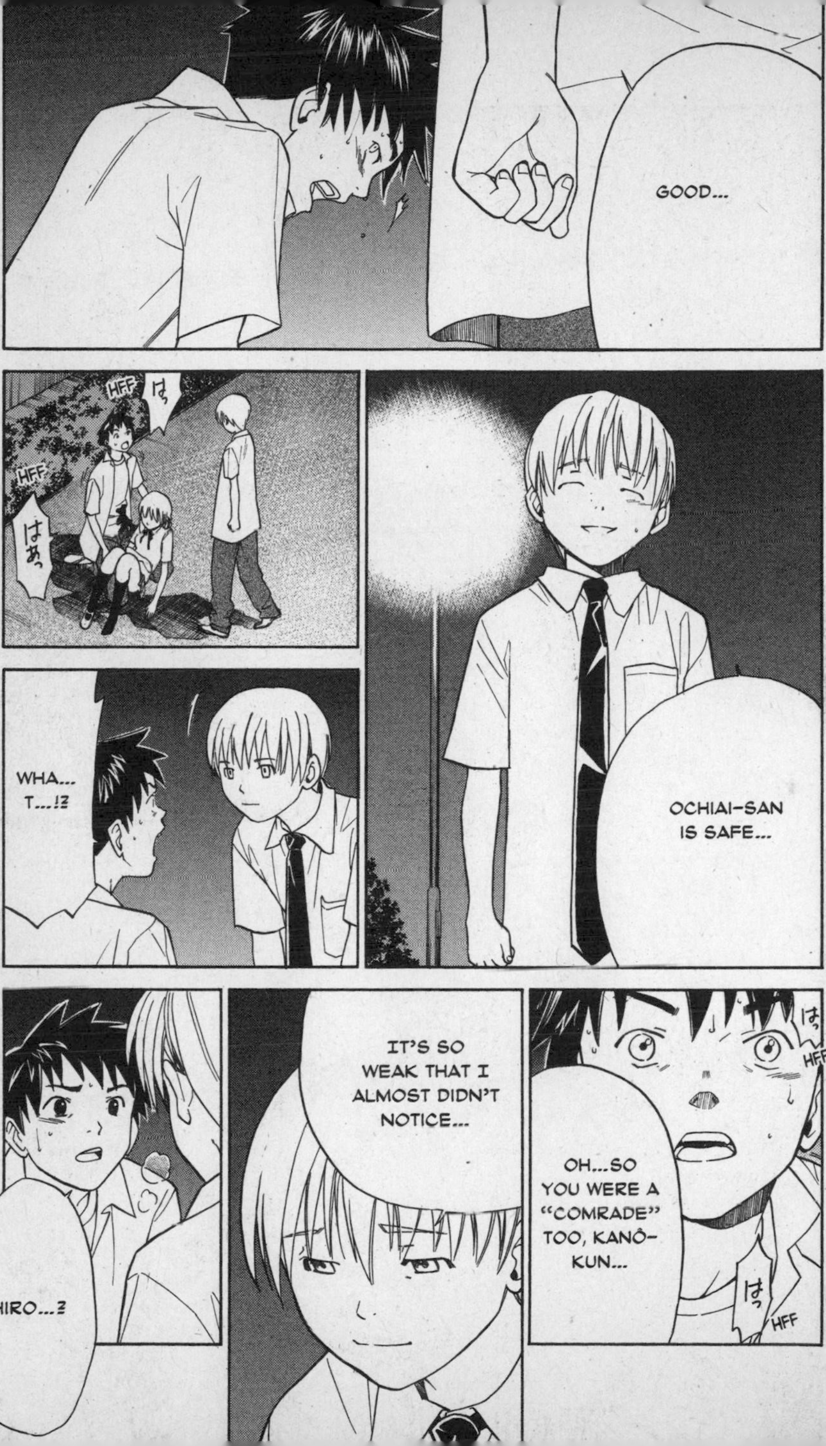
GOOD...
OCHIAI-SAN IS SAFE...
HFF
は
HFF
はあっ
WHA... T...!?
はっ
HFF
OH...SO YOU WERE A "COMRADE" TOO, KANÔ-KUN...
はっ
HFF
IT'S SO WEAK THAT I ALMOST DIDN'T NOTICE...
HIRO...?

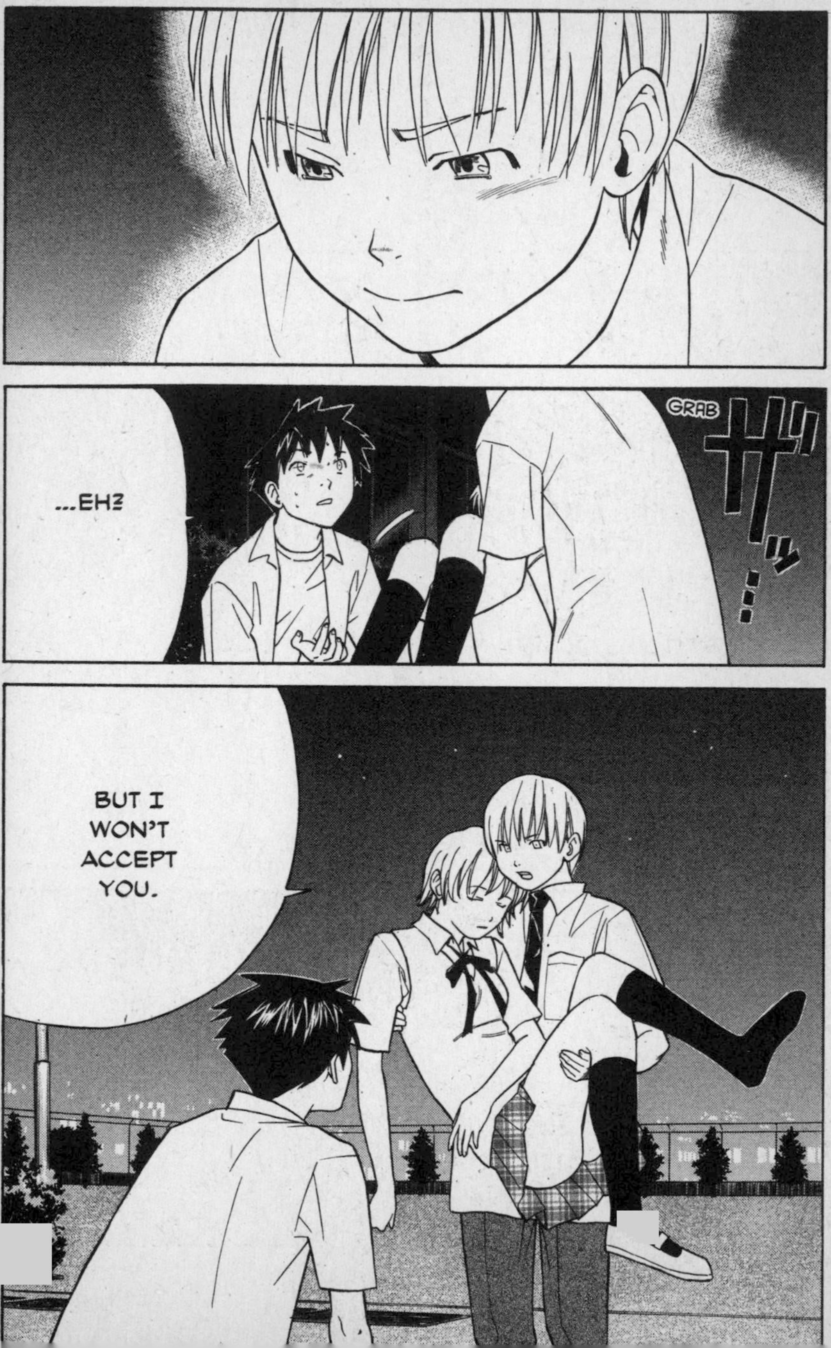
GRAB
ザッ‥
...EH?
BUT I WON'T ACCEPT YOU.

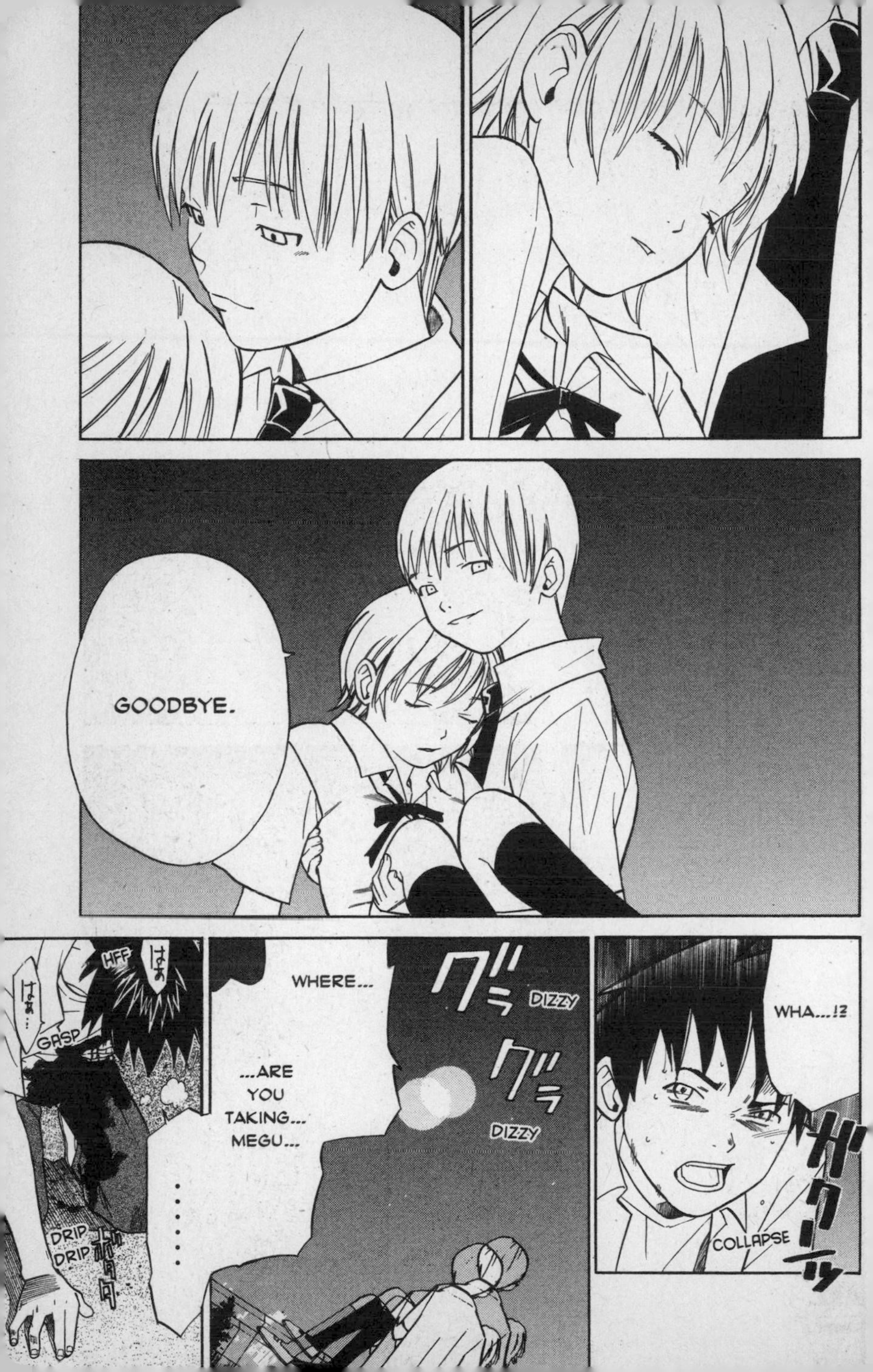
GOODBYE.
WHA...!?
COLLAPSE
WHERE...
...ARE YOU TAKING... MEGU...
DIZZY
DIZZY
......
HFF
GASP
DRIP DRIP

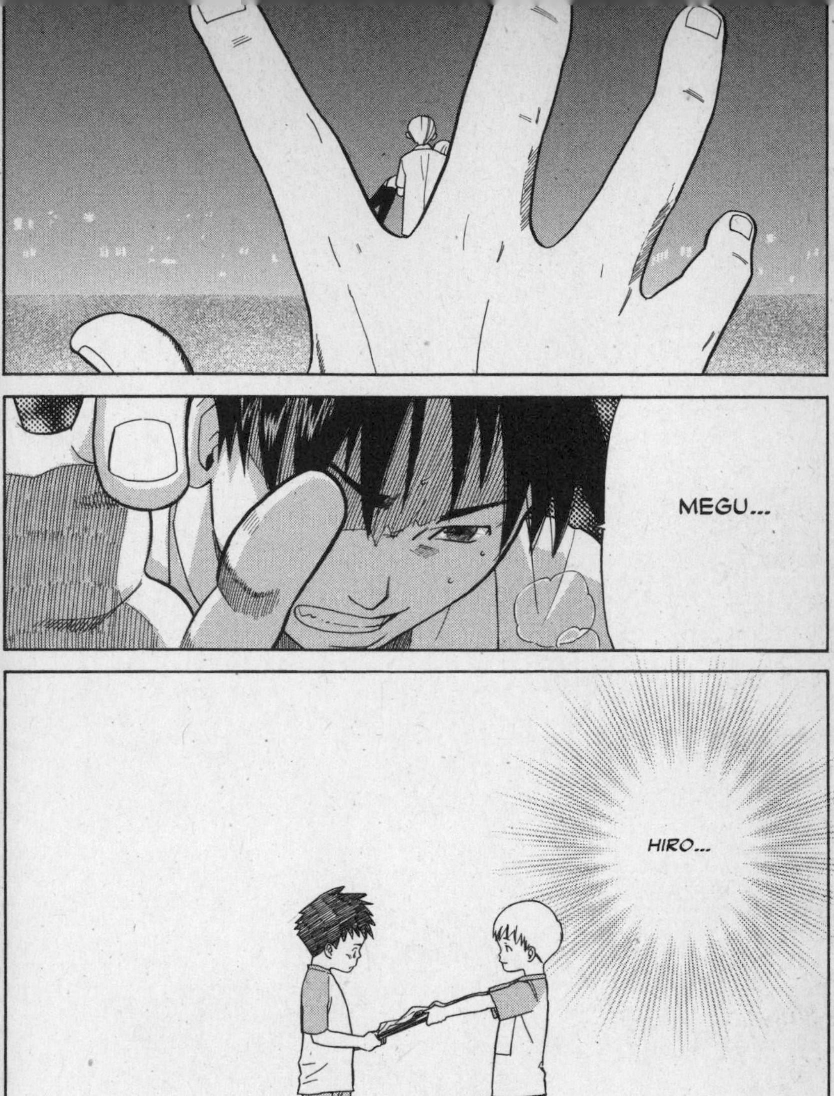
MEGU...
HIRO...

Chapter 3/ End

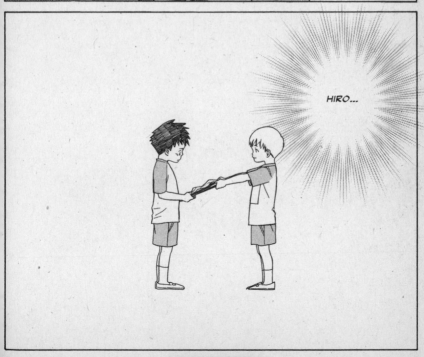

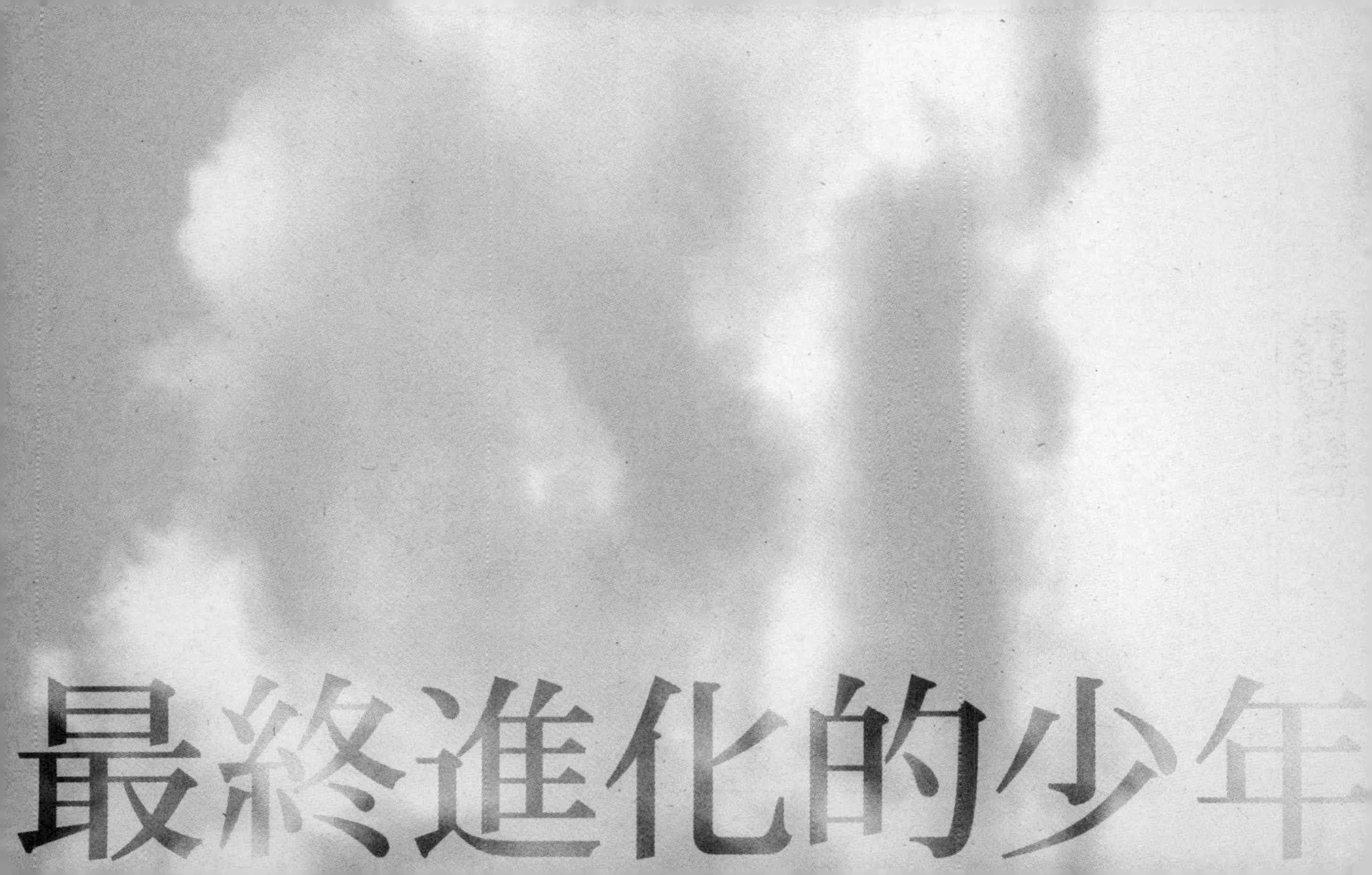
最終進化的少年

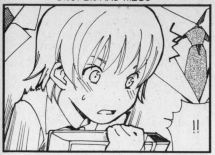

Light Visual Manga 1

DING DING...

GROPER AND MEGU

!!
...HUH? WHAT?
A GROPER!?
SO...
HOW DID IT FEEL...?!

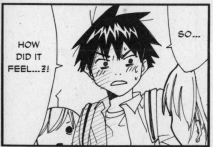

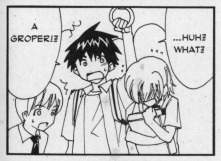

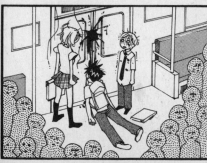

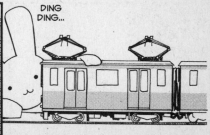

ALIVE...THE END

WHIP

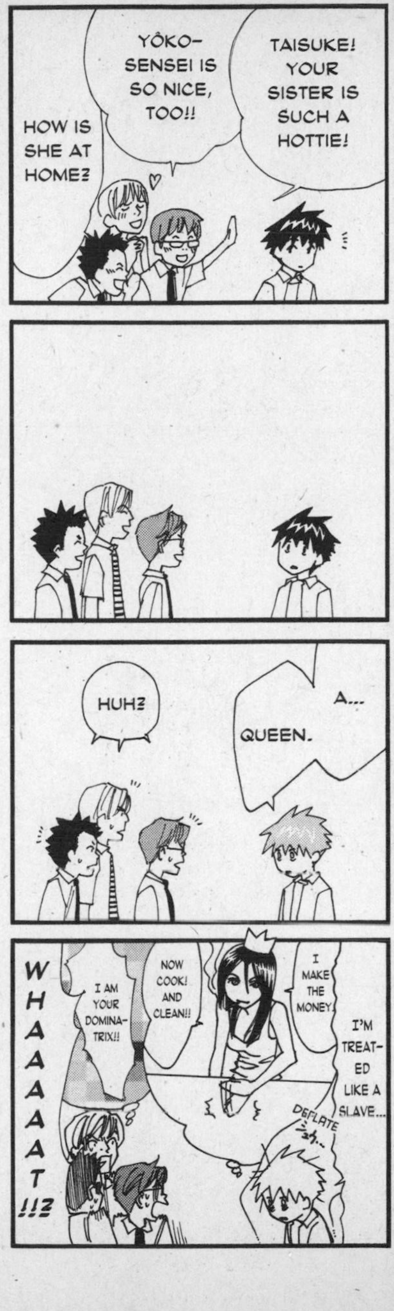
TAISUKE! YOUR SISTER IS SUCH A HOTTIE!
YÔKO-SENSEI IS SO NICE, TOO!!
HOW IS SHE AT HOME?
A... QUEEN.
HUH?
I MAKE THE MONEY.
I'M TREATED LIKE A SLAVE...
NOW COOK! AND CLEAN!!
I AM YOUR DOMINATRIX!!
DEFLATE
WHAAAAAAT!!?

CANDY

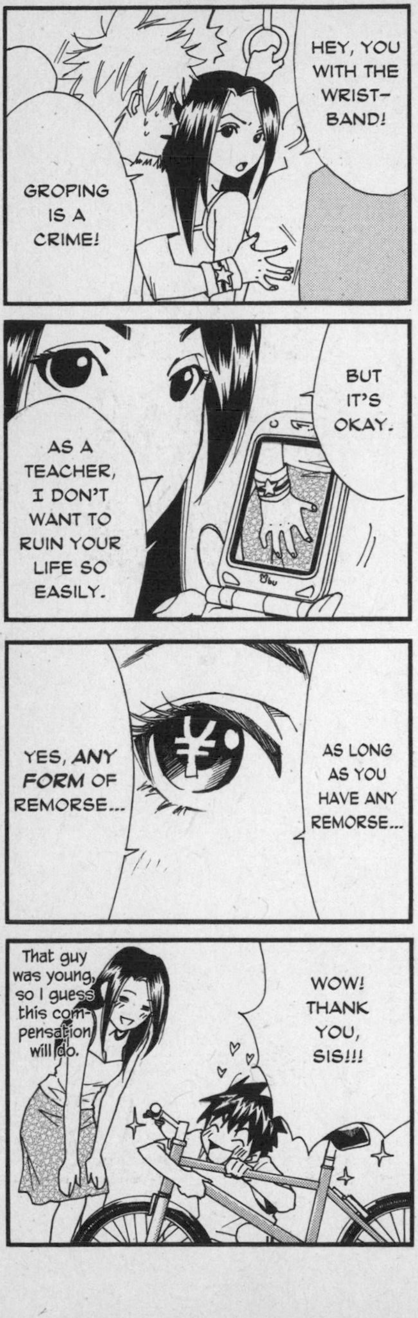
HEY, YOU WITH THE WRISTBAND!
GROPING IS A CRIME!
BUT IT'S OKAY.
AS A TEACHER, I DON'T WANT TO RUIN YOUR LIFE SO EASILY.
AS LONG AS YOU HAVE ANY REMORSE...
YES, ANY FORM OF REMORSE...
WOW! THANK YOU, SIS!!!
That guy was young, so I guess this compensation will do.

MALE FANTASIES

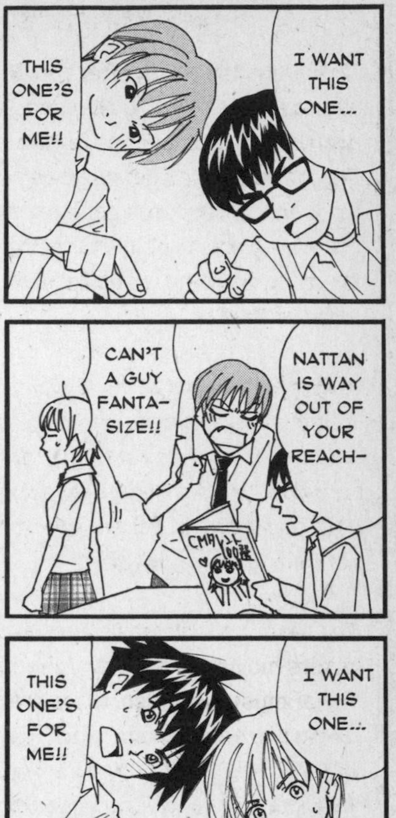
I WANT THIS ONE...
THIS ONE'S FOR ME!!
NATTAN IS WAY OUT OF YOUR REACH–
CAN'T A GUY FANTA-SIZE!!
I WANT THIS ONE...
THIS ONE'S FOR ME!!
SANMA FOR 20 CENTS APIECE IS WAY OUT OF YOUR REACH–
I think I'll set-tle for some eggs...
CAN'T A GUY FANTA-SIZE!!

THESE GUYS ARE PATHETIC IN A DIFFERENT SORT OF WAY.

RECOLLECTION

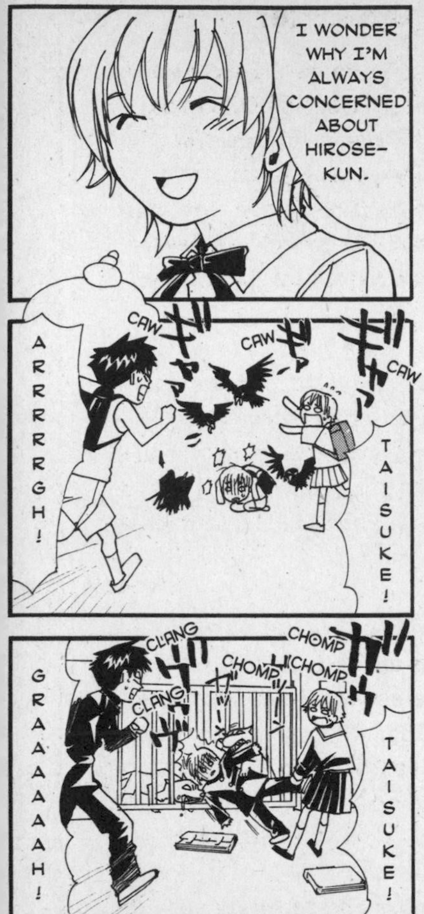
I WONDER WHY I'M ALWAYS CONCERNED ABOUT HIROSE-KUN.
TAISUKE!
CAW
CAW
CAW
ARRRRRGH!
TAISUKE!
CHOMP
CHOMP
CHOMP
CLANG
CLANG
GRAAAAAAAH!
TAISUKE!
GROWL
GROWL
HELL NO!!!

Greetings from the Writer

To tell you the truth, after concluding the series that I drew and wrote for the *Monthly Magazine's Special Issue GREAT*, I really wanted to write a series for the main flagship title, the *Monthly Magazine*. But, although I was a budding manga artist, my artistic skills weren't good enough for a flagship title, and with my slow pace, I couldn't possibly draw fast enough to meet the monthly deadline, so as a result, I decided to team up with a different artist.

And, it was the right decision. A rookie artist, Adachitoka, who has great talent and potential, cooked up a mouthwatering, alluring meal with dazzling graphics based on my scripts, and served it up on a great dish called the *Monthly Magazine*. Yes, all I did was provide the raw materials, and we ended up with great brain food! How amazing!

But *Alive* is not an easy meal to prepare. There are many characters moving in different directions at once, and the story is full of mysteries. Also, there are interesting themes which are zesty spices —"to live" and "to die." Can living just for the sake of living, without having any objectives, be categorized as truly living? Or is it simply another form of death? Well, these are just a few of the concepts that need to be included in this series.

Be that as it may, I will continue to do my best to make this series a success, so I hope readers like you will continue to support our endeavors. Thank you.

Writer: Tadashi Kawashima

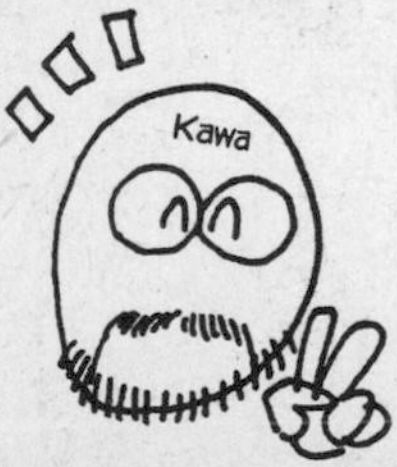
Kawa

Err, this is really personal, but Furu-chan, Nishihara, Big Sis Nami, MIYA-chan, everyone at TABOO, Tani-yan, Ken-chan, Hota-san, everyone at Mizake, everyone at Team Bindaray, and everyone at Lion, associates, friends, my sempais, I'm finally published in a tankobon! You'll all buy it, right?

Translation Notes

Japanese is a tricky language for most Westerners, and translation is often more art than science. For your edification and reading pleasure, here are notes on some of the places where we could have gone in a different direction in our translation of the work, or where a Japanese cultural reference is used.

Itadakimasu, page 22

Itadakimasu is a Japanese greeting customarily said before meals. It means, "Thank you for this meal."

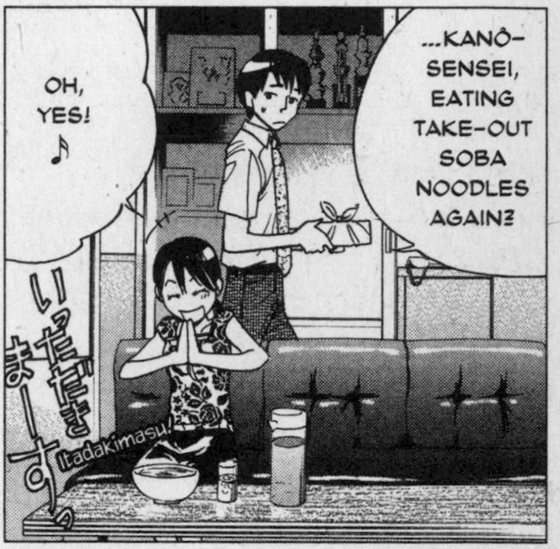
...KANÔ-SENSEI, EATING TAKE-OUT SOBA NOODLES AGAIN?
OH, YES! ♪
いただきまーす
Itadakimasu!

Hiepita, page 92

Hiepita is a brand of fever-cooling strip, usually placed on the forehead. It is similar to the ICY HOT patches used for muscle soreness.

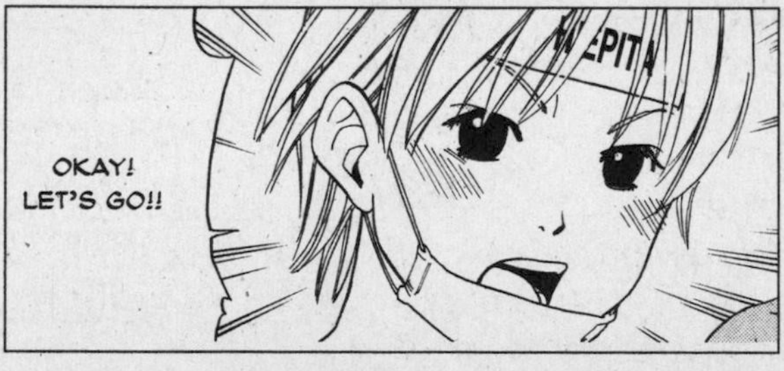
OKAY! LET'S GO!!

Katsudon, page 142

Katsudon is a pork cutlet bowl, a relatively cheap Japanese version of a fast food dish that is sometimes served in prison. The price is comparable to the price of a McDonald's value meal.

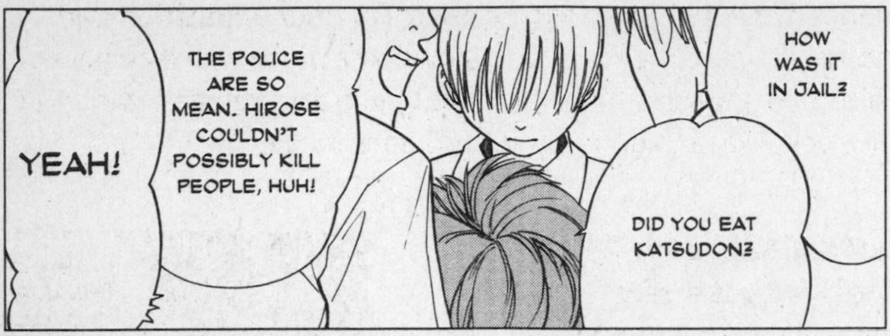
HOW WAS IT IN JAIL?
DID YOU EAT KATSUDON?
THE POLICE ARE SO MEAN. HIROSE COULDN'T POSSIBLY KILL PEOPLE, HUH!
YEAH!

Name tape, page 144

Handmade name tapes are sewn onto school PE clothes in Japanese schools. In this example, 1–3, 1 means first grade of elementary school, and 3 is the class number. The student's name (full or just the last name) and class number are usually on name tapes.

Kattsun, Hiropi, Kochan, page 154, 156

Kattsun is a nickname for Katsumata, Hiropi is a nickname for Hirose, and Kochan is a nickname for Kouchou-sensei, which means school principal in Japanese. Shortening names and adding suffixes like –tsun, –pi, –chan, etc. indicates the speaker's adoration of or affection for the person being addressed.

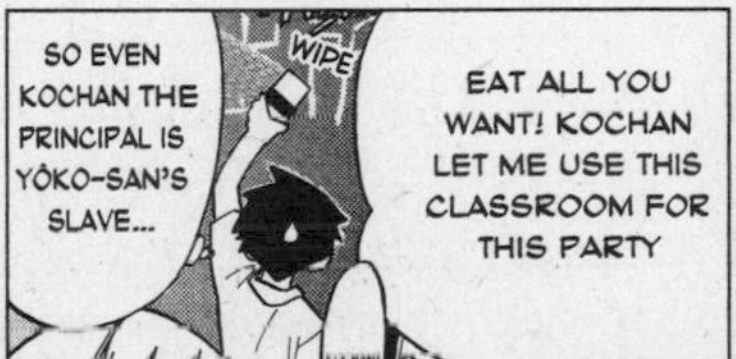
EAT ALL YOU WANT! KOCHAN LET ME USE THIS CLASSROOM FOR THIS PARTY
KOCHAN!
SO EVEN KOCHAN THE PRINCIPAL IS YÔKO-SAN'S SLAVE...
WIPE

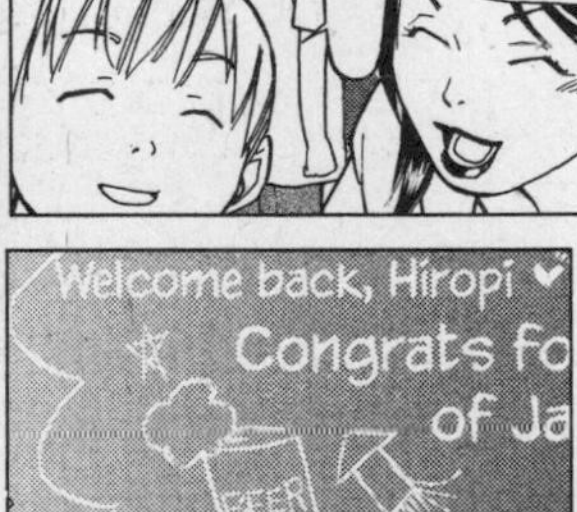
Welcome back, Hiropi ♥
Congrats fo
of Ja
BEER

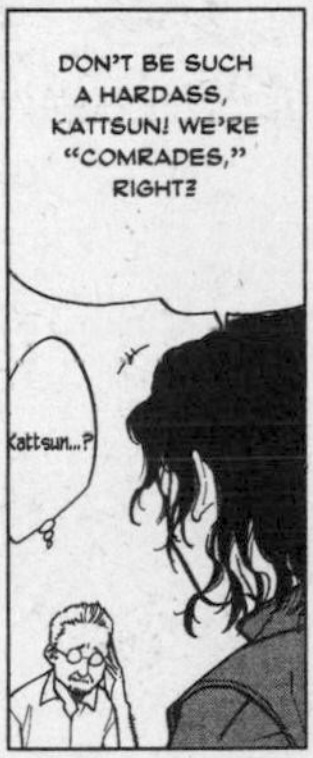
DON'T BE SUCH A HARDASS, KATTSUN! WE'RE "COMRADES," RIGHT?
Kattsun...?

Nattan, page 196

Nattan is a shortened form of a girl's name, possibly Natsumi or Natsuko.

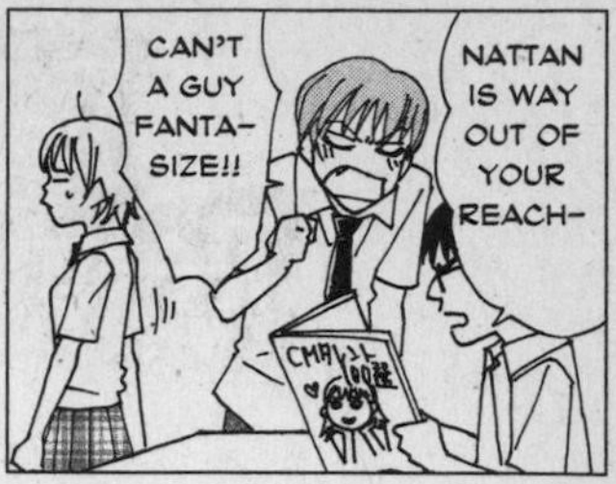
NATTAN IS WAY OUT OF YOUR REACH—
CAN'T A GUY FANTA-SIZE!!

Sanma, page 196

Sanma is a Pacific saury fish.

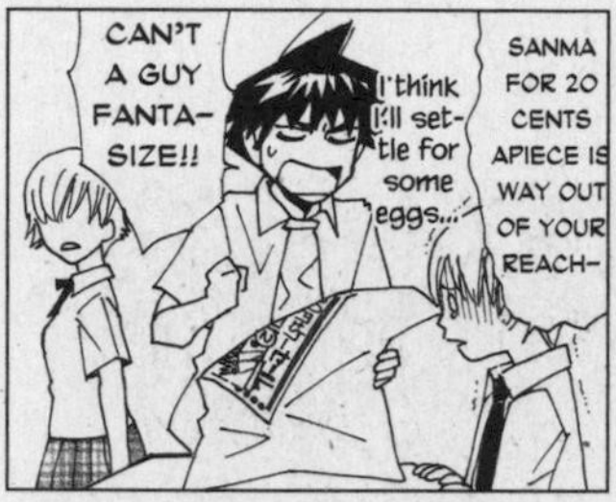
SANMA FOR 20 CENTS APIECE IS WAY OUT OF YOUR REACH—
I think I'll set-tle for some eggs...
CAN'T A GUY FANTA-SIZE!!